"Victoria Smirkova has written the story of the pivotal *exempla* collection of the Middle Ages. By contrast to Caesarius' very long book of 300,000 words, her book is concise but comprehensive. She tells the fascinating story of *exempla* before and after Caesarius *Dialogue* and traces the book's Cistercian roots and reception by Cistercians and others from Caesarius' time to our own. For anyone interested in *exempla*, Cistercians, or Caesarius, this book is required reading."

— Hugh Feiss, OSB

"Victoria Smirnova offers us a thorough, philologically accurate, and enjoyable history of Caesarius of Heisterbach, his stories, and their fortune from the twelfth century to the present day. Both an in-depth study of the *Dialogus miraculorum* and an introduction to Cistercian exemplary literature, *Medieval Exempla in Transition* is an outstanding work. Clearly written and meticulously researched, this volume will be a required reading for all scholars and students of the Cistercian world."

— Stefano Mula, Middlebury College

"Victoria Smirnova's fascinating and carefully researched study of the reception history of Caesarius of Heisterbach's *Dialogue on Miracles* illustrates the myriad ways that Caesarius's collection of stories captures the imagination of its readers. Smirnova tracks the communities who copied, printed, modified, interpreted, and translated Caesarius's text, and she guides us through its manuscript and printed history from the thirteenth century to the present day. This is important reading for the study of monasticism and religious life but also for the investigation of medievalism and the modern reuse of medieval texts."

— Martha G. Newman, Professor of History and Religious Studies, The University of Texas at Austin

CISTERCIAN STUDIES SERIES:
NUMBER TWO HUNDRED NINETY-SIX

Medieval *Exempla* in Transition

Caesarius of Heisterbach's *Dialogus miraculorum* and Its Readers

Victoria Smirnova

α

Cistercian Publications
www.cistercianpublications.org

LITURGICAL PRESS
Collegeville, Minnesota
www.litpress.org

A Cistercian Publications title published by Liturgical Press

Cistercian Publications
Editorial Offices
161 Grosvenor Street
Athens, Ohio 45701
www.cistercianpublications.org

Cover design by Tara Wiese. Caesarius Heisterbacensis. Dialogus miraculorum. Nördl. Rheinland. 14. Jh., 2. Drittel. Signatur: Ms. C 27, f. 1 r. Die Handschrift ist Leihgabe der Stadt Düsseldorf an die Universitäts- und Landesbibliothek Düsseldorf.

1   2   3   4   5   6   7   8   9

Library of Congress Cataloging-in-Publication Data

Names: Smirnova, Victoria, author.
Title: Medieval exempla in transition : Caesarius of Heisterbach's
    Dialogus miraculorum and its readers / Victoria Smirnova.
Description: Collegeville, Minnesota : Cistercian Publications/
    Liturgical Press, [2023] | Series: Cistercian studies series; two
    hundred ninety-six | Includes bibliographical references and index.
    | Summary: "This study follows the transmission and reception
    of Caesarius of Heisterbach's Dialogus miraculorum (1219–1223),
    a Cistercian collection of miracles and memorable events, from the
    Middle Ages to the present day. It ranges across different media
    and within different interpretive communities and includes brief
    summaries of a number of the exempla"—Provided by publisher.
Identifiers: LCCN 2022026667 (print) | LCCN 2022026668 (ebook) |
    ISBN 9780879071301 (trade paperback) | ISBN 9780879071325
    (epub) | ISBN 9780879071325 (pdf) | ISBN 9780879072964 (pdf)
Subjects: LCSH: Caesarius, of Heisterbach, approximately 1180–
    approximately 1240. Dialogus miraculorum. | Miracles. | Exempla.
    | BISAC: RELIGION / Monasticism
Classification: LCC BT97.3.C343 S65 2023 (print) | LCC BT97.3.C343
    (ebook) | DDC 282.09/02—dc23/eng/20220712
LC record available at https://lccn.loc.gov/2022026667
LC ebook record available at https://lccn.loc.gov/2022026668

To Oleg Bolotov

whose unwavering support and constant encouragement

made writing this book possible

Contents

PART THREE: The Way into Modernity

Abbreviations

AASS	Acta Sanctorum
CCCM	Corpus Christianorum, Continuatio Mediaevalis. Turnhout: Brepols Publishers
CCSL	Corpus Christianorum, Series Latina. Turnhout: Brepols Publishers
CF	Cistercian Fathers series, Cistercian Publications
CS	Cistercian Studies series, Cistercian Publications
CSQ	*Cistercian Studies Quarterly*
Dialogus	Caesarius of Heisterbach, *Dialogus miraculorum*
Dist.	*Distinctione*
Exordium	Conrad of Eberbach, *Exordium magnum Cisterciense*
HD	*Homiliae Dominicales*
ISTC	Incunabula Short Title Catalogue
Liber	Herbert of Clairvaux, *Liber visionum et miraculorum Clarevallensium*
PL	Patrologiae cursus completus, Series Latina. Ed. J.–P. Migne
SCh	Sources Chrétiennes. Paris: Éditions du Cerf

List of Images

Acknowledgments

I would like to express my gratitude to all the librarians who provided assistance to me in Germany, Austria, France, Belgium, and Poland. I am extremely grateful to Marie Anne Polo de Beaulieu and Stefano Mula for assisting me in revising the manuscript before publication and offering many excellent suggestions. I would also like to thank Marjorie Burghart for her advice in paleography. Thanks also to Elena Koroleva for her friendly support. I am deeply grateful to Cistercian Publications in general for agreeing to publish this monograph, and to Marsha Dutton in particular for editing the manuscript with great skill and care.

Introduction

Caesarius was very old when he died. But since the monk
was a brave man who had helped many people, his good
spirit can appear to this day in the old cloister ruins. There
he meets his old friend Schandor, who, being a dragon,
can live a thousand years and even more. They have
many things to tell one another.[1]

This passage from the German children's book by Wilfried
Esch, titled *Schandor und Cäsarius: Geschichten und Abenteuer
des Cäsarius von Heisterbach und des Drachen Schandor* ("Schandor and Caesarius: Stories and Adventures of Caesarius of
Heisterbach and Schandor the Dragon") features Caesarius
(1180–1240), a monk and master of novices in the Cistercian
abbey of Heisterbach (in Latin, Vallis Sancti Petri), not very far
from Bonn. Caesarius is primarily known as the author of the
Dialogus miraculorum (1219–1223),[2] one of the most compelling
and successful medieval collections of miracles and memorable

[1] Wilfried Esch, *Schandor und Cäsarius: Geschichten und Abenteuer des Cäsarius
von Heisterbach und des Drachen Schandor* (Bonn: Free Pen, 2002), 2. Unless
otherwise noted, all translations in this volume are mine (VS).

[2] *Caesarii Heisterbacensis Dialogus miraculorum*, 2 vols., ed. Josephus Strange
(Cologne-Bonn-Brussels: J. M. Heberle, 1851), hereafter *Dialogus*. Studies on
the *Dialogus* are numerous; for a historiographical overview, see Victoria
Smirnova, Marie Anne Polo de Beaulieu, and Jacques Berlioz, eds., *The Art
of Cistercian Persuasion in the Middle Ages and Beyond*, Studies in Medieval and
Reformation Traditions (Leiden: Brill, 2015), 1–28 (introduction). Some stories
from the *Dialogus* may have been written down before Caesarius; see Horst
Schneider, introduction to *Dialogus miraculorum: Dialog über die Wunder*, 4 vols.,

events. It is hard to imagine any other medieval author (let aside the author of a didactic *exempla* collection)[3] who could have become the sympathetic protagonist of a twenty-first-century children's book.

Not much is now known about Caesarius himself. The information that scholars use to reconstruct his biography is provided almost exclusively by his own writings,[4] and specifically by the *Dialogus miraculorum*, which contains a number of precious biographical details. He also compiled, toward the end of his life, the so-called *Epistola catalogica*, in which he enumerated, in chronological order, his thirty-six literary works.[5]

Caesarius was born in around 1180 to a well-to-do family from or near Cologne. He began his education in the school of Saint Andrew there, then continued it in the cathedral school. While still in his youth, he started writing sermons and biblical

---

ed. and trans. Horst Schneider and Nikolaus Nösges, Fontes Christiani 86 (Turnhout: Brepols, 2009), 1:62–63.

[3] Jacques Le Goff defines *exempla* as "brief stories presented as authentic and destined to be inserted in a discourse (as a rule, a sermon) in order to convince the audience of a salutary lesson"): see Claude Bremond, Jacques Le Goff, and Jean-Claude Schmitt, *L'Exemplum*, Typologie des sources du Moyen Âge Occidental 40 (Turnhout: Brepols, 1982, re-ed. Turnhout: Brepols, 1996), 37–38. Other scholars have since offered their own definitions, see p. xxi, n. 20, below.

[4] With the notable exception of a 1221 document that mentions Caesarius as a master of novices in Heisterbach: see Falko Neininger, "Caesarius von Heisterbach in Walberberg," in *Arbor amoena comis. 25 Jahre Mittellateinisches Seminar in Bonn, 1965–1990*, ed. Ewald Könsgen (Stuttgart: Franz Steiner, 1990), 207–28. See detailed biographical summaries in Jacques Berlioz, "Césaire de Heisterbach," in *Dictionnaire encyclopédique du Moyen Âge*, ed. André Vauchez (Paris: Éditions du Cerf, 1997); Karl Langosch, "Caesarius von Heisterbach," in *Die deutsche Literatur des Mittelalters: Verfasserlexikon*, 2nd ed. (Berlin: de Gruyter, 1978); Fritz Wagner, "Caesarius von Heisterbach," in *Lexikon des Mittelalters* (Munich and Zurich: Artemis & Winkler, 1983); introduction to Smirnova, et al., *The Art of Cistercian Persuasian*, 6–10.

[5] Alfons Hilka, ed., *Die Wundergeschichten des Caesarius von Heisterbach*, 2 vols. [1 and 3; vol. 2 was never published], Publikationen der Gesellschaft für Rheinische Geschichtskunde 43 (Bonn: Hanstein, 1933), 1:2–7, here 3.

commentaries. In 1199 he entered the Cistercian abbey of Heisterbach,[6] and as a monk, he continued to write. About ten years later, he started to work on his large homiletic collection, *Moralitates evangeliorum*. Its first part—*De infantia Salvatoris*—was finished before 1219. Somewhere around this time, Caesarius became the master of novices at Heisterbach.

As Caesarius himself related in the prologue to the *Dialogus*, his pedagogical activity included telling the novices stories of miracles that had recently happened in the Cistercian Order.[7] His pupils, as well as other brothers (including the abbots of Heisterbach and Marienstatt)[8] urged him to write these stories down in order to preserve them.[9] Caesarius therefore interrupted his writing of the *Moralitates evangeliorum* and dedicated himself to the *Dialogus*.

The *Dialogus* contains around eight hundred *exempla*, interwoven in a dialogue between a novice (*Novicius*) and a senior monk (*Monachus*) regarding different aspects of the *vita regularis* and major points of church doctrine. The work is divided into twelve parts (*distinctiones*), roughly following the progression of monastic life from the moment when people enter the monastery (the first part is dedicated to their *conversio*) until their death (the last part is entitled *de praemio mortuorum*). Caesarius's stories are taken mainly from oral sources. He had a predilection for material that circulated among his fellow Cistercians, but he also included stories from the world outside

---

[6] On Heisterbach see Swen H. Brunsch, *Das Zisterzienserkloster Heisterbach von seiner Gründung bis zum Anfang des 16. Jahrhunderts* (Siegberg: Franz Schmitt, 1998).

[7] *Cum ex debito iniunctae sollicitudinis aliqua ex his quae in ordine nostro nostris temporibus miraculose gesta sunt et quotidie fiunt, recitarem noviciis* (*Dialogus* vol. 1, p. 1).

[8] Henry, the abbot of Heisterbach from 1208 to 1244, and Herman, the abbot of Marienstatt, Heisterbach's daughter house, from 1215 to around 1223. Herman was the first abbot of Heisterbach and one of Caesarius's major sources.

[9] *rogatus sum a quibusdam cum instantia multa, eadem scripto perpetuare* (*Dialogus* vol. 1, p. 1).

the cloister, narrated by, among others, priests, canons, knights, and religious women. A large part of the *Dialogus* material is original and features in his collection for the first time.

About a year before the completion of the *Dialogus*, Caesarius left the post of the master of novices. From 1222–1223 he was followed in the post by a monk called Gottfried, whom Caesarius mentions in the *Dialogus* (X.42).[10] Having finished the *Dialogus*, Caesarius returned to the composition of the Sunday Homilies (the second part of the *Moralitates evangeliorum*). He finished this part before 1224–1225, and the third part—homilies for the saints' feasts—at some point after 1226. He was a popular author. At the request of the archbishop of Cologne, Henry of Müllenark, he composed the *Vita* of his predecessor Engelbert, murdered on November 7, 1225, and some ten years later, in 1236, he was asked by Ulrich, prior of the Teutonic Order in Magdeburg, to compose the Vita of Saint Elizabeth of Hungary.[11] Interestingly, Caesarius's hagiographic writings are limited to these two pieces. As for *exempla* collections, the only one he wrote besides the *Dialogus*—the *Libri VIII miraculorum*[12]—remained unfinished, with only two of the projected eight books written between 1225 and 1227. Praised as a champion of Cistercian storytelling, Caesarius was apparently more of a homilist.

Nothing is certainly known about Caesarius's monastic career after he left the post of the master of novices. The belief that he became a prior is widespread, but erroneous.[13] Cae-

---

[10] Vol. 2, p. 247; textual references to the *Dialogus* refer to *distinctio* and chapter numbers unless identified, as here, by volume and page number.

[11] The *Vita sancte Elyzabeth Lantgravie*, ed. Albert Huyskens, in Hilka, ed., *Wundergeschichten*, 3:344–81. On the hagiography of Saint Elizabeth, see also Ottó Gecser, "Lives of Saint Elizabeth: Their Rewritings and Diffusion in the Thirteenth Century," *Analecta Bollandiana* 127 (2009): 62.

[12] Hilka, ed., *Wundergeschichten*, 3:15–128.

[13] For further details, see p. 225, nn. 48, 49. See also Brian P. McGuire, "Friends and Tales in the Cloister: Oral Sources in Caesarius of Heisterbach's *Dialogus miraculorum*," *Analecta Cisterciensia* 36 (1980): 173.

sarius probably remained a simple monk for the rest of his life, dedicating himself to writing. He did travel extensively, mostly accompanying his abbot or his prior.[14] His last attested journey took place in 1233, when he visited Marburg and reported on the crowds of pilgrims visiting the tomb of Elizabeth of Hungary.[15] Caesarius died around 1240,[16] at the age of sixty.

Caesarius's life as we know it today lacked adventures that might fascinate modern readers. Rather, the image of a gifted storyteller and dedicated teacher emerges from the *Dialogus*, one that continues to capture the imagination, shaping our perception of him and his work. In fact, in the German children's book, Caesarius and his dragon friend Schandor do not have conventional adventures but instead exchange stories.

The *Geschichten und Abenteuer des Cäsarius von Heisterbach und des Drachen Schandor* represents only one chapter in the long and fascinating history of the reception of Caesarius's most famous work. Designed primarily for use within Caesarius's immediate community, the *Dialogus* soon acquired a much wider readership. Its manuscript tradition is impressive. More than sixty Latin manuscripts containing full or abridged versions survive, in addition to numerous excerpts found in other *exempla* collections. In the fifteenth century, the *Dialogus* was translated into Dutch and German. Over a number of centuries, different communities with different identities and contexts found it worth reading and copying. Caesarius's *exempla* were appreciated not only by Cistercians, but also by Canons and Canonesses Regular, Carthusians, Benedictines, Dominicans, and Franciscans. A number of his stories, migrating from one

---

[14] For more detailed information see Brunsch, *Das Zisterzienserkloster Heisterbach*, 147–50.

[15] Hilka, ed., *Wundergeschichten*, 3:384.

[16] On the date of Caesarius's death, see Fritz Wagner, "Studien zu Caesarius von Heisterbach," *Analecta Cisterciensia* 29 (1973): 84; and Langosch, "Caesarius von Heisterbach," col. 1154.

exempla collection to another, reached even wider audiences, ranging from Mexico[17] to Russia.[18]

Transmission of the *Dialogus* was not limited to the Middle Ages. In the fifteenth century, the collection passed into print, and not once, but twice: in 1475 by Ulrich Zell, a pioneer printer from Cologne, and in 1481 by Johann Koelhoff the Elder, Zell's colleague and competitor. In the age of the Reformation, Protestants severely criticized the *Dialogus*, prompting apologetic defenses by Catholic editors and publishers. Despite this controversy, two more editions confirmed its popularity. The first one, by Jacob Fischer, was reprinted no fewer than three times—in Cologne in 1591 and in 1599, and finally in Antwerp in 1605. The second of the later editions was published in 1662 by Bertrand Tissier, a Cistercian from Bonnefontaine Abbey (Reims diocese), in the second volume of his *Bibliotheca Patrum Cisterciensium*.

With its abundance of historical details, the *Dialogus* was already in the seventeenth century appreciated as a reliable source of information on the history of the Cistercian Order. But this fact did not prevent Caesarius from being ridiculed a century later for being naive, gullible, and utterly superstitious. Only during the nineteenth century did the *Dialogus* gain renewed interest among historians and the general public with the rediscovery of the Middle Ages. Today most readers of the *Dialogus* are surely medievalists reading it as part of their research, but even this very specific audience experiences delight and a vivid emotional reaction while listening to Caesarius's *exempla* when they are narrated during a conference. Thanks

---

[17] Danièle Dehouve, *L'évangélisation des Aztèques ou le pécheur universel* (Paris: Maisonneuve & Larose, 2004), with a preface by Marie Anne Polo de Beaulieu; see also Danièle Dehouve, "Caesarius of Heisterbach in the New Spain (1570–1770)," in Smirnova, et al., *The Art of Cistercian Persuasion*, 242–68.

[18] Marie Anne Polo de Beaulieu and Victoria Smirnova, "Visual Preaching in Russia (17th–19th Century)," in *Preaching and New Worlds: Sermons as Mirrors of Realms Near and Far*, ed. Timothy J. Johnson, Katherine Wrisley Shelby, and John D. Young (London: Routledge, 2018), 201–26.

to numerous modern translations into German, Caesarius has had the rare chance to be claimed by popular culture. Besides the *Geschichten und Abenteuer des Cäsarius von Heisterbach und des Drachen Schandor*, several historical adventure novels feature Caesarius as a character. Some websites dedicated to prophecies cite one allegedly by Caesarius,[19] and several years ago, it was even possible to buy a figurine of Caesarius at his writing desk, resembling the monument erected in 1991 not far from the ruins of the Heisterbach abbey, in commemoration of its most famous son (see Figure 1, p. xxii).

While the study below reveals a great deal about the *Dialogus* as a tool of religious formation and a source of reading pleasure, it also explores a number of the theoretical questions that have recently been raised in the field of medieval *exemplum* scholarship. In the last decades, there has been what may be called a pragmatic turn—an increasing shift of emphasis from the *exemplum* as a specific type of narrative to *exemplarity*, that is, to its pragmatic function and communicative intention.[20] In accord with the ever-growing interest in problems of belief and "making believe" (*faire-croire*),[21] researchers in medieval

---

[19] For example, *bibliotecapleyades.net* and *catholicprophecy.org*. See below, p. 263, n. 25.

[20] Jean-Yves Tilliette defines the *exemplum* as "un mode de persuasion qui prend la forme du récit" (Jean-Yves Tilliette, "L'exemplum rhétorique: questions de définition," in *Les* Exempla *médiévaux: nouvelles perspectives*, ed. Jacques Berlioz and Marie Anne Polo de Beaulieu [Paris: Honoré Champion, 1998], 65). Discussions of the nature of *exempla* are summarized in Nicolas Louis, "*Exemplum ad usum et abusum*: définition d'usages d'un récit qui n'en a que la forme," in *Le récit exemplaire (1200–1800): Actes du XXIIIᵉ colloque international de la Société d'Analyse de la Topique Romanesque, Belley 17–20 septembre 2009*, ed. Madeleine Jeay and Véronique Duché (Paris: Classiques Garnier, 2011), 17–36. See also the introduction to Jacques Berlioz, Pascal Collomb, and Marie Anne Polo de Beaulieu, eds., *Le Tonnerre des exemples: Exempla et médiation culturelle dans l'Occident médiéval* (Rennes: Presses Universitaires de Rennes, 2010), 11–15.

[21] The popular French term *faire-croire* can be translated loosely as "making believe" or "causing someone to believe" and refers to a complex process that involves different strategies and means of persuasion, both religious and rhetorical.

Figure 1.
The statue of Caesarius made by Ernemann Sander in Königswinter-
Oberdollendorf. Source: Wikimedia Commons.

exempla more and more often ask questions like "What makes a narrative an example that may be used as an efficient instrument of didactic conversion?" "How it is possible to make someone believe in a story and instill faith with a story?" "What strategies of rhetorical and religious persuasion does it involve?"[22]

The construction of exemplarity is usually studied in terms of different narrative and rhetorical strategies used by compilers of *exempla* collections or by preachers who insert *exempla* in their sermons. Compilers or preachers initiate and perform the process of exemplification for their audiences. For example, they can put a particular story into a new moral or doctrinal context, give it a new interpretation, and supply it with a salutary lesson. Or they can establish a parallel between the story in question and another story or event, and in so doing make it topical.[23] However, the processes of exemplification do not end here. The *exemplum* is meant to be efficacious,[24] that is to say that its message should be understood, accepted, internalized, and performed by the audience. Caesarius himself demonstrated such a response. When he accompanied Gevard, the abbot of Heisterbach in 1195/6–1208 from the monastery of Walberberg[25] to Cologne, the abbot told him about the appearance of the Virgin Mary, Saint Anne, and Mary Magdalene to the harvesting monks in Clairvaux and her comforting them.[26] Caesarius was so moved by the story that he promised the

---

[22] See the introduction to Smirnova, et al., *The Art of Cistercian Persuasion.*

[23] Anne Duprat, "Pestes et incendies: l'exemplarité du récit de témoin aux XVIe–XVIIe siècles," in *Construire l'exemplarité: Pratiques littéraires et discours historiens (XVIe –XVIIIe siècles)*, ed. Laurence Giavarini (Dijon: Éditions universitaires de Dijon, 2008), 63–83.

[24] Jacques Berlioz, "Le récit efficace: l'*exemplum* au service de la prédication (XIIIe–XVe siècles)," *Mélanges de l'École française de Rome, Moyen Âge-Temps modernes* 92 (1980/1): 113–46.

[25] Walberberg was a monastery of Cistercian nuns under the authority of Heisterbach.

[26] On this *exemplum*, see Stefano Mula, "Les *exempla* cisterciens du Moyen Âge, entre philologie et histoire," in *L'Œuvre littéraire du Moyen Âge aux yeux*

abbot that he would not make profession anywhere but at Heisterbach (*Dialogus* I.17).

This kind of reaction to *exempla* should not be taken for granted. It would be wrong to imagine that audiences passively absorbed a preacher's teaching without reflection or evaluation. Medieval sources offer abundant evidence of people's reactions to preaching, ranging from enthusiastic reception and similarly vivid disapproval to boredom and sleep.[27] Besides, there was always danger of misinterpretation. Caesarius tells a story about a priest's mistress who, fearing for her own salvation, interrupted a sermon about sins and their punishments in hell and asked the preacher what awaited the concubines of priests in the afterlife. The preacher, knowing this woman to be naive, jokingly responded, "They will be damned, unless they enter a burning furnace." She understood the message literally and threw herself into a furnace (*Dialogus* VI.35). On a less extreme level, Caesarius warns the Novice not to take miracles as examples, that is, not to understand an exceptional case—a miraculously accepted written confession[28]—as an excuse to imitate it by making his own confession in writing.

Neither listening to sermons nor reading didactic texts implied a passive absorption of a proposed lesson. In fact, the *exemplum* usually tells a very specific story that could only be transmitted if it also bore a general meaning relevant to many people.[29] It is no wonder that *exempla* often use indefinite pronouns like *quidam* or *quaedam* to designate their protagonists, as if to tell the audience, "this certain man or certain woman

---

de l'historien et du philologue, ed. Ludmilla Evdokimova and Victoria Smirnova (Paris: Classiques Garnier, 2014), 377–92.

[27] Jacques Berlioz and Marie Anne Polo de Beaulieu, "The Preacher Facing a Reluctant Audience According to the Testimony of Exempla," in *Medieval Sermon Studies* 57, no. 1 (2013): 16–28.

[28] *"Simile aliquid legitur de Karolo Imperatore in Vita sancti Aegidii; sed miracula non sunt in exemplum trahenda"* (*Dialogus* III.27).

[29] Pierre-Antoine Fabre, "Readings/Lessons of the *Exemplum,*" in Smirnova, et al., *The Art of Cistercian Persuasion,* 280–81.

might just as well be you."[30] To internalize the story, the listeners or readers should accept this parallel and admit that they could indeed be that person. By doing so, they could retranslate the general to the particular, so creating a new meaning that they could further perform, for example as penitence. The will to teach a salutary lesson should meet a reciprocal will to be taught, to internalize the lesson and act accordingly.

Medieval readers, like modern ones, actively took what they needed from the text, reconfiguring what they discovered through their reading for their own purpose. This process was especially true for didactic works aiming to improve morals and to change behavior, since they required intensive spiritual work and a great deal of interaction with the text. An author may assign a ready meaning to any given story, but it is the readers' task to make an *exemplum* from it: to construct exemplarity within their own context of socially grounded reading and interpretative practices, varying from community to community, from century to century.

The notion of the community is crucial. If the idea of individual reception is difficult—if even possible—to grasp, especially for the Middle Ages, it is possible to understand a global readership, in Maura Nolan's words, as a community created by intersecting contexts:

> Texts do not exist in isolation. Each written work is embedded in a wide variety of contexts—literary, historical, geographical, social, political, religious—and derives its meaning in part from the intersection of those contexts in the reader's experience of the text. . . . that intersection [may be understood] as a "community": a social, sometimes affective grouping that both intentionally and unintentionally makes meaning.[31]

---

[30] Tilliette, "L'exemplum rhétorique," 65.

[31] Maura Nolan, introduction to *The Text in the Community: Essays on Medieval Works, Manuscripts, Authors, and Readers*, ed. Jill Mann and Maura Nolan (Notre Dame, IN: University of Notre Dame Press, 2006), 1–10, here 1.

The members of such a community share a common discourse (Latin, for example, or a set of Bible references) and a set of practices (scribal, pedagogical, devotional) that shape each individual reading of the texts.[32] Because of various negotiations among members of a community or communities, the process of making meaning continues to evolve long after the initial experiences of the text.

Studying the manuscript and print transmission of an *exempla* collection within different communities makes it possible to reach a fuller understanding of the medieval *exemplum*—this multifaceted narrative form that defies definition. The *Dialogus*, with its long and complex reception history, can serve as an excellent case study. My aim is therefore not only to answer the question of the identity of Caesarius's readers and the way the *Dialogus* was transmitted through different media, but also to understand how different communities exemplified Caesarius's stories. To put it otherwise, how did a collection of stories vigorously promoting the Cistercian way of life in terms of both power and God's approval become compelling and efficacious in different contexts of belief and "making believe"?

The first part of the present book explores the particularities of Cistercian storytelling to put the *Dialogus* in context and to understand how Cistercians themselves perceived and assigned exemplary meaning to their stories. The second part focuses on the manuscript transmission of the *Dialogus* and its reception in different religious communities from the thirteenth to the fifteenth centuries. Because of this focus, I inevitably concentrate on the manuscripts with known provenance, aware that I must omit a number of manuscripts whose provenance is unknown from the scope of this study, no matter how important they might be for the work's textual history. In

---

[32] Nolan, introduction to *The Text in the Community*, 1.

both the first and the second parts, I pay special attention to the signs of scribes' and readers' activity. The *exemplum* was often an object of a specific kind of reading: active and pragmatic.[33] To become an *exemplum*, the narrative must be found in the text and then put into another context, be it a sermon, a new *exempla* collection, a social practice (such as teaching or spiritual conversation), or an individual one (such as meditation, imitation, or examination of conscience). To facilitate finding the narrative, *exempla* in manuscripts are often signaled by means of paragraph signs, initials (lombards), rubrics, or marginal signs, left by scribes or by readers. The marginal notes help to highlight stories for future readers, and therefore to express and to share reading experiences within a community. They say, *You should note this story! It's a good exemplum! It was important for me, and it will be useful for you.* By paying attention to manuscript annotations, one can better understand the complex dynamics between individual and collective in the reception of the *Dialogus*. Usually a communal property, a medieval manuscript can still bear traces of individual reading choices.

In addition to the manuscripts themselves, in what follows I analyze medieval library catalogues that mention the *Dialogus*, not only to trace manuscripts that are now lost, but because such catalogues can also reveal how the book in question was perceived by the community of reception. Works that modern scholars would call *exempla* collections were often in the past classified under different categories. Sometimes such collections were placed with sermons and sermon aids, sometimes with the books on moral theology, history, or monastic rules.[34] As Stephen Kelly and John J. Thompson observe, "Imagining the book as an object always under conditions of process in the Middle Ages—always, in other words, being

---

[33] Victoria Smirnova, "L'*exemplum* médiéval dans une perspective codicologique (XIIIe–XVe siècle)," *Revue Mabillon* 85 (2013): 27–59.
[34] Smirnova, "L'exemplum médiéval," 42.

remade and reconfigured by the cultural demands of its makers, readers, and owners—demotes the idea of the book as material object in favour of the idea of the book as a site of diverse activities and concerns."[35] Questions of how exactly the *Dialogus* as an object was used in different communities may never be answered. Was it used for example to teach novices, or to compose sermons, was it borrowed by monks for individual reading, or read in a group? But one can at least try to understand how it was imagined.

The third part of this book is devoted to early modern, modern, and contemporary reception of the *Dialogus*. The change of media during "the printing revolution" (Elizabeth Eisenstein's expression)[36] could not but affect the transmission of the *Dialogus*. Certainly many religious communities continued to read it in printed form, and to the extent possible I examine the provenance of incunabula of the *Dialogus*. But it is harder to trace print copies of the *Dialogus* to specific communities than those surviving in manuscripts, especially for seventeenth-century editions. In this portion of the book, therefore, I shift the focus from particular communities that possessed the *Dialogus* to discussions about the work and about Caesarius himself, as these inquiries form an important part of the work regarding transmission and reception during the Reformation. Interestingly, in this period Roman Catholic reception of the *Dialogus* was sometimes critical, as editors and publishers reexamined its narrative theology[37] and often found it inconsistent with Catholic doctrine. To understand early

---

[35] Stephen Kelly and John J. Thompson, "Imagined Histories of the Book: Current Paradigms and Future Directions," in *Imagining the Book*, ed. Stephen Kelly and John J. Thompson, Medieval Texts and Cultures of Northern Europe 7 (Turnhout: Brepols, 2005), 5.

[36] Elizabeth Eisenstein, *The Printing Revolution in Early Modern Europe* (Cambridge: Cambridge University Press, 2005).

[37] On the concept of narrative theology in relation to the *Dialogus* see Victoria Smirnova, "Narrative Theology in Caesarius of Heisterbach's *Dialogus miraculorum*," in Smirnova, et al., *The Art of Cistercian Persuasion*, 121–42.

modern reception of the *Dialogus*, it is important to examine how Caesarius's readers dealt with the challenges posed by his often-unorthodox narratives. Another important consequence of the change of media from manuscript to print was the stability of the text. That is, printing left very little room for intervention and interaction with the text during its transmission. Certainly readers left notes on margins, but major interventions became an editorial prerogative. The development of the paratext in early modern books (prefaces, indices, etc.) created new ways of conveying the editor's view of the text and of shaping and controlling readers' responses. I therefore pay particular attention to the composition of new editions of the *Dialogus* and to the way their paratexts framed the text and encouraged a particular reading.

I further touch briefly on how the *Dialogus* was studied from the nineteenth century onward and also on the popular reception of the *Dialogus* and its author from the nineteenth century, when the ruins of Heisterbach Abbey became part of the German romantic landscape, to twenty-first-century medievalism with its playful and bold appropriations of medieval imagery.

From the thirteenth century to the present, different ways of reading *exempla* collections, of internalizing their lessons, and of enjoying their narrative material have emerged and disappeared. An in-depth study of the transmission and reception of Caesarius's *Dialogus miraculorum* can help to clarify both the diversity and continuity of the way what Canadian novelist Nancy Huston calls our "fabulating species"[38] shares experiences and emotions, creates identities, and transfers knowledge by telling and responding to one another's stories.

---

[38] Nancy Huston, *L'espèce fabulatrice*, Un endroit où aller Series (Arles: Actes Sud, 2008).

PART ONE

The White Monks and Their Stories

1

Cistercian Storytelling in the Twelfth and Thirteenth Centuries

Caesarius of Heisterbach's *Dialogus miraculorum*, though exceptional in many regards, continues an established tradition of collecting exemplary stories, especially miracles and visions, that originated in oral storytelling. Stories of local provenance already hold an important place in the first known Cistercian *exempla* collection, the *Collectaneum exemplorum et visionum Clarevallense*, compiled in Clairvaux under the prior John who was in charge in 1171 to 1179.[1] The predominance of the oral tradition is even more apparent in the slightly later *Liber visionum et miraculorum Clarevallensium (Liber)* by Herbert of

---

[1] *Collectaneum exemplorum et visionum Clarevallense e codice Trecensi 946*, ed. Olivier Legendre, CCCM 208 (Turnhout: Brepols, 2005). A first version was probably completed before 1174. The formal *terminus ad quem* is 1181, but the completion of the collection probably took place shortly after 1174 (see Legendre's introduction to *Collectaneum exemplorum*, XXXIV–XLIII). The *Collectaneum* contains, besides local exemplary stories, the long and detailed *Expositio misse* (chap. 29), *sententie satis utiles et necessarie de decretis et sententiis sanctorum* (chaps. 105–27), and visions of Elisabeth of Schönau and of Tnugdal (chaps. 11–12, about one third of the volume). It also contains stories taken from the *Dialogi* of Gregory the Great, *Historia ecclesiatica gentis anglorum* by the Venerable Bede, *Liber de corpore et sanguine Domini* by Paschasius Radbertus, and other works (see Legendre, ed., *Collectaneum exemplorum*, "Fontes exemplorum," 383–434).

Clairvaux (completed in 1178):[2] of 165 total chapters, 147 are from oral sources.[3] The *Exordium magnum Cisterciense*, compiled before 1221[4] by Conrad of Eberbach[5] to present the foundation of Cîteaux and its growth, as well as to legitimize and defend the success of the Order against its detractors, also heavily relies on oral storytelling. The early collections of "monastic folklore" themselves quickly became sought-after written sources. Conrad of Eberbach largely borrows from Herbert's *Liber*, as well as from the *Collectaneum*, and even the compiler of the so-called *Collectio exemplorum Cisterciensis*,[6] which is distinguished from other Cistercian collections of the first quarter of the thirteenth century by its clear preference for written, mostly non-Cistercian, sources, draws heavily from Herbert's collection.[7]

Brian Patrick McGuire connects the beginning of the exemplary genre in the Cistercian milieu with the oral tradition

---

[2] On the relationships between two collections, see Legendre, introduction to *Collectaneum exemplorum*, LXXXVI–XCIII.

[3] Herbertus Turritanus, *Liber visionum et miraculorum Clarevallensium*, ed. Giancarlo Zichi, Graziano Fois, and Stefano Mula, CCCM 277 (Turnhout: Brepols, 2017), LXXIV–LXXVI. Hereafter *Liber*.

[4] The first four books (of six) were probably written during the 1180s. The work was completed between 1206 and 1221 (see Bruno Griesser, introduction to Conradus Eberbacensis, *Exordium magnum Cisterciense, sive Narratio de initio Cisterciensis Ordinis*, ed. Bruno Griesser, CCCM 138 [Turnhout: Brepols, 1997], 33*–36*). Hereafter *Exordium*.

[5] Conrad was a monk in Clairvaux under the abbots Peter Monoculus (1179–1186) and Garnier of Rochefort (1186–1193), before moving to Eberbach (a daughter house of Clairvaux near Mainz), where he became abbot.

[6] The collection, compiled by an anonymous Cistercian between 1200 and 1220, survives in Paris MS., Bibliothèque nationale de France, lat. 15912 (see *Collectio exemplorum Cisterciensis in codice Parisiensi 15912 asseruata*, ed. Jacques Berlioz and Marie Anne Polo de Beaulieu, CCCM 243 [Turnhout: Brepols, 2012]).

[7] On the sources of *Collectio*, see the Introduction to the *Collectio exemplorum Cisterciensis*, XXIII–XXIX, as well as the article by Brian P. McGuire, "The Cistercians and the Rise of the Exemplum in Early Thirteenth Century France: A Reevaluation of Paris BN MS. Lat. 15912," *Classica et Mediaevalia* 34 (1983): 211–67.

developed after the canonization of Saint Bernard. He argues that the telling and writing down of stories that circulated among Cistercian houses can be seen as part of a strategy to cope with the death of Bernard by collecting memories about him, but also about other Cistercian monks, their fights with temptations, and the miraculous consolations they received. These stories were meant, as he writes, "to encourage monks who may have come to feel they had lost a sense of the meaning of their existence."[8]

By reading Cistercian *exempla* collections, one grasps how the question of what it meant to be a Cistercian was raised, nuanced, and answered through the telling of stories, or, to put it otherwise, how the stories circulating in the Cistercian milieu served as tools to shape the Order's collective mentality and identity.[9] Exemplary stories helped to familiarize the monks with written and unwritten rules within the communities, such as, for instance, how to act in case of the death of a brother[10] or how to make a proper confession.[11] They touched upon many

---

[8] Brian P. McGuire, "Les mentalités des Cisterciens dans les recueils d'exempla du XIIe siècle: une nouvelle lecture du *Liber visionum et miraculorum* de Clairvaux," in *Les* Exempla *médiévaux: nouvelles perspectives*, ed. Jacques Berlioz and Marie Anne Polo de Beaulieu (Paris: Honoré Champion, 1998), 107–45. The quotation comes from the English summary of the article on 107. See also Brian P. McGuire, "Cistercian Storytelling—A Living Tradition: Surprises in the World of Research," CSQ 39 (2004): 281–309, esp. 288–90 on the emergence of the Cistercian storytelling tradition.

[9] On the notion of collective identity, see Russell Spears, "Group Identities: The Social Identity Perspective," in *Handbook of Identity Theory and Research*, vol. 1, *Structures and Processes*, ed. Seth J. Schwartz, Koen Luyckx, and Vivian L. Vignoles (New York-Dordrecht-Heidelberg, et al.: Springer, 2011), 201–24.

[10] Stefano Mula, "Herbert de Torrès et l'autoreprésentation de l'ordre cistercien dans les recueils d'*exempla*," in *Le Tonnerre des exemples:* Exempla *et médiation culturelle dans l'Occident médiéval*, ed. Jacques Berlioz, Pascal Collomb, and Marie Anne Polo de Beaulieu (Rennes: Presses Universitaires de Rennes, 2010), 187–200, see esp. 198–99 for the conclusion.

[11] Caesarius insists in the *Dialogus* (III.23–25) that a monk should make a general confession to the abbot, *secundum consuetudinem ordinis*.

issues of monastic life, such as sexual temptations,[12] and provided a pattern of decent behavior within the Cistercian community by inviting their listeners to learn from both positive and negative examples.[13] From the *Dialogus* one can deduce a great deal about Cistercian practices of oral communication.[14] For example, the telling of stories played a crucial role in the period of the novitiate as an efficient tool for monastic socialization, to use McGuire's expression.[15] Caesarius more than any other Cistercian writer

---

[12] McGuire, "Les mentalités des Cisterciens," 110–13.

[13] On the crucial role of stories in the organization of the religious life, see also Markus Schürer, *Das Exemplum oder die erzählte Institution: Studien zum Beispielgebrauch bei den Dominikanern und Franziskanern des 13. Jahrhunderts*, Vita regularis 12 (Münster: LIT, 2005). See also Thomas Füser, "Vom *exemplum Christi* über das *exemplum sanctorum* zum 'Jedermannsbeispiel': Überlegungen zur Normativität exemplarischer Verhaltensmuster im institutionellen Gefüge der Bettelorden des 13. Jahrhunderts," in *Die Bettelorden im Aufbau. Beiträge zur Institutionalisierungsprozessen im mittelalterlichen Religiosentum*, ed. Gert Melville and Jörg Oberste, Vita regularis 11 (Münster: LIT, 1999), 27–106.

[14] I do not aim here to discuss in detail the notion of orality in its theoretical implications. The concept itself is not new in the domain of medieval studies; see, for example, Karl Reichl, "Plotting the Map of Medieval Oral Literature," in *Medieval Oral Literature*, ed. Karl Reichl (Berlin-Boston: De Gruyter, 2012), 3–68, though monastic storytelling is not discussed there. Monastic oral practices are analyzed in more depth in Steven Vanderputten, ed., *Understanding Monastic Practices of Oral Communication (Western Europe, Tenth–Thirteenth Centuries)* (Turnhout: Brepols, 2011); see especially the article by Marie Anne Polo de Beaulieu, "Traces d'oralité dans les recueils d'*exempla* cisterciens," 139–57. See also (with an emphasis on the institutional control of oral communication in the Cistercian milieu), Victoria Smirnova, "Narrative Theology in Caesarius of Heisterbach's *Dialogus miraculorum*," in *The Art of Cistercian Persuasion in the Middle Ages and Beyond*, ed. Victoria Smirnova, Marie Anne Polo de Beaulieu, and Jacques Berlioz (Leiden: Brill, 2015), 121–42, esp. 136–40; and Victoria Smirnova, "Raconter des histoires dans une communauté soumise au silence: les Cisterciens et leurs *exempla* (XIIe–XIIIe s.)," *L'Atelier du CRH*, forthcoming.

[15] Brian P. McGuire, "Friends and Tales in the Cloister: Oral Sources in Caesarius of Heisterbach's *Dialogus miraculorum*," *Analecta cisterciensia* 36 (1980): 191.

stresses the importance of storytelling for newcomers. As he declares in the Prologue, he put into the *Dialogus* the stories he was accustomed to narrate to the novices. He also relates his own experience of the novitiate through the stories he had heard, and not only from his master of novices (VII.13, 14) or senior monks (II.22), but also from other novices (I.3; IV.49), who, like Caesarius himself, were learning what it meant to be a Cistercian.

Further, the monks of different ranks actively exchanged stories, as one can tell from the information provided by Caesarius on how he came to know one or another story. Edifying stories were among the few subjects permitted for conversation in a Cistercian monastery.[16] In a community subjected to the strict observance of silence, the spiritually edifying storytelling provided a rare opportunity to discuss feelings, to maintain friendships, and to experience and internalize the fraternal *caritas* as crucial element of their identity.[17] Caesarius does not specifically address the issue of monastic friendships (though his stories reveal a great deal about emotional relationships in a monastic context).[18] But in his few mentions, the sentiments

---

[16] Around ten years after the composition of the *Dialogus*, in 1232, the General Chapter published a statute against illicit conversations. During *colloquia*, monks were only allowed to talk about miracles or about saints, pronounce edifying words, or evoke topics that served the salvation of the soul (Joseph-Marie Canivez, ed., *Statuta Capitulorum Generalium Ordinis Cisterciensis ab anno 1116 ad annum 1786*, vol. 2 [Louvain: Revue d'Histoire Ecclésiastique, 1934], 102 [1232, no. 5]): *Propter collationes illicitas de medio tollendas, statuitur ut quando monachi causa solatii ad colloquium ab ordinis custode vocantur, illud colloquium sit de sanctorum miraculis, de verbis aedificatoriis, et de his quae pertinent ad salutem animarum.*

[17] On Cistercian friendships, see Brian Patrick McGuire, "The Cistercians and the Transformation of Monastic Friendships," *Analecta Cisterciensia* 37 (1981): 1–69. See also McGuire, "Cistercian Storytelling," 304–7.

[18] On friendly male-female relationships (as reported by Caesarius), see McGuire, "The Cistercians and the Transformation," 28–36. On friendship between novices, see Brian P. McGuire, "Taking Responsibility: Medieval Cistercian Abbots and Monks as their Brother's Keepers," *Citeaux* 39 (1988): 261–63.

of friendship and fraternal charity are clearly linked to the sharing of stories.

In chapter thirty of the fourth *distinctio* (IV.30), Caesarius narrates the visions and temptations of Christian, a monk from Heisterbach, whose health was so bad that he was granted permission to stay in the chapter room during Solemn Vigils. Christian, however, almost never took advantage of this permission, and at Matins he even stayed in the church longer than was required for the sick. Approached by Henry (the future abbot of Heisterbach, but at that time a simple monk), Christian reluctantly mentioned a consolation that God had bestowed upon him, and Henry continued to question him, because they had a special friendship (*de speciali praesumens amicitia*). Henry finally obtained the answer: Christian saw angels and Christ himself moving in the choir during the psalmody. In *distinctio* V.4, Caesarius says that Herman (the first abbot of Heisterbach) conveyed to him his visions of the devil out of great charity (*ex multa caritate*). Adam, a monk from the Loccum abbey, aware of Caesarius's passion for modern miracles, *ex multa caritate* told him about his own miraculous healing (VII.24).

By sharing stories, their own or those heard elsewhere, different members of the Cistercian community not only contributed to the group narrative about the Order, but also claimed their place in it. Caesarius relates, for example, that lay brothers shared their spiritual experiences with monks. Some lay brothers took the initiative to approach the prior or even the abbot[19] to talk about their visions, overstepping the boundary—both spatial and hierarchical—that separated "two monasteries," the expression of the Cistercian in Idung of Prüfening's *Dialogus inter Cluniacensem monachum et Cisterciensem*.[20] So, for example,

[19] See *Dialogus* VIII.43, in which a lay brother from Himmerod reports his vision to the abbot Herman.

[20] "*Nos modo habemus infra ambitum monasterii duo monasteria: unum scilicet laicorum fratrum, et aliud clericorum*" ("*Dialogus inter Cluniacensem monachum et Cisterciensem*," III.43, ed. Robert B. C. Huygens, in *Le moine Idung et ses deux*

once an unnamed lay brother described as being simple came from a grange to Herman, then the prior of Himmerod, Heisterbach's mother abbey,[21] and said that he wanted to talk with him in secret (IV.96). When Herman gave him permission, the lay brother narrated his dream. He reported that he had seen a column with an iron spike driven into it, and on the spike hung a very beautiful crown. Then he saw a beautiful man who took the crown from the spike, gave it to him, and said, "Take it to that monk (naming the monk),[22] because he has deserved it this very night." Having heard this account, Herman understood that the monk in question had overcome a very strong temptation.

Another group within the Cistercian Order that benefited from the booming storytelling activity were nuns, whose difficult integration into the Order is still a matter of discussion among scholars.[23] In the *Dialogus*, Caesarius tells not only stories about nuns, but also stories related by nuns (fifteen altogether), from for example Gertrude, the abbess of Hoven

---

ouvrages *"Argumentum super quatuor questionibus"* et *"Dialogus duorum monachorum"* [Spoleto: Centro italiano di studi sull'alto medioevo, 1972], 463). On the separateness of life and functions of monks and lay brothers, see James France, *Separate but Equal: Cistercian Lay Brothers, 1120–1350*, CF 246 (Collegeville, MN: Cistercian Publications, 2012), 89–172. It should be noted that the *Usus conversorum* requires of lay brothers a strict observation of silence, stating, for example, *"Insuper in suo dormitorio et refectorio omnino silentium teneant, et preter hec in omnibus locis aliis, nisi forte iussu abbatis uel prioris de necessariis loquantur, uel etiam ipsius cellararii, si tamen hec potestas cellarario data fuerit"* (Chrysogonus Waddell, *Cistercian Lay Brothers: Twelfth-century Usages with Related Texts*, Cîteaux: Commentarii cistercienses, Studia et Documenta 10 [Brecht: Cîteaux, 2000], 65, chap. VI).

[21] Herman was the abbot of Heisterbach from 1189 to 1195/96.

[22] Caesarius omits the name, although he knew the monk personally.

[23] Among many works on this subject, see, for example, Alexis Grélois, "Clairvaux et le monachisme féminin, des origines au milieu du XVe siècle," in *Le temps long de Clairvaux: Nouvelles recherches, nouvelles perspectives (XIIe–XXIe siècle)*, ed. Alexis Grélois and Arnaud Baudin (Paris: Somogy, 2016), 155–82.

(VIII.82),[24] and Petrissa, a nun from Walberberg (V.54). Caesarius thus portrays nuns as having a certain level of storytelling agency, and conveys monks' willingness to listen to
women's stories and to learn from them. Through storytelling,
the members of the Cistercian community experienced and
expressed acceptance of one another.

Thus Cistercian storytelling as portrayed by Caesarius had
a strong communal aspect. It promoted and nourished emotional attachment and commitment to the group and supple-
mented particular events with explanations and interpretations
that served to construct a powerful and compelling image of
the Cistercian way of life. It is a fascinating area of research that
has helped—and will certainly continue to help—our understanding of the Cistercian phenomenon in general. But one of
the most fascinating things about the Cistercian storytelling
of the twelfth through the beginning of the thirteenth century
is what Karl Reichl has called its written "fixation" or "textu-
alization"[25]—to put it in other words, the fact that a predominantly literate society[26] judged oral tradition important enough
to invest time, administrative action, and money in it.

Manuscript production was expensive and time consuming.
Along with that, Cistercian book production was strictly controlled. According to the statute promulgated by the General
Chapter in 1134, no abbot or monk or novice could write a
book without permission of the General Chapter.[27] In 1175, the

---

[24] Hoven (Marienborn) was a female Cistercian monastery in Zülpich
(North Rhine-Westphalia), founded in 1188.

[25] Reichl discusses the concept in Reichl, "Plotting the Map," 8–10.

[26] On the interactions between oral and written traditions in the Cistercian
milieu, see McGuire's observations on Caesarius's written sources: "Written
Sources and Cistercian Inspiration in Caesarius of Heisterbach," *Analecta
Cisterciensia* 35 (1979): 227–82, and especially the section titled "Cistercian
Models: The Lives of Bernard and Herbert's *Liber miraculorum*" (266–74).

[27] Canivez, *Statuta Capitulorum Generalium*, vol. I (Louvain: Revue
d'Histoire Ecclésiastique, 1933): 26 (1134, art. LVIII): "*Nulli liceat abbati, nec
monacho, nec novitio, libros facere, nisi forte cuiquam in generali capitulo concessum
fuerit.*"

Chapter issued another statute controlling book production, this one stating that abbots who had written sermons and other texts were to submit their works for approval during the next General Chapter.[28] It is not known which incident gave occasion to the statute of 1175, or whether both statutes were actually observed.[29] Henry, the abbot of Heisterbach at the time, was at least supposed not only to approve Caesarius's project but also to take the necessary steps to obtain the permission from the General Chapter.

Once collected in a book, what had been known as monastic folklore therefore gained a new importance and authority. Compilers claimed the relevance of their works to monastic formation and presented them as much-needed reading material on a par with such bestsellers as the *Vitae Patrum*. The anonymous compiler of the *Collectaneum*,[30] the first known Cistercian *exempla* collection, reported that he had searched for examples relevant to monastic temptations and their remedies in the treatises of doctors of the church but found them nowhere except in the *Vitae Patrum*.[31] In accordance to what was recommended by Cistercian treatises of spiritual advice, and specifically the obligation to learn,[32] monks were eager to

---

[28] Canivez, *Statuta Capitulorum Generalium* I:84 (1175, no. 31): *"Abbates qui sermones et alias scripturarum compilationes fecerunt eadem opuscula sua in proximo Capitulo representent."*

[29] Cistercians might not have strictly complied with these statutes. See Hans D. Oppel, "Die exemplarischen Mirakel des Engelhard von Langheim: Unterschungen und kommentierte Textausgausgabe (Teildruck)," Würzburg University, PhD dissertation, 1978, 66.

[30] Or one of the compilers; the book was probably a collective effort: *"Denique liber iste proprium non habet auctorem; nam plures fuerunt; qui que in eo scripta sunt, stilo singuli proprio tractaverunt"* (*Collectaneum exemplorum et visionum Clarevallense*, 6).

[31] *"Etsi non omnes uel integre, tamen multorum tractatus legi doctorum et non recolo me inuenisse in eorum scriptis exempla multa de hujuscemodi temptamentis, uel eorum remediis. . . . nisi in Vitas Patrum in quadam collectione"* (*Collectaneum exemplorum et visionum Clarevallense*, 286).

[32] Caroline Walker Bynum, Docere Verbo et Exemplo: *An Aspect of Twelfth-Century Spirituality*, Harvard Theological Studies 31 (Missoula, MT: Scholar Press, 1979).

find material that would be beneficial for their spiritual progress. Caesarius indeed often describes himself and his fellow monks as actively looking for edifying stories.

Abbots or priors, for example, sometimes used their authority to compel sick or dying monks to share their spiritual experiences. In *distinctio* VII.16, Caesarius tells of Christian, a monk in Himmerod, who once became ill and was placed in the infirmary. He was visited there by his son, also a monk in the same community. Christian started to tell his son about the visions he had seen, and Gevard, then an infirmarian in Himmerod and later the abbot of Heisterbach, told the prior. The prior first purposely asked Christian (*"ex industria,"* as Caesarius points out), if he had something to confess. Christian answered that he had already made his confession. Then the prior said, *"Rogo ut aliquid mihi dicatis ad aedificationem"* ("I ask you to tell me something edifying"). This time Christian, complying with the request, shared his vision of the Virgin Mary and Christ in monastic habits.

The writing down of edifying stories circulating in the monastic milieu turned them into examples to learn from, available to every literate brother. The compilers strengthened the relevance of their stories for the community and increased the teaching potential of individual experiences by imposing interpretations upon them through morals and comments, or by interweaving them with other stories, thus enhancing their mutual meaning. Even in collections without an obvious structure, stories often form thematic clusters, providing readers with opportunities to explore issues of current interest. For instance, Engelhard of Langheim allows himself a certain lack of structure in the collection addressed to the nuns of Wechterswinkel (1188–1190): *"Debueram in textu consequentias querere, similia similibus comparare, sed facio quod infantulus, quidquid in buccam primum venerit, prius loquor"* ("I should have sought to make the text more consistent, and to compare similar to similar, but instead I proceed like a child, and what comes first to the mouth I will talk about first").[33] Engelhard's stories, however, tend to appear in thematic groups: the sacrament of the altar (chapters 2–7), remedies against temptations (chapters 8–11), and stories in defense and praise of the Cistercian Order (chapters 22 and 24–35).[34]

As the prologues to Cistercian *exempla* collections show, the recording of recent miracles and visions also had a pronounced historiographical and memorial dimension. The most evident example is the *Exordium*, which strives to offer a global vision of the history of the Order. In the prologue, Conrad of Eberbach describes his purpose as follows: "*Et nunc intentus scrutare uoluminis huius / Textum, quo plene ualida pandam ratione / Principium celebris uitae, quae gaudia caelis / Parturit et terris parat incrementa salutis*" ("And now [reader], pay heed and carefully examine / The text of this volume, / By which I shall plainly and with compelling reasoning disclose / The origin of this celebrated [Cistercian] way of life, / Which to the joys of heaven gives birth / And on earth prepares the seeds of salvation").[35] Conrad begins with a brief presentation of monastic history from Christ to the foundation of Cîteaux, then moves on to the history of Clairvaux, told through the stories of its abbots (and especially Saint Bernard), high-ranking and simple monks, both literate and illiterate, and lay brothers.[36] To sum it up,

---

[33] Cited in Oppel, *Die exemplarischen Mirakel*, 79. On Engelhard's *Miracula*, see Bruno Griesser, "Engelhard von Langheim und sein Exempelbuch für die Nonnen von Wechterswinkel," *Cistercienser-Chronik* 70 (1963): 55–73.

[34] Oppel, *Die exemplarischen Mirakel*, 78.

[35] *Exordium magnum Cisterciense*, 3. English translation cited from Conrad of Eberbach, *The Great Beginning of Cîteaux: A Narrative of the Beginning of the Cistercian Order*, trans. Benedicta Ward and Paul Savage, ed. E. Rozanne Elder, CF 72 (Kalamazoo, MI: Cistercian Publications, 2012), 39.

[36] Books I to IV. Clairvaux's stories occupy books II to IV and are arranged according to the Order's hierarchy, not chronologically. The last two books are a collection of edifying stories on different aspects of monastic life, organized thematically. Their geographical scope is wider than the stories in the rest of the volume, including Germany and Italy, and a number of *exempla* are not monastic.

Conrad tells the story of Cistercian success, highlighted by numerous miracles and exemplary devotion.

Unlike the *Exordium*, the *Dialogus* does not intend to follow a chronological order, but its historical overtone is nevertheless unmistakable. As Caesarius states in his Prologue, his aim in the *Dialogus* is to save from oblivion the miraculous events that had happened and were continuing to happen in the Cistercian milieu. Interestingly, he explains his decision to add to the *Dialogus* some of the stories from the *Liber miraculorum* of Himmerod,[37] the mother abbey of Heisterbach, through the same lens of preserving history: *"Duo haec capitula, sicut et quinque reliqua quae sequuntur, a quodam reperi notata, qui se ea quae dicta sunt vidisse et audivisse commemorat; quae perire non sum passus"* ("These two chapters, as well as five that follow, I found written elsewhere by someone who recalls having seen and heard the events. I could not stand to let them perish") (XI.3).

The historical purpose of the *Dialogus* was recognized very early by Caesarius's fellow Cistercians. Alberic of Trois-Fontaines († 1252), primarily known for his chronicles, in around 1229 made a collection of excerpts from the *Dialogus* (totaling sixty-one *exempla*), organized chronologically and indicating dates, using Caesarius's hints. The title of the compilation, *Adbreviatio relationum fratris Cesarii, monachi de Valle santi Petri*, given probably by Alberic himself, emphasizes the historical value of Caesarius's stories.[38] The *Dialogus* apparently enjoyed an early appreciation in the cradle of Cistercian *exemplum* tradition.

---

[37] Griesser dates the *Liber* to after 1213 ("Ein Himmeroder *Liber miraculorum* und seine Beziehungen zu Caesarius von Heisterbach," *Archiv für mittelrheinische Kirchengeschichte: nebst Berichten zur kirchlichen Denkmalpflege* 4 [1952]: 259).

[38] Stefano Mula, "*Exemplum* and Historiography: Alberic of Trois-Fontaines' Reading of Caesarius's *Dialogus miraculorum*," in Smirnova, et al., *The Art of Cistercian Persuasion*, 143–59.

Cistercian exemplary stories appeal to the communal sense of the past, and some reworkings and changes introduced by the Cistercians during the transmission of the earlier *exempla* collections can be interpreted as attempts to make them more relevant for the target community. In the last quarter of the thirteenth century, an anonymous compiler from Fürstenfeld in Bavaria decided to eliminate from Herbert's *Liber* all stories not directly related to the Cistercian Order.[39] He also changed the order of chapters according to the Order's hierarchy: the rearranged collection started with the stories about abbots, followed by the stories about monks and novices, and so on (possibly indicating some influence by the *Exordium*, whose second, third, and fourth books are arranged in a similar way). The compiler excerpted Herbert's *Liber* from the manuscript belonging to Aldersbach, the mother house of Fürstenfeld.[40] Interestingly, he decided not to copy the *Vita* of Saint Brendan, which precedes the *Liber* in Aldersbach's exemplar. Instead, after the *Liber* he added a small *exempla* collection originating from Ebrach (Fürstenfeld's grandmother house).[41]

Ebrach's original *Libellus miraculorum* (1219–1227), containing seven miracles about monks from Cîteaux, Clairvaux, and Ebrach, does not survive. The collection was later copied by an anonymous monk, probably from Aldersbach,[42] who added

---

[39] See Munich MS., Bayerische Staatsbibliothek, Clm 6914. This short version of the *Liber* was published in *Herbert von Clairvaux und sein Liber miraculorum: die Kurzversion eines anonymen bayerischen Redaktors*, ed. Gabriela Kompatscher-Gufler (Bern: Lang, 2005).

[40] Munich MS., Bayerische Staatsbibliothek, Clm 2607.

[41] On this collection see Hans D. Oppel, "Eine kleine Sammlung cisterciensischer Mirakel aus dem 13. Jahrhundert," *Würzburger Diözesangeschichtsblätter* 34 (1972): 5–28. Munich MS. Bayerische Staatsbibliothek, Clm 6914, also contains the life of Saint Erasmus (by another hand), books II–III of the *Collationes patrum* (by yet another hand), and book inventories from 1312, 1313, and 1314.

[42] He refers to Ebrach Abbey as "our mother" (see Oppel, "Eine kleine Sammlung," 6–7): "*quia ad alia, que in honorabili matre nostra, domo scilicet Eberacensi.*" The sentence comes from chapter II, *De beata Agatha virgine, que*

three more miracles: a vision of an unknown Franciscan nun who saw the Cistercian Order having the superior position in heaven, a vision of Agatha from Himmelspforten (a Cistercian monastery under the care of Ebrach), and the eucharistic vision of Rudolf, monk in Kaisheim. This enlarged version is the one copied into the Fürstenfeld manuscript.

Interestingly, the first two stories about female visionaries already circulated in the vernacular. The author had received them written on a leaflet from some unnamed Cistercian nuns (*in quadam cedula michi concessa a devotis quibusdam nostri ordinis monialibus . . . vulgaribus verbis scriptam legissem*). Although he had doubts about Agatha's vision, a certain nun assured him that she had spent some time in Himmelspforten and had seen Agatha there, and that the related version was authentic. The author took that opportunity to question the nun about some details of the story and then retold both visions in Latin. Later he even traveled to Himmelspforten with his abbot and spoke with the nuns there. At first he hesitated to bring up the subject of Agatha's visions, but encouraged by the abbot, he asked one nun "*submissa voce*" ("in a low voice") about Agatha. At once, almost all nuns present confirmed the veracity of the miracle and added more detail about Agatha's pious life.[43] The editor's engagement is quite remarkable, but no more so than the storytelling agency of the nuns who not only made the vision circulate but also took action to assure its veracity.

Despite a similar premise—the first-person narrator receives a written version of a vision, has doubts, and investigates further—the vision of Rudolf, added by the monk from Aldersbach to the Ebrach collection of miracles, was in all likelihood written by another person. MS. Munich Bayerische Staatsbibliothek, Clm 6914, from Fürstenfeld, in fact transmits the so-

---

fuit in claustro monialium ordinis Cisterciensis quod dicitur Celi porta, published separately by Bruno Griesser, "Agatha von Himmelspforten, eine unbekannte Cistercienserin des 13. Jahrhunderts," *Cistercienser-Chronik* 59 (1952): 111.

[43] Griesser, "Agatha von Himmelspforten," 110–11.

called short version of the *Visio Rudolfi*, which is also to be found in MS. Munich, Bayerische Staatsbibliothek, Clm 28165, from Kaisheim.[44] The long version, transmitted in four manuscripts,[45] is not a first-person account. It clearly states, however, that it was Eberhard I von Rohrdorf, abbot of Salem from 1191 to 1240, who questioned Rudolf about his vision and later published it in Salem.[46] The similarities between the two versions suggest that the short version was written by Eberhard as well.[47] The vision of Rudolf apparently circulated in leaflets, as is implied by the words, "*et alii quamplures ipsam visionem transcripserunt*" ("many other persons copied this vision").[48]

The rapid circulation of written miracles between related or neighboring abbeys is noticeable in the case of both Aldersbach and Salem. Additionally, Caesarius himself testifies in chapter IX.41 of the *Dialogus* that a priest from Himmerod wrote him about the eucharistic vision of a lay brother. The leaflet- and letter-exchange was arguably an important part of Cistercian storytelling practices, though little known because of the scarcity of surviving evidence.

Miracles and visions also enhanced the community's image. The author of the Ebrach collection, for instance, presents his monastery as follows: "*In Erbipolensis ecclesie dyocesi est celebre monasterium quod dicitur Eberach, cuius odor bone opinionis et*

---

[44] The manuscript from Kaisheim was used in the edition by Andrea Liebers; see "Rigor ordinis—Gratia amoris. I," *Cîteaux* 43 (1992): 175–81.

[45] Paul Gerhard Schmidt, ed., "Luzifer in Kaisheim: Die Sakramentsvision des Zisterziensers Rudolf (ca. 1207) und Abt Eberhard von Salem," in *Litterae Medii Aevi: Festschrift für Johanne Autenrieth zum 65. Geburtstag*, ed. Michael Borgolte and Herrad Spilling (Sigmaringen: Thorbecke, 1988), 191–201. See also Andrea Fleischer, *Zisterzienserabt und Skriptorium: Salem unter Eberhard I. von Rohrdorf (1191–1240)* (Wiesbaden: Reichert, 2004), 195–218.

[46] On Eberhard and the *Visio Rudolfi* see p. 47 below.

[47] See Liebers, "Rigor ordinis. I," 174. Oppel, however, does not exclude the possibility that it was written by the same person (the monk from Aldersbach) as the first two visions (Oppel, "Eine kleine Sammlung," 8).

[48] Oppel, "Eine kleine Sammlung," 25–26.

sancte conversationis est notus Deo in omni loco sicut odor agri pleni cui benedixit Dominus [Genes. 27, 27]" ("In the Diocese of Würzburg, there is a famous monastery called Ebrach, whose odor of good fame and saintly way of life is known to God and all around, like the smell of a field that the Lord has blessed").[49] The local miracles have no less importance than those experienced by monks from Cîteaux and Clairvaux: the scribe from Aldersbach who copied the *Liber* mentions the persons as equally admirable *"de diversarum ordinis nostri ecclesiarum, id est Clareuallensis, Cysterciensis, Eberacensis"*[50] ("from the different houses of our Order, that is Clairvaux, Cîteaux, and Ebrach").

The anonymous compiler of the *Liber miraculorum* of Himmerod similarly commemorates saintly members of his community, shaping the image of Himmerod as a place receiving special grace and protection from God:

> *Ab initio fundationis domus nostre constat hoc in loco uiros fuisse magnificos, dilectos a Deo et hominibus, quorum memoria in benedictione est adhuc. Quos illuminauit et ditauit lumen uerum, quod illuminat omnem hominem, alios scientia, alios prudentia, alios eruditionis facultate, alios uisionum consolatione.*

> (It is known that, from the very foundation of our house, there were eminent men, loved by God and by others, whose memory is blessed up to now. The true light that illuminates all people enlightened and enriched them, some with knowledge, some with prudence, some with capacity to teach, some with consolation by visions.)[51]

By collecting miraculous stories from their own communities, compilers reinforced the sense that the choice to join the monastery in question was especially rewarding. The message was clear: God rewarded his beloved Cistercians with his wonders,

---

[49] Oppel, "Eine kleine Sammlung," 21.
[50] Griesser, "Agatha von Himmelspforten," 111.
[51] Griesser, "Ein Himmeroder Liber miraculorum," 260.

even in modern times when miracles were rare compared to the time of the first Christians.

The reader of a Cistercian *exempla* collection was expected not only to accept the narrated events (usually miraculous) as an important part of communal history and identity, but also to develop some degree of affective bond and sense of solidarity with the storyteller and the protagonists of the tales. As the compiler of the *Collectaneum* stresses, his stories require "*fidem*

. . . , *non racionem; assensum, non argumentum; simplicem animum, non scrupulosum; deuotum, non uersutum; amicum, non insidiosum; credulum, non dubium; flexibilem, non obstinatum*" ("faith, not reason; assent, not argument, a simple soul, not captious; devout, not cunning; credulous, not doubtful; flexible, not obstinate").[52] The Cistercian strategy of making believe (*fairecroire*) relied on the communal emotion of brotherly or sisterly love that enhanced acceptance of the stories and their salutary message. Engelhard of Langheim in the afterword (*Apologeticum scriptoris*) to his collection of miracles for the nuns in Wechterswinkel declares that charity has persuaded him to write and that he expects the same charity and trust from his readers: "*Eadem* [caritas] *persuasit, ut scriberem: persuadeat et legentibus, ut adhibeant fidem et que honesta sunt horum dignaque imitatu, venerentur in aliis et exhibeant in se ipsis*" ("This same charity persuaded me to write; let it persuade readers to embrace faith and to venerate in others and show in themselves virtuous things that are worthy of being imitated").[53]

One can deduce a great deal about the modes of construction of exemplarity in Cistercian *exempla* collections by analyzing their prologues and other authorial interpolations, which often offer glimpses into the image of an ideal audience and modes of reception intended by the compilers. The content of *exempla* collections also reveals the interests of their readers and the

---

[52] *Collectaneum exemplorum et visionum Clarevallense*, 5.

[53] See Joseph Schwarzer, "Vitae und Miracula aus Kloster Ebrach," *Neues Archiv fur Deutsche Geschitskunde* 6 (1881): 521.

way a community nurtured and supported these interests. The initial reception of the early collections rested on adherence to a communal narrative, emotional investment in the group, and a shared sense of the past. It would, however, be incorrect to imagine the Cistercian reception and transmission of the *Dialogus* in light of the early tradition alone. The majority of the surviving Cistercian manuscripts of the *Dialogus* date from the fourteenth and fifteenth centuries. A closer look at Cistercian *exemplum* production after the *Dialogus* is indispensable for understanding how the white monks managed their extremely rich storytelling tradition from the middle of the thirteenth century onward, so to grasp the social and cultural dynamics related to the consumption of exemplary stories.

2

Cistercian *Exempla* Production in the Late Thirteenth through Fifteenth Centuries

The late-medieval Cistercian *exempla* collections are unfortunately insufficiently researched[1] and have not gained the attention and visibility enjoyed by the early collections, even giving the impression that the Cistercian *exemplum* tradition ended with the *Dialogus*. But Cistercians in fact continued to collect edifying stories. Jean-Thiébaut Welter has already identified at least three collections composed in the fourteenth

---

[1] On late-medieval Cistercian collections, see Victoria Smirnova, "De l'histoire à la rhétorique: Les recueils d'*exempla* cisterciens du Moyen Âge tardif," in *L'Œuvre littéraire du Moyen Âge aux yeux de l'historien et du philologue*, ed. Ludmilla Evdokimova and Victoria Smirnova (Paris: Classiques Garnier, 2014), 393–408. The *Sertum florum moralium* (see below) has been discussed in Marie Anne Polo de Beaulieu, "L'image du clergé séculier dans les recueils d'*exempla* (XIIIᵉ–XVᵉ siècles)," in *Le clerc séculier au Moyen Âge, actes du XXIIᵉ congrès de la Société des Historiens Médiévistes de l'Enseignement Supérieur Public, Amiens, juin 1991* (Paris: Publications de la Sorbonne, 1993), 61–80; Marie Anne Polo de Beaulieu, "L'exemplarité cistercienne," in *Les Cisterciens et la transmission des textes (XIIᵉ–XVIIIᵉ siècles)*, ed. Thomas Falmagne, et al. (Turnhout: Brepols, 2018), 271–72.

century,[2] though only one, the so-called *Liber lacteus*, was recently edited (regrettably only partially).[3]

In the times of booming mendicant *exempla* collections, the Cistercian *exemplum* tradition, as we know it from earlier times, might seem to have become sporadic and feeble, but it was far from being completely extinct. The General Chapter encouraged the collecting of miracles that took place in the Order: a statute from 1325 ordered that monks collect such miracles and submit them to the General Chapter, where they were to be written down and then diffused in the *scripta publica*.[4] About a century later (in 1439 and 1447), the General Chapter promulgated further statutes urging abbots to promote the collecting of stories about their pious and saintly monks and nuns.[5]

In Germany and Austria in particular, the compiling of local collections commemorating the devotion and spiritual experiences of community members continued to be observed. In the previous chapter, I mentioned MS. Munich, Bayerische

---

[2] Jean-Thiébaut Welter, *L'Exemplum dans la littérature religieuse et didactique du Moyen Âge* (Paris-Toulouse: Occitania, 1927). These are the *Lacteus Liquor* (279–81), the *Libellus exemplorum* (285–86), and the *Sertum florum moralium* (325–28). Welter's attribution of the *Liber ad status* to a Cistercian compiler (272–75) is apparently incorrect. Recent studies show that the *Liber ad status* was probably compiled by Rambert of Bologna, a Dominican theologian and bishop of Castello near Venice († 1308); see Caroline Guillaume, "Édition d'un recueil d'*exempla* du XIVe siècle, le *Speculum exemplare* ou *Liber ad status*," PhD dissertation, École des chartes, 1991, 22–23.

[3] *Liber lacteus: eine unbeachtete Mirakel- und Exempelsammlung aus dem Zisterzienserkloster Stams (Innsbruck, ULB, Cod. 494)*, ed. Daniela E. Mairhofer (Badenweiler: Bachmann, 2009). Mairhofer gives only the *incipits* and *explicits* of each *exemplum* and identifies their sources and parallel texts.

[4] Joseph-Marie Canivez, ed., *Statuta Capitulorum Generalium Ordinis Cisterciensis ab anno 1116 ad annum 1786* (Louvain: Revue d'Histoire Ecclésiastique, 1935), 3:370 (1325, No. 2): "*generale Capitulum ordinat et diffinit quod miracula facta vel facienda in locis Ordinis universi, per personas Ordinis generali Capitulo regulariter et lucide referantur, et ibidem in scriptis publicis redigantur.*"

[5] Canivez, *Statuta Capitulorum generalium* (Louvain: Revue d'Histoire Ecclésiastique, 1936), 4:488–89 (1439, no. 98), and *Statuta Capitulorum generalium*, 4:603 (1447, no. 4).

Staatsbibliothek, Clm 6914, originating from Fürstenfeld, which contains the short version of Herbert's *Liber visionum et miraculorum Clarevallensium (Liber)* and the *Libellus miraculorum* from Ebrach. In the end of the thirteenth or beginning of the fourteenth century, this manuscript was copied in Stams abbey in Tirol.[6] The Stams scribe added to the manuscript the collection of stories compiled by Rudolf, the abbot of Stams from 1289.[7] The collection comprises ninety-eight miracles performed in Stams by Saint John the Baptist: *Miracula, que in Stams a Domino per beatum Johannem perpetrantur.*

In Waldsassen (one of the earliest Cistercian foundations in Bavaria), Abbot Johannes de Cubito (1313–1325) collected lives, deeds, and mystical experiences of monks of his abbey under the title *De vita venerabilium monachorum monasterii sui liber*. He dedicated his work to Peter of Zittau, the abbot of Königsaal (Zbraslav), near Prague. As Johannes stated in his dedication, Peter had previously told him or written to him about the lives, morals, and *exempla* of devoted persons from his own abbey.[8] Inspired by Johannes's book of the glorious deeds of monks from Königsaal, Peter in turn wrote his own book of such stories.[9] Unfortunately, Peter's collection, entitled *Liber secretorum Aulae regiae*, survived only as part of his *Chronicon Aulae Regiae*. Interestingly, Peter presented the writing of exemplary stories as a more practical occupation than mystical studies and practices; however, he regarded the alternation between the two as commendable and meritorious.[10]

---

[6] Stams, Zisterzienserkloster, Archiv, Cod. 6 (Cod. 67).

[7] On Rudolf, see Fritz Peter Knapp, "Ein vergessener Tiroler Autor des Spätmittelalters: Rudolf von Stams († 1294), Sprache und Dichtung," in *Sprache und Dichtung in Vorderösterreich*, ed. Guntram A. Plangg and Eugen Thurnher (Innsbruck: Wagner, 2000), 99–110.

[8] *"De vita venerabilium monachorum monasterii sui liber,"* in *Bibliotheca ascetica antiquo-nova*, ed. Bernhard Pez (Regensburg: Peetz, 1725; repr. 1967), 8:467.

[9] Cited in Johann Loserth, *Geistlichen Schriften Peters von Zittau* (Vienna: Gerold in Komm., 1881), 5.

[10] *"Solet itaque homo quilibet virtuosus studium suum secundum circumstancias temporis alternare, ut nunc ad sublimia, nunc ad humilia, nunc ad mistica, nunc*

The compiling of an ample new *exempla* collection for Cistercians was not the only way to perpetuate stories circulating in the monastic milieu. An author could insert one or two miracle stories between other works, or add them at the end of the manuscript, which did not need to be a collection of *exempla*. For example, in the manuscript of the *Speculum historiale* from Salem (Heidelberg, MS. Cod. Sal IX, 41I, written around 1300), fol. 200^v contains, along with the mark of provenance and pen trials, a short note readable only in ultraviolet light: "*Johannes Mollitor et fr. Petrus Burster loquentes . . .* [illegible] *et apparuit eis spiritus sanctus in forma columbe . . .* [illegible]" ("Johannes Mollitor and Petrus Pürster talking . . . and the Holy Spirit appeared to them in the form of a dove").[11]

There was, however, another strong tendency in late medieval Cistercian *exempla* production: a propensity to privilege written sources over oral ones. Some collections draw upon monastic sources in general, such as the *Vitae Patrum* and the *Dialogi* of Gregory the Great, and Cistercian sources in particular, such as Herbert of Clairvaux, Conrad of Eberbach, and Caesarius of Heisterbach. Examples are the so-called *Libellus exemplorum*, dating from the second half of the fourteenth century,[12] and the *Vitae sive gesta sanctorum et venerabilium patrum monasterii in Hemmenrode*, compiled in Himmerod in 1459 (London, British Library, Add. MS. 21616). The latter collection is particularly interesting, since it consists of the extracts from

---

etiam se grossiora transferat ad exempla" (cited in Loserth, *Geistlichen Schriften*, 5).

[11] Wilfried Werner, *Die mittelalterlichen nichtliturgischen Handschriften des Zisterzienserklosters Salem*, Kataloge der Universitätsbibliothek Heidelberg 5 (Wiesbaden: Reichert, 2000), 253.

[12] The *Libellus exemplorum* originates in the German-speaking area. Its identification as Cistercian is based on one *exemplum* (fol. 87, n. 12) that presents Cistercian monks as being from the same religious order as the compiler: "*in ordine nostro.*" See Welter, *L'exemplum*, 285–86. For abridged summaries of the stories, see John Alexander Herbert, *Catalogue of Romances in the Department of Manuscripts in the British Museum* (London: Trustees of the British Museum, 1910), 3:581–97.

the *Dialogus* relative to the abbey of Himmerod, as the compiler himself states in the prologue.[13] Indeed the *Dialogus* speaks often of the saintly monks of Himmerod; its impact on the history and image of Heisterbach's mother abbey appears to have been profound and lasting.

Another fascinating late medieval Cistercian collection originates from the abbey of Altzella in Saxony (MS. Leipzig, Universitätsbibliothek, Cod. 841, copied in 1452). It contains Cistercian miracles—fifty-eight in all—that are said to have been depicted on the walls of the cloister: "*Miracula ordinis Cysterciensis conscripta et depicta in monasterio Celle sancte Marie in ambitu*" (fols. 122^r–32^r). Unfortunately, the pictures do not survive, which is all the more sad because in Western Europe exemplary stories were rarely illustrated.[14] Whether the Altzella wall paintings were unique or others existed in other places, also lost but without written description, remains unknown. Judging by the content of this collection, the paintings, accompanied by texts, depicted saintly men and women of the Order, both less and well known, and even anonymous. Some of those paintings were apparently traditional images of saints,

---

[13] Fol. 4^r: "*multifarie multisque desideriis olim affectus, ut uitas siue gesta sanctorum patrum nostrorum, videlicet monachorum et conuersorum huius claustri in unum opusculum compilarem, que diuersis locis seu distinctionibus a bone memorie Cesario Heisterbacensi sparsim in suo dialogo sunt collecta.*"

[14] For some exceptional cases, see Marie Anne Polo de Beaulieu, "Recueils d'*exempla* enluminés: textes et images pour une rhétorique de la persuasion," in *La légitimité implicite: Le pouvoir symbolique en Occident (1300–1640)*, ed. Jean-Philippe Genet, 2 vols., Éditions de la Sorbonne (Paris-Rome: École française de Rome, 2015), 1:423–56; Julie Jourdan, "Les *exempla* en image: Du *Jeu des échecs moralisés* au *Ci nous dit*," in *Quand l'image relit le texte: Regards croisés sur les manuscrits médiévaux*, ed. Sandrine Hériché-Pradeau and Maud Pérez-Simon (Paris: Presses Sorbonne Nouv., 2013), 233–46. On the images accompanying Russian translations of medieval Western *exempla*, see Marie Anne Polo de Beaulieu and Victoria Smirnova, "Visual Preaching in Russia (17th–19th Century)," in *Preaching and New Worlds: Sermons as Mirrors of Realms Near and Far*, ed. Timothy J. Johnson, Katherine Wrisley Shelby, and John D. Young (London: Routledge, 2018), 201–26.

for example, Saint Robert of Molesme: the manuscript's chapter about him contains only a brief summary of his virtues and the commemoration of the institution of the Order in 1098. Other paintings could have been more narrative and dynamic, depicting miraculous visions of the members of the Order.

The Altzella collection draws upon written sources, including the *Dialogus*. The second miracle in the collection is already a rewriting of chapter I.35 about a Benedictine monk named Geoffrey, who became a Cistercian of exemplary life (he is in fact introduced as *sanctus*) and even enjoyed some miraculous visions. The *Dialogus* is not cited as the source of the story. Other stories taken from the *Dialogus* are numbers 4 (VII.52, the famous vision of Mary protecting members of the Cistercian Order under her mantle), 37 (VIII.11), 44 (IV.53), 46 (XI.13), 47 (VII.38), 49 (XI.17), 50 (XI.19), 51 (X.5), 52 (XII.43, about a holy abbess), and 53 (VII.21, about the saintly nun Christina). The use of Caesarius's *exempla* as mini-*vitae* suitable for the gallery of portraits of saintly persons can be seen as part of the same pronounced hagiographic tendency in the late medieval Cistercian *exempla* production that resulted in the Waldsassen, Königsaal, and Himmerod collections.

Other Cistercian *exempla* collections from the same period, however, privilege neither Cistercian written sources nor oral stories about members of the Order. To put it in other words, these latter collections, almost devoid of specific Cistercian content, are barely recognizable as written by Cistercian monks. Indeed, the identification of their origin often turns out to be problematic. This is especially the case of two fourteenth-century collections that are closely related to each other: the *Liber lacteus* and the *Lacteus liquor*.[15]

---

[15] According to Welter, the *Lacteus liquor* is an "alter ego" or a "corrected version" of the *Liber lacteus* (Welter, *L'Exemplum,* 279). Daniela Mairhofer argues that both works are versions of a still unknown *exempla* collection composed around 1330 (Mairhofer, *Liber lacteus*, 26–27). The *Lacteus liquor* was the more successful of the two and survives in at least twenty-one manu-

Both collections lack any explicit mention of oral sources,[16] and as for the written ones, half of the *exempla* from both *Liber lacteus* and the *Lacteus liquor* are taken from the famous *Legenda aurea* by Jacobus of Voragine,[17] with Cistercian sources in a definite minority. The compiler of the *Liber lacteus* mentions a certain *Liber visionum* (probably Herbert's *Liber*) as a source of only four *exempla*,[18] and a further eight *exempla* whose source is not acknowledged have more or less exact parallels in Herbert's *Liber*.[19] As for the works of Caesarius, Mairhofer indicates eight *exempla* with parallels in the *Libri VIII miraculorum*,[20] and one with a parallel in the *Dialogus*.[21] A few more stories originate in the *Dialogus*,[22] but all are substantially altered and contain no reference to Caesarius.

Taking into account the borrowings from the *Legenda aurea*, the extensive praise for Saint Francis and Saint Dominic, and the criticism of Benedictine and Cistercian monks expressed in one *exemplum*,[23] Adolph Franz and Jean-Thiébaut Welter

---

scripts, whereas *Liber lacteus* has been preserved in only two manuscripts (see Mairhofer, *Liber lacteus*, 22–23, nn. 32–33).

[16] Mairhofer, *Liber lacteus*, 31.

[17] The *Legenda aurea* is never mentioned as a source. On the *Liber lacteus*'s sources see *Liber lacteus*, 31. Other favorites of the compiler are *Vitae patrum*, the *Dialogi* by Gregory the Great, and the fables of Odo of Cheriton.

[18] Nos. 260, 308, 395, and 499. Only two of them, however, 260 and 308, are present in Herbert's *Liber*. No. 499 is a version of *Dialogus* IV.90.

[19] Three of them also figure in the *Exordium*.

[20] Seven of those are not in fact by Caesarius, but from the later addition to the collection; see *Die Wundergeschichten des Caesarius von Heisterbach* (Bonn: Hanstein, 1937), 3:9–11. The only exception is chapter 365, which appears to have been inspired by one *exemplum* from the *Libri VIII* (I.6 in Hilka's edition: *Die Wundergeschichten*, vol. 3, p. 25). The *exemplum* from the *Liber lacteus*, however, diverges from Caesarius's (as Mairhofer indicates).

[21] No. 369 in Mairhofer's edition = *Dialogus* III.6. The text in the *Liber lacteus* differs significantly from the version in the *Dialogus*.

[22] For example No. 367 = *Dialogus* III.2; No. 372 = *Dialogus* III.6; No. 373 = *Dialogus* III.39; No. 499 (mentioned above, note 18) = *Dialogus* IV.90.

[23] No. 476 in Mairhofer's edition: "*Quoniam Cysternienses (!) habent cupiditatem templarii superbiam and nigri monachi sibi luxuriam maritaverunt*"

identified the compiler of the *Liber lacteus* as a member of a mendicant order.[24] By contrast, Welter argues that the compiler of the *Lacteus liquor* was a Cistercian because Saint Bernard is called *pater noster* in one *exemplum* (a phrase absent from the *Liber lacteus*).[25] It should be noted, however, that the *exemplum* criticizing the Cistercian Order is also present in the *Lacteus liquor*,[26] and, as Mairhofer points out, the praise for Saint Benedict and Saint Bernard is no less pronounced in the *Liber lacteus* than the praise for the mendicant saints. This being said, the *exempla* about Bernard are taken, as textual comparison suggests, from the *Legenda aurea* and not from his Cistercian *Vitae*.[27] There is thus no hard evidence for the places of origin of the *Liber lacteus* and *Lacteus liquor*, and one should be cautious about attributing them to the Cistercian Order, although the majority of fourteenth-century manuscripts of both collections are indeed of Cistercian origin or provenance.[28]

Luckily, the attribution of the fourteenth-century *Sertum florum moralium*[29] to the Cistercian Order is certain, thanks to two colophons. One of them (in Paris MS., Bibliothèque nationale de France, lat. 13475) presents the compiler as a student in the Collège de Saint Bernard in Paris,[30] and the other (Bern MS., Burgerbibliothek, 410) even reveals his name: Symon de

---

(Mairhofer, *Liber lacteus*, 216). The source of the story (not indicated in the text) is the *Parabolae* of Odo of Ceriton, ed. Léopold Hervieux, *Les Fabulistes latins depuis le siècle d'Auguste jusqu'à la fin du moyen âge*, vol. 4, *Eudes de Chériton et ses dérivés* (Paris: Firmin-Didot, 1893), 325 (no. CLIII).

[24] Adolph Franz, *Drei deutsche Minoritenprediger aus dem 13. und 14. Jahrhundert* (Freiburg: Herder, 1907), 124. Welter, *L'Exemplum*, 276.

[25] See Heiligenkreuz, Zisterzienserstift, Cod. 323, fol. 119vb.

[26] See the chart of comparisons in Mairhofer, *Liber lacteus*, 56.

[27] Mairhofer, *Liber lacteus*, 136–40.

[28] Mairhofer, *Liber lacteus*, 22–23, nn. 32, 33.

[29] Welter, *L'Exemplum*, 325–28.

[30] "*Explicit Sertum florum moralium distractorum per ordinem alphabeti, collectorum per quendam monachum cisterciensis ordinis, studentem parisiis in domo sancti Bernardi, anno Domini m^o cccm^o xlvi^o*" (fol. 120^v).

Valle Virenti.[31] On the basis of the Bern manuscript, Charles-Victor Langlois identified the compiler as Simon de Vauvert,[32] an identification that is somewhat confusing, because Vauvert was actually a Charterhouse. Cistercian bibliographer Charles De Visch († 1666) credited the authorship of the *Sertum* to a Simon de Valle Lucenti.[33] The name given by De Visch corresponds to the entries in the Clairvaux library catalog (1472) identifying the compiler of the *Sertum* as Simon from Vauluisant (a daughter-house of Cîteaux).[34]

Without colophons, however, the identification of the *Sertum florum* as a Cistercian *exempla* collection would be difficult, if not impossible. The collection, which contains not only exemplary stories but also non-narrative elements like comparisons or maxims, is organized alphabetically around about 150 terms relevant to moral instruction (vices, virtues, abstract concepts of doctrinal interest, such as *adulatio, confessio, fortitudo, laus, mors*), on the model of the more famous *Alphabetum narrationum*

---

[31] *"Explicit hoc sertum florum moralium collectorum parisiis in monte uirenti per fratrem symonem de valle virenti anno verbi incarnati m⁰ cccm⁰ xlvi⁰"* (fol. 71ᵇ).

[32] Charles-Victor Langlois, "Simon de Vauvert," *Histoire littéraire de la France*, vol. 37 (Paris: Imprimerie nationale, 1938), 507–8.

[33] *"Simon de Valle Lucenti composuit librum qui intitulatur: Sertum florum moralium compilatum a Simone monacho de Valle Lucenti, scholari S. Bernardi, anno Domini 1346"* ("Auctarium D. Caroli de Visch ad Bibliothecam Scriptorum ordinis Cisterciensis," ed. Joseph-Marie Canivez, in *Cistercienser-Chronik* 39 [1927]: 43–44).

[34] "L 66. *Item ung autre volume contenant Sertum florum composé per dominum Symonem de Valle Lucenti ordinis Cisterciensis secundum ordinem alphabeti"* and "L 67. *Item ung autre samblable volume au precedent nommé aussi Sertum Florum* . . . . *Lequel livre fut aussi composé par ledit Symon de Val Luisant"* (André Vernet and Jean-François Genest, *La Bibliothèque de l'abbaye de Clairvaux du XIIe au XVIIIe siècle*, vol. 1, *Catalogues et répertoires* [Paris: CNRS, 1979], 190). Both manuscripts are now lost. The catalogue of the Vauluisant library probably mentions the *Sertum florum* under the title *"Promptuarium florum variorum doctorum, scilicet Ambrosii, Augustini, Iohannis Chrisostomi et Senecae moralis iuxta ordinem alphabeti,"* without the author's name. See *La bibliothèque de l'abbaye cistercienne de Vauluisant: histoire et inventaires*, ed. François Bougard and Pierre Petitmengin (Paris: CNRS, 2012), 112.

(1297–1308) of Arnold of Liège. As in the *Alphabetum*, the entries in the *Sertum florum* usually have cross-references to other entries in the collection to which the story can also be relevant, introduced by the formula *hoc valet ad.*

The *exempla* in the *Sertum florum* come predominantly from learned classical and medieval sources. Simon declares that he used the works of Aristotle, Livy, Valerius Maximus, Seneca, Flavius Josephus, Orosius, Fulgentius, Avicenna, Albert the Great, and many others. An attentive reading shows, however, that Simon, like many other medieval compilers, cites second hand, most often from unacknowledged intermediate sources like the *Speculum morale* of Vincent of Beauvais or the *Liber de natruris rerum* by Thomas of Cantimpré.[35] *Exempla*, especially those extracted from writings on natural history, are often accompanied with ample moralizations.

As for specific Cistercian elements, the reference to the *Exordium magnum* ("*Legitur in quodam libro de iniciis cisterciensis ordinis*"[36]) looks promising at first sight; it turns out, however, that the immediate source is the *Speculum morale* of Vincent of Beauvais.[37] Saint Bernard is cited, though rarely in comparison to other sources, and the compiler inserted praise for Bernard in the special rubric dedicated to him.[38] As for the oral tradition, Simon presents one *exemplum* with the formula "*audivi recitari.*" The story itself, which has nothing to do with the Cistercian Order, reports an exemplary saying of Robert II of Burgundy († 1306), who is said always to have kept in memory the inevitability of death. In short, the Cistercian Simon of

---

[35] A dozen *exempla* have no indication of a source, the majority coming from the *Tractatus de diversis materiis praedicabilibus* by the Dominican Stephen of Bourbon.

[36] Paris MS., Bib. nat., lat. 13475, fol. 62ᵛ.

[37] Vincentius Bellovacensis, *Speculum doctrinale*, II, I pars 3 (Douai: Bibliotheca Mundi, 1624; repr. Graz: Akademische Druck -u. Verlagsanstalt, 1964), 818.

[38] *Bernardus* (fol. 14ʳ in the Paris manuscript): "*In Bernardo fuit obediencia Noe fides Abrahe Joseph providencia,*" etc.

Vauluisant draws upon neither Cistercian *exempla* collections nor the Order's oral tradition and makes no references to contemporary Cistercian life.

In the Late Middle Ages, then, the early Cistercian *exempla* collections were still used as written sources for compiling new collections, especially in Germany and Austria. But the big influential *exempla* collections of the mendicants, which had already proved their efficacy in doctrinal instruction, were gaining a foothold as a new narrative pool for other collectors to draw upon and imitate. Late medieval library catalogues (from Cîteaux and Clairvaux, for example) attest to the popularity of collections such as the *De oculo morali* by Peter of Limoges, the *Bonum universale de apibus* by Thomas of Cantimpré, and, of course, the *Alphabetum narrationum* by Arnold of Liège, among Cistercians.[39]

The growing interest of white monks in the *exemplum* as a discursive tool for the instruction of others rather than as a tool of monastic identity formation is not surprising, given all the changes that were taking place within the Order that affected both Cistercian practices and self-image. Along with new attitudes to university education and training,[40] the intensified involvement of Cistercian monks in the *cura animarum* is apparent, including preaching, which had previously been prohibited.[41] Despite the original ban on Cistercian acquisition

---

[39] For more details on the *exempla* collections in Cistercian libraries, see chap. 8 below.

[40] On Cistercian education see Barry O'Dwyer, "The Problem of Education in the Cistercian Order," *Journal of Religious History* 3 (1965): 238–45; Louis J. Lekai, *The Cistercians: Ideals and Reality* (Kent, OH: Kent State University Press, 1977), 77–90. As Lekai points out, in the Late Middle Ages the image of the Cistercian ascetic who spent his day in prayer and hard manual labor was replaced by that of the scholarly monk, dividing his working hours between school and library (*The Cistercians*, 79).

[41] For more details see Bede K. Lackner, "Early Citeaux and the Care of Souls," in *Noble Piety and Reformed Monasticism*, ed. E. Rozanne Elder, Studies in Medieval Cistercian History 7, CS 65 (Kalamazoo, MI: Cistercian Publications, 1981), 52–67.

and administration of parish churches,[42] late medieval monasteries often received them as gifts. Heisterbach Abbey, for example, had a church in Dordrecht, and in 1259, a monk from Heisterbach was already responsible for the *cura animarum* there.[43] At the end of the fifteenth century, the scale of Cistercian involvement in pastoral care outside the monastery apparently became fairly high; Jean de Cirey, the reforming abbot of Cîteaux, even insisted in his *Articuli parisienses seu Instrumentum reformationis Ordinis Cisterciensis* (1493) that monks should be dissuaded from engaging in it, "unless asked by very important persons whom it was impossible to refuse without censure."[44]

Even though preaching outside the monastery was generally forbidden,[45] the practice persisted, as is shown by the numerous issues of unauthorized preaching brought up at the General Chapters.[46] The establishing of Cistercian colleges

---

[42] Repeated several times, for example, in 1234; see Canivez, *Statuta Capitulorum generalium*, vol. 2 (Louvain: Revue d'Histoire Ecclésiastique, 1934), 126 (1234, no 1).

[43] Richard Knippig, *Die Regesten der Erzbischöfe von Köln im Mittelalter*, vol. 3/1, *1205–1261* (Bonn: Hanstein, 1909), 273 (no. 2034). The land near Dordrecht was given to Heisterbach by Dietrich VII of Holland († 1203) and his wife Aleidis, together with the patronage of Saint Mary Church in Dordrecht.

[44] *"nisi esset pro tam notabilibus personis quod sine reprehensione denegari non posset."* *Articuli Parisienses* are published in *Nomasticon Cisterciense seu antiquiores Ordinis Cisterciensis constitutiones* (Paris: Alliot, 1664), 683 (art. XIII).

[45] Thus the General Chapter of 1191 reprimanded the abbot of Aiguebelle for preaching in secular churches (Canivez, *Statuta capitulorum generalium* [Louvain: Revue d'Histoire Ecclésiastique, 1933] 1:137–138 [1191, no 20]).

[46] For example, in 1198, 1199, 1200, 1201, 1212, etc. There were, of course, famous exceptions, such as the involvement of the white monks in preaching the Crusades under papal order. Among numerous works on this subject, see Monique Zerner, "L'abbé Gui des Vaux-de-Cernay, prédicateur de croisade," in *Les cisterciens en Languedoc*, Cahiers de Fanjeaux 21 (1986): 183–204; Beverly Kienzle, "Hélinand de Froidmont et la prédication cistercienne dans le Midi (1145–1229)," in *La prédication en pays d'Oc (XIIᵉ–début XVᵉ siècle)*, Cahiers de Fanjeaux 32 (1997): 37–67; Jessalynn Bird, "The Religious's Role in a Post-Fourth-Lateran World: Jacques de Vitry's *Sermones ad status* and

contributed to the development and acceptance of public preaching. In 1285, the abbey of Kamp received permission to have a church open to the public in their college in Cologne, with the right to preach.[47] Did Cistercians use mendicant *exempla* in their preaching? It is difficult to know, since Cistercian written sermons are almost devoid of *exempla*, with a few notable exceptions, including Caesarius's own sermons.[48] However, a fifteenth-century manuscript from the Cistercian abbey of Wilhering in Upper Austria contains a small collection of miracles presented as follows: "*Secuntur miracula valde pulcra et ad credendum possibilia que quidem miracula in sermonibus popularibus multos possunt edificare et corda perversorum in melius mutare et ad penitenciam peragendum peccatorum suorum provocare*" ("The miracles that follow are very beautiful and easy to believe. If used in popular sermons, they can edify many; they can change for the good the hearts of the corrupt and incite them to do penance for their sins").[49] This *incipit* could, however, have been copied from another manuscript, not necessarily one of Cistercian origin.

The success of Dominicans and Franciscans as "masters of speech" (to use Nicole Bériou's happy expression[50]) clearly sparked the interest of Cistercians in their art of persuasion through stories. This interest affected the transmission and reception of the *Dialogus* both negatively and positively. On the one hand, the *Dialogus*—along with other early Cistercian

---

Historia occidentalis," in *Medieval Monastic Preaching*, ed. Carolyn Muessig (Leiden: Brill, 1998), 215–18.

[47] See Friedrich Michels, *Geschichte und Beschreibung der ehemaligen Abtei Camp bei Rheinberg: nebst Notizen aus einer alten geschriebenen Urkunde, welche die Abtei und Umgegend betreffen* (Crefeld: Funcke, 1832), 136.

[48] See the introduction to the *Fasciculum moralitatis: Omelie morales de Infantia Saluatoris*, ed. Victoria Smirnova, Prague Medieval Series (Prague: Karolinum Press, forthcoming).

[49] Wilhering, Zisterzienserkloster, Cod. IX 96, 15th century, fol. 279ᵛ.

[50] Nicole Bériou, *L'Avènement des maîtres de la Parole: La prédication à Paris au XIIIᵉ siècle*, 2 vols. (Paris: Institut d'Études Augustiniennes, 1998).

exempla collections—may have become somewhat less compelling as reading and study material than were the widely acclaimed mendicant compilations. On the other hand, famous Dominican authors like Arnold of Liège and Johannes Gobi not only made great use of the *Dialogus* in their collections but also cited Caesarius as their source,[51] credit that could have further reinforced Caesarius's *auctoritas* among his fellow Cistercians.

---

[51] See Elisa Brilli, "The Making of a New Auctoritas: The *Dialogus miraculorum* Read and Rewritten by the Dominican Arnold of Liège (1297–1308)," in Smirnova, ed., *The Art of Cistercian Persuasion*, 161–82; and Marie Anne Polo de Beaulieu, "*Dialogus miraculorum*: The Initial Source of Inspiration for Johannes Gobi the Younger's *Scala coeli*?" in *The Art of Cistercian Persuasion*, 183–210.

3

Cistercian Manuscripts of the
Dialogus miraculorum

Who were the Cistercian readers of the *Dialogus*? The following is the list of its surviving manuscripts of Cistercian origin or provenance:

Be1   Berlin, Staatsbibliothek zu Berlin, Preußischer Kulturbesitz, Hdschr. 328, second half of the 14th century—Himmerod (Clairvaux line)

Br1   Brussels, Bibliothèque Royale de Belgique, II 1067 (2121), 14th century—Aulne (Clairvaux line)

Dü1   Düsseldorf, Universitäts- und Landesbibliothek, MS. C 26, 13th–14th century. Dist. II–XII[1]—Heisterbach (Clairvaux line)?

Dü2   Düsseldorf, Universitäts- und Landesbibliothek, MS. C 27, 14th century—Altenberg (Morimond line)

Eb   Wiesbaden, Hauptstaatsarchiv, Abt 22, 535/6 [a] (fragment), 13th century—Eberbach (Clairvaux line)

Ha   The Hague, Koninklijke Bibliotheek, 73 E 36, first half of the 15th century—Eiteren (Morimond line)

---

[1] In MS. Dü1, the *Dialogus* is bound with the *Homiliae de Passione Domini* by Caesarius, fol. 1r–24v. Two quires from the beginning of *Dialogus* were lost, so the manuscript begins with II.3. Two quires in the end (fols. 191–210) date from the 14th century.

H	Heidelberg, Universitätsbibliothek, Cod. Sal. IX, 46, beginning of the 14th century. Dist. I-VI—Salem (Morimond line)
I	Innsbruck, Universitäts- und Landesbibliothek Tirol, Cod. 185, before 1341—Stams (Morimond line)
L	Leipzig, Universitätsbibliothek, Cod. 445, first half of the 15th century—Altzella (Morimond line)
M1	Munich, Bayerische Staatsbibliothek, Clm 2687, first third of the 14th century (1328)—Aldersbach (Morimond line)
Na	Namur, Musée Provincial des Arts anciens du Namurois, Fonds de la Ville, 52, 15th century—Jardinet (Clairvaux line)
R	Rein, Zisterzienserstift, Cod. 58, first quarter of the 15th century (1414)—Rein (Morimond line)
T2	Troyes, Bibliothèque municipale, 592, last third of the 15th century (1471–1472)—Clairvaux
T1	Troyes, Bibliothèque municipale, 641, 15th century—Clairvaux
Z	Zwettl, Zisterzienserstift, Cod. 131, 15th century. Dist. I–X—Zwettl (Morimond line)

Lost or unidentified manuscripts

The inventory (1511/1512) from Walderbach Abbey in Bavaria mentions a *Liber visionum beate virginis Marie, item dyalogus Cesarii etc., in pergamento scripti*, and a *Dialogus Cesarii monachi ordinis Cisterciensis, in pergamento scriptus*.[2]

The list both confirms the importance of the *Dialogus* to Cistercian readers persisting far beyond the thirteenth century and

---

[2] *Mittelalterliche Bibliothekskataloge Deutschlands und der Schweiz*, vol. 4/1, *Bistümer Passau und Regensburg*, ed. Bernhard Bischoff and Christine Elisabeth Ineichen-Eder (Munich: Beck, 1977), 538–39.

invites us to question the assumptions about its popularity. The *Dialogus* is often labeled as a medieval bestseller, which would imply a much wider readership within the Order than it actually had. Its success seems in fact to have been confined to the region corresponding to Northern France, the Netherlands, Belgium, Germany, and Austria. Cistercian readership of the *Dialogus* was apparently limited to monks from monasteries in the lines of filiation of Clairvaux and Morimond. Some of the surviving manuscripts that belonged to the monasteries of Morimond affiliation (e.g., MS. H, MS. I, and MS. M1) transmit a particular version of the *Dialogus* that is characterized by an important number of omissions and abridgments, but also by several additions. I refer to this abridged contaminated version as Version B, to distinguish it from the full version of the text, or Version A. The manuscripts from Altzella (MS. L) and Rein (MS. R) transmit yet another version of the text, based on Version B. Although this version—Version C—retains some of the added stories from Version B, it is much more concise than Version B. The manuscript from Zwettl presents an extremely abridged version of the text, the "*excerpta* version," or Version E. Finally, the fragment from Eberbach transmits yet another shortened version (Version D).[3]

The dynamics of Cistercian readership of the *Dialogus* are best illustrated by comparing its pattern of transmission with those of another two bestselling *exempla* collections: the *Liber visionum et miraculorum Clarevallensium (Liber)* by Herbert of Clairvaux and the *Exordium magnum Cisterciense (Exordium)* by Conrad of Eberbach.

---

[3] Versions B through E are discussed below in chapters 4–6.

Cistercian Manuscripts of Herbert's *Liber miraculorum*[4]

Graz, Universitätsbibliothek, MS. 421, middle of the 14th century—
Neuberg (Morimond line)

Heidelberg, Universitätsbibliothek, Cod. Sal. IX, 19, second quarter of the 13th century (after 1235)—Salem (Morimond line)

Heiligenkreuz, Zisterzienserstift, Cod. 177, end of the 13th century—Heiligenkreuz (Morimond line)

Leipzig, Universitätsbibliothek, Cod. 1332, middle of the 15th century—Altzella (Morimond line)

Leipzig, Universitätsbibliothek, Cod. 842, end of the 15th century (1496)—Altzella (Morimond line)

London, British Library, Add. MS. 15723, end of the 13th century (the part with the Liber)—Cîteaux?

Munich, Bayerische Staatsbibliothek, Clm 2607, end of the 12th, beginning of the 13th century—Aldersbach (Morimond line)

Munich, Bayerische Staatsbibliothek, Clm 6914, middle of the 13th century—Fürstenfeld (Morimond line)

Paris, Bibliothèque nationale de France, lat. 3175, first quarter of the 13th century—Notre-Dame de Bonport (Cîteaux line)

Rein, Zisterzienserstift, Cod. 69, 13th century—Rein (Morimond line)

Stams, Zisterzienserkloster, Archiv, Cod. 6 (Cod. 67), end of the 13th—beginning of the 14th century—Stams (Morimond line)

The distribution of the production of the *Liber* is revealing. The surviving manuscripts show an important contribution of the Morimond line to the transmission of the *Liber*, both its copying and its re-working. The manuscript Munich, Bayerische Staatsbibliothek, Clm 2607, produced in the scriptorium

---

[4] According to the critical edition, Giancarlo Zichi, Graziano Fois, and Stefano Mula, eds., Herbertus Turritanus, *Liber visionum et miraculorum Clarevallensium*, CCCM 277 (Turnhout: Brepols, 2017), XII–LIV.

of Aldersbach, granddaughter of Morimond, was copied shortly after the lost Clairvaux original had been compiled. The short version of the *Liber* also originated in a monastery of Morimond affiliation (Fürstenfeld, discussed above). That the majority of the surviving manuscripts date from the thirteenth century is a sign of the early success of the book. By contrast, only two surviving Cistercian manuscripts of the *Dialogus* date from this period. A number of monasteries that had the *Liber* also possessed the *Dialogus*. In those cases, Caesarius's work was usually copied somewhat later (Stams) or much later (Aldersbach) than Herbert's. Apparently it was the *Liber* that first caught the attention of German and Austrian Cistercians, and it may have heightened their interest in *exempla* collections.

Cistercian Manuscripts of the *Exordium magnum*[5]

Brussels, Bibliothèque Royale de Belgique, II 1077 (3872), 13th century—probably Aulne (Clairvaux line)

Brussels, Bibliothèque Royale de Belgique, 412–14 (3873), 15th century—Moulins (Clairvaux line)

Cambrai, Bibliothèque municipale, 860 (764), 13th century—probably Vaucelles (Clairvaux line). Anne Bondéelle-Souchier, however, considers the attribution to the Vaucelles abbey insufficiently justified.[6]

Dijon, Bibliothèque municipale, 594 (olim 349), 14th century—Cîteaux

Innsbruck, Universitäts- und Landesbibliothek Tirol, Cod. 25, 14th century—Stams (Morimond line)

Karlsruhe, Badische Landesbibliothek, Hs. 1016, 13th century—Salem (Morimond line)

---

[5] According to the edition by Bruno Griesser, *Exordium magnum Cisterciense*, CCCM 138 (Turnhout: Brepols, 1997), Nᵒˢ 7*–25*.

[6] Anne Bondéelle-Souchier, *Bibliothèques cisterciennes dans la France médiévale. Répertoire des abbayes d'hommes* (Paris: CNRS, 1991), 315.

Karlsruhe, Generallandesarchiv, 143, end of 16th–beginning 17th century, before 1604—Salem (Morimond line)

Laon, Bibliothèque municipale, 331, 13th century—Foigny (Clairvaux line)

Lille, Bibliothèque municipale, 446, 15th century—Loos (Clairvaux line)

Lille, Bibliothèque municipale, 447, 17th century (1643)—Loos (Clairvaux line)

Marienstatt, Klosterbibliothek, K f. 3, 15th century—Marienstatt (Clairvaux line)

Munich, Bayerische Staatsbibliothek, Clm 7992, 13th century—Kaisheim (Morimond line)

Oxford, Bodleian Library, Cod. Laud Misc. 238, first quarter of the 13th century—Eberbach (Clairvaux line), then Marienhausen, a Cistercian nunnery under the care of Eberbach

Paris, Bibliothèque de l'Arsenal, 1156 (25 H. L.), 17th century—Feuillants (Paris)

Paris, Bibliothèque nationale de France, nouv. acq. lat., 2044, 17th century (1660)—Bernardines of the Precious Blood, rue de Vaugirard, Paris

Wiesbaden, Hessische Landesbibliothek, Hs. 381, first quarter of the 13th century—Eberbach (Clairvaux line)

The distribution of the *Exordium* among Cistercian houses follows the trends observed earlier. The area of its readership is essentially the same as that of the *Dialogus* and the *Liber*, and both the Clairvaux and the Morimond lines of filiation play a crucial role in its transmission. It is not surprising to see the already familiar names of Stams and Salem among monasteries possessing the *Exordium*: these two abbeys possessed manuscripts of all three bestselling Cistercian *exempla* collections. As in the case of the *Liber*, the number of surviving thirteenth-century manuscripts of the *Exordium* is considerable. By contrast, the number of fourteenth-fifteenth-century manuscripts of the *Exordium* is lower than those of the *Dialogus*. The *Exor-*

dium's popularity, as manuscript production shows, persisted far beyond the Middle Ages, certainly in the houses that already had earlier manuscripts (Salem and Loos), but also among members of new Cistercian congregations like the Feuillants or the Bernardines of the Precious Blood.

Further analysis of the manuscript distribution of the *Dialogus, Liber,* and *Exordium* among Cistercian houses shows that the monasteries involved in the production and transmission of Cistercian *exempla* collections were often closely related. One can certainly recognize the branch of Ebrach (Morimond's daughter), with its daughters Aldersbach, Rein, and Eiteren, and its granddaughter Fürstenfeld (the daughter of Aldersbach). Then there was a remarkably active branch of Lucelle (Morimond's granddaughter via Bellevaux), its daughters Salem and Kaisheim, and its granddaughter Stams (daughter of Kaisheim). Finally, there is the pair Heiligenkreuz (Morimond's daughter) and its daughter Neuberg.

With regard to the filiation of Clairvaux, the picture is somewhat different. The monasteries in that line that possessed Cistercian *exempla* collections were predominantly daughters of Clairvaux. Very few abbeys within the Clairvaux line formed readership clusters like those that can be observed within the filiation of Morimond.[7]

The relationships among affiliated abbeys were crucial with regard to the transmission of books within the Order. The mother abbey was supposed to provide its daughters with the

---

[7] The exceptions are Himmerod and its daughter Heisterbach; Eberbach and Marienhausen, which is a female monastery under the care of Eberbach; and the abbeys of Aulne, Moulins, and Jardinet with their rather complicated affiliation history. Initially Jardinet was a female monastery under the care of Aulne. In 1441 the female monastery was dissolved and reformed as male when it was re-founded by monks from Moulins. However, Jardinet remained under the authority of Aulne until 1460. Moulins itself was initially a female monastery, re-founded in 1414 by monks from Aulne and Villers.

necessary books[8] and could further lend exemplars for copying or allow visiting monks to copy them. For example, the Fürstenfeld copy of the *Liber* was made from the exemplar belonging to Aldersbach, Fürstenfeld's mother, and the *Libellus miraculorum* from Ebrach was copied at its daughter Aldersbach and later its granddaughter Fürstenfeld. In the same vein, an exemplar of the *Exordium* that belonged to Moulins was probably copied from the manuscript in Aulne after its re-foundation.[9]

For their part, mother abbeys often paid attention to their daughters' book production and, if necessary, attempted to control it. Testimony exists concerning Morimond's early interest in the *exempla* collections of the affiliated abbeys, all the more important because the library of Morimond itself ended up being dispersed and lost.[10] According to a letter exchange between Engelhard of Langheim and Erbo II, the abbot of the

---

[8] See Canivez, *Statuta capitulorum generalium* (Louvain: Revue d'Histoire Ecclésiastique, 1933), 1:15 (1134, art. 12): "*Duodecim monachi cum abbate tertiodecimo ad coenobia nova transmittantur: nec tamen illuc destinetur donec locus libris, domibus et necessariis aptetur, libris dumtaxat missali, Regula, libro Usuum, psalterio, hymnario, collectaneo, lectionario, antiphonario, graduali.*" Fontfroide abbey gave its daughter Valbonne an impressive number of sixty books (see Anne Bondéelle, "Trésor des moines: Les Chartreux, les Cisterciens et leurs livres," in *Histoire des bibliothèques françaises*, vol. 1, *Les bibliothèques médiévales du VIe siècle à 1530*, ed. Claude Jolly and André Vernet [Paris: Promodis, 1989], 64–81, here 70, 71, and 79–80, n. 46).

[9] Unfortunately, Bruno Griesser did not include the manuscript from Moulins in his stemma. For the arguments concerning the proximity of two manuscripts, see Xavier Hermand, "*Scriptoria* et bibliothèques dans les monastères cisterciens réformés des Pays-Bas méridionaux au XVe siècle," in *Les cisterciens et la transmission des textes (XIIe–XVIIIe siècles)*, ed. Thomas Falmagne, et al. (Turnhout: Brepols, 2018), 116.

[10] Morimond was plundered many times, and its library was dispersed at the end of the eighteenth century. All inventories are post-medieval and incomplete. For example, an inventory dated May 4, 1790, mentions only nine manuscripts. The twenty-six known surviving manuscripts from its library contain no *exempla* collection.

Benedictine abbey of Prüfening,[11] a notary of the abbot of Morimond, probably during a visitation journey,[12] saw the *Libellus*[13] of Engelhard held by Erbo. The notary was not pleased to see the book in a Benedictine house without the knowledge and permission of the abbey of Morimond (the grandmother of Langheim). When the notary reached Langheim, he demanded that the abbot get Erbo's copy back (it was apparently the only one existing) to take it to Morimond.[14] Erbo complied with the request.[15]

It is thus no wonder that one finds the *Liber* from Himmerod in a manuscript that is believed to be from Clairvaux (Florence, Biblioteca Medicea Laurenziana, Ashburnham 1906, the only surviving copy of the collection)[16] and a manuscript of the *Dialogus* originating from Heisterbach's mother, Himmerod (MS. Be1). Unfortunately, no manuscripts of confirmed Heisterbach origin survived, and it is impossible to prove direct transmission. According to a probe collation, the manuscript from

---

[11] The letters survived in the manuscript Zwettl, Zisterzienserstift, Cod. 13. They were published by Bruno Griesser, "Engelhard von Langheim und Abt Erbo von Prüfening," *Cistercienser-Chronik* 71 (1964): 22–37.

[12] At the time, the visitation could be done not by the abbot but by his delegate. See Canivez, *Statuta Capitulorum Generalium* 1:115 (1189, no. 31). Oppel supposes that the notary first visited Cistercian houses in Austria, then headed for Langheim in Upper Franconia, making a stopover in Prüfening.

[13] Composed before 1186 and now considered to be lost.

[14] Griesser, "Engelhard von Langheim und Abt Erbo," 25–26: "*Responsio apollogetica Engelhardi monachi. . . . Notarius abbatis morimundensis libellum nostrum uidit apud uos, abbati nostro locutus est, inde arguens, obsecrans et increpans talia se celari, saturandum primum filios et sic aliis expendendum, se filium ordinis iniuriatum, quem tale, apud nos cum esset, latuisset opusculum, rogare uel nunc, ut afferret libellum sibi; gloriosum ei fore, si afferret, gratum et utile cunctis qui legerent.*"

[15] Griesser, "Engelhard von Langheim und Abt Erbo," 26.

[16] Bruno Griesser, "Ein Himmeroder *Liber miraculorum* und seine Beziehungen zu Caesarius von Heisterbach," *Archiv für mittelrheinische Kirchengeschichte: nebst Berichten zur kirchlichen Denkmalpflege* 4 (1952): 257.

Himmerod does share the majority of distinctive variants with MS. Dü1, which may have originated from Heisterbach.[17] The manuscripts containing the *Dialogus* from the abbeys of Jardinet (Na) and Aulne (Br1) originated in the same mother-daughter dynamics. These manuscripts are almost identical, and that the manuscript from Jardinet was copied from the exemplar at Aulne cannot be excluded.[18] The manuscript from Jardinet was corrected with the help of another manuscript, which had perhaps once belonged to Villers. In fact Caesarius's stories were included in the so-called *Gesta sanctorum Villariensium*,[19] compiled in Villers, with a first recension from before 1333 and the second before 1459. It is therefore safe to assume that this abbey had an exemplar of the *Dialogus*, now unfortunately lost.

This being said, the majority of surviving manuscripts show mostly horizontal exchanges between abbeys, often but not necessarily belonging to the same branch of the Cistercian filiation tree.[20] Other factors were crucial as well, ranging from geographical proximity to personal connections between monks. For example, the manuscript from the Altenberg abbey of the Morimond filiation line (Dü2) is close to MS. Dü1 and even closer to MS. Be1 from Himmerod, with which it shares a number of important lacunae. That is not surprising given

[17] Agata Mazurek and Irmgard Siebert, *Die mittelalterlichen Handschriften der Signaturengruppe C in der Universitäts- und Landesbibliothek Düsseldorf* (Wiesbaden: Harrassowitz, 2012), 170.

[18] On the activities of the Jardinet scriptorium in the context of contemporary reform taking place at Jardinet, see Hermand, "*Scriptoria* et bibliothèques."

[19] Georg Waitz, ed., *Gesta Sanctorum Villariensium*, in *Monumenta Germaniae Historica: Scriptores* 25 (Hannover, Germany: Hahnsche Buchhandlung, 1880), 220–35.

[20] A study on the Aldersbach scriptorium brings to light similarities between the abbey's manuscripts and those from the Cistercian monasteries of Ebrach, Rein, Wilhering, Heilsbronn, Heiligenkreuz, and Zwettl. See Donatella Frioli, *Lo scriptorium e la biblioteca del monastero cisterciense di Aldersbach* (Spoleto: Centro Italiano di Studi sull'Alto Medioevo, 1990), 321–52.

that the abbey of Altenberg, situated near Cologne, had close connections to both Heisterbach and Himmerod, as is suggested by a number of documents mentioning abbots of these monasteries acting as witnesses or mediators in conflicts.[21]

Another interesting case is the manuscript containing Herbert's *Liber* from Stams. It was copied from the exemplar originating from Fürstenfeld. Although Stams and Fürstenfeld belong to different branches of the Morimond filiation line, they were closely connected. Fürstenfeld was founded in 1263 by Louis II, Duke of Bavaria, the brother of Elizabeth of Bavaria. Some years later, in 1273, Elizabeth and her husband Meinhard II of Tyrol founded Stams as a family burial place. It is possible that Fürstenfeld was initially meant to be the mother house of Stams but was too weak to start a new foundation. Instead, the abbey of Kaisheim was chosen as the mother house, probably because it had strong connections to the Staufen family. Conradin, Elizabeth's son, made several donations to Kaisheim and even mentioned it in his will on the day of his execution in Naples, October 29, 1268. Fürstenfeld, however, remained a model for Stams, whose foundation charter was in fact modeled on that of Fürstenfeld.[22]

In many other cases, however, the patterns of exchange are difficult to detect, because certain links in the textual transmission are missing, and Cistercian networks of manuscript production and exchange were fairly complex. For example, the

---

[21] See Swen H. Brunsch, *Das Zisterzienserkloster Heisterbach von seiner Gründung bis zum Anfang des 16. Jahrhunderts* (Siegberg: Franz Schmitt, 1998), 313–18. In 1267 and 1269 Abbot Dietrich from Altenberg was asked to help Heisterbach, which was at the time in a difficult financial situation. See Canivez, *Statuta Capitulorum Generalium* (Louvain: Revue d'Histoire Ecclésiastique, 1935), 3:53 (1267, no. 42). And see Canivez, *Statuta Capitulorum Generalium*, 3:75 (1269, no. 34). See also Hans Mosler, *Altenberg* (Neustadt an der Aisch: Schmidt, 1959), 43–44.

[22] Ulrich Köpf, "Zisterziensische Spiritualität in Tirol: Die Anfänge von Stift Stams," in *Von der Via Claudia Augusta zum Oberen Weg. Leben an Etsch und Inn; Westtirol und angrenzende Räume von der Vorzeit bis heute*, ed. Reiner Loose (Innsbruck: Wagner, 2006), 187.

manuscripts of the *Dialogus* from Stams and Aldersbach (different lines of the Morimond family) were copied from the same unknown exemplar.[23] Again, the manuscripts of the *Exordium* originating from the abbeys of Keisheim and Stams (mother and daughter houses) are not directly related, though they belong to the same branch of the textual tradition.[24]

Despite all the differences, the three best-selling Cistercian *exempla* collections have strong similarities in their transmission. The geography of their readership is roughly the same, and in many cases their reception communities are characterized by a pronounced interest in collecting and writing down exemplary stories. The filiation lines of Clairvaux and Morimond were most active in *exempla* production.[25] Some monasteries that possessed a manuscript of the *Dialogus* are also known to have produced their own collections, such as Clairvaux, Himmerod, Eberbach, Altzella, Stams, Salem, and probably Kaisheim.

Salem near Konstanz is an excellent example of a German abbey with a passion for collecting exemplary and miracle tales. During the abbacy of Eberhard I von Rohrdorf (1191–1240), a considerable number of *miracula* and *visiones* were copied in Salem's flourishing scriptorium, including its own small collection of miracles from shortly after 1223, from MS. Heidelberg, Universitätsbibliothek, Cod. Sal. IX, 31 (fols. 97^r–113^r).[26] The abbot's interest in Cistercian storytelling clearly

---

[23] See the *stemma codicum* in Karl Drescher, ed., *Hartliebs Übersetzung des* Dialogus Miraculorum *von Caesarius von Heisterbach* (Berlin: Weidmannsche Buchhandlung, 1929), xi.

[24] See Griesser's stemma in *Exordium magnum Cisterciense*, 33*.

[25] The only exception is Vauluisant, the daughter of Cîteaux (see the *Sertum florum moralium*, see pp. 28–31 above). No *exempla* collection is known to have been compiled in the lines of Pontigny and La Ferté.

[26] The collection was edited by Andrea Liebers, in "Rigor ordinis - Gratia amoris," *Cîteaux* 43 (1992): 162–220 (introduction), and *Cîteaux* 44 (1993): 36–151 (edition and commentaries). It should be noted, however, that these miracles are not local. The same manuscript contains the *Visio Edmundi monachi de Eynsham* (on this vision see Thomas Ehlen, ed., *Visio Edmundi monachi*

manifested itself when he undertook a journey to Kaisheim (Salem's sister abbey) to speak with a visionary named Rudolf. Appealing to Rudolf's obedience, Eberhard questioned him about his visionary experiences. Eberhard then narrated the *Visio Rudolfi* to the monks of his abbey, where it was written down.[27] One can easily see the parallels between this situation and the scenes from the *Dialogus* where abbots or priors used their authority to obtain an edifying story from sick or dying monks. Remarkably, Eberhard himself is said to have had visions. As the *Tractatus super statu monasterii Salem* (written shortly after 1337) relates, when the abbey was in a particularly difficult situation, the Virgin Mary appeared to the abbot and persuaded him not to dissolve the convent, but to preserve it whole.[28] Another of Eberhard's visions is mentioned by Dietrich of Apolda in his *Vita S. Dominici*:[29] one night, God appeared

---

de Eynsham: interdisziplinäre Studien zur mittelalterlichen Visionsliteratur [Tübingen: Narr, 1998]). Among the manuscripts produced by Salem's scriptorium during this period, besides Herbert's *Liber* and probably the *Exordium*, is the *Liber de miraculis sanctae Mariae* earlier ascribed to Boto of Prüfening in MS. Heidelberg, Cod. Sal. IX, 23 (Franz Josef Worstbrock, "Boto von Prüfening," in *Die deutsche Literatur des Mittelalters: Verfasserlexikon*, vol. I, ed. Kurt Ruh [Berlin: De Gruyter, 1978]). For more details about Eberhard and Salem book production, see Andrea Fleischer, *Zisterzienserabt und Skriptorium: Salem unter Eberhard I. von Rohrdorf (1191–1240)* (Wiesbaden: Reichert, 2004).

[27] "*Ne igitur auditoris animum diuitius suspendamus, ad narrationem visionis, sicuti venerabili domino Eberhardo, abbate tunc temporis in Salem referente audivimus, qui ab eo utique, qui eam vidit monacho, sicut gesta est, infirmitate corporis valida detento, obedientia coacto cognovit, accedamus*" (Fleischer, *Zisterzienserabt und Skriptorium*, 198 [the edition of the *Visio Rudolfi* according to MS. Heidelberg, Cod. Sal. IX, 26, is on pp. 197–211]). Eberhard himself probably wrote the short version of this vision (see Paul Gerhard Schmidt, "Luzifer in Kaisheim. Die Sakramentsvision des Zisterziensers Rudolf (ca. 1207) und Abt Eberhard von Salem," in *Litterae Medii Aevi: Festschrift für Johanne Autenrieth zum 65. Geburtstag*, ed. Michael Borgolte and Herrad Spilling [Sigmaringen: Thorbecke, 1988], 194).

[28] Franz Joseph Mone, *Quellensammlung der badischen Landesgeschichte*, 4 vols. (Karlsruhe: G. Macklot, 1863), 3:29.

[29] AASS, Augusti (Antwerpen, 1733), 1:596.

to Eberhard in a dream and said that he would send him horses for shoeing. The next day, when two Dominican friars came to Salem, Eberhard welcomed them and, having understood the meaning of the dream, provided them with shoes and clothes.

Eberhard's passion for miracles and visions definitely influenced Salem's culture. The *Dialogus* was copied (or acquired?) later, under Abbot Ulrich II von Seelfingen (1282–1311), who also supported book production in the abbey. And even under his successor, Konrad von Enslingen (1311–1337), who was rather careless with books,[30] Salem's library seems to have acquired a certain "new book" of *Miracula ordinis*, given to the Benedictines in Einsiedeln as guaranty for the loan of Abelard's *Sic et Non*. MS. Einsiedeln, Stiftsbibliothek 300 (439) reads, "*Iste liber est monasterii S. Mariae de Heremitis et debet restitui fratri Heinrico de Ligertia*[31] *thesaurario eiusdem monasterii*" ("This book belongs to the monastery of Saint Mary in Einsiedeln and should be returned to brother Henry of Ligerz, the treasurer of this same monastery"), then, in a different hand: "*Et ipse debet restituere dominis de Salem unum novum librum qui intitulatur Miracula ordinis*" ("And he, in his turn, should return to the monks of Salem one new book entitled *Miracula ordinis*"). This *Miracula ordinis* cannot be confidently identified. MS. Heidelberg, Universitätsbibliothek, Cod. Sal. IX, 19, containing Herbert's *Liber*, has an inscription on its back saying, *Vita s. Elizabeth et miracula ordinis Cisterciensis*. It was, however, produced as early as the second quarter of the thirteenth century. Could it still be described as new? Was there another copy of Herbert's *Liber*, or a similar collection? In any case, the mention

---

[30] According the *Tractatus super statu monasterii Salem* (shortly after 1337), the abbot used to send his relatives to different *studia* at the abbey's expense and supplied them with books, none of which was returned. See Mone, *Quellensammlung*, 3:38.

[31] *Catalogus codicum manu scriptorum qui in bibliotheca monasterii Einsidlensis O. S. B. servantur*, vol. 1, ed. Gabriel Meier (Leipzig: Harrassowitz, 1899), 275. Henry of Ligerz (1303–1356), was a treasurer and librarian in Einsiedeln.

of this "new book" shows that monks from Salem still found Cistercian *exempla* collections worthy of investment, despite the abbot's negligence toward the library. Establishing the full textual tradition of the *Dialogus* is beyond the scope of this study. However, some scribal interventions help to define the manuscript families and therefore to cast more light on the transmission of the *Dialogus* among Cistercians as well as adding some historical context. The first variant to mention is a curious early rewriting that is found, among others, in MS. Dü1, dating from the thirteenth century.[32] In chapter XII.3, instead of *"Non est diu quod Hermannus Lantgravius filius praedicti Lodewici mortuus est"*[33] ("Not long ago the Landgrave Herman, son of the aforementioned Ludwig, died"), we read *"Non est diu quod alter quidam princeps Allemanie mortuus est"* ("Not long ago a certain prince from Germany died"). Caesarius's usual style suggests the more detailed version to be closer to the original. The variant *Hermannus Lantgravius* is attested in another thirteenth-century manuscript, though not of Cistercian provenance: MS. Utrecht, Universiteitsbibliotheek, Cat. 176, from the monastery of Regular Canons of Saint Mary and the Twelve Apostles in Utrecht (Ut1). It seems therefore that at some point—as early as in the thirteenth century—the name of Landgrave Herman I of Thuringia († 1217) was replaced with "a certain prince from Germany." Both the manuscripts from Altenberg (Dü2) and from Himmerod (Be1) share the *"quidam princeps"* variant. It is also present in the manuscripts from Aulne (Br1) and Jardinet (Na), and in the manuscripts transmitting versions B and C of the *Dialogus*.

---

[32] Except fol. 191ʳ to fol. 210ᵛ, from the 14th century. The fragment in question belongs to the 13th century. See Agata Mazurek, *Die mittelalterlichen Handschriften der Signaturengruppe C in der Universitäts- und Landesbibliothek Düsseldorf* (Wiesbaden: Harrassowitz, 2012), 170–73.

[33] As in Strange's edition.

Both manuscripts originating from Clairvaux Abbey (T1 and T2, both late fifteenth century), as well as the manuscript from Eiteren (Ha, also fifteenth century) have the variant chosen by Strange. Clairvaux early on acquired an exemplar of the *Dialogus* whose *terminus ante quem* is the the composition of the *Adbreviatio relationum fratris Cesarii* (around 1229) by Alberic of Trois-Fontaines († 1252). The manuscripts from Clairvaux could derive from an earlier version than the one preserved in MS. Dü1, although they date from a later period. But why remove the name of the Landgrave? There is no obvious answer to this question. It should, however, be remembered that Herman I was the father of Ludwig IV (the husband of Saint Elizabeth of Thuringia, also venerated as a saint). Herman also founded the Saint Katherine Abbey of Cistercian nuns in Eisenach, which was under the care of the abbey of Pforta. The *exemplum* in question presents him as a damned sinner, a walking dead man inhabited by the devil for many years, an image that the scribe may have seen as inappropriate.

So, shortly after the completion of the *Dialogus*, its manuscript tradition split into two families: "*Hermannus*" and "*Quidam princeps.*" From the latter family, more branches developed. One of them is characterized by a variant reading in chapter VI.31. This is a story about a recluse who complained to Master Johannes about having lost her God. Johannes jokingly suggested that she search carefully in her cell: the Lord had probably fallen into some hole. The simple woman did as directed and found her devotion anew. This Master Johannes—mentioned several times in the *Dialogus*—was scholasticus in Xanten, dean of the collegiate church of Mary in Aachen, and later abbot of Saint-Trond and of Deutz († 1228).[34] The manuscripts from Altenberg (Dü2) and Himmerod (Be1) present him as "*Magister Johannes, nunc Abbas sancti Trudonis*" (the variant

---

[34] On Johannes of Xanten, see Ingo Runde, *Xanten im frühen und hohen Mittelalter: Sagentradition—Stiftsgeschichte—Stadtwerdung* (Cologne-Weimar-Vienna: Böhlau Verlag, 2003), 446–47.

retained by Strange), whereas the manuscripts from Clairvaux, Eiteren, Aulne, and Jardinet, and all the manuscripts containing the B and C versions, have *Magister Johannes decanus Aquensis*. In this case it appears that the variant *Magister Johannes decanus Aquensis* is the older one. Johannes indeed became abbot of Saint-Trond in 1222,[35] and *distinctio* VI, as Brian McGuire convincingly suggests, was completed by 1221. The correction of *"decanus Aquensis"* into *"nunc Abbas sancti Trudonis"* could therefore have been made as early as between 1222 and 1228.[36] Finally, there is an interesting variant in chapter II.24, a story about a Jewish girl who became pregnant by a cleric who misled the whole Jewish community into thinking that she was carrying their Messiah. To their great confusion, the girl gave birth to a daughter. According to the manuscripts from Clairvaux, Eiteren, Altenberg, and Himmerod, this story happened in Worms (*"In civitate, ut opinor, Wormacia"*), though in the manuscripts from Aulne and Jardinet , and in all manuscripts containing Versions B and C, it happened in Liège (*"in civitate Lemovicensi"*).

To sum up, one can tentatively divide the textual tradition of the *Dialogus* into two families: *"Hermannus"* and *"Quidam princeps."* From the latter family, a new branch developed, with the reading *abbas sancti Trudonis* (manuscripts Dü1, Dü2, Be1), and then still another branch, containing the reading *in civitate Lemovicensi*. The probe collation confirms this distribution of manuscripts.

This branch has another particularity worth mentioning. In the manuscripts from Aulne (Be1) and Jardinet (Na) the Novice

---

[35] See Hubert Kesters, "Jan van Xanten, Kruistochtprediker en Abt van Sint-Truiden," *Ons Geestelijk Erf* 28 (1954): 5–26.

[36] Johannes became the abbot of Deutz before February 14, 1226. However, the papal legate, Konrad of Porto, gave him permission to continue as the abbot of Saint Trond. See Joseph Milz, *Studien zur mittelalterlichen Wirtschafts- und Verfassungsgeschichte der Abtei Deutz* (Cologne: Wamper, 1970), 240.

is called *Apollonius* and the Monk *Cesarius* in *distinctiones* VII to XII. The name *Apollonius* was common in the Cologne region, and in Heisterbach Abbey there was in fact a monk named Apollonius. According to Friedrich Lau, this Apollonius originated from the Spiegel patrician family from Cologne and had a brother named Bruno, who was also a monk in Heisterbach.[37] There is unfortunately no proof that this Apollonius was the prototype for the Novice in the *Dialogus*. Both the Aulne and the Jardinet manuscripts date from the fifteenth century, but the name of the Novice himself appears much earlier. In his *Alphabetum narrationum* (1297–1308), Arnold of Liege relates the story of a child who was kidnapped and raised by wolves, walked on all fours, and howled like them. He attributes the story to a certain "Apollonius."[38] Arnold based this chapter on the exact words of a reply made by the Novice in the *Dialogus* (X.66),[39] and used a manuscript with Apollonius as the name of the novice. The evidence provided by the *Alphabetum narrationum* therefore sets a *terminus ante quem* for this particular branch. Perhaps the reason that the Novice's name is present only in the second part of the *Dialogus* (*distinctiones* VII–XII) is that the first part of the archetype of this particular branch was lost before having been copied, as the *Dialogus* often circulated in two volumes: *distinctiones* I–VI and VII–XII. The only manuscript that has both names in the first part is MS. Michaelbeuern, Benediktinerstift, Man. cart. 90 (from the fifteenth century), which contains excerpts from *distinctiones* I, II, III, IV, and VII of the *Dialogus* (Version C).

---

[37] Friedrich Lau, "Das Kölner Patriziat bis zum Jahre 1325, II," in *Mitteilungen aus dem Stadtarchiv von Köln* 10/26 (1895): 149. See also Brunsch, *Das Zisterzienserkloster Heisterbach*, 386.

[38] Arnoldus Leodiensis *Alphabetum Narrationum*, ed. Elisa Brilli, CCCM 160 (Turnhout: Brepols, 2015), 261.

[39] "*Ego quendam iuvenem vidi, qui in infantia a lupis fuerat raptus, et usque ad adolescentiam educatus, ita ut more luporum supra manus et pedes currere sciret, atque ululare.*"

Both Versions B and C of the *Dialogus* descend from the branch with the variant *in civitate Lemovicensi.* However, since all known manuscripts transmitting these versions (except the fifteenth-century manuscript from Michaelbeuern) do not name the interlocutors, one can assume that their archetype appeared after the introduction of the *in civitate Lemovicensi* variant, but before the Monk and the Novice were named Caesarius and Apollonius. In the chapters below, I discuss both versions in detail.

4

Version B of the
Dialogus miraculorum

As was mentioned earlier, some of the surviving manuscripts of the *Dialogus* that belonged to the monasteries of Morimond affiliation—namely MSS. H, I, and M1—transmit Version B of the *Dialogus*.[1] Version B originates from the south of Germany or Austria, probably from a region close to Alsace, as is suggested by its replacement of *Alna* (Aulne Abbey, in the diocese of Liège) by *Alsacia* in chapter XI.65: "*Cum in Alsacia in domo ordinis nostri.*"[2] In the textual tradition, this version belongs to the branch with the variant *in civitate Lemovicensi*, of the "*Quidam princeps*" family.[3]

[1] All cited manuscripts containing the *Dialogus*, with sigla, are listed in Appendix I, pages 275–78.

[2] This variant is present in all manuscripts of the group containing all XII *distinctiones*, e.g., MS. M1.

[3] The *stemma codicum* of this version was published by Karl Drescher on the basis of Alfons Hilka's preparatory works for his planned critical edition of the *Dialogus*; see Karl Drescher, ed., Einleitung to *Hartliebs Übersetzung des* Dialogus Miraculorum *von Caesarius von Heisterbach* (Berlin: Weidmannsche Buchhandlung, 1929), xi. One of the manuscripts transmitting this version served as the basis for the German translation made by Johannes Hartlieb before 1467. Some of the surviving manuscripts of this branch were unknown to Hilka; his *stemma*, however, provides a useful basis for the present study.

Omissions and abridgments in Version B

Version B is characterized by an important number of omissions and abridgments, as well as by several additions to Caesarius's text. It also changes Version A's chapter numbering at the beginning of *distinctio* IV, as a certain Johannes (the compiler of Version B?) explains: "*Sciendum quod ista distinctio non habuit capitula [in] se distincta sed ut prudens lector et diligens cito inueniat quod desiderat ego Iohannes studui breuiter aliqua sibi intitulare*" (MS. H, from Salem, fol. 74ʳ). Version A of the *Dialogus* structures the fourth *distinctio* according to the seven deadly sins, from *superbia* to *luxuria*, and in the manuscripts it was often highlighted with rubrics or running titles.[4] Johannes kept this structure but started the chapter numbering over with each new section of sins.

Version B omits a number of chapters in the following *distinctiones*:[5] II (chap. 35), III (chaps. 19, 28, 39, 41, 43–45, 48, 51), IV (chaps. 15, 17, 23, 65–67), VII (chap. 18), and XII (chap. 16). In some cases, the ending of an omitted chapter, announcing the following story, is moved to the previous chapter better to maintain the inner logic of the section. For example, the conclusion to III.19 ("*De hoc tibi dicam manifestum exemplum a quodam ordinis nostri abbate mihi relatum*" ["About this I am going to tell you a manifest *exemplum* that was related to me by an abbot of our Order"]) has been moved to III.18, where it replaces the original conclusion ("*Quod autem damnandis confessio tribuat veniam, praesto est exemplum*" ["Here is an *exemplum* (saying) that confession grants pardon to those who are to be damned"]). Such replacements show that the editor worked with a specific editorial project in mind while respecting Caesarius's method of connecting the stories.

---

[4] Running titles already appear in the thirteenth-century MS. Dül.

[5] Chapter numbers are given according to the Strange's edition unless otherwise specified.

It is difficult to know why some of the stories were omitted. Sometimes, on the other hand, the reasons seem clear. For example, IV.15 may have been dropped because it contains a severe criticism of Christians and their vicious life by a virtuous Saracen (Nur ad-Din, emir of Damascus and Aleppo) and could therefore have been seen as scandalous. It is not, however, clear why the compiler omitted chapters 65, 66, and 67 in the same *distinctio*, since they relate the exceptional charity of monks from Heisterbach, Himmerod, and an unnamed Cistercian abbey in Westphalia. Did the idea of sharing the food with poor laymen and laywomen during the famine come to seem too radical over time?

Partial omissions also occur in the texts, mostly in *distinctiones* III (towards its second part), IV, VII, VIII, XI (from chapter 45), and XII. In *distinctiones* III and IV omissions usually take place in the exchanges between the Monk and the Novice that contain short theological commentaries (for example, in IV.22[6]) or references to previous chapters (for example, III.38[7] and IV.10[8]). In other cases, the editor dropped some elements of long chapters containing multiple stories, as in III.33 about Simon de Alna.[9]

In the seventh *distinctio* the omissions become more common and at the same time more consistent. The editor often omits names of persons (especially those of the secondary characters, but sometimes also of the protagonists),[10] additional

---

[6] Here the compiler omits *"Lingua inquietum malum est . . . propter vitam vero utrumque pervium fecit."*

[7] The compiler skips *"Item quod quidam ex sola Dei misericordia . . . Ausculta."*

[8] In this chapter, the compiler omits *"Alii dicebant . . . qui dispensatorem dolose circumvenit."*

[9] The *lacunae* are [*notarius quidam . . . esse comperimus*] and [*hoc eum posse nosse . . . defectus ille suppleatur*].

[10] For example (omissions in square brackets), in VII.35: *"Miles quidam iuvenis ac delicatus in Hemmenrode ante annos paucos est conversus* [*vocabulo Henricus*]*,"* and VII.36: *"Eodem tempore quo Daniel . . . quidam monachus* [*Henricus nomine*]*."*

information about their positions,[11] and indications of place.[12]
He usually drops any additional information Caesarius gave
about the source of the story in question, as well as references
to previous chapters.[13] Some omissions were apparently due
to censorial intervention. In VII.32, for example, Caesarius tells
a story about the Virgin Mary's curing a knight from a sinful
passion by giving him a kiss. The editor removed a part of the
dialogue between the Virgin and the knight (as somewhat too
playful?),[14] as well as the line saying that the Virgin compelled
the knight to kiss her (*"et coegit eum"*).

This same editorial strategy can be observed in *distinctio*
VIII. The editor here omitted, for example, the exchange between the Monk and the Novice about two crosses venerated
in Heisterbach (one from Apulia and the other from St. Sophia
in Constantinople), probably perceived as too local and irrelevant (VIII.30). However, it seems that in this *distinctio* he retained more details, including some references to the previous
chapters (see, for example, chapters 45 and 46).

Surprisingly, few to no omissions of this kind take place in
distinctiones IX and X, but they reappear after *distinctio* XI.45.
The last *distinctio* (XII) is heavily abridged and contains some
elements of rewriting, in chapter 8, for example. This relatively
short story tells about Flemish travelers who sailed near Mount
Vulcan, where the entrance to the Hell was located. When they

---

[11] For example, in VII.39: "*Post mortem Abbatis nostri [Gevardi], . . . quod
dominus Henricus [tunc Prior . . .] in Abbatem consecrandus.*"

[12] VII.46: "*In [introitu] Frisia [iuxta civitatem Gruningen] coenobium*"; and
VII.50: "*In domo quadam Hispaniae ordinis nostri [quae Pumerane vocatur] duo
adolescentes sunt conversi.*"

[13] In VII.35 the scribe skips "*De his a me requisitus idem Henricus, non nega-
vit . . . . Novicius: Bene recordor huius capituli.*"

[14] "*Placetne tibi species mea? Dicente milite, nunquam pulchriorem te vidi; illa
subiunxit: Sufficeret tibi si me posses habere uxorem, necne? Cui cum responderet:
Cuilibet Regi bene sufficeret species tua, et beatus iudicaretur tuo consortio; subiecit
illa . . . .*"

heard a voice announcing the arrival of a certain Siward (the head of the Lechenich municipality), an old friend of the Devil, they noted the day and the time. Upon their return, they visited Lechenich and learned that Siward had died on that very day. In Version B, the story in question became both less detailed and more explicit. The editor omitted the information about the position and origin of Siward, as well as the action taken by the Flemish travelers, but added Siward's sins and eventual punishment. Here is the comparison of the two versions (the rewriting is in boldface):

Version A, ed. Strange	Version B
Alio tempore quidam Flammingi cum mare transirent, de eodem monte Vulcano vocem huiusmodi audierunt: Bonus amicus noster Sywardus hic venit, suscipite illum; qui cum multo stridore missus est in Vulcanum. Nam et ipse scultetus fuerat in Leggenich. Illi notantes tempus et nomen personae, reversi villam iam dictam intraverunt, et cum de sculteto requirerent, eum eadem die et hora qua vocem audierunt in mari, obisse repererunt. Nam et ipse homo pessimus erat, sicut superior.	Alio tempore quidam flemmingi de eodem monte talem vocem audierunt: Bonus amicus noster hic venit **qui multum laborauit in superbia in avaricia et luxuria. Fessus est, faciamus ei balneum.** Nam et ipse homo pessimus erat, sicut superior. (MS. M1, fol. 218ᵛ)

Why such inconstancy in editorial strategy? It seems plausible that it was a result of the work of at least two scribes who copied different quires of the exemplar, one of whom took the initiative to generalize Caesarius's stories somewhat and make them more concise (unless he just wanted to save time and effort).

Additions to Version B

Additions mostly occur in the first six *distinctiones*. They are stories interpolated after the following chapters: II.9, II.34, III.12, IV.68, IV.103, and V.30.[15] Another three stories are added after the sixth *distinctio*, without any changes in chapter numbering. These nine stories, which are those most discussed here, are summarized in Appendix II below. Finally, seven stories are added after the formal *Explicit* of the *Dialogus*.[16] This small collection of miracles (mostly unknown, with the exception of the famous story of Udo of Magdeburg, a fictional bishop who ignored all warnings and signs from God and was beheaded for his sins by the sentence of the divine court) forms a sort of an annex to the *Dialogus* that is present in all full manuscripts of this version.[17]

The majority of the interpolated stories are so skillfully interwoven into Caesarius's text that they do not stand out. They correspond thematically to the preceding ones, sometimes being slight local variations. For example, the story added after IV.68 tells about the Benedictine abbey of Saint Mathias in Trier, which once lost its wealth, being punished by God for having rejected the poor, especially, as a wise old monk explained to his brethren, those from the Cistercian Order. The abbey resumed its charitable activity and became prosperous again. In order to atone for the lapse, the Benedictines from St. Mathias even built a house for the Cistercians: "*Commemorato tandem consilio edificauerunt ordini Cysterciensi domum sicut hodierna die ibidem cernitur*" ("In view of this advice, they built a house for

---

[15] Chapter numbers are those of Strange's edition.

[16] E.g., fol. 228^r–32^r in MS. M1.

[17] The stories added after the end of *distinctio* XII were published by Karl Hopf in his short article "Sieben Wundergeschichten aus dem XIII. Jahrhundert," *Germania: Vierteljahrsschrift für deutsche Altertumskunde* 16 = Neue Reihe, Jg. 4 (1871): 308–16. Hopf's transcription was made from MS. Königsberg, Staats- und Universitätsbibliothek, N. 1080 (lost in WWII). The journal is available online: http://opacplus.bsb-muenchen.de/title/6701624/ft/bsb 10812522?page=316. My edition of the aforementioned nine exempla is to be published on-line in the database ThEMA: http://thema.huma-num.fr/.

the Cistercian Order that can still be seen today").[18] This story is in fact a rewriting of *Dialogus* IV.68, which also tells of an unnamed Benedictine abbey that became impoverished after having neglected the duty of hospitality and then, thanks to the *Date* and *Dabitur* parable, amended its ways. But Caesarius did not include Cistercians in the category of the poor neglected by these Benedictines.

Sometimes, in order to accommodate the interpolations better and to preserve the inner logic of the *distinctio* in question, the closing exchange between the Monk and the Novice from a preceding chapter was moved to follow an insertion, as in the case of the story added after II.9. The story tells of the abbot of Murbach, a Benedictine abbey in Alsace, who waged wars and plundered cemeteries, like Bishop Luitpold (Leopold) of Worms († 1217), protagonist of II.9, who usurped the diocese of Mainz and sacked it during the dispute for the German throne between the House of Hohenstaufen and the House of Welf. When the soldiers of the unnamed abbot of Murbach protested the plundering of a cemetery, he responded with the same words as Luitpold to his men: "*si ossa mortuorum tollitis, tunc primum cimiteria spoliatis*" ("only if you have carried out the bones of the dead, then you will have plundered the cemetery"). The dialogue between the Monk and the Novice that initially closed the previous chapter now follows the interpolation. The editor also changed the original story, increasing the emphasis on the reconciliation of Luitpold (who initially supported King Philip and went to Italy to fight the pope) with the church, and adding at the end, "*Dicitur tamen quod in ultimo multum pro ecclesia laborauerit et quod ab Innocentio papa laudatus fit*" ("It is said that in the end he worked hard for the church and was praised by Pope Innocent") (MS. H, fol. 33ʳ).

To complete the story about a counterfeiter of coin and his partner killed by the devil (interpolated after V.30) the editor himself wrote the closing dialogue: "*Novicius: Valde miror quod dyabolus ianuis clausis non venit ad illos sicut solet ad tales uenire qui talia operantur. Monachus: Quod in publico uenit hoc factum est ad exemplum multorum falsariorum et ut ceteri metum habeant. Hic illud daviticum impletum est: Da illis secundum opera eorum et secundum nequiciam adinuentionum ipsorum* [Ps 27:4]" (V.31; MS. H fols. 139ᵛ–140ᵛ [here 140ᵛ]). ("Novice: I wonder why the devil did not go after them behind closed doors, as he usually comes after those who do such things. Monk: He did this in public to give an example to many false coiners and to put fear into others. So these words of David came true: Give them according to their works, and according to the wickedness of their inventions"). This interpolation explicitly mentions its oral source: "*narrauit nobis Hermannus monachus noster*" ("Our monk Herman told us").

Five of the six interpolated stories are introduced by a first-person narrator, and three contain a first-person address to the interlocutor. For example, the story interpolated after III.12 reads, "*Referam tibi adhuc aliud memoria dignum quod a uiro religioso nomine Bernhardo Salzeburgensi canonico audiui*" ("I will tell you another memorable story that I have heard from a religious named Bernhard, a canon from Salzburg").[19] The intention of imitating Caesarius could not be more obvious.

Two of the three stories added after the sixth *distinctio* are also introduced by the first-person narrator: "*Referente abbate de Willeheringen in Austria Cysterciensis ordinis nuper cognouimus*" ("Through the abbot of Wilhering, a house of the Cistercian Order in Austria, we recently learned") (MS. H, from Salem, fol. 177ʳ), and "*Retulit nobis idem abbas*" ("The same abbot told us") (MS. H, fol. 74ᵛ). However, these three stories do not correspond thematically to the sixth *distinctio*, which is

---

[19] Fol. 57ʳ in MS. H, from Salem. See also "*Referam tibi huic simila*" (H, fol. 48ᵛ); "*Retulit nobis abbas Petrus Noui Castri*" (H, fol. 100ʳ); "*Qvantum operetur castitas et oratio ex subiecto doceberis exemplo. Retulit nobis unus de minoribus fratribus*" (H, fol. 118ʳ).

dedicated to the virtue of simplicity, and they are not connected to the previous chapter by any association.[20] The first added story is about a priest who celebrated Christmas Eve with his family in an inappropriately jolly way. The next day during Mass, he could not find the sacramental bread and wine. The second story is about a cleric whose lewdness was repulsive even to the demons. And the last is a story about a knight who was led by his dead suzerain into a place where he met some important persons enduring the pains of purgatory, who asked him to deliver a message to their friends and relatives.

Origin of the changes

Where exactly and when were these abridgments and interpolations in the *Dialogus* made? Were they done at the same time and by the same person? Numerous elements point to Alsace. I have already mentioned the replacement of *Alna* with *Alsacia*, as well as the story concerning the belligerent abbot of the Alsacian abbey of Murbach. Additionally, the story interpolated after IV.68 is related by the abbot of Neubourg (daughter of Lucelle), also situated in Alsace (MS. H, fol. 100ʳ). The abbot is presented by name—Peter—and, according to the compiler, he later became the abbot of Morimond: *"Retulit nobis abbas Petrus Noui Castri postea in Morimundo."* It is however not easy to identify this Peter. Neubourg had two abbots by this name before the early fourteenth century, with the *terminus ante quem* set by the oldest manuscript containing this version. The best known is Peter I, abbot from 1196 to 1214. First a canon in Trier, he became a monk in Himmerod, the mother house of Heisterbach, with its rich storytelling tradition. According to the 1648 necrology of the abbey,[21] Peter died in 1214. It is

---

[20] Caesarius often deviates from the main theme when the end of the narrated story triggers some association.

[21] *Necrologium Neocastrense anno 1648 compilatum a Mich. Strohmeyer* (Archives départementales du Bas-Rhin, H 1066).

therefore doubtful that he was elected abbot of Morimond in the same year. However, a certain abbot P. of Morimond seemed to have assisted the General Chapter in 1214.[22] Was there a confusion between two Peters? Or is the date provided by the Necrology wrong? But perhaps Peter died shortly after the election. Unfortunately, the succession of the abbots of Morimond is not sufficiently attested for the period from 1200 to 1241.[23] The other Peter is known to have been in charge of the Neubourg abbey in 1261.[24] No Peter (or P.) is attested as abbot in Morimond in the following years.

In addition to the stories set in Alsace, there are others connected to other locations. One comes from a story told by a canon from Salzburg named Bernhard. His story is about demons from Cyprus who raped virgins sent as tribute to a king from the region of Syria Maritima (MS. H, fols. 57^r–58^r). It is interpolated after III.12, which has a similar subject: demons having intercourse with women.[25] The point of connection between Salzburg and the Alsace region could have been the Salem abbey near Konstanz, founded in 1136/37 as a daughter house of Alsatian Lucelle. Salem was taken under protection of the archbishop of Salzburg in 1201, during the controversy over the German throne.[26] A document from 1237 emphasizes the long-term friendship between the abbey and the canons of the Salzburg cathedral: "*magna . . . familiaritas inter nos et ven-*

---

[22] Canivez, *Statuta capitulorum generalium*, 1:430 (1214, no 62). According to Angel Manrique, *Cisterciensium seu verius ecclesiasticorum annalium a condito Cistercio* (Lyon: G. Boissat et L. Anisson, 1642), 1:520, the abbot of Morimond from 1200 to 1238 was Guido I. Manrique mentions no Peter as abbot of Morimond in the thirteenth century.

[23] See Archdale Arthur King, *Cîteaux and her Elder Daughters* (London: Burns & Oates, 1954), 350–52.

[24] Antoine Wathlé and Claude Muller, *Notre-Dame de Neubourg: Histoire d'une abbaye cistercienne de Basse-Alsace* (Dauendorf: Chez l'auteur, 2016), 152.

[25] III.12 in Strange's edition: "*Exemplum de Hunis, et de Merlino, et quod in filiis incuborum sit veritas humanae naturae.*"

[26] See Alberich Siwek, *Die Zisterzienserabtei Salem: der Orden, das Kloster, seine Äbte* (Salem: Erzb. Münsterpfarramt, 1984), 143–44.

erabiles Salzburgensis chori canonicos iam dudum viguit" ("Great
. . . familiarity flourished between us and the venerable canons of Salzburg for a long time").[27]

One story (the one about the counterfeiters of coin inserted
in *distinctio* V) is attributed—also in a very Caesarius-like
manner—to a monk named Herman, from the same monastery.
The event took place in Weiler, now part of the city of Cologne.
Herman, then a priest, used to celebrate Mass there and knew
the protagonists: *"in eadem uilla celebrauit et illos bene nouit vnde
dicturus sum"* ("he celebrated Mass in the same town and knew
the people about whom I am going to speak") (MS. H, fol.
139ᵛ). The church is probably Saint Cosmas and Damian, which
belonged to the Saint Kunibert collegiate church from 1135.[28]
Herman could therefore have been a canon in Saint Kunibert,
and in 1250 documents do attest a certain Herman.[29] It is not,
however, possible certainly to identify either the Herman in
question or the monastery that he entered.

Two stories added after the end of *distinctio* VI were told, as
I have already mentioned, by a certain abbot of Wilhering, in
Upper Austria, which was founded in 1146 as a daughter of
Rein Abbey. In 1185, Wilhering became the daughter of Ebrach.
A third story is said to have happened *"uix infra tres menses"*
("just three months ago"), and the date is explicitly spelled out
in the end: *"Acta sunt hec anno domini mᵒ ccᵒ lviijᵒ"* ("this happened in the year 1258").[30] The abbot who told the story can
therefore be identified as Abbot Ernest (1246–1270). In the
story, a knight, led by his dead suzerain, meets the bishop of

---

[27] Andreas von Meiller, ed., *Regesta archiepiscoporum Salisburgensium: inde
ab anno MCVI usque ad annum MCCXLVI: Conrad I., Eberhard I., Conrad II.,
Adalbert, Conrad III. und Eberhard II.* (Vienna: Gerold, 1866), 270.

[28] Peter Kürten, *Das Stift St. Kunibert in Köln vom Jahre 1453 bis zur Auflösung*
(Cologne: Janus, 1990), 40–41, 255.

[29] Klaus Militzer, *Kölner Geistliche im Mittelalter*, vol. 1: *Männer* (Cologne:
Historisches Archiv, 2003), 291.

[30] Added by a different hand in MS. H (fol. 178ʳ); the date is present in all
the manuscripts containing this story.

Würzburg, the count of Enchirsberge (Erichsberg?),[31] and the count of Hohenlohe (Honloch). The story also mentions an abbot of Ebrach: the knight initially refuses to go with the dead man without having consulted the abbot, and later—after having been heavily burned by purgatory fire—is transported to Ebrach Abbey to die.

As for the seven *exempla* added after *distinctio* XII, they originated mostly in northwest Germany, that is, from the same region as the majority of Caesarius's stories. For example, the first one tells about Count Wilhelm III († 1218) of Jülich in North Rhine-Westphalia (*De comite de Gůlich*), while the fourth (*De monacho submerso in Reno*) mentions Saint Alban's Abbey and Saint Jacob's Abbey in Mainz as well as Eberbach. It was the abbot of this last one, here named Benimundus (for Reimundus?),[32] who found the body of the drowned monk. The fifth story, *De puella quam dyabolus rapuit et nutriuit*, is said to have happened in "*Brabancia in quadam uilla*" ("a certain town in Brabant"). Only one *exemplum* out of seven (*De periculo excommunicationis*, the sixth) indicates its source, which is again Alsatian. The story was narrated by "*Gotfridus, uenerabilis abbas Noui Castri quod est cenobium in Alsacia ordinis Cysterciensis*" ("Geoffrey, the venerable abbot of Neubourg, which is a monastery of the Cistercian Order in Alsace").[33] In the abbey of Neubourg, there were at least two abbots named Geoffrey in the thirteenth century: Geoffrey II (1242–1248) and Geoffrey III (1252–1261? 1280?).[34] Therefore, by all appearances, the seven stories were added at some point between 1242 and 1280, with the *terminus ante quem* being the end of the abbacy of Geoffrey III.[35]

---

[31] *Sic* in MS. H. MSS. I and M1 have Erchirberge.

[32] Could it be Rimund, abbot of Eberbach in 1228–1247?

[33] Fol. 152ʳ in MS. I, which originated at Stams.

[34] Between 1261 and 1280 two other persons were mentioned as abbots: Peter, in 1261 (see pp. 63–64 above), and Engelhard, in 1268.

[35] Wathlé and Muller, *Notre-Dame de Neubourg*, 152.

It now seems possible to conclude that the stories indicating their oral sources—the abbots of Neubourg and Wilhering—were told at slightly different times: in or slightly after 1214 or around 1261 (the interpolation made after IV.68); in 1258 (one of the three stories added after *distinctio* VI); between 1242 and 1248/1252 and 1280 (one of the seven stories added at the end of the *Dialogus*). The differences in how the additional stories were integrated into the *Dialogus* (skillfully interwoven within a *distinctio* or simply appended after it) lead us to assume that they were not added at the same time. But in which order? Much-needed insight is provided by manuscripts that are close to those of Version B but have some substantial and therefore revealing differences:

Be2   Berlin, Staatsbibliothek zu Berlin - Preußischer Kulturbesitz, MS. theol. fol. 95. Provenance unknown.

Bs   Basel, Universitätsbibliothek, B VIII 18, from Saint Margarethental, Basel.

Gd1   Gdańsk, Biblioteka Gdańska Polskiej Akademii Nauk, MS. 2155. Provenance unknown.

Gd2   Gdańsk, Biblioteka Gdańska Polskiej Akademii Nauk, Ms. Mar. F. 198. Provenance unknown.

The Berlin manuscript (Be2) has additions after the sixth and the twelfth *distinctiones*, but not those imitating Caesarius except for one story interpolated after II.34—the final chapter of the *distinctio*. Its text is not abridged, and the chapter numbering in *distinctio* IV is as usual. It contains no mention of Johannes, and in XI.65 *Alna* is not replaced with *Alsacia*. The *Vita* of the monk Hugo from the Cistercian abbey of Tennenbach is also added to the seven stories at the end of the *Dialogus*.[36] Hugo died in 1270, which serves as the *terminus post quem* for this addition; the addition certainly originated at the Cistercian

---

[36] Franz Josef Mone, ed., *Quellensammlung der badischen Landesgeschichte* (Karlsruhe: G. Macklot, 1867), 4:65–75.

abbey of Tennenbach (the daughter of Salem), situated in Baden-Württemberg, not far from the oft-mentioned Neubourg. Another story is added after *distinctio* XII.56 (fols. 284^v– 85^r), with the *incipit "Legitur de quodam uiro sancto qui cum quadam die dominica transiret quandam uillam in francia"* ("We read about a certain holy man who, one Sunday, went past a certain town in France"). It is about a demon who, through the mouth of a possessed woman, declares that he is ready to sustain every possible torment to see again the face of God, whose ineffable clarity he then describes. The interlocutor of the demon is presented as an anonymous holy man. The same story, however, is found in the *Promptuarium exemplorum* by Johannes Herolt († 1468), where the man is presented as *"Magister Jordanus frater ordinis praedicatorum"* (certainly the Blessed Jordan of Saxony).[37]

On the other hand, MS. Gd1 has the interpolations imitating Caesarius in the first part. The story inserted after IV.103 is found again after the eight stories (including the *Vita Hugonis*) added after *distinctio* XII. It is presented as *"notabile bonum licet non sit de ordine libri huius"* ("a remarkable good [story] although it is not a part of this book"). The additions to *distinctio* VI are present, but they are inserted before VI.37 (the last chapter in this section). As in the Berlin manuscript (Be2), the text in question is not abridged, and there is no mention of Johannes in *distinctio* IV. *Alna* in XI.65 is not replaced by *Alsacia*. The addition in *distinctio* XII is present.

The other manuscript from Gdańsk (Gd2) is remarkable in many regards. It has no stories imitating Caesarius's style in the first part, except for the one at the end of the second *distinctio*, written on an inserted folio. The three stories added after *distinctio* VI are also on inserted folios. The additions within and after *distinctio* XII are the same of MS. Gd1 (including the *Vita Hugonis* and the *notabile bonum*). There are no omis-

---

[37] Johannes Herolt (Discipulus), *Sermones Discipuli de Tempore . . . cum promptuario exemplorum* (Cologne, 1504), *Gaudia caeli* I.

sions or abridgments, no replacement of *Alna* with *Alsacia*. This manuscript is very peculiar from a textual point of view. Its second part was probably copied from a manuscript close to MS. Gd1 and possibly from Gd1 itself.[38] Its first part, however, deviates from it, except for the stories on the added folios, which are, once again, very close to Gd1. I presume that the first six *distinctiones* of MS. Gd2 were copied from an unidentified or now lost manuscript textually close to MS. Be2. The exemplar for the first part apparently lacked interpolations, so some were added later on inserted folios.

MS. Bs, from Basel, transmits Version B, with the addition of the *Vita Hugonis* and the story recounted above about the holy man who talked with a demon about the face of God (inserted in *distinctio* XII). Specific to this manuscript is the interpolation made after XII.35, which contains the vision of Gûta from Günterstal (the nunnery under the care of Tennenbach), absent from the other manuscripts that I have consulted.

To sum up, it seems that the earliest additions to this version of the *Dialogus* were the story added after II.34 and those added after *distinctio* VI; it is not clear in what order they were added—probably not all at once. It is possible that the seven stories after *distinctio* XII were added at around the same time. The majority of the stories imitating Caesarius's style were therefore added after 1258 (the *terminus post quem* for the additions made after *distinctio* VI), except for the already mentioned addition after II.34 and the *notabile bonum* in the Gdańsk manuscripts, which was later placed after IV.103. At some point after all the stories imitating Caesarius had been interpolated into the text, an abridged version of the text was created, possibly by a scribe named Johannes. Then, after 1270, an anonymous compiler, certainly from Tennebach, added the *Vita Hugonis* and, probably, the story after XII.56.

---

[38] The *Dialogus* frequently circulated in two parts.

The fact that Be2 does not have additional stories in Caesarius's style (except for the one after II.34), while Gd1 has them, while both also transmit the *Vita Hugonis* and the interpolation in *distinctio* XII, absent in Version B, can be explained by their having been copied from two volumes belonging to closely related but different branches of the textual tradition, as is the case of MS. Gd2. As for the Basel manuscript (Bs), it transmits basically the same version as MSS. H, I, and M1. Further, it contains two more interpolations in *distinctio* XII and the *Vita Hugonis*. It is possible that the copyist of the Basel manuscript amended the text by adding these stories from another exemplar.

Version B was therefore not a single-shot initiative of one person. Different monks from different houses of the Morimond line added new stories to the *Dialogus*. They worked in various ways, from making discernible additions (for example, with the *notabile bonum* clearly marked as not being part of the original) to carefully inserting new stories into Caesarius's text. Although the abridgments in Version B were probably made by the same person, this attitude towards the *Dialogus* was certainly not exceptional, as is shown by manuscripts of Cistercian provenance discussed below.

5

Version C of the *Dialogus miraculorum*

Two manuscripts, Rein, Zisterzienserstift, Cod. 58 (R), and Leipzig, Universitätsbibliothek, Cod. 445, from Altzella (L), transmit another version of the text different from that found in Version A, this one based on Version B. Version C is much more concise than Version B. However, it also keeps some of the stories added in Version B. Version C does not mention Johannes at the beginning of *distinctio* IV, and chapter numbering, when present, follows the usual order (MS. L has the numeration, but MS. R does not).

The omissions and abridgments in this version are numerous. In the first *distinctio*, for example, the following chapters are omitted: 7, 13, 17, 18, 20, 23, 24, 32, 34, part of 39, and 40–43; the second *distinctio* omits chapters 4, 6, 7, 17, 19–22, 25–30, and 33–35; the third *distinctio* omits chapters 3, 4, part of 6, 7–12, 17–20, 24, 28–31, 33, 35, 38–45, 48, 51, and 53, and so on in the other *distinctiones*.

The editor of Version C made an effort to ensure that its omissions would not disturb the inner logic of the *Dialogus*, just as had the one who had introduced abridgments in Version B. The Version C editor also replaced and/or edited the closing dialogues of the chapters that followed or preceded deleted chapters, and deleted parts of long chapters. One example occurs in III.6, about a demon who stalked a virgin from Brabant while revealing the sins of other people. He was visible only to the virgin, but everyone could hear him. Many people

interrogated the demon, among them a man who wanted to
speak to him but was afraid that the demon would reveal his
sins in public. The man confessed his sins, while however keeping the intention to sin further. The demon easily found that
out and exposed the man, much to his embarrassment. The
editor omits all the information about the virgin from Brabant,
as well as the digression concerning the demon's inability to
say the *Pater noster* properly. The retained part of the chapter
starts with *"Fuit vir quidam, qui supradictum demonem nimis
videre desiderans"* ("There was a certain man who very much
wanted to see the aforementioned demon") (MS. R, fol. 19ᵛ)
and directly follows the previous chapter, III.5, about a Premonstratensian canon whose unconfessed sins were disclosed
by a demon through the mouth of a demoniac. Version C therefore implies that the unnamed man spoke with same demon
as did the Premonstratensian canon, as is not the case in the
original story. The logic of the narrative is however left undis-
turbed, and the two chapters fit thematically even better.

The editor also omits details relative to characters and
places, as well as indications of sources. An example occurs in
the opening passage of II.5. In Version A it begins, *"Dominus
Conradus, quondam Episcopus Halberstadensis, anno praeterito
retulit nobis historiam satis mirabilem, quam contigisse dicebat ante
paucos annos in regno Franciae. Erat ibi sacerdos quidam"* ("Dom
Konrad, the former bishop of Halberstadt, last year told us
quite a wonderful story, which he said happened several years
ago in the kingdom of France. There was there a certain
priest"). In Version C this beginning becomes simply *"Sacerdos
quidam erat in regno Francie"* ("In the kingdom of France, there
was a certain priest" MS. R, fol. 11ᵛ). In comparison to Version
B, the abridgments in Version C are more radical. The full version of VII.35 in Version A has *"Miles quidam iuvenis ac delicatus
in Hemmenrode ante annos paucos est conversus vocabulo Henricus"*
("A certain young and delicate knight named Henry entered
Himmerod a few years ago"); Version B omits only *"vocabulo
Henricus,"* whereas Version C reads, *"Miles quidam iuuenis et
delicatus in quadam domo ordinis nostri est conuersus"* ("A certain

young and delicate knight entered a certain house of our order") (MS. R, fol. 67ʳ).

This compact version, however, keeps some interpolations, namely the story in *distinctio* II about the abbot of Murbach, the story at the end of *distinctio* IV about a young woman who made a vow of chastity, and the story in *distinctio* V about false coiners killed by the devil. Of the three stories at the end of *distinctio* VI, MS. R keeps two (the second one about a lecherous cleric and the third one about the knight who encountered his dead suzerain), and MS. L only one (the third, about the knight).

MS. L from Altzella deserves special attention. It has both similarities to and differences from the Rein manuscript. Judging by the probe collation, it basically transmits Version C, but some of the stories omitted from that version are present here, and there are some changes in the order of chapters. For example,[1] chapter I.34 (about a cleric necromancer who became a Cistercian after having seen the punishment of Landgrave Ludwig in Hell) is not omitted, but inserted at the end of chapter I.27, about the same Landgrave Ludwig—so becoming manuscript chapter 19, fols. 12ʳ–13ʳ. After this chapter the editor placed the thematically appropriate I.33, also about a necromancer converted to the Cistercian way of life (now manuscript chapter 20, fol. 13ʳᵛ).[2]

What I find most fascinating about this manuscript is its numerous and various additions of its own in almost every *distinctio*, except *distinctiones* VI and X. They are usually inserted singularly or in small clusters, especially in *distinctiones* IV and VII. After the final chapter of the twelfth *distinctio* of

---

[1] The chapter numbers and titles here are given according to Strange's edition if not stated otherwise.

[2] This story, although present in Version C, differs slightly from the one in other manuscripts. It begins with *In arte nigromancie cuius titulus mors anime scribitur*—the definition of necromancy given by Caesarius in his *Homiliae dominicales*—where he reused this *exemplum*. See *Fasciculus moralitatis venerabilis fr. Caesarii, Heisterbacencis monachi*, ed. Joannes A. Coppenstein (Cologne: P. Henningius, 1615), 2:34.

the *Dialogus* (*De coelesti Jerusalem et gloria sanctorum* [On the heavenly Jerusalem and the glory of the saints]) come thirty-seven additional stories (fols. 261^r–74^r). The first story is added as chapter 36 without interruption. The following stories were originally not numerated[3] but accompanied by rubrics, a pattern that to some extent mimics the structure of the *Dialogus* itself: *de contritione, de peccatrice conversa, de temptatione gule, de temptatione avaritie, de demonibus, de simplicitate, de beata virgine, de visionibus, de corpore Christi, de morientibus, de elemosina, de passione, de premiis iustorum, de pena malorum, de gloria beatorum* (on contrition, on the converted [female] sinner, on the temptation of gluttony, etc.). This appended material amounts to an independent *exempla* collection and recalls the additions made after *distinctio* XII in Version B.

The additions to MS. L are mostly exemplary stories (though with non-narrative pieces as well)[4] from written sources. Many added *exempla* circulated widely in the Middle Ages and can easily be found in or traced to well-known collections such as the *Bonum universale de apibus* by Thomas of Cantimpré, *Fabulae et parabolae* by Odo of Cheriton,[5] the *Liber miraculorum Beatae*

---

[3] Hereafter numeration is that of the manuscript.

[4] For example, a string of seven *similitudines* on *otiositas* in *distinctio* IV.54–59 (fols. 79^v–91^r): "*Prima similitudo. Attende homo quod tu es in medio maris . . . hec de pigris otiosis siue accidiosis dicta sufficiant.*" In the same *distinctio* there is a treatise on *luxuria*, "*Cui assimilabo luxuriosum? Similis est pavoni . . . . Qui comedit semel in die vivit sicut angelus, qui bis sicut homo, qui plus sicut bestia*," chap. 104 (fols. 111^r–15^r). This text can be found in MS. Zeitz, Stiftsbibliothek 37 (olim Cod. XIII). The short treatise has a number of *similitudines* and well-known *exempla* on lust, such as that of a hermit pursued by a courtesan. Faking consent, he suggested that they sin in the marketplace. When the woman refused, the hermit explained that they were no less hidden from God there than in the desert. The *exemplum* originated in the *Vita S. Ephraem* and is also present in the *Vitae Patrum* (PL 73:916AB), as well as in many medieval *exempla* collections.

[5] The story from IV.77, fol. 101^r (numerated as in the manuscript) came from the *Bonum universale de apibus* (Douai: B. Belleri, 1627), II.56.2. The same *distinctio*, IV.105 (fol. 115^r), contains a popular parable about a fool who put a cat in his chest to protect the cheese against mice. This parable can be found,

Mariae Virginis,[6] *Vitae fratrum,*[7] and *Tabula exemplorum.*[8] Others can be found in still unpublished collections.[9] But one of the major sources of additions is Cistercian, namely the *Liber miraculorum* by Engelhard of Langheim, written for the nuns from Wechterswinkel (1188–1190).[10]

---

for example, in Odo de Ceritona, *Fabulae et parabolae,* 21, ed. Léopold Hervieux, *Les fabulistes latins depuis le siècle d'Auguste jusqu'à la fin du moyen âge,* vol. 4, *Eudes de Cheriton et ses dérivés* (Paris: Firmin-Didot, 1896), 194.

[6] Some *exempla* are added to *distinctio* VII, e.g., chap. 58, fol. 172[r], "*Quidam clericus Carnotensium urbe degebat, qui erat levis moribus*" (n° 1343 in Poncelet's index of Marian miracles), and the following chapter, 59: "*Alter clericus in quodam loco commorabatur*" (n° 69 in Poncelet's index) (Albert Poncelet, "Miraculorum B.V. Mariae, quae saec. VI–XV latine conscripta sunt Index," *Analecta Bollandiana* 21 [1902]: 241–360).

[7] XII.38 (fol. 264[v])—Gerardus de Fracheto, *Vitae fratrum ordinis praedicatorum* (Louvain: Charpentier & Schoonjans, 1896), 211 (IV.22.3).

[8] XII.45 (fol. 266[v])—Jean-Th. Welter, ed., *La tabula exemplorum secundum ordinem alphabeti: Recueil d'exempla compilé en France à la fin du XIII*[e] *siècle* (Paris-Toulouse: Occitania, 1926), 20 (n° 64).

[9] XII.64 (271[v]): "*Duo fratres religiosi ad visitandum limina sanctorum olim pariter gradientes.*" This *exemplum* can be found in Berlin, Staatsbibliothek zu Berlin - Preußischer Kulturbesitz, theol. lat. fol. 611, fol. 529[v], which contains a small collection of twenty-two *exempla* entitled "*Hic incipiunt se rumores ex libris sanctorum compilati ex ore predicancium et veriditorum hominum collecti sunt diuina reuelacione scriptisque commendati sunt de Wern a Hugone.*" Also XII.39 (fols. 264[v]–65[v])—*Miles quidam nec deum nec homines timens coniugem habuit satis fidelem*—is present in MS. Soest, Wissenschaftliche Stadtsbibliothek, Cod. 31/32.

[10] There are fourteen added stories, among them I.21 (MS. L, fol. 13[v]–14[v]), in Engelhard: *De duobus nicromanticis* (fol. 162[r]–163[v]); II.21 (MS. L, fol. 39[r]–40[r]), in Engelhard: *De Petro episcopo* (fol. 160[r]–161[r]); III.20 (MS L, fol. 53[v]–55[r])—in Engelhard: *De Pontio episcopo et monacho eius* (fol. 138[v]–140[v]); IV.16 (MS. L, fol. 64[v]–65[r])—in Engelhard: *De monacho iracundo* (fol. 147[rv]). Folio numbers cited here for Engelhard's additions come from MS. Munich, Bayerische Staatsbibliothek Clm 13097 (end of the 12th century, available online). On this copy of Engelhard's *Liber miraculorum,* see Bruno Griesser, "Engelhard von Langheim und sein Exempelbuch für die Nonnen von Wechterswinkel," *Cistercienser-Chronik* 70 (1963): 55–73; and Hans D. Oppel, "Die exemplarischen Mirakel des Engelhard von Langheim: Untersuchungen und kommentierte Textausgausbe (Teildruck)," PhD dissertation, Würzburg University, 1978, 77–85.

Remarkably, in MS. L some additional stories originate from Caesarius's writings, sometimes from his homilies, but also from the *Dialogus* itself. For example, the added chapter IV.99 tells a story about a certain virgin from France who had a severe carnal temptation and was liberated from it by reciting a psalm verse suggested by an angel (fol. 109ʳ). She was then overtaken by the temptation of blasphemy and complained about it to the angel. The angel responded that it is impossible for any human being to live without temptation and that the virgin had to choose between carnal temptation and blasphemy. The virgin took the first one. This story is an epitome of an *exemplum* first used by Caesarius in his *Homiliae de infantia Salvatoris*[11] and then in VIII.42 of the *Dialogus*. The latter is part of Version C and as such appears in the Altzella manuscript L (VIII.20; fols. 191ᵛ–92ʳ), so IV.99 is a duplication. IV.99 is distinct from both the *Homiliae* and the *Dialogus*. It apparently originated in an as-yet-unidentified *exempla* collection.[12] Thematically, it also fits perfectly at the end of *distinctio* IV, which is dedicated to the sin of *luxuria*.

Another example of the reintroduction of stories from the *Dialogus* via another source is the story about a certain Master Thomas, theologian, who was lying on his deathbed and saw a devil standing in the corner. Master Thomas exhorted the devil to tell him what harmed him the most. The demon replied that there is nothing in the church that harms and weakens devils as much as frequent confession (XI.38). This story was used by Arnold of Liège in his *Alphabetum narrationum* under the rubric *Confessio*. Arnold's redaction of the story is found inserted in III.10 of the manuscript (III.4 in Strange's

---

[11] See *Fasciculus moralitatis*, 1:73.

[12] It is possible that the *Homiliae de infantia Salvatoris* served as a source for additions. The vision of the monk Gottschalk from IX.2 (fol. 205ʳᵛ in the manuscript) is repeated as VII.46, on fol. 174ᵛ. This vision first appeared in the *Homiliae* (*Fasciculus moralitatis*, 1:59). The version of VII.46 is closer to the *Homiliae* and was probably taken from there.

edition). The inserted story presents Master Thomas as not only *theologus*, but also as *"predicator egregius"* ("famous preacher"; see fol. 47ᵛ). The original story is still in its place in *distinctio* XI (chapter 22 in the manuscript, fol. 245ᵛ).

An important number of stories added after *distinctio* XII— eleven in total—are borrowed either directly or indirectly from Caesarius's *Homiliae dominicales*,[13] written just after the completion of the *Dialogus*. Because in this homiletic cycle Caesarius reused many *exempla* from the *Dialogus*, some of these added stories have doubles in the main text of the *Dialogus*.[14]

The compiler of the manuscript found it necessary to explicate Caesarius's first-person references in the *exempla* originating in the *Homiliae dominicales*. In the *Homiliae dominicales* one story reads, *"Retulit michi domina Mechtildis, magistra in Fussenich, quod dicturus sum"* ("Lady Mechtildis, superior in Füssenich, related to me the story that I am going to tell")

---

[13] *Fasciculus moralitatis*, vols. 2 and 3.

[14] These are chapters 41 on fol. 265ᵛ (*Homiliae dominicales* [HD] III.27); 42 on fol. 265ᵛ (HD III.78, corresponding to *Dialogus* XI.19—this chapter is present in the Altzella manuscript as XII.8, fol. 231ᵛ); 43 on fol. 265ᵛ–66ʳ (HD III.46); 44 on fol. 266ʳᵛ (HD III.58 corresponding to V.18, here omitted); 49 on 267ᵛ (HD II.2); 50 on 267ᵛ (HD II.5, corresponding to X.16, omitted in the manuscript, and corresponding partially to VII.38, present as chapter VII.31–34 on fol. 161ʳ–163ʳ, the part in question being omitted in the manuscript); 56 on fol. 269ᵛ (HD III.37, partially corresponding to VII.20, present in the manuscript as VII.16–17, fols. 153ᵛ–155ʳ); 62 on fols. 270ᵛ–271ʳ (HD III.133); 69 on fol. 273ʳ (HD III.11); 70 on 273ʳᵛ (HD II.16) and 71 on fol. 273ᵛ (HD III.42 corresponding to XII.6, present in the manuscript as XII.5, fols. 250ᵛ–251ʳ). In the references to the *Homiliae dominicales*, Roman numerals indicate the volumes in Coppenstein's edition, and Arabic numerals indicate the pages. The first readers of the *Homeliae dominicales* did not approve of an abundance of *exempla* inserted in sermons, as Caesarius himself admits in the postscript to the *Moralitates euangeliorum* (a large cycle that includes the *Homiliae dominicales*). He therefore decided to abstain from this practice in his further homiletic works: *"et quia hoc quibusdam minus placuit, in omeliis de sollempnitatibus sanctorum hoc ipsum caui."* Coppenstein published postscripts as *Altera Epistola Monitoria Venerabilis Caesarij in Homilias suas Dominicales ac Festiuales ad lectorem* (ed. Coppenstein, vol. I). This introductory part of the edition is not paginated.

(HD III.11). This indication of the story's source was changed in MS. L as follows: *"Retulit michi Cesario de Haysterbach monacho Mechtildis magistra sanctimonialium"* ("Mechtildis, the nuns' superior, related to me, Caesarius of Heisterbach"). The first-person element was retained but apparently judged insufficiently clear, even though the context of the *Dialogus* already implied that the narrator was Caesarius. It is possible that the additions after *distinctio* XII were perceived by the compiler of the Altzella manuscript (L) as an independent collection, despite their lacking a proper *incipit*, rather than as part of the *Dialogus*.

Within the framework of this study it is impossible to discuss in detail each additional story that made its way into the Altzella manuscript. I will focus on two of them—I.27 and VII.62—to provide an additional glimpse into the compiler's strategy in dealing with written sources.

Chapter I.27 results from a curious combination of two written sources: the *Dialogus* (I.40 in Strange's edition) and Engelhard's *Liber miraculorum* (fols. 163ᵛ–167ʳ).[15] It contains the *Vita of Saint Hildegund*, a monk from Schönau known as Joseph, who was discovered after her death to be a woman.[16] The *Vita* is omitted in other manuscripts transmitting Version C. In MS. L, the beginning of the chapter is the same as in *Dialogus* I.40: *"In civitate Misia* [sic pro Nussia] *que quinque miliariis distat a Colonia ciuitate magna ciuis habitauit"* ("In Neuss, a town five miles from the big city of Cologne, lived a citizen," fol. 17ʳᵛ).

---

[15] The *vita* is published in Joseph Schwarzer, "Vitae und Miracula aus Kloster Ebrach," in *Neues Archiv der Gesellschaft für ältere deutsche Geschichtskunde zur Beförderung einer Gesamtausgabe der Quellenschriften deutscher Geschichten des Mittelalters* 6/3 (1881): 516–21.

[16] On Hildegund's *Vita* in the *Dialogus* see Brian P. McGuire, "Written Sources and Cistercian Inspiration in Caesarius of Heisterbach," *Analecta Cisterciensia* 35 (1979): 247–54. See also Martha G. Newman, "Real Men and Imaginary Women: Engelhard of Langheim Considers a Woman in Disguise," *Speculum* 78, no. 4 (2003): 1184–1213; and Martha G. Newman, *Cistercian Stories for Nuns and Monks: The Sacramental Imagination of Engelhard of Langheim* (Philadelphia: The University of Pennsylvania Press, 2020).

The part describing Hildegund's adventures on the way to Verona when she was sent to deliver a message from the archbishop of Cologne to the pope is omitted or, to be more exact, summarized as follows: *"Tandem post multis quas passa est tribulationes et mortis euasionem sicut ipsa cum ageret in extremis plenius manifestauit, ut postea dicemus, cum ad partes Alemanie fuisset reversa, abbatem de Schonouia instanter rogauit ut in monasterium suscipitur"* ("However, after many tribulations and a near escape from death, as she herself related in detail while lying on her deathbed—we will come to it later—she returned to Germany and begged the abbot of Schönau that she might be accepted in the monastery") (MS. L, fol. 17^v).

The compiler then returns to copying from the *Dialogus* and describes the life of Hildegund, disguised as a man, in the abbey of Schönau until her final illness. Thereafter it is Engelhard's text that is used as the source. In Engelhard's version, the dying Hildegund tells the prior the events of her life in the first person. Remarkably, the episode in which Hildegund was framed for a robbery, sentenced to be hanged, and then acquitted is again taken from the *Dialogus*, as is the conclusion of the *Vita*, which describes how the monks from Schönau searched for the real name of Brother Joseph and learned that she was called Hildegund (fol. 20^v–21^r). This final revelation is absent in Engelhard's text, which is in fact the earliest version of the *Vita*, written immediately after Hildegund's death in 1188.[17]

Chapter VII.62 (fols. 173^r–174^r) relates the famous vision of a monk who saw his fellow Cistercians under the cloak of the Virgin Mary (VII.59 in Strange's edition). It has the following postscript on f. 174r: *"Predictam visionem vidit quidam heremita sicut predictum est per omnia. Quem conversus in Walcheym quidam Kuno nomine de Altenburch bene novit et cum eo locutus est. Qui conversus cum fuerat miles ducis Ludowici cuius predictus heremita fuerat consors"* ("A certain hermit saw the aforesaid vision. A lay brother from Waldheim, named Kuno, from Altenburg, knew

---

[17] Oppel, "Die Exemplarischen Mirakel," 84–85.

this hermit well and spoke with him. The lay brother had been a knight of Duke Ludwig, at a time when the hermit was the duke's associate"). The abbey in question was probably Buch Abbey in Saxony, situated not far from Waldheim. Buch Abbey had close relationships with the Burgraves of Altenberg. Duke Ludwig, mentioned in the text, was probably one of the Landgraves of Thuringia (where Altenburg is located). A more precise identification is unfortunately not possible.

There is, however, an interesting parallel in another manuscript from Altzella, MS. Leipzig, Universitätsbibliothek, Cod. 841, containing the collection *Miracula ordinis Cisterciensis conscripta et depicta in monasterio Celle sanctae Mariae in ambitu*.[18] This famous vision is copied on fol. 123r with a postscript: *"Eandem visionem ut Cesarienses miraculorum gesta testant quidam heremita habuit et reuelauit"* ("A certain hermit had and revealed the same vision, as the [book of] miracles from Kaisheim [Lat. *Caesarea*] testifies"). There was, it seems, a collection of miracles originating at Kaisheim Abbey (so far unidentified), where a hermit is said to have had a vision of Mary.[19] Apparently it was important for the editor of MS. L to add yet another source of the emblematic vision promoting the special relationships between Mary and her friends the Cistercians.

The compiler's manner of adding new stories to the *Dialogus* is somewhat similar to the one encountered in Version B. For example, after the *exemplum* about Bishop Luitpold and the abbot of Murbach, the Altzella compiler adds two more *exempla*: II.27, on the cleric who said German bishops could not be

---

[18] On this collection see above, p. 48.

[19] The collection of stories added after *distinctio* XII of the *Dialogus* opens with the vision of Rudolf from Kaisheim (fols. 261ʳ–263ᵛ). The version of the famous vision in the Altzella manuscript differs from those published elsewhere (see Andrea Fleischer, *Zisterzienserabt und Skriptorium: Salem unter Eberhard I. von Rohrdorf (1191–1240)* [Wiesbaden: Reichert, 2004], 195–218; and Andrea Liebers, "*Rigor ordinis—Gratia amoris*," *Cîteaux* 43 [1992]: 175–81). It is possible that it originated in the same collection of miracles as the vision of the hermit.

saved (fol. 30ʳ), and II.28, on a monk from Clairvaux who did not consent to become a bishop (fol. 30ʳᵛ). Both chapters are absent from other manuscripts containing Version C. The closing dialogue from the story of Luitpold is placed after the new additions (*"Saepe quosdam vidimus cadere, et per poenitentiam resurgere"* ["We often see some people fall and rise again through penance"]). The added stories correspond thematically to the *distinctio* in which they are inserted, and they often echo the chapters they follow (as in this case, the problems with being a bishop).

The compiler of the Altzella manuscript (L) also undertook some rewriting in imitation of Caesarius's style, to integrate the additions better. As one example, IV.31 in the manuscript (fols. 69ᵛ–70ʳ) is taken from Engelhard of Langheim's *Liber miraculorum* (*"De monacho studioso in choro"*). Engelhard presents the story in the previous chapter of his book (*"Quod sancta Maria cuidam uisa est"*) as follows: *"Bezlino nostro teste scriptum sit hoc quod ille nobis de Francia rediens abtulit et in laude monachorum illorum et in nostri forma recitare consuevit. Adiecit adhuc quod studiosis in choro fiduciam prebeat et negligentibus excitet diligentiam"* ("This story was written down according to the testimony of our Bezlin [Becelinus in other manuscripts], who brought it from France and used to tell it in praise of those monks and for our own instruction. He added to this story another one that will encourage those who are assiduous in choir and who urge the negligent ones to be more diligent").[20] In the Altzella manuscript the line reads, *"Audi de hoc exemplum memoria dignum quod frater Becelinus monachus in Lancheym de Francia rediens attulit"* ("In relation to this, listen to this *exemplum* that brother Becelinus, monk in Langheim, brought from France") (fol. 69ᵛ), with the typical second-person address used by Caesarius.

---

20 Fol. 146ʳ in MS. Munich, Bayerische Staatsbibliothek, Clm 13097.

To sum up, MS. L from Altzella provides yet another telling example of the interplay between Version C's tendency both to abridge and to generalize; the compiler aimed not just to smuggle some stories into Caesarius's text here and there, but instead systematically to enrich it with new elements, including some stories omitted in Version C. He also rearranged some chapters in order to group together *exempla* about the same person, or about those with the same principal theme, probably because of the influence of mendicant *exempla* collections arranged in alphabetical order by subject. It is possible that the editor used an unknown *exempla* collection from Kaisheim. He may also have had connections to Ebrach, since the name of Eberbach Abbey is often confused and replaced with that of Ebrach (*Eberbacensis: Eberacensis; In Eberbacho: In Eberaco*), for example in IX.54 (IX.46 in the manuscript, fol. 220ᵛ) and X.5 (X.3 in the manuscript, fol. 224ᵛ). Fascinating in its own right, the Altzella manuscript is also important evidence of the lasting transmission among Cistercians of Engelhard's *Liber miraculorum*, all the more relevant because of the small number of surviving manuscripts of that work.[21]

The question about Version C is whether it was of Cistercian origin. This version is usually found in non-Cistercian manuscripts, especially in Benedictine ones,[22] and Cistercian manuscripts of this version are in a clear minority. They also do not include the oldest manuscript of known provenance, MS. Sankt Paul im Lavanttal, Benediktinerstift, Cod. 61/4 (MS. Pl), dating from 1394, which once belonged to the Canons Regular from Neunkirchen am Brand. Nonetheless, both MS. R, a Cistercian manuscript from Rein, and MS. Pl have some readings in common with the full version different from those in other manu-

---

[21] Munich, Bayerische Staatsbibliothek., Clm 13097, fols. 133ᵛ–167ʳ; Paris, Bibliothèque nationale de France, nouv. acq. lat. 2627, fols. 228ᵛ–242ʳ; Poznań, Miejska Biblioteka, 173; Zwettl, Zisterzienserstift, Cod. 13, fols. 228ʳ–233ᵛ.

[22] See below p. 160.

scripts of Version C. The Rein manuscript also retains two of the three additional stories after *distinctio* VI from Version B, and MS. Pl has all three of them, whereas all other manuscripts have only one. MS. R appears therefore to be close to the archetype of Version C; it is not impossible that this version is due to the initiative of German Cistercian monks, probably from the Morimond filiation.

6

Versions D and E of the
Dialogus miraculorum

One early German manuscript points to the fact that the abridgement of the *Dialogus* took place at the very beginning of its Cistercian transmission: the Fragment Abt 22, 535/6 [a], from the Wiesbaden Hauptstaatsarchiv, originated at Eberbach Abbey and is dated as early as the first half of the thirteenth century. It is a consecutive bifolium, with both its outer sides (including half of the outer columns) and lower part unfortunately cut away. The fragment was used as an envelope for Eberbach's tribute register, which dates from 1634.

This fragment contains several stories from the end of *distinctio* VI (chaps. 27–37). Surprisingly for such an early witness, its version of Caesarius's text is heavily abridged. Here is, for example, the comparison of the beginning of VI.35 in Version A, Version C, and the fragment (Version D):[1]

---

[1] The *exemplum* in question is the one discussed earlier, about the priest's concubine who interrupts the preacher.

Version A: Strange VI.35	Version C (MS. R, fol. 58^v)	Version D (Eberbach fragment)
Sacerdos quidam, sicut mihi retulit quidam vir religiosus, cum die quadam multis praesentibus sermonem haberet de peccatis et poenis gehennae, mulier quaedam verba eius interrumpens, eo quod territa esset et compuncta, sic ait.	*Sacerdos quidam cum die quadam multis presentibus sermonem haberet de peccatis et penis gehenne, mulier quedam uerba eius interrumpens, eo quod territa esset et compuncta, sic ait.*	*Sacerdoti cuiusdam concubina in sermone cuiusdam predicatore compuncta clamauit dicens. . .*

Version D, though short, does not omit the dialogical frame, and it even contains additions imitating Caesarius's style. The fragment contains what looks like a life of a saint, accompanied by a dialogue between the Monk and the Novice and introduced with a second-person address: "*uobis recitabo*." The story is probably related to Worms ("*egregius Wormacie*"), but all other details have been lost in the unfortunate cropping of the folios.

The state of this fragment makes it impossible to compare it more thoroughly with other manuscripts of the *Dialogus*. Judging by its identification of Johannes from Xanten as "*decanus Aquensis*" (see above, pp. 50–51) the fragment is at least not directly related to the manuscripts from Alternberg and Himmerod. It is unclear whether or not some chapters were omitted in this version.

MS. Zwettl, Zisterzienserstift, Cod. 131, from Zwettl in Lower Austria (a daughter of Heiligenkreuz) (MS. Z), transmits yet another heavily abridged version of the *Dialogus* (fols. 1^r–65^v). As in the Eberbach fragment, the *exempla* in this manuscript were rewritten and abridged. Here, for example, is the beginning of I.3 in Strange's edition, chapter 1 in MS. Z:

Version A: Strange I.3[2]

Retulit mihi frater Godefridus monachus noster, quondam canonicus sancti Andreae in Colonia, cum essemus simul in probatione, rem dignam memoria. Asserebat sibi a quodam monacho Claraevallis bene noto relatum, quendam clericum actu trutanum, quales per diversas vagari solent provincias, venisse ad Claramvallem, non quidem zelo ordinis, sed ut aliquid monasterio raperet sub pallio religionis. Factus itaque novicius, cum per totum annum probationis suae insidiaretur ornamentis ecclesiae, et propter diligentem custodiam satisfacere nequivisset cordis sui malitiae, haec intra se cogitabat: Cum factus fuero monachus, et licuerit ministrare, sine nota ac labore ipsos calices subtraham, sicque recedam.[3]

Version E: MS. Z, fol. 4[r]

Clericus quidam de talibus quales per diuersas prouincias solent discurrere aut vagari venit ad Claramvallem, non quidem zelo ordinis sed gratia quippiam accipiendi. Tempore ergo probacionis sue religiose conuersatus est vt saltem post professionem ad ornamenta ecclesie nullo suspiciente secure posset accedere.

Version E has only ten *distinctiones*, as the incipit announces: "*Opus istud decem partes continet. Prima pars agit de conuersione, secunda de contricione,*" etc. (MS. Z, fol. 4[r]). The general prologue to the *Dialogus*, the prologues to all *distinctiones*, the non-narrative chapters, and the dialogue between the Monk and the Novice are omitted. Many chapters are also eliminated. For example, of the first *distinctio* this version retains only chapters 3, part of 6, 27, 32, 34, 35, 37, and 40. In all, Version E,

---

[2] Neither Version B nor C abridges this part.

[3] This story tells of a vagabond clerk who joined Clairvaux in order to steal some liturgical treasure. But the treasure was well guarded, and as a novice, he had no access to it, so he decided to become a monk and steal it later.

often associated with *exempla* from other sources, has between 131 and 164 chapters, depending on the manuscript.[4] Fortunately, it is possible to trace the origin of this version. The end of the fourth *distinctio*, after IV.103, has one more story, which is also found in Versions B and C, about a young woman who took a vow of chastity. In this manuscript it is titled *De uirgine cui parentes bona sua abstulerunt* (On a virgin whose relatives stole her possessions) (fols. 35^v–36^v). The presence of the *Vita Hildegundis* (fols. 6^v–9^r), absent from Version C, shows that this version derives from Version B. The last *exemplum* from the *Dialogus* included in Version E is X.53 (as in Strange's edition), suggesting that the archetype of this version was copied from a truncated manuscript.

After the final *exemplum* from the *Dialogus*, the Zwettl manuscript adds, without interruption, seventeen additional miracles, *notae*, and comparisons (fols. 65^v–71^r). These are mostly pieces that circulated widely with no specific relation to the Cistercian Order. Among them are two miracles from the popular *Liber miraculorum Beatae Mariae Virginis* (fols. 66^r–67^r),[5] and a variant of the vision of Saint Fursey, whose soul was claimed by devils for having accepted the clothing of a damned man (fol. 67^r).[6] These additions, however, are specific to the Zwettl manuscript and do not form an integral part of Version

---

[4] Version E is transmitted by the following manuscripts, none of which is of confirmed Cistercian origin or provenance: Colmar, Bibliothèque municipale 57 (24) (fols. 1^r– 42^v); Cologne, Historisches Archiv, *W 67 (fols. 1^r–68^v); Eichstätt, Universitätsbibliothek, Cod. st. 450 (fols. 213^v– 45^v); Munich, Bayerische Staatsbibliothek, Clm 3593 (fols. 180^r–298^r); Vorau, Augustiner-Chorherrenstift, Cod. 172 (olim CXV), (fols. 1r–59^v); London, British Library, Add. MS. 18346 (fol. 2^r–44^r); Berlin, Staatsbibliothek zu Berlin - Preußischer Kulturbesitz, MS. lat. qu. 107 (fol. 215^r–341^r); Cologne, Historisches Archiv, GB 8° 194 (fol. 1^r–132^v).

[5] *"Homo quidam diues vnicum habuit filium"* and *"In quodam cenobio erat quidam monachus secretarius officio."* See also Albert Poncelet, "Miraculorum B.V. Mariae, quae saec. VI–XV latine conscripta sunt Index," *Analecta Bollandiana* 21 (1902): 241–360, n°s 699 and 468 respectively.

[6] *"Quidam erat heremita sanctus qui habebat tunicam ab usurario."*

E. Other manuscripts containing this version append different collections to Version E.[7] The Zwettl manuscript mentions neither the author, Caesarius, nor the title of the work, whereas other manuscripts of unknown or non-Cistercian provenance transmitting this version usually acknowledge Caesarius's authorship. For example, MS. Vorau, Augustiner-Chorherrenstift, Cod. 172 (olim CXV), has an inscription by a contemporary hand on fol. 1[r]: "*Incipit Cesarius. Excerpta sunt ex Cesario.*" The question of whether Version E is of Cistercian origin remains open. MS. Z is the only known manuscript of this version that was certainly owned by a Cistercian house.[8] It is also the oldest, dating from around 1300.[9] Version E itself derives from the undoubtedly Cistercian Version B. Its Cistercian origin, though impossible to prove, can definitely not be excluded.

The transmission of the *Dialogus* among Cistercian houses (and especially in the Morimond line) is characterized by the scribes' (or, better, editors') active interaction with the texts. Far from being a fixed, unchangeable entity, the *Dialogus* was systematically enriched with new *exempla*, from both written and oral sources. These changes happened along with abridgment and generalization of the text. Cistercian scribes-editors

---

[7] For example, in the Vorau manuscript, to the *Dialogus* have been added chapters 1–35 of the famous collections of Marian miracles *Liber miraculorum Beatae Mariae Virginis* (with the *incipit* "*Ad omnipotentis Dei laudem cum sepe recitentur miracula sanctorum*"). In MS. Colmar, Bibliothèque municipale, 57 (24), after the *explicit* of the *Dialogus* (*Expliciunt exempla excerpta de Cesarie* [sic], fol. 42[v]) there follows a collection of twenty-eight *exempla* from the Cistercian milieu (*Alia exempla*). A similar collection of twenty-eight *exempla* appears in MS. Eichstätt, Universitätsbibliothek, Cod. st. 450, but it is placed before Version E of the *Dialogus* (fol. 209[v]–213[v]).

[8] Eichstätt, Universitätsbibliothek, Cod. st. 450 is also possibly of Cistercian origin.

[9] Charlotte Ziegler and Joachim Rössl, *Zisterzienserstift Zwettl: Katalog der Handschriften des Mittelalters*, vol. 2, *Codex 101–200* (Vienna-Munich: Schroll, 1985), 83–84.

removed details that had certainly been appealing to the Heisterbach community and its surroundings but that had become less significant for monks in a South German or Austrian house of the Morimond line. There was clearly a demand for making individual stories more generic, more generally applicable. This tendency, attested as early as the first half of the thirteenth century, coincides with the growing interest of the Cistercians in mendicant *exempla*, and with the changes in Cistercian *exempla* production itself as discussed above.

7

Cistercian Readers Interacting with the *Dialogus miraculorum*

The process of exemplification of a particular story could be—and often was—expressed through highlighting it in the manuscript with marginal notes, additional rubrics, or other means.[1] The manuscripts of *exempla* collections used by preachers, such as the famous *Alphabetum narrationum*, often contain many notes to allow the quick finding of (*statim invenire*) an appropriate story and placing it in the required context.[2] Monastic *exempla* collections appear to be much less annotated than do those explicitly intended as preaching aids. Private monastic reading, however, did not exclude interactions with the text, and some Cistercian manuscripts of the *Dialogus* have readers' notes that contribute to a better understanding of the reception of the book within the Order, both personally and communally. By making their own annotations, readers not only highlighted what was significant for them but also—given the fact that in a monastery books were usually in communal possession—influenced the reading experience of those who read the book after them.

---

[1] See Victoria Smirnova, "L'*exemplum* médiéval dans une perspective codicologique (XIIIᵉ–XVᵉ siècle)," *Revue Mabillon* n.s. t. 24 = t.85 (2013): 27–59.

[2] See also Richard H. Rouse and Mary A. Rouse, *Preachers, Florilegia and Sermons: Studies on the* Manipulus florum *of Thomas of Ireland* (Toronto: Pontifical Institute of Mediaeval Studies, 1979).

The list of heavily annotated Cistercian manuscripts of the *Dialogus* is relatively short:

Br1   Brussels, Bibliothèque Royale de Belgique, II 1067 (2121). *Notae* by several hands, *maniculae*

Dü1   Düsseldorf, Universitäts- und Landesbibliothek MS. C 26. *Notae* by one hand, marginal rubrics by another hand, *maniculae*

H   Heidelberg Cod. Sal. IX, 46. *Notae* by two different hands, marginal rubrics by two different hands, braces on margins

I   Innsbruck, Universitäts- und Landesbibliothek Tirol, Cod. 185. *Notae* by one hand, marginal rubrics by two different hands, braces on margins

M1   Munich, Bayerische Staatsbibliothek, Clm 2687. *Notae* by several hands (including that of the scribe), rubrics, *maniculae*

Each of these manuscripts conveys a unique view—or, better, views—on the text, which reflect what a reader found interesting, rather than offering a discernible Cistercian agenda. Recognizing this individuality and diversity, I outline here some of the common themes running through these manuscripts.

Unsurprisingly, Cistercian readers highlighted stories related to different aspects of the *vita regularis* and its practices. In MS. H, from Salem, a fifteenth-century reader highlighted a metaphor of the monastic life as one long bearing of the cross with the marginal rubric "*in* [*crucem?*] *assignificatio hec bona*" ("this is a good explanation on the cross"),[3] and an image of

---

[3] Fol. 5ᵛ. The highlighted passage is from I.6: "*Qui compunctus et Spiritus sancti unctione intus instructus crucem suscepit, non tamen transmarine illius expeditionis sed ordinis, salubrius iudicans longam crucem imprimere menti, quam breuem zonam ad tempus assuere uesti.*" A similar idea is emphasized on the same folio with a brace by another hand: "*Monachorum uita regulariter uiuentium tota crux est.*"

monastic conversion as a transition from one battle to another with the rubric *"militia secularis in spiritualem sic conuertatur vide"* ("see how the secular soldiery is converted to the spiritual one").[4] Reflecting on conversion, this reader agreed with the Novice that no reason to enter the monastery, even one insignificant at first sight, should be deprecated, and wrote on the margin of I.29, at fol. 15^r, *"minima non paruipendenda"* (fol. 15^r). It is no wonder that in I.33, with the rubric *"commendatio ordinis,"* he marked praise of the Cistercian Order spoken by a dead necromancer who appeared to his friend and tried to convince him to change his ways. To the living man's question about which path he should take, the dead man answered, *"Non est uia securior, quam ordo Cysterciensis, neque inter omne genus hominum pauciores descendunt ad inferos, quam persone ordinis illius"* ("There is no way more secure than the Cistercian Order, and among those who go to hell, the persons from this Order are in absolute minority") (fol. 17^r).

Similarly, a reader of MS. B1 from Aulne marked with a *nota* in I.3 the sentence *"Habitus monachi virtutem habet baptismi"* ("The habit of a monk has the power of baptism") (fol. 4^r). Another reader of the same manuscript drew a *manicula* to the saying in IV.64 of Archbishop Philip of Cologne († 1191) concerning the foundation of Heisterbach (and—by extension—of every Cistercian house): *"nulli nocerent, cum multis prodessent"* ("They harm no one but are useful to many") (fol. 91^r).

In MS. Dü1, a reader left *notae* on different subjects, among them how a novice miraculously overcame his aversion to the poor monastic food (fol. 89^r, IV.80), how Christ showed his disdain to a monk who used to doze in choir (fol. 72^r, IV.29), and how dangerous it is to disobey one's abbot (fol. 209^r, X.9). A reader of the Salem manuscript (H) left a *nota* drawing attention to the problem of the public display of inner devotion,

---

[4] Fol. 19^v, I.36 in the manuscript (I.37 in Strange's edition). It is a story of a knight who came to Himmerod in full armor, which he put down at the altar of Virgin Mary and became a monk.

and specifically the Monk's answer to the question of the Novice of whether it is dangerous to want to display signs of contrition. The Monk replies that it depends on the intention of the person (*"secundum intencionem"*): it can be meritorious if one wants to instruct others while being humble in heart, but otherwise it is not (fol. 41ʳ; II.21 [23 in the MS.]). Another reader of the same manuscript emphasized with the rubric *"cogitatio in oratione talis debet esse"* ("what one should think while praying") the advice given by the monk Geoffrey of Villers: *"Nichil debetis dicere in oratione, sed tantum cogitare de Saluatoris natiuitate, passione, resurrectione et aliis que uobis nota sunt"* ("You should say nothing while praying, but meditate on the nativity of Christ, his passion, resurrection, and other things you know") (fol. 18ᵛ; I.35).

In MS. M1 many marginal *notae* highlight *exempla* about the struggles of monastic life: challenges of humility,[5] and choir duty as a potential source of pride,[6] but also the dangers of sloth,[7] the necessity to control oneself even while sleeping,[8]

---

[5] For example, on fol. 49ᵛ, a *nota* and a *manicula* draw attention to chapter IV.6 (in Strange's edition) about a monk who overcame the temptation of pride by drinking the water that had been used to wash the dirty laundry.

[6] On fol. 50ʳ a *nota* accompanies IV.8, about a monk from Monte Cassino who sang beautifully while blessing the candles during the Easter Vigil and disappeared shortly after: no one ever knew whether he had been abducted by a demon or by an angel. On the verso of the same folio, another *exemplum* concerning the chant (IV.9, about the devil who gathered in a bag the voices of clerics singing with pride) has an additional marginal rubric, *de cantu*. On fol. 83ʳ a *nota* highlights the Monk's conclusion: *"Ex quo colligitur, quod magis placet humilis cantus cum cordis deuocione, quam voces eciam in celum arroganter exaltatare"* (V.5).

[7] A *nota* on fol. 56ʳ marks the Novice's question, *"Estne accidia, in choro dormire?"* (IV.31); on the same page the same hand emphasizes a story about a sleepy lay brother. Another lay brother saw a cat (the devil) sitting on the head of the second lay brother and closing his eyes with its paws (IV.33).

[8] Fol. 125ᵛ has a *nota* in VII.14 pointing to the Monk's conclusion after telling of the apparition of the Virgin Mary in the dormitory (VII.14). She blessed the monks sleeping in the right manner while ignoring those sleeping *inordinate* (without shoes or with the belt loose). Caesarius concludes, *"Dormientes et peccare possumus et mereri."*

and the ever-lurking temptation to apostasy.[9] The austere Cistercian discipline is indeed a constant temptation, as a certain prelate said to Caesarius: *"Non audeo intrare in tentationem"* ("I do not dare enter temptation" IV.47). A reader of the manuscript marked this saying with a *nota* on fol. 59[v].

Another common point among different manuscripts is the appreciation expressed by their readers for the theological and moral *sententiae* scattered through the *Dialogus*, and especially for the questions and observations of the Novice and answers of the Monk. A reader of manuscript H marked with *notae* the observation on the power of contrition,[10] the elements of the justification of sinners,[11] and the definition of perfect charity.[12] There is also a rubric *"predestinatio"* marking the Novice's

---

[9] A *nota* on fol. 62[r] points to the Novice's remark: *"Puto etiam nonnullos monachos de apostasia temptari"* (IV.54).

[10] On fol. 24[r] a *nota* highlights the following: *"Minima contritio maximam delet culpam, perfecta uero culpam simul tollit et penam"* (II.1). This *sententia* is also marked in MS. M1; see fol. 14[r].

[11] On fol. 24[v], a reader highlights four elements of the justification of sinners: *"In iustificatione peccatoris dicunt quatuor concurrere: gratie infusionem, motum surgentem ex gratia et libero arbitrio, contritionem, peccatorum remissionem"* (II.1). This passage comes from the *Sententiae* of Peter of Poitiers (III.2) (Petrus Pictaviensis, *Sententiarum libri quinque*, III.2; PL 211:1044A). On the use of early scholastic treatises in the *Dialogus*, see Victoria Smirnova, "Narrative Theology in Caesarius of Heisterbach's *Dialogus miraculorum*," in *The Art of Cistercian Persuasion in the Middle Ages and Beyond*, ed. Victoria Smirnova, Marie Anne Polo de Beaulieu, and Jacques Berlioz (Leiden: Brill, 2015), 121–42. See also my introduction to *Fasciculum moralitatis: Omelie morales de Infantia Saluatoris*, ed. Victoria Smirnova, Prague Medieval Studies Series (Prague: Karolinum Press, forthcoming).

[12] A *nota* on fol. 34[r] points to the following definition: *"Quando mens non est sibi conscia alicuius peccati mortalis siue uenialis, [libera] non solum est a culpa, sed etiam a pena"* (II.10). In the same chapter, a reader of the manuscript from Aulne (Br1) highlighted with a *nota*, *"Et puto, si sepedictus clericus decessisset in tali statu, minime sensisset penam purgatoriam, quia perfecta caritas consumit plumbum et stipulam, culpam et penam"* (fol. 30[r]). The concept of the augmentation of charity was widespread in medieval theological and pastoral literature; see Nicole Bériou, ed., *Les sermons et la visite pastorale de Federico Visconti archevêque de Pise, 1253–1277* (Rome: École française de Rome, 2001), 1045, n. 2. See also Smirnova, introduction to *Fasciculum moralitatis*.

demand to illustrate the difficult concept of predestination with scriptural authorities, and the Monk's answer (fol. 13ᵛ; I.26). In the manuscript from Aldersbach (M1) different readers call attention to the Novice's questions about confession,[13] the nature of children born from demons,[14] what mice consume when they nibble a Host,[15] and proverbial sayings such as *"Sterilis est terra sine pluuia, et absque fructu liberum arbitrium sine gratia"* ("The earth is sterile without rain, and free will is fruitless without grace") (fol. 14ᵛ, II.1) and *"sicut mutata sunt tempora ita et homines"* ("As time has changed, so have people) (fol. 108ʳ, VI.7). Readers also highlighted quotations from authorities serving to clarify one or another complicated issue, for example, Augustine's opinion on late penance (II.13)[16] and on those who take the sacrament or celebrate Mass without respect (I.55).[17]

---

[13] See fol. 42ʳ, where a *nota* draws attention to the question of the Novice, *"Item quero, si confitens confessori prodere debeat personam, cum qua peccauit?"* (III.27). This question is also marked in the Stams manuscript (I) with the marginal note *"quod confitenti non liceat prodere personam peccati consortem et exemplum de clerico et sanctimoniali"* on fol. 30ᵛ.

[14] On fol. 35ᵛ, a *nota* in red ink marks the Novice's question about whether the children of humans and demons would be judged in the Last Judgment (III.12), and the Monk's response, citing the opinion of a certain highly educated man.

[15] See fol. 172ᵛ. A *nota* points to the question, *"Quod est queso quod mures vel vermes in sacramento altaris comedunt?"* (IX.11).

[16] Fol. 21ʳ in MS. M1. See Augustinus Hipponensis [?], *Sermo CCCXCIII de Poenitentibus* (PL 39:1713–15). In the same manuscript a *nota* on fol. 108ʳ draws attention to Gregory the Great's commentary on Job 12:4: *"super quem locum dicit Gregorius: Justorum simplicitas deridetur, quia ab huius mundi sapientibus puritatis uirtus, fatuitas creditur. Omne enim quod innocenter aguntur* [sic], *ab eis procul dubio stulticia putatur. Et quicquid in opere veritas approbat, carnali sapientia* [sic] *fatuum sonat."* See Gregorius Magnus, *Moralia in Iob*, 10.XXIX.48, ed. Marcus Adriaen, CCSL 143 (Turnhout: Brepols, 1979), 571.

[17] On fol. 223ᵛ of MS. Br1, a reader marked the *auctoritas* of Augustine: *"Idcirco dicit Augustinus super illum locum: Dederunt in escam meam fel, de crucifixoribus eius: Quibus similes sunt indigne, inquit, sumentes et conficientes. Grauius enim peccant contemnentes Christum regnantem in celis, quam qui crucifixerunt ambulantem in terris"* (see *Enarrationes in psalmos* 68.33, ed. Eligius Dekkers

The *Dialogus* is also full of content that is not specifically monastic. Many of its stories are about life outside the cloister, and Cistercian readers seem to appreciate this dimension of Caesarius's work. A reader of MS. Dü1 highlighted stories about usurers,[18] criticisms against bishops[19] and against Christians in general,[20] miraculous effects of confession,[21] punishment of cunning persons and rogues (fol. 135ᵛ [VI.23]; fol. 136ʳ [VI.24, 25]), healing effects of the Host (fol. 201ʳ [IX.43, 44]), etc. The Salem manuscript (H) has rubrics concerning usury and the punishment of robbers[22] as well as necromancy,[23] and the Aldersbach manuscript (M1) has usury-related *notae*.[24]

Sometimes the reading of the *Dialogus* seems to have taken a pastoral turn, toward *cura animarum*. Although readers of

and Johannes Fraipont, CCSL 39 [Turnhout: Brepols, 1956], 922, cited by Caesarius probably via Petrus Cantor, *Verbum Abbreviatum* 1.25, ed. Monique Boutry, CCCM 196 [Turnhout: Brepols, 2004], 204).

[18] Fol. 37ᵛ and 39ʳ: II.32 (31) and 34 (33) respectively. (When they differ, chapter numbers in parentheses refer to Strange's edition.) In II.34, the reader also marked the Novice's comment: "*Videtur mihi usura multum esse defectiue nature, quia raro ad tertiam siue quartam illam durare uidemus generacionem*" (fol. 39ʳ).

[19] On fol. 36ᵛ a *nota* marks two passages. The first is from II.28 (27): "*Omnia credere possum, sed non possum credere quod unquam aliquis episcopus Alemannie possit saluari.*" On the same page, the reader highlighted a passage from II.29 (28): "*Ad hoc, inquit, iam deuenit status ecclesie, ut non sit digna regi, nisi a reprobis episcopis.*"

[20] On fol. 68ʳ a *nota* draws attention to the beginning of IV.15, a reflection on the loss of Jerusalem to the Saracens. The harsh criticism of Christians who do not observe Christian law (expressed, remarkably, by a noble pagan) is highlighted with a *nota* and a *manicula* on fol. 68ᵛ.

[21] Fol. 41ᵛ (III.2), fol. 42ʳ (III.3), fol. 46ʳ (III.13), fol. 47ʳ (III.14), and fol. 48ʳ (II.15).

[22] Fol. 32ʳ: "*predonum pena*" and "*usurarius*" (II.8 [7]).

[23] Fol. 16ᵛ: *nota de nigromanticis* (II.33).

[24] On fol. 18ᵛ a *nota* by the scribe marks this exchange between the Monk and the Novice on the fact that usury never rests from sin. In the same manuscript, a *nota* by another hand on fol. 29ᵛ highlights the fact that money gained from usury had devoured the money of a monastery (II.34).

manuscript I from Stams marked some monastic elements,[25] they apparently had a predilection for stories about laymen and secular clergy. For example, on fol. 58^r a *nota* marks the famous *exemplum* about little demons riding on the tail of a fancy dress (V.7); on fol. 69^r a *nota* by the same hand draws attention to the story about a canon mocked by the devil (V.53); on fol. 80^r a *nota* by another hand, a *manicula*, and a rubric *nota obedientia* highlight the story of the priest's concubine who entered a burning furnace after being told to do so—jokingly— by a preacher (VI.35). On fol. 147^r a *nota* and a *manicula* point to the Novice's question, *"Quid sentis de missis?"* ("What do you think about the Masses [for the Dead]"), asked in XII.32 (31 in the manuscript), about a phantom who said he preferred alms to prayers for his soul. The beginning of this chapter is marked by another *manicula* by a different hand. Also in *distinctio* XII, a rubric to chapter 57 (55 in the manuscript) insists that one should not refuse last communion and anointing to those who ask for it.[26]

A curious reader of the manuscript from Stams (I) drew on fol. 85^v a *manicula* with a manchette saying *"medicina"* in order to draw attention to a passage from VI.16 (19 in the manuscript). The chapter narrates the life of Christian, a monk from Himmerod, and the passage in question relates an event that happened before Christian's conversion. Christian, a student at the time, was staying overnight in the house of a woman whose daughter suffered from scabies on her head. The woman, persuaded that students know all sorts of things, urged Christian to help her daughter. Defeated by her insistence, Christian invented a balm that, as Caesarius declares, was not at all suitable for this illness. However, thanks to Chris-

---

[25] For example, a story about the Virgin Mary's visit to a monks' dormitory (VII.14) is marked with a *nota bene* on fol. 85^r.

[26] Fol. 149^v: *"nota exemplum propter sacramentum non denegare cuiquam vnctionem petenti."*

tian's simplicity, it worked. One wonders whether the monks from Stams ever tried to reproduce this medicine.

I truly hope that they did not try another dubious remedy, mentioned in I.14 and marked by another hand with "*nota medicina*" on fol. 4ᵛ. In this chapter Caesarius tells a story about a novice named Leonius who after leaving the Cistercian Order led a sinful life, then finally became ill and lost his sanity. To cure his frenzy, his relatives ripped apart living puppies and put their still warm flesh on Leonius's forehead. A different reader from Stams marked with a marginal note "*exemplum*" (fol. 75ʳ) the passage from VI.10 describing robbers' putting servants of a house to sleep with the help of black magic—by hanging a cadaver's spinal column under the roof.

Different readers annotating the same manuscript usually parallel or complement one another's view by highlighting similar or different aspects of the book. Sometimes, however, they apparently disagreed, as in manuscript Br1 from Aulne, where annotations left by two readers reflect curiously on the content of VIII.51. It is the story of two nuns, the first of whom adored John the Evangelist and the other John the Baptist. The nuns constantly argued about which saint was greater. Finally, John the Evangelist and John the Baptist appeared to their respective admirers. John the Evangelist announced that John the Baptist was greater than he, and *vice versa*. The nuns exchanged their visions, asked one another's pardon, and reconciled. In the manuscript, a *nota* on fol. 192ʳ marks the words of John the Baptist: "*Soror, noveris sanctum Johannem Evangelistam me maiorem*" ("You should know, Sister, that John the Evangelist is greater than I"). On the same folio a *manicula* by another hand marks the words of John the Evangelist: "*Soror, scias beatum Johannem Baptistam longe maiorem esse me*" ("Sister, you should know that John the Baptist is far greater than I").

The reader who drew the *manicula* was apparently himself an admirer of John the Baptist. On folio 193ʳ he drew another *manicula* pointing to the passage from VIII.52 where John the Baptist appeared to a disrespectful canon from Bonn and kicked him in the stomach. In the next chapter, one more *manicula* calls the reader's attention to a story of a certain merchant's managing to buy the arm of John the Baptist for 140 pounds of silver. One wonders whether the two readers of the manuscript accepted the moral of the story proposed by Caesarius, or just took what they needed, namely, praise for their preferred saint.

The annotated manuscripts of the *Dialogus* confirm the long-lasting currency of Caesarius's insights about monastic life, as well as the importance of pastoral and theological reflections expressed both in narrative and in non-narrative exchanges between the Monk and the Novice. Certainly Cistercian manuscripts show a tendency towards abridgment or even elimination of the dialogical frame of the *Dialogus*,[27] but in general, the way Caesarius framed his stories remained compelling in the long run. I would argue that the success of Caesarius's *exempla* collection was in no small measure due to its non-narrative, dialogical elements. The dialogue between the Monk and the Novice proved to be an efficacious tool to convey a religious message, one highly appreciated by readers looking for clear and concise answers to pointed theological and moral questions. The *Dialogus* is a complex and multifarious work, and Cistercian readers definitely enjoyed its diversity, ranging from complex theological concepts to curious *mirabilia*.

---

[27] See above, pages 57–58, 71–72, on Versions C and E.

8

The *Dialogus miraculorum* and Other *Exempla* Collections in Cistercian Libraries

Medieval and early modern library catalogues and booklists are indispensable for the study of the transmission and reception of a particular work. They not only attest the presence of the book in question in one library or another, but they also reveal how the book was imagined by its readers: how they described it, and among which texts and under what title they placed it. Catalogues from the time also provide an additional glimpse into the reading habits and trends of a given community. Although my main focus here is on the *Dialogus* and other Cistercian *exempla* collections, it is useful to consider the presence of other *exempla* collections in medieval Cistercian libraries to better contextualize the interest that the white monks took in mendicant *exempla* production.[1]

Unfortunately, not many medieval or late-medieval monastic catalogues were made, despite the 1459 General Chapter's explicit exhortation to do so,[2] and even fewer survived

---

[1] On the subject of *exempla* collections in Cistercian libraries, see also Marie Anne Polo de Beaulieu, "L'exemplarité cistercienne," in *Les Cisterciens et la transmission des textes (XIIe–XVIIIe siècles)*, ed. Thomas Falmagne, et al. (Turnhout: Brepols, 2018), 239–84.

[2] Joseph-Marie Canivez, ed., *Statuta Capitulorum Generalium Ordinis Cisterciensis ab anno 1116 ad annum 1786* (Louvain: Revue d'Histoire Ecclésiastique,

the turmoil of the Thirty Years' War, the Napoleonic wars, and finally secularization. The content of some libraries relevant for this study can only be guessed from what is usually a small number of surviving manuscripts. No catalogue and very few manuscripts of the Heisterbach monastic library survived. Its mother house, Himmerod, had an extremely rich library; in 1453 it reportedly had around 2000 books,[3] of which only around 150[4] are now traceable. As in the case of Heisterbach, there is no surviving catalogue.

Some medieval library and early modern catalogues have luckily come down to the present day; among them are those from Cîteaux, Clairvaux, Pontigny, Stams, Altzella, and Eberbach. The German abbeys and then Cîteaux and its daughters, Pontigny and Clairvaux,[5] show which *exempla* collections

---

1937), 5:33 (1459 n° 41): "*Praecipitur omnibus et singulis patribus abbatibus, quatinus habeant inventoria omnium et singulorum librorum et iocalium monasteriorum utriusque sexus sibi subditorum.*"

[3] According to the note made by Matthias Agricius († 1613); see Ambrosius Schneider, "Skriptorium und Bibliothek der Cistercienserabtei Himmerod im Rheinland: zur Geschichte klösterlichen Bibliothekswesens im Mittelalter," *Bulletin of the John Rylands Library* 35 (1952/53): 155–205. Agricius mentions two inventories, now lost (see Schneider, "Skriptorium und Bibliothek der Cistercienserabtei," 162).

[4] Ambrosius Schneider, "Skriptorium und Bibliothek der Abtei Himmerod, bearb. von Fritz Wagner," *Libri Pretiosi: Mitteilungen der Bibliophilen Gesellschaft Trier* 6 (2003): 4–12.

[5] The book holdings of La Ferté and Morimond were dispersed: it is difficult to judge their actual content. La Ferté, the first of the four great daughter houses of Cîteaux, suffered from plunderers and fires during the Wars of Religion. The surviving evidence of La Ferté's book collection dates from as late as the eighteenth century and mentions no medieval *exempla* collection. Among eight manuscripts that can surely be attributed to La Ferté, as well as among sixteen manuscripts of uncertain attribution to the abbey, there are also no *exempla* collections (see Anne Bondéelle-Souchier, *Bibliothèques cisterciennes dans la France médiévale: Répertoire des abbayes d'hommes* [Paris: CNRS, 1991], 155–57). Morimond was also plundered many times, with its library dispersed; all inventories are modern and partial. The twenty-six surviving manuscripts attributed to the abbey include no *exempla* collections (see Bondéelle-Souchier, *Bibliothèques cisterciennes*, 217–23).

caught the interest of the first monasteries of the Order. Their interest can be interpreted as confirmation of the success and relevance of the collections for the Cistercian community. The abbeys of Cîteaux and Clairvaux also had exceptional means of producing and acquiring books, even in times of economic distress, and often their abbots were renowned intellectuals and bibliophiles. The content of their libraries may offer some clues on questions of the extent and ways in which the new intellectual aspirations of the Order in the late Middle Ages affected the transmission and reception of *exempla* collections, and may therefore help to put into perspective the observations made in the previous chapters.

Stams Abbey

Stams Abbey, in Tirol, founded in 1273 as a daughter house of Kaisheim, had its own scriptorium and library, the content of which is relatively well known thanks to several surviving inventories. The most relevant for the present study is the catalogue from 1341, which lists 230 titles.[6] It survives in MS. Stams, Zisterzienserkloster, Cod. 28 (fols. 61^r–62^r).[7]

The Stams inventory follows *grosso modo* the traditional medieval book classification scheme, especially in the beginning. It starts with the Bible and biblical commentaries, followed by

---

[6] There was also an inventory from 1295, listing the books that some monks were permitted to keep (150 titles in all, with no *exempla* collections) (see Anton Dörrer, "Weitere mittelalterliche Bücherlisten aus Tirol," *Zentralblatt für Bibliothekswesen* 56 [1939]: 329–34; the catalogue composed by Wolwgang Lebersorg, a monk in Stams, in around 1600; the catalogue by Anton Roschmann from 1739, and the so-called Übergabekatalog from 1808, made during the secularization of the abbey (see Sieglinde Sepp, "Neuzeitliche Quellen zur Stamser Bibliotheksgeschichte," *Innsbrucker historische Studien* 6 [1983]: 81–127).

[7] Published by Anton Dörrer, "Mittelalterliche Bücherlisten aus Tirol," *Zentralblatt für Bibliothekswesen* 51 (1934): 247–50. The photos of the pages containing the inventory can be seen at https://www.univie.ac.at/paecht -archiv-wien/ki/stams/cod_28/cod_28.htm.

the writings of church fathers and medieval theologians. Then, rather incoherently, come hagiography, historiography and homilies, liturgy, law, medicine, and liberal arts. Quite remarkably, the *Dyalogus Cesarii* is mentioned toward the beginning of the list, where authorities such as Augustine, Gregory the Great, and Bernard are grouped, between sermons of Peregrinus of Opole and Vincent of Beauvais's *Speculum historiale*. Herbert's *Liber* is harder to spot, not least because the manuscript tradition did not retain the author's name. It appears further in the catalogue, among liturgical books, sermons, and hagiography, under the title *Miracula ordinis*,[8] preceded by the *Collationes patrum* and followed by the *Parvum Passionale*. Neither the *Exordium* nor the *Liber Lacteus* is listed in the 1341 catalogue. As for mendicant *exempla* collections, the catalogue mentions the *Alphabetum narrationum*[9] among sermon collections, grouped toward the end.[10] The *Liber de exemplis sacre Scripture* is in the middle of the list, among different *summae* and treatises such as *Lucidarius, Biblia beate Virginis, Benedictionale*, and Giles of Rome's *De Regimine principum*.

The *Exordium* is featured in the 1600 catalogue by Wolwgang Lebersorg, under the title *Institutiones Ordinis Cisterciensis*,[11] but neither the *Dialogus* nor Herbert's *Liber* appears, despite the fact that they were still present in the library at that time. Lebersorg, master of novices and librarian, was perhaps not aiming to make an inventory of all the library's possessions, but rather to present it as a study library meeting the demands

---

[8] This is MS. Stams, Zisterzienserkloster, Archiv, Cod. 6 (Cod. 67), which also contains the anonymous miracle collection from Ebrach and the *Miracula, que in Stams a Domino per beatum Johannem perpetrantur*, collected by Rudolf, the third abbot of Stams.

[9] MS. Innsbruck, Universitäts- und Landesbibliothek Tirol, Cod. 350.

[10] There is also a mention of the as-yet-unknown or unidentified *Adaptiones exemplorum* in the same section.

[11] The catalogue is arranged alphabetically by author. The *Exordium* is placed among the anonymous books, *Cathalogus librorum qui suorum authorum nomina non prae se ferunt* (Sepp, "Neuzeitliche Quellen," 125).

of humanist scholars, and selected the books accordingly.[12] He did not apparently perceive the *Dialogus* as pedagogically relevant or valuable enough, or sufficiently scholarly, to be mentioned, unlike the *Exordium*, which had some institutional importance. Besides the *Exordium*, the only *exempla* collection he lists is the *Speculum exemplorum*.

Lebesorg's catalogue provides call numbers for around two-thirds of the titles. The system of call numbers, introduced earlier, offers a glimpse into the categorizing of the books undertaken after 1341. Some books originating in the Stams library still have call numbers indicated on the covers, among them Innsbruck, Universitäts- und Landesbibliothek Tirol, Cod. 185 (*Dialogus*), which has the call number E 3. The letters E–F comprise mostly sermons in Latin or German.[13] The *Exordium*, with the call number L 3, is placed among the books on sacraments, ascetica, and Marian devotion (letters K–L). The *Liber lacteus* (R 27) is grouped with the works from classical antiquity, rhetoric, and arts (letters P–Q). The *Speculum exemplorum* has the call number P 9 (the letter P comprises mostly books on church and profane history). Finally, the *Alphabetum narrationum*, with the call number M 10, is placed, surprisingly, among the books on law (letters L–N).

Since the 1341 catalogue has a rather loose structure, the order in which manuscripts are mentioned does not necessarily reflect their usage or whether they were perceived as similar. It should however be noticed that the *Dialogus* and Herbert's *Liber* are not grouped together within what is more or less defined as the same thematic section, contrary to what a modern reader, accustomed to think about Cistercian *exempla* collections as belonging together, would expect. Similarly, the Late Medieval–Early Modern system of call numbers puts all *exempla* collections into different categories. The classification of Cistercian *exempla* collections was clearly a complex matter.

---

12 Sepp, "Neuzeitliche Quellen," 86–87.
13 Sepp, "Neuzeitliche Quellen," 85.

Eberbach Abbey

Eberbach Abbey in the Rheingau, a direct foundation of Clairvaux (1136), once had a rich library, of which only 195 manuscripts are now traceable with certainty. Its most comprehensive catalogue was compiled in 1502 under the abbot, Martin Rifflink (1498–1506), by the sub-prior, Nicolaus of Eltville, and the abbot's chaplain, Johannes of Saint Goar.[14] The catalogue lists an impressive number of 754 volumes (1230 titles in total). Such a large collection required a capacious space. Already in 1470, Eberbach's book collection was divided in two parts: the so-called *libraria major* and the *libraria minor*. In the *libraria major* the books were chained to lecterns, while in the *libraria minor* they were apparently kept in cabinets of different sizes.[15] The content of the *libraria minor* consisted mostly of patristic and medieval theological works, as well as some volumes on history, hagiography, and preaching. The placement of these books in the *libraria minor* was probably purely practical: there was not enough space for them (and especially for the patristic works, often in multiple exemplars) in the *libraria major*. In 1480, under Abbot Johannes Bode from Boppard, a dedicated building was constructed over the western part of the cloister;[16] however, according to the 1502 catalogue, Eberbach's book collection remained divided into two parts. In each *libraria*, the books were organized more or less thematically according to call numbers: from *A* to *Z* in the *libraria major* and from *a* to *h* in the *libraria minor*.

---

[14] The catalogue was published by Nigel Palmer in his book, *Zisterzienser und ihre Bücher: die mittelalterliche Bibliotheksgeschichte von Kloster Eberbach im Rheingau* (Regensburg: Schnell & Steiner, 1998). The so-called *Reinische Gesamtcatalog*, dating from the 1470s (MS. Basel, Universitätsbibliothek, F VI 53), lists a number of books from Eberbach, mostly patristic. No *exempla* collection is mentioned (see Palmer, *Zisterzienser und ihre Bücher*, 227–30).

[15] Palmer, *Zisterzienser und ihre Bücher*, 182.

[16] Palmer, *Zisterzienser und ihre Bücher*, 182.

Unsurprisingly, the *Exordium*, finished when Conrad was abbot of Eberbach, is mentioned twice under the title *De initio ordinis Cisterciensis*, with both call numbers T7 (in the *libraria major*) and d27 (in the *libraria minor*). The former manuscript has been identified as MS. Oxford, Bodleian Library, Cod. Laud Misc. 238 (from the first quarter of the thirteenth century). The latter, long considered to be lost,[17] did in fact survive. It is MS. Wiesbaden, Hessische Landesbibliothek, Hs. 381 (also from the first quarter of the thirteenth century). According to Bruno Griesser, it could be the archetype of the *Exordium's* textual tradition.

Interestingly, in the manuscript now in Oxford, Eberbach's *ex libris* from the fifteenth century was erased and a new one was appended: that of Marienhausen, a monastery of Cistercian nuns near Aulhausen under the care of Eberbach. Marienhausen was reformed in 1493; it is possibly in this reform context that the *Exordium* was given to the nuns. As I mentioned above, the *Dialogus* was copied in the abbey of Jardinet after its reform. Despite the scarcity of evidence, it seems that *exempla* collections may have played a certain role in the reforms that some Cistercian houses underwent in the fifteenth century.

As for the *Dialogus*, the Eberbach catalogue includes it under the call numbers V 12 (the first volume, also comprising the *Gesta et origo Saxonum* by Widukind of Corvey) and V 13 (the second volume) in the *libraria major*. The fragment Abt 22, 535/6 [a] from Wiesbaden Hauptstaatsarchiv (thirteenth century) is believed to be what remains of the first part. However, the surviving fragment contains a considerably shortened text of the *Dialogus* (Version D), and it is questionable whether

---

[17] Griesser, introduction to Conradus Eberbacensis, *Exordium magnum Cisterciense, sive Narratio de initio Cisterciensis Ordinis*, ed. Bruno Griesser, CCCM 138 (Turnhout: Brepols, 1997), 9*. See also Ferruccio Gastaldelli, "A Critical Note on the Edition of the *Exordium Magnum Cisterciense*," CSQ 39, no. 3 (2004): 311–20.

such a concise version would have been transmitted in two volumes.

It is striking that the *Dialogus* and the *Exordium* were listed in different sections of the catalogue. The T section (featuring the *Exordium*) includes commentaries on monastic rules, *exempla* collections, and revelations (like the *Vitae patrum*, the *Alphabetum narrationum*, and the *Liber scivias* by Hildegard of Bingen), as well as books on theology and spirituality (for example, *De potestate ecclesiastica* by Jean Gerson, or *Horologium sapientiae* by Henry Suso). The *Dialogus* would have fit perfectly into this section. But instead, it is in the next one, designated with letter V, comprising primarily historiographic writings and works from Classical Antiquity, like Justinus's *Epitome in Trogi Pompeii historias*, Comestor's *Historia scholastica*, and Cicero's *Orationes*.

Could it be that the *Exordium*, written by the abbot of Eberbach, was perceived as a book that not only narrated events that had happened centuries ago but also guided and informed the contemporary life of the Eberbach community, similar to commentaries on monastic rules and treatises of spiritual direction? The presence of the *Dialogus* in the historical section should not be surprising, given Caesarius's efforts to provide an event-related context for most of his stories. One may also recall the chronological rearrangement of the *Dialogus* made by Alberic of Trois-Fontaines.[18]

There is a non-Cistercian parallel to Eberbach's cataloging decision. In the catalogue of the library of Saint Margaret Charterhouse in Basel, composed by Georg Carpentarius around 1520,[19] the *Dialogus* is ranged in the *"armarium tertium principale veteris bibliothece . . . sub littera C comprehendens libros siue codices historiales epistolares atque poeticos et quicquid id generis ad eosdem referri potest"* ("The third principal cupboard of the old

---

[18] See above, p. 14.

[19] MS. Basel, Universitätsbibliothek, AR I 2, available online https://www.e-codices.unifr.ch/fr/description/ubb/AR-I-0002/HAN.

library . . . under the letter C, comprising historical, epistolary, and poetical books or codices, and whatever can fit into these categories," fol. 19ᵛ), and more precisely the fifth subdivision of the *armarium* (*armarium speciale*), with books like Vincent of Beauvais's *Speculum historiale* and Sallust's *De bello Catilinario et Jugurthino*, together with the *Alphabetum narrationum*[20] and the *Vitae Patrum*. The third *armarium generale* held other hagiographic works, such as the *Lombardica historia* (the famous *Golden Legend*) and *exempla* collections like the *Speculum exemplorum*, which were evidently perceived as pertaining to historiography.

By contrast, the fourth *armarium*, containing "*sermones sive materias predicabiles pro diuini uerbi declamatoribus perutiles*" ("sermons or preaching material very useful for those who proclaim the Word of God") (fol. 33ʳ) does not include any independent *exempla* collection,[21] despite the fact that the prologues of both the *Alphabetum narrationum* and the *Speculum exemplorum* present the works in question as preaching aids.

According to Eberbach's catalogue, Dominican *exempla* collections seem to have been highly appreciated in Eberbach. The *De oculo morali* by Peter of Limoges, for example, is mentioned three times, in the sections comprising preaching aids, commentaries on *Sententiae*, and books on canon law (M4), commentaries on monastic rules, *exempla* collections, and revelations (T3), and sermon collections (ʒ14), with the manuscripts categorized according to the first work each contains. An unidentified manuscript with the *Alphabetum narrationum* and the *Exempla sacrae scripturae* is placed in the same section as the *Exordium* (T14), probably because the *Alphabetum*, the first work in the manuscript, starts with "*Antiquorum Patrum exemplo didici nonnullos ad uirtutes inductos fuisse narrationibus edificatoriis et exemplis*" and is presented in the description as the *Narrationes patrum*. The catalogue also mentions the *Gesta*

---

[20] Described as "*Narratorium de exemplis per ordinem alphabeti.*"
[21] Only "*Sermones Discipuli de tempore et sanctis cum promptuario*" (fol. 26ʳ).

Romanorum with the call number X 13, in the section comprising theological works and *distinctiones*, but also works of Meister Eckhart. The library probably also held the *De dono timoris* by Humbert of Romans (Z 13). The cited *incipit Quoniam plus exempla* corresponds in fact to that of the *De dono timoris*, but the work is presented in the catalogue as *Sermones de tempore et de sanctis*. Section Z lists mostly sermon collections.

Altzella Abbey

The library of Altzella Abbey, founded in 1162 by Otto II, margrave of Meissen, and populated in 1175 by monks from Pforta, enjoyed its most flourishing period under the humanist abbot Martin von Lochau (1501–1522). The library catalogue dating from 1514, however, was made not by a member of the monastic community, but by an outsider: the humanist Georg Spalatin († 1545), secretary of the Saxon Elector Frederick the Wise.[22] Frederick designated Spalatin to head his new library, established in 1512. The cataloging of the library of Altzella, as well as of some other monasteries,[23] was definitely part of this assignment.

Spalatin's catalogue describes rather accurately the system of bookkeeping already in use in the abbey. According to the catalogue, Altzella's book collection, numbering 957 volumes, was kept in *pulpita* (lecterns with shelves); each of those was

[22] Ludwig Schmidt, "Beiträge zur Geschichte der wissenschaftlichen Studien in sächsischen Klöstern. Altzelle," *Neues Archiv für sächsische Geschichte und Altertumskunde* 18, Heft 3/4 (1897): 201–72. The edition of the catalogue (part I—Theology and Philosophy) is on 229–68. On the Altzella library, see Gerhard Karpp, "Bibliothek und Skriptorium der Zisterzienserabtei Altzelle," in *Altzelle: Zisterzienserabtei in Mitteldeutschland und Hauskloster der Wettiner*, ed. Martina Schattkowsky and André Thieme (Leipzig: Leipziger Univ.-Verl., 2002), 193–233.

[23] On this subject, see Franzjoseph Pensel, *Verzeichnis der altdeutschen und ausgewählter neuerer deutscher Handschriften in der Universitätsbibliothek Jena* (Berlin: Akademie-Verlag, 1986), 4–11.

marked with capital letters of different colors: red for theology and philosophy (774 volumes in 21 lecterns), green for medicine (108 volumes in 5 lecterns). The books on law (75 in total) had no specific color. This classification system was apparently recent, introduced by the abbot Martin von Lochau, probably on account of Spalatin's mission.[24] The abbey's collection was certainly richer than it appears from the catalogue; it does not mention liturgical books, which were kept separately.

In contrast to the catalogues from Stams and Eberbach, the catalogue from Altzella arranges Cistercian *exempla* collections in a more conventional manner. The *Dialogus* (featured as *Dyalogus Cesarii Cisterciensis*)[25] and Herbert's *Liber visionum et miraculorum Clarevallensium* (*Miracula ordinis Cisterciensis*) are placed one after another in the *Nonum pulpitum sub littera I* (numbers 11 and 10 respectively),[26] with works of Saint Bernard, his *vita*, and *flores* from his works.[27] In the same lectern are kept lives of some other saints, for example, *Vita s. Elisabeth libri VIII* (I 20), spiritual and theological treatises, such as the famous *Malogranatum* (I 15–16), as well as other collections of miracles and visions, for example, *Miracula collecta de multis* (I 28),[28] *Revelaciones sancte Brigide* (I 18–19), *Liber spiritualis*

---

[24] Schmidt, *"Zur Geschichte der wissenschaftlichen Studien,"* 204.

[25] MS. Leipzig, Universitätsbibliothek, Cod. 445.

[26] There two manuscripts of the *Liber* in Altzella; see supra, p. 38, but only one corresponding entry is to be found in the catalogue.

[27] Cf. the inventory of Heiligenkreuz, dating between 1363 and 1347, which places Herbert's *Liber* (*Visiones Clarevallensium, no. 14 in septimo assere*) together with the *Vita* of Saint Bernard and his letters and sermons. See *Mittelalterliche Bibliothekskataloge Österreichs*, ed. Theodor Gottlieb, et al., vol. 1, *Niederoesterreich* (Aalen: Scientia, 1915), 22–33. However, in the somewhat later *Tabula pro bibliotheka Sancte crucis* from 1381 (*Mittelalterliche Bibliothekskataloge Österreichs*, 1:40–74) Herbert's *Liber* was grouped differently, with the *Vite Sanctorum*, 70.

[28] MS. Leipzig, Universitätsbibliothek, Cod. 817 (14th–15th century). On fol. 2^r–103^v there is a collection of miracles from different sources. On fol. 107^{rv} is another small collection of miracles by a later hand (15th century) that has some Cistercian stories.

gracie sive revelaciones s. Mechtildis virginis (I 30), and *Visiones Tundali et Georgii cum aliis variis et utilissimis tractatulis* (I 27). The latter is MS. Leipzig, Universitätsbibliothek, Cod. 841, containing the aforementioned collection of Cistercian miracles depicted on the walls of the cloister.

Altzella's library catalogue mentions only one Dominican *exempla* collection: the *Liber apum* (*Bonum universale de apibus* by Thomas of Cantimpré), placed in the *Sextum pulpitum sub littera F*, which contains mostly works of Augustine, but also some sermons and treatises related to the *cura animarum* (*Tractatus de confessione pulcherrimus* and *Manuale prelatorum et confessorum*) and preaching (*Alphabetum predicantium*, a dictionary of theological subjects for the use of preachers).

All three catalogues show diverse conceptualizations of the *exempla* collections. Some of them look familiar, but others are surprising. The question to what extent these differences also imply different reading assumptions and conventions is not easy to answer with certainty. But the catalogues offer an interesting glimpse into the way Cistercian storytelling in its written form was juxtaposed with other modes of accessing the past or with other tools for spiritual instruction. Each catalogue highlights different aspects of Cistercian *exempla* collections, their historicity, their relevance to Bernard's heritage, or their actual use as hagiographic sources.

Cîteaux and Its First Daughters

Cîteaux Abbey

Cîteaux's library catalogue—*Inventarium librorum monasterii Cistercii*—was composed between 1480 and 1482[29] by Abbot Jean de Cirey (1476–1501), hailed as *bonus abbas*[30] and even as

---

[29] The catalogue survives in MS. Dijon, Bibliothèque municipale, 610, published in Auguste Molinier, et al., eds., *Catalogue général des manuscrits des bibliothèques publiques de France*, vol. 5, *Dijon* (Paris: Plon, 1885), 339–452.

[30] Denis de Sainte-Marthe, ed., *Gallia Christiana in provincias ecclesiasticas distributa* (Paris: Coignard, 1728), 4:1005.

the column that prevented the ruin of Cîteaux.[31] A man of learning (he gained his doctorate from the University of Paris in 1470), bibliophile, and writer, Jean de Cirey was abbot of Theuley (1468–1475), then of Balerne (1475–1476), and finally of Cîteaux. He is primarily known for his reform activities, which resulted in the acceptance of his ambitious program for general reform—*Articuli Parisienses*—by the General Chapter in 1494.[32]

The *Inventarium* of Jean de Cirey lists an impressive number of about 1200 volumes belonging to Cîteaux. The catalogue was compiled before the construction of the special library building (completed in 1509 under Jacques de Pontailler, Cirey's successor), when the books were stored in different places: at Cîteaux itself (in the cloister, novitiate, infirmary, dormitory, and abbot's private apartments [n°s 1 to 1073]), in the abbot's *studorium* in the nearby priory of Gilly (n°s 1074 to 1184), and in the abbey's townhouse in Dijon (n°s 1185–1200). The *Inventorium* follows this system and therefore offers an interesting glimpse into the eventual usage of the books by different groups within the monastery.

The *Dialogus* does not appear among the books listed in the catalogue. In fact, there are only two Cistercian *exempla* collections mentioned in a clear way: the *Exordium* and the *Sertum florum moralium*. The *Liber* of Herbert of Clairvaux may also have been in Cîteaux's library; it is presumably number 635 (the numeration is continuous through the catalogue), described as *"Parvus liber incatenatus ad analogium cathedre in opposito capituli, continens vitam sancte Elizabeth de Sconaugia, quedam miracula beate Marie et Soliloquia beati Augustini et Anselmi"* ("a small book chained to the reading desk opposite the chapter house, containing the Life of Saint Elisabeth of

---

[31] *"Ne rueret Cistercium columna fuit."* Angel Manrique, *Cistercienses seu verius ecclesiasticae annales a condito Cistercio* (Lyon: Boissat & Lavrent, 1642), 1:487.

[32] See Emilia Jamroziak, *The Cistercian Order in Medieval Europe: 1090–1500* (London: Routledge, 2015), 244–45.

Schönau, some miracles of the Blessed Virgin Mary, and *Solilo-quies* of blessed Augustine and Anselm").[33] It is usually associated with MS. British Library, Add. 15723 (from the thirteenth century).[34] The fact that the book was chained to a reading desk in the cloister[35] implies that it was often consulted by the brethren.

The *Exordium* is listed under number 600 as "*Unum volumen satis magnum, continens narrationem Cisterciensis ordinis*" ("One volume, big enough, containing the story of the Cistercian Order"). It was stored with the books chained to the third reading desk near the chapter house, as is indicated in the title of the section: "*Isti libri sunt incathenati super analogiis ante capitulum*" ("These books are chained above the reading desks in front of the chapter house" [n°s 590–607]). The manuscript in question survived and is now known as MS. Dijon, Bibliothèque municipale, 594 (*olim* 349). It dates from the fourteenth century and probably originated at Igny, a daughter house of Clairvaux.[36] It is unclear how the manuscript ended up in Cîteaux, but its importance for the community is clearly suggested by its placement near the very heart of the monastic "lived social space," that is, the chapter house.[37]

It was not, however, one of the early Cistercian *exempla* collections, but the *Sertum florum moralium* by Simon de Vauluisant that seems to have been in highest demand among the readers of Cîteaux. The catalogue mentions it three times,

---

[33] *Catalogue général des manuscrits*, 5:405.

[34] On this manuscript, see Herbertus Turritanus, *Liber visionum et miraculorum Clarevallensium*, ed. Giancarlo Zichi, Graziano Fois, and Stefano Mula, CCCM 277 (Turnout: Brepols, 2017), XLVIII–L.

[35] Section *In parvis analogiis claustri* (n°s 635–39).

[36] See Yolanta Załuska, *Manuscrits enluminés de Dijon*, Corpus des manuscrits enluminés des collections publiques des départements Series (Paris: CNRS, 1991), 233, n° 226.

[37] See Philippe Cordez, "Le lieu du texte: Les livres enchaînés au Moyen Âge," *Revue Mabillon* 17 (2006): 75–103, esp. 78–90 ("Espaces communs, textes fondateurs: de la Parole divine au droit local").

under numbers 693, 841, and 1093. The first manuscript, listed in the section *"Libri legendi in conventu seu dividendi fratribus ad legendum"* ("Books to be read in community or to be distributed among brothers for reading"), was intended for ordinary monks, while the other two belonged to the abbot's private collection and were kept separately in his apartment (*"In studorio nostro apud Cistercium"*) and in his study in the residence at Gilly priory (*"In studorio nostro Gilleii"*) respectively.

The success of the learned *Sertum florum* is not surprising if one considers the impressive number of bestselling *exempla* collections, mostly mendicant ones, in the possession of the library of Cîteaux. Two collections were stored in the dormitory (the section *In quarta banca de latere dormitorii* in the catalogue): the *Tractatus de diversis materiis praedicabilibus* by Stephen of Bourbon (n° 182), and *De oculo morali* by Peter of Limoges (n° 193). Then at least five popular *exempla* collections belonged to the abbot's library: the *Liber de exemplis sacrae scripturae* (n[os] 807 and 810), the *Gesta Romanorum* (n° 833), the *Bonum universale de apibus* (n° 834), the *Alphabetum narrationum* (n° 836), and the *De ludo scaccorum* (n[os] 850 and 851). Finally, among the books kept in the abbot's study in Gilly there were another copy of the *Liber de exemplis sacrae scripturae* (n° 1125) and a certain *Liber de exemplis naturalibus* (n° 1081).

It seems that mendicant *exempla* collections were highly appreciated by the learned abbot as study sources and aids, along with model sermons, biblical concordances, books of *distictiones, florilegia*, and other preaching and pastoral tools located in the *studoria*. By contrast, early Cistercian *exempla* were intended for ordinary monks, whose reading activities were more conservative and less oriented toward scholarly concerns than the abbot's. Among the books *"extracti de libraria ad usum cotidianum conuentus"* ("taken from the library for the daily use of the brethren," n[os] 561–89) and books *"legendi in conventu seu dividendi fratribus ad legendum"* ("to be read in community or to be distributed among the brothers for reading," n[os] 640–747), one indeed finds mostly biblical books, homilies of the church fathers, hagiographical collections, and devotional treatises.[38]

The catalogue by Dom Cirey is a useful reminder of the heterogeneity of Cistercian readership, and therefore of the coexistence of different reading trends and habits even within a single monastery, especially in times when both the practical and the intellectual life of the abbot was becoming more and more separated from that of the ordinary monks.[39]

Pontigny Abbey

Pontigny, the second daughter of Cîteaux, founded in 1114, was sacked by Protestants in 1567 and 1569.[40] Despite considerable losses caused by fires and plundering, Pontigny's book collection[41] partially survived the turmoil and remained in place until the French Revolution. In 1791, by the decision of the administrative directory of the Yonne department, the books judged "valuable" were transferred to Auxerre, and others were sold by public auction. Officially, only printed books in a bad state were destined for the auction; however, some manuscripts were sold as well.[42]

The only surviving medieval inventory of Pontigny's library dates from the third quarter of the twelfth century and is

[38] On the "conservative nature" of Cîteaux's library, see David N. Bell, "The Library of Cîteaux in the Fifteenth Century: *Primus inter pares* or *Unus inter multos,*" *Cîteaux: Commentarii Cistercienses* 50 (1999): 107.

[39] On the changes in the abbot's role in the late medieval period, see Emilia Jamroziak, "Cistercian Abbots in Late Medieval Central Europe: Between the Cloister and the World," in *The Prelate in England and Europe 1300–1560*, ed. Martin Heale (Woodbridge: Boydell and Brewer, 2014), 240–57.

[40] King, *Cîteaux and her Elder Daughters*, 185–86.

[41] On Pontigny's book collection see Monique Peyrafort-Huin, *La bibliothèque médiévale de l'abbaye de Pontigny (XIIᵉ–XIXᵉ siècles): histoire, inventaires anciens, manuscrits* (Paris: CNRS, 2001); on its physical library, see Terryl N. Kinder, "Where was Pontigny's Library?" *Cîteaux: Commentarii Cistercienses* 53 (2002): 269–303.

[42] Peyrafort-Huin, *La bibliothèque médiévale*, 210–12.

beyond the temporal scope of the present study. I therefore use the comprehensive inventory composed in 1778 by Jean Depaquy, the last abbot of Pontigny. It lists 326 titles,[43] among which is no Cistercian *exempla* collection.[44] By contrast, the catalogue mentions two Dominican collections under number 76 (the numeration is continuous though the catalogue).[45] The manuscript containing the *Liber de exemplis sacrae scripturae* and the *Alphabetum narrationum* has been identified as MS. Auxerre, Bibliothèque municipale, 36 (third quarter of the fourteenth century).[46] Number 280 in the inventory, identified as MS. Auxerre, Bibliothèque municipale, 243 (second half of the fourteenth century), contains among many other works the *De oculo morali* by Peter of Limoges, not mentioned in the description given by Dom Depaquy.[47]

Currently, 164 surviving manuscripts have been identified as originating from Pontigny.[48] Among them only 24 date from the period relevant to the present study. Those 24 were apparently not copied in the abbey's *scriptorium*,[49] but were purchased or received as donations on a rather irregular basis. The diminished book-related activity of the abbey is not surprising given all the economic troubles that Pontigny faced

---

[43] *Catalogus librorum bibliothecae Pontiniacensis digestus a F. Joanne Depaquy Pontiniacensi religioso, M DCC LXXXVIII* (Auxerre: Bibliothèque municipale, MS 260ᶦ), ed. Peyrafort-Huin, in *La bibliothèque médiévale*, 342–79. The inventory of the possessions of Pontigny made in 1790 states that there were 380 manuscripts (this number probably includes not only books but also archival documents). See Peyrafort-Huin, *La bibliothèque médiévale*, 210.

[44] The manuscript mentioned in the inventory made by François-Xavier Laire (1791) under number 253 ("*Exordia ordinis Cisterciencis; et Regula hujus ordinis*") probably contains the *Exordium Cistercii* and the *Exordium parvum*, not the collection of Conrad of Eberbach (Peyrafort-Huin, *La bibliothèque médiévale*, 416).

[45] Peyrafort-Huin, *La bibliothèque médiévale*, 348.

[46] Peyrafort-Huin, *La bibliothèque médiévale*, 477–78.

[47] On this manuscript, see Peyrafort-Huin, *La bibliothèque médiévale*, 493–94.

[48] Peyrafort-Huin, *La bibliothèque médiévale*, 459–94.

[49] Peyrafort-Huin, *La bibliothèque médiévale*, 162–64.

in the Late Middle Ages, marked by a series of famines and plagues, including outbreaks of the Black Death. The number of monks sank dramatically. In 1342 there were twenty-nine brothers, and only sixteen in 1366, including the abbot.[50] Cistercian *exempla* collections were definitely not on Pontigny's priority purchase list at that time. By contrast, the fact that the *Liber de exemplis sacrae scripturae* and the *Alphabetum narrationum* made it to the abbey's library in the fourteenth century emphasizes their appeal to a large audience, including French Cistercians.

Clairvaux Abbey

By far the most famous daughter of Cîteaux, the abbey of Clairvaux (founded in 1115), not only rivaled its mother house in the richness of its library, but surpassed it. Unfortunately, no inventory survives to attest to the early period of *exempla* production and reception at Clairvaux, the cradle of the tradition.[51] However, other evidence exists to show the eagerness with which monks from Clairvaux gathered miracle stories at the end of the twelfth and beginning of the thirteenth centuries. The *Adbreviatio relationum fratris Cesarii, monachi de Valle santi Petri* by Alberic of Trois-Fontaines attests to the early presence of the *Dialogus* in Clairvaux.[52] Another interesting example is provided by Herbert of Clairvaux, in the so-called *Narratio Herberti, abbatis coenobii Morensis, de libro Miraculorum S. Bernardi,*

---

[50] Peyrafort-Huin, *La bibliothèque médiévale*, 119–22.

[51] In fact, there are only a few documents related to the content of Clairvaux's library before the end of the fifteenth century: a fragment of the twelfth-century catalogue (too early for the scope of the present study), a list of the books borrowed by Lambert Uppenbrouck, originally a monk from Clairvaux and a new abbot of Dunes (1337), and two donation lists by Jacques d'Audeloncourt (1351 and 1359). See André Vernet, *La bibliothèque de l'abbaye de Clairvaux du XIIe au XVIIIe siècle*, vol. 1, *Catalogues et répertoires* (Paris: CNRS, 1979), 13–22.

[52] On this matter see above, p. 14.

per insigne miraculum servato.[53] Herbert reports that he once accompanied Peter Monoculus, the new abbot of Clairvaux (1179–1186), in his visitation journey to the ecclesiastical province of Reims. In the abbey of Valroy, a granddaughter of Clairvaux, they found a collection of Bernard's miracles, absent from Clairvaux. They took the collection along with seven other books for copying. On the way back, near Longpont, the horse carrying the bag with manuscripts fell into a pond. In an hour, the horse, its rider, and the bag were pulled from the water. All the books were heavily damaged, except for the book of miracles, which appeared dry and intact. The saved collection is now known as *liber VI* of the *Vita prima* of Saint Bernard, or *Miracula S. Bernardi in itinere Germanico patrata* ("Miracles performed by Saint Bernard in Germany").

The most comprehensive inventory of Clairvaux's library, listing 2318 volumes, was made for Pierre de Virey († 1506), the abbot from 1471 to 1496. A man of learning and a great bibliophile,[54] Dom Virey became a monk at Maizières (a daughter house of La Ferté near Beaune). He was then sent to study at the Collège de Saint Bernard in Paris. In 1451–1453, Dom Virey obtained the degree of Biblical Bachelor, and in 1453–1455 the degree of Bachelor of Sentences. In 1460 he received both a teaching license and the degree of *magister theologiae*. After serving as abbot of Chaalis from 1458 on, he became the abbot of Clairvaux in 1471.

In 1472, Dom Virey took care of the cataloging of Claivaux's vast book collection. As the analysis of the surviving working copy suggests (MS. Troyes, Bibliothèque municipale, 2299), it was Jean de Voivre, Clairvaux's prior from 1480 to 1499, who not only acted as the principal scribe but was also the author/

---

[53] *Historia miraculorum in itinere Germanico patratorum,* in *Monumenta Germaniae Historica, Scriptores* (in folio), vol. 26, *Ex rerum Francogallicarum scriptoribus,* ed. Georg Waitz (Hannover: Hahn, 1882), 121.

[54] See André Vernet, "Un abbé de Clairvaux bibliophile: Pierre de Virey (1471–96)," *Scriptorium* 6, no. 1 (1952): 76–88.

editor of the library catalogue, working for the abbot and under his direction.[55] At around the same time, a new, more elegant copy of the catalogue was made for the abbot's personal use (MS. Troyes, Bibliothèque municipale, 521).

The catalogue arranged the library's books into twenty-four relatively well-defined thematic groups, designated by the letters of the alphabet from A (*Biblia* and *biblica*) to Ɔ and + (liturgical books).[56] Some entries were left empty in order for eventual accommodation of new books. The working copy also occasionally indicates the provenance of books (including those copied anew under the abbot's command), their intended use—for example, to be read in the infirmary or during collation—and their placement, for example, *in armaria juxta librariam* (in the cupboards near the library).

The valuable additional information coming from the working copy gives a glimpse into Dom Virey's acquisition politics. During his years of studying in Paris, he acquired around thirty volumes, mostly by well-known philosophical and theological authors—Aristotle, Thomas Aquinas, and Giles of Rome, for instance—but also sermons by Johannes de Sancto Geminiano, Jean Gerson, and Jacobus of Voragine.[57] Once he became abbot of Clairvaux, Pierre de Virey noticeably changed his preferences. He began to commission the copying of books relevant to monastic spiritual formation, for example, the *Liber exceptionum* by Richard of Saint-Victor, the lives of Saint Bernard and Saint Malachy, and two commentaries on the Rule of Benedict, one by Johannes de Turrecremata[58] and one by an anonymous author.

---

[55] See Vernet, *La bibliothèque de l'abbaye de Clairvaux*, 1:33–34.

[56] On the cataloging system see Vernet, *La bibliothèque de l'abbaye de Clairvaux*, 1:31–33.

[57] On the books owned by Dom Virey, see Vernet, "Un abbé de Clairvaux bibliophile," and Vernet, *La bibliothèque de l'abbaye de Clairvaux*, 1:27–29.

[58] He commissioned another three copies of this *Expositio regulae* as gifts to the Cistercian houses of Cambron, Chaalis, and Loos (*La bibliothèque de l'abbaye de Clairvaux*, 1:28).

One of the books commissioned by Dom Virey was the *Dialogus*. It is listed under the call number P. 30:

> *Item ung autre beau volume contenant le Dyalogue Cesarii monachi en .xii. distinctions, commençant on tiers feullet* || *criter vallis illa, et finissant on penultime illius longi* || *Ainsi signé. Quem scribi fecit domnus Petrus de Vireyo abbas Clarevallis.*

("Then another beautiful volume containing the Dialogue by the monk Caesarius in twelve parts, beginning on the third folio || *criter vallis illa*, and ending on the penultimate *illius longi* || Herewith signed. Commissioned by Pierre de Virey, the abbot of Clairvaux.")[59]

The manuscript, now in the Municipal Library of Troyes (MS. 592 [here T2]), is in fact a "beautiful volume." It was written on parchment in a neat *textualis formata* and adorned with parti-colored red and blue flourished initials (4–5 lines) in the beginning of each *distinctio*. To emphasize its relevance for the Clairvaux community, the scribe added a postscript in red indicating where in the book to find *exempla* about Saint Bernard.[60]

Another manuscript of the *Dialogus* owned by Clairvaux (Troyes, Bibliothèque municipale, 641 [here T1]) is not mentioned in the 1472 catalogue.[61] This codex gives a completely different impression from the beautiful T2. It was written on paper in *cursiva currens*, in a single column with plain initials.

---

[59] *La bibliothèque de l'abbaye de Clairvaux*, 1:231.

[60] Fol. 292ʳ: "*Nota quod loquitur auctor iste de sancto Bernardo Clarevallis abbate in prima distinctione capitulo viii° ix° xvi° et xix°. Item in secunda distinctione capitulo iii° et xvii°. Item in tertia distinctione capitulo viii° et xxxix°. Item in iiiia distinctione capitulo i° et vii°.*"

[61] Only the catalogue from 1664 (*La bibliothèque de l'abbaye de Clairvaux*, 1:641–82) mentions two manuscripts of the *Dialogus*: one under number 421 (*Dialogi sive historiae Caesarii Histerbatensis* [sic]) and the other under 465 (*Dialogus Caesarii Hesterbacensis de diversis miraculis*). As the working copy of the 1472 catalogue does not have a blank entry after the mention of the *Dialogus*, it seems that there was no intention of eventually adding MS. 641 to the catalogue.

So far as I was able to ascertain from a sample collation, T2 could have been copied directly from T1 after the latter was corrected against a now-unidentified or lost exemplar.

The library's catalogue mentions the *Exordium* just after the *Dialogus*, with call number P 31. This book is also said to have been commissioned by Dom Virey: *"Et hunc librum fecit scribi etiam prefatus dominus Petrus abbas Clarevallis"* ("And this book was also commissioned by the aforementioned Pierre, the abbot of Clairvaux.")[62] No mention is made of the volume's quality. Unfortunately, the manuscript is now lost.

In the catalogue, the letter P, under which both the *Dialogus* and the *Exordium* are listed, heads the section entitled *"Libri communes proprium titulum non habentes"* ("Common books without proper titles,") call numbers O5 –Q7. It features books that were apparently difficult to classify. The section has rubrics, indicated on the margins in the working copy, for example, *"Mariale," "De preparatione cordis," "Beleth," "Ad predicandum,"*[63] *"Exempla," "Alphabetum narrationum," "De virtutibus and viciis," "De apibus," "Cesarius,"* and *"De exordio"* (the last three are indications for the rubricator, overlooked or left undone). That being said, the rubrics do not always cover the whole content of the sections. For example, about thirty titles come between the rubrics *De exordio* and *De virtutibus et viciis*, titles mostly of mendicant *exempla* collections, but also collections of deeds and sayings of ancient philosophers, lives of saints, treatises on confession, fables, etc.[64]

The importance of Cistercian *exempla* collections for Clairvaux's reading program, promoted by Dom Virey, is obvious. Both copies of the *Dialogus*, as well as the *Exordium*, were made

---

[62] *La bibliothèque de l'abbaye de Clairvaux*, 1:231.

[63] Under this rubric are books like *Auctorités et examples sur la Bible* (P2), Interpretations of Hebrew names (P3, P4, P5, P6), Exposition of the Canon of the Mass (P11), etc., and *Somme magistri Jacobi de Vitriaco de plusieurs exemples de la Saincte Escriture et des meurs des hommes comparees aux choses naturelles* (P8, not identified). See *La bibliothèque de l'abbaye de Clairvaux*, 1:227–29.

[64] *La bibliothèque de l'abbaye de Clairvaux*, 232–34.

in the period when book-related activities in French Cistercian abbeys, including Clairvaux, significantly declined. Indeed, only 3% of the surviving manuscripts from Clairvaux date from the fifteenth century,[65] which makes the abbot's choice to invest in the copying of the *Dialogus* and the *Exordium* all the more significant.

The attention paid to the two indisputable bestsellers was not however granted to other Cistercian *exempla* collections, which seem to have been overlooked—or at least not explicitly mentioned—during the cataloguing of Clairvaux's library. The 1472 catalogue mentions neither Herbert of Clairvaux's *Liber* nor Goswin's *Liber miraculorum*[66] nor the *Adbreviatio* by Alberic of Trois-Fontaines. Even if Goswin's *exempla* collection was already lost by the time the catalogue was made, Herbert's *Liber* was certainly still in the abbey's library. For his 1660 *editio princeps* of Herbert's *Liber*, Pierre-François Chifflet used a manuscript then at Clairvaux but now untraceable.[67] The only surviving copy of the *Liber* from Himmerod is found in MS. Florence, Biblioteca Medicea Laurenziana, Ashburnham 1906, which is believed to be from Clairvaux,[68] but the catalogue contains no identifiable mention of it.

---

[65] See Jean-François Genest, "*La bibliothèque de Clairvaux de Saint Bernard à l'humanisme,*" in *Histoire de Clairvaux: Actes du colloque de Bar-sur-Aube/ Clairvaux, 22 et 23 juin 1990* (Bar-sur-Aube: Némont, 1992), 124.

[66] It was mentioned in Alberic of Trois-Fontaines's *Chronicon Clarevallense*; see Stefano Mula, "Gossuinus e il *Chronicon Clarevallense,*" *Herbertus* 2 (2000): 91–94; and Stefano Mula, "I frammenti del *Liber Miraculorum* di Gossuinus: Edizione dal ms. Firenze, Laurenziana, Ashburnham 1906," *Herbertus* 3 (2002): 7–16.

[67] Herbertus Turritanus, *Liber visionum et miraculorum*, LXXXVI–XCII. On the manuscript see also Stefano Mula, "Le Chronicon Clarevallense, la littérature exemplaire et l'ancienne bibliothèque de Clairvaux au XIIIᵉ siècle," in *Les cisterciens et la transmission des textes (XIIᵉ–XVIIIᵉ siècles)*, ed. Thomas Falmagne, et al. (Turnhout: Brepols, 2018), 37–51.

[68] Bruno Griesser, "Ein Himmeroder Liber miraculorum und seine Beziehungen zu Caesarius von Heisterbach," *Archiv für mittelrheinische Kirchengeschichte: nebst Berichten zur kirchlichen Denkmalpflege* 4 (1952): 257.

Why the catalogue does not mention extant manuscripts is unclear. But the miscellaneous Ashburnham codex seems to be a collection of working copies, not at all elegant, and initially left even without a binding.[69] MS. T1 of the *Dialogus* in fact gives the same impression of a working copy, probably perceived as not worth mentioning in the new catalogue, or perhaps omitted by mistake. The only manuscript with an early Cistercian *exempla* collection other than the *Dialogus* and the *Exordium* listed in the 1472 catalog is MS. Troyes, Bibliothèque municipale, 946, described, in fact, as being *"beau et bien escript"* ("beautiful and elegantly written"), and containing the unique surviving copy of the *Collectaneum Clarevallense*. The manuscript is mentioned among *exempla* collections (call number P 26), but its description covers only the content of the first part (fols. 5^v–113^r): *"Item ung autre beau et bien escript volume contenant en .iiii. livres plusieurs Miracles de Nostre Dame, et de plusieurs autres sainctz et saictes et plusieurs visions, et l'Exposition du canon de la messe"* ("Then another beautiful and elegantly written volume, containing in its four parts numerous miracles of the Virgin Mary and many other saints, both male and female, and numerous visions and the Exposition of the Canon of the Mass").[70] The *exempla* with Cistercian content are predominantly in parts II–IV (fols. 113^r–181^r). No wonder the *Collectaneum Clarevallense* remained unidentified a long time, even though the manuscript in question was known to scholars.[71]

As for the late medieval *exempla* collections, the 1472 catalogue mentions two copies of the *Sertum florum* by Simon de Vauluisant in the section *Exceptiones et flores doctorum* (call numbers L 66 and L 67), probably because of its title. The importance of the book was emphasized with the rubric *Sertum florum*. Unfortunately, both manuscripts are lost.

---

[69] See Mula, "Le Chronicon Clarevallense," 44–55.

[70] *La bibliothèque de l'abbaye de Clairvaux*, 230.

[71] See Brian McGuire, "A Lost Clairvaux Exemplum Collection Found: The *Liber visionum et miraculorum* Compiled under Prior John of Clairvaux (1117–1179)," *Analecta Cisterciensia* 39 (1983): 26–62.

Like Cîteaux's library catalogue, Clairvaux's lists an impressive number of mendicant *exemplum* collections. The rubric *Exempla* opens with the *Tractatus de diversis materiis praedicabilibus* (call number P 17). Then under the same rubric comes the *Summa collationum* by the Franciscan John of Wales (P 19)[72] and a certain *Summa de communi statu* (P 20), probably the *Liber ad status* by the Dominican Rambert of Bologna. Afterwards, under the rubric *Alphabetum narrationum*, the catalogue mentions five manuscripts of the famous collection (P 21–P 25). Then comes the *Bonum universale de apibus* by Thomas of Cantimpré (P 28). According to the catalogue entry, the *Bonum universale* was commissioned by the abbot, a clear sign of the importance of this Dominican *exempla* collection for Cistercian monastic formation. Finally were *De dono timoris* by Humbert of Romans (P 33), *De oculo morali* by Peter of Limoges (P 41 and 42), and *De ludo scaccorum* by Jacobus de Cessolis (P 56).

It is not possible to tell exactly how the books from the section *Libri communes proprium titulum non habentes* were read, since there is no additional information in this regard. The preaching context suggests itself, although it is unclear whether these books actually served as preaching tools: probably not. The Clairvaux library catalogue is the only one that draws together Cistercian and mendicant collections under the rubric *exempla*, which follows the rubric *Ad predicandum*. Only the *Sertum florum moralium* is listed separately. Were Cistercian *exempla* collections perceived as being similar to mendicant ones because they also belonged to the global narrative stock used by preachers and moralists? Or, rather, were mendicant *exempla* collections supposed to be read as edifying books, like the *Bonum universale* commissioned by the abbot among other books relating to monastic spirituality? Both options seem possible.

As the library catalogues from Cîteaux, Pontigny, and Clairvaux suggest, interest in Dominican *exempla* collections was

---

[72] P 18 is left empty.

strong among Cistercians. These collections were often acquired or copied in difficult times of economic stagnation and troubles, when both acquisition and production of books diminished greatly in the French Cistercian milieu, even in the richest abbeys. It is tempting to assume that the new intellectual and pastoral aspirations of the Cistercian Order made the early Cistercian *exempla* collections less appealing in comparison to Dominican ones, or to the *Sertum florum moralium*, which enjoyed a considerable success in the intellectual centers like Cîteaux and Clairvaux. To some extent that is true.

However, the 1472 catalogue of Clairvaux's library shows that exactly in this period, a learned abbot considered collections such as the *Dialogus* and the *Exordium* to be valuable additions to the reading program of his monks. He himself may have read other kinds of books (maybe the Dominican *exempla* collections, present in the catalogue of Cîteaux's library), while his monks still enjoyed Caesarius's stories.

The centuries-old traditions persisted even in the most renowned humanistic centers as, for example, in Aduard (Adwert) abbey, near Groningen (the daughter of Klaarkamp), which Goswinus van Haelen († 1530) praised as "academia."[73] The abbey indeed flourished under the abbot Henricus van Rees (1450–1485). It had a large number of well-educated monks and a rich library, which attracted noblemen and scholars from all over Friesland, including, for example, Rudolf Agricola († 1485). In this same period the *Dialogus* was read in the abbey's refectory, as we know from the biography of the theologian-philosopher John Wessel Gansfort († 1489).[74] Master

---

[73] *Erat ea tempestate Adwert non tam monasterium quam Academia* (Wessel Gansfort, *Opera*, ed. Petrus Pappus à Tratzberg [Groningen: Iohannes Sassius, 1614], **4ʳ). See Percy Stafford Allen, *The Age of Erasmus: Lectures delivered in the Universities of Oxford and London* (Oxford: Clarendon Press, 1914), 7–32.

[74] Wessel Gansfort, *Life and Writings; Wessel Gansfort (1419–1489) and Northern Humanism*, ed. Fokke Akkerman, Gerda C. Huisman, and Arie Johan Vanderjagt (Leiden: Brill, 1993). The biography was written after 1561 by Albertus Hardenberg. It is published in *Wessel Gansfort, Opera*, ***ʳ–***5ʳ.

Wessel often visited Aduard and actively participated in the teaching of younger monks, as well as joining in erudite debates with learned senior monks.[75] He used to eat in the abbey's refectory and listen to the devotional reading. Among the books read in the refectory at that time was the *Dialogus*: "*Habet ordo Cisterciensis librum Dialogorum Caesarii valde ineptum, qui in coenobiis ejusdem ordinis solebant ad mensam legi: nam novitas delectabat monachos parum peritos*" ("The Cistercian Order has a book of dialogues by Caesarius, rather foolish, and they used to read it at mealtime in the monasteries of this order, because novelty pleased ignorant monks"). Wessel believed the *Dialogus* to be absurd and even dangerous and unsuitable for reading in a Cistercian refectory. He derided the reading of this "*valde ineptus*" ("rather foolish") book, and Caesarius began to be dismissed. The *Exordium* suffered the same fate.[76]

This passage from Wessel's biography not only shows the appeal of the *Dialogus* to the Aduard community and its controversial reception among Northern humanists. It also offers a glimpse in how the *Dialogus* was read, the only direct evidence we have. Unfortunately, Aduard's library was destroyed by fire in 1580, so it is not possible to learn more about its monks' reading habits. But it is not unlikely that refectory reading of the *Dialogus* was a common practice in the region where it circulated the most.

---

[75] Jaap van Moolenbroek, "Wessel Gansfort as a Teacher at the Cistercian Abbey of Aduard: The Dismissal of Caesarius of Heisterbach's *Dialogus miraculorum*," in *Education and Learning in the Netherlands, 1400–1600*, ed Koen Goudriaan, Jaap van Moolenbroek, and Ad Tervoort (Leiden: Brill, 2003), 114–23.

[76] "*Ad illam semper auscultabat Wesselus, et subinde sauve ridebat. Rogatus causam dicebat: Rideo crassa mendacia. Praestaret Sacras literas et Bernhardi devotalia fratribus proponi: nam haec praeter ineptiam etiam multa periculosa continent . . . . Adwerdiae autem post illam admonitionem coepit contemni Caesarius, et jam omnino obsoletus est, ut et liber de illustribus viris Ordinis Cisterciensis quem vocabat monastico labore concinnatas nugas*" (Wessel Gansfort, *Opera*, ***ʳᵛ).

The Cistercian *exemplum* tradition, born in Clairvaux, did not end with the well-known and large collections such as the *Exordium* or the *Dialogus*. It continued to engage Cistercian monks throughout the Middle Ages and beyond, for both reading and writing practice. The addition of new stories to the *Dialogus* during its transmission among German and Austrian houses of the Morimond line is a case in point. German and Austrian Cistercians not only actively copied the *Dialogus*, but also interacted with it through abridgments and additions. Apparently intensive storytelling exchanges among related monasteries created both supply and demand for miracle narratives, and some of those narratives were perceived important enough to be added to the *Dialogus*. The interaction of writing, reading, and oral storytelling ensured the continuous appropriation of the *Dialogus* as a repository of Cistercian memories and as an efficient tool to perpetuate and to transmit captivating stories, both local and non-local.

In conformity with the ever-growing interest in exemplary figures from the communal past, encouraged by the General Chapter, Cistercian reception of the *Dialogus* showed a clear tendency towards "hagiographisation." Caesarius's work was used in Himmerod to compile a new collection of *Vitae sive gesta sanctorum et venerabilium patrum monasterii in Hemmenrode*. In Altzella, it provided material for the gallery of saintly Cistercian monks and nuns depicted on the cloister walls. The same is true for the *Exordium*. Usually in the early manuscripts entitled *Narratio ordinis Cisterciensis*, in the fifteenth century it acquired the title *Liber de viris illustribus Ordinis Cisterciensis*.[77]

The *Dialogus* could also have been used as tool to support inner reform (for example, in Jardinet) or to refresh communal spirituality (as at Clairvaux under Abbot Pierre de Virey). The

---

[77] For example, in MS. Kopenhagen, Kongelige Bibliotek, Gl. Kgl. Saml. 174, 15th century (which also contains *Vitas fratrum* by Geraldus de Fracheto), or MS. Paris, Bibliothèque nationale de France, nouv. acq. lat., 364, 14th or 15th century.

early Cistercian *exempla* collections were apparently supposed to help the monks to find new inspiration in examples from the glorious period of Cistercian history. In a sense, early Cistercian *exempla* collections thus became new *Vitae* or *Collationes Patrum*. Many issues discussed by Caesarius remained topical for his late medieval readers, as their notes suggest. Even if the *Dialogus* lost its immediacy with passing time, it powerfully evoked the Cistercian Golden Age and therefore continued to be capable of engaging readers, especially in the period after the Great Schism (1378–1417), which caused the unfortunate division of the Order.

Library catalogues suggest that Cistercians were sensitive to the individuality of each *exempla* collection, though the question of to what extent Cistercian librarians' different categorizations implied different reading assumptions and conventions assigned to different collections may never be answered. Despite all indications of common perceptions, the relevance of the *Dialogus* to each community of reception and therefore to the "exemplarity" of each also resulted from often incomprehensible and elusive individual choices and preferences.

PART TWO

Outside Cistercian Walls

9

Regular Canons as Readers of the *Dialogus miraculorum*

Canons Regular, priests living according to the rule of Saint Augustine,[1] actively participated in the transmission of the *Dialogus*, matching Caesarius's fellow Cistercians. In contrast to Cistercian monks or mendicant friars, the Canons Regular are not particularly famous for having compiled many *exempla* collections. Their contribution to the medieval narrative pool is, however, far from negligible. It is sufficient to mention Jacques de Vitry († 1240),[2] the famous preacher praised by his contemporaries for the extensive use of *exempla*.[3] Collections of exemplary stories excerpted from his sermons were already circulating in the thirteenth century (for example, in MS. Paris, Bibliothèque nationale de France, lat. 16515).

---

[1] Jean Châtillon, *Le mouvement canonial au Moyen Âge: réforme de l'Église, spiritualité et culture*, Bibliotheca Victorina 3 (Paris-Turnhout: Brepols, 1992). There were different orders of Canons Regular, but unless I specify differently, I treat them as one group.

[2] On Jacques de Vitry and the Augustinian priory of Saint Nicolas d'Oignies, see Edoardo Formigoni, "Jacques de Vitry et le prieuré d'Oignies," in *Autour de Hugo d'Oignies*, ed. Robert Didier and Jacques Toussaint (Namur: Société archéologique de Namur, 2003), 37–45.

[3] Humbertus de Romanis, *De dono timoris*, ed. Christine Boyer, CCCM 218 (Turnhout: Brepols, 2008), 4. "*Magister Iacobus de Vitriaco, . . . predicando per regnum Francie et utens exemplis in suis sermonibus, adeo totam Franciam commouit quod non extat memoria aliqua ante uel postea sic mouisse.*"

In her seminal work *Docere verbo et exemplo*, Caroline Walker Bynum shows the importance assigned by the Canons Regular to teaching one's fellows, within the cloister and outside, both by word (*verbo*) and by personal example (*exemplo*) of impeccable conduct.[4] But what was the role played by storytelling in this teaching? Jacques de Vitry often introduced his *exempla* with the word *audivi*, implying an oral source; however, unlike Caesarius, he gave no details on exactly how he had obtained the story in question.

Luckily, Peter of Cornwall († 1221), prior of Holy Trinity London, who between 1200 and 1206 compiled the so-called *Liber revelationum*,[5] was more talkative. The *Liber revelationum* is a vast collection of 1077 chapters, dedicated to visions of the afterlife. It was compiled, as Peter announced in the Prologue, to persuade the unbelieving that the world was ruled by the Providence of God, that good and bad angels existed, and that the soul lived after the death of the body.[6] The only extant copy is MS. London, Lambeth Palace Library, 51. It was probably made under the author's supervision.

Although Peter drew mostly upon famous works like the *Dialogi* of Gregory the Great and Bede's *Historia ecclesiastica*, he also included in the *Liber* some stories that he himself had heard,[7] sometimes with an acknowledgment of the source. Peter's informants mentioned by name or profession were people from outside Holy Trinity priory: laymen,[8] monks,[9]

---

[4] Caroline Walker Bynum, Docere verbo et exemplo: *An Aspect of Twelfth-Century Spirituality* (Missoula, MT: Scholars Press, 1979).

[5] Edition and English translation in Robert Easting and Richard Sharpe, eds., *Peter of Cornwall's Book of Revelations* (Toronto: Pontifical Institute of Mediaeval Studies; Bodleian Library, 2013).

[6] *Peter of Cornwall's Book*, 74, Prol.: *"quia nonnulli sunt qui Deum non esse putantes . . . nec alia spiritualia et inuisibilia esse credant, ego Petrus ecclesie sancte Trinitatis Lundonie minister ad utilitatem multorum . . . reuelationes et uisiones spirituales . . . in hoc unum uolumen redegi."*

[7] In the edition these stories are grouped in chapters 5, 6, and 7.

[8] *Peter of Cornwall's Book*, 88, Prol. *"uilla qui dicitur Horpintona qui mihi Petro qui hec scribo, narrare solebat."*

[9] II.888: *Peter of Cornwall's Book*, 316–21, chap. 7.

canons,[10] and parish priests. One of the most active was William, the parish priest of Lessness (Kent), whose church was a property of the priory. William used to ask his acquaintances to appear to him after death, as they did a number of times.[11] Impressed by descriptions of punishments in the afterlife, William decided to amend his ways and joined the Cistercian Order.

Not only did Peter of Cornwell mention Cistercians with sympathy and respect, but he included in the *Liber* eleven stories that had originated in the Cistercian abbey of Stratford Langthorne in Essex, also known as (West) Ham Abbey, the daughter house of Savigny (Clairvaux line).[12] Five stories have indications of their sources: Precentor Hervey,[13] Abbot Benedict,[14] and lay brother Roger.[15] There is no clear evidence to show whether Peter wrote these stories or used an already extant *exempla* collection. In any case, Cistercian storytelling was of great interest and utility to a Canon Regular on a mission of religious instruction.

Storytelling exchanges between Cistercians and Canons Regular were also attested by Caesarius. Canons Regular of different orders are mentioned in the *Dialogus* on several occasions, not only as protagonists of exemplary stories, but also—four times in all—as informants. Thus a certain canon told Caesarius about his fellow canon who, being ill, had slept with a woman on the advice of a physician (or rather of the

---

[10] II.897: *Peter of Cornwall's Book*, 334–37, chap. 7. According to this passage, the story related by Brother Marc, prior of Lessness, may have reached Peter of Cornwall in written form.

[11] I.204: *Peter of Cornwall's Book*, 260–67, chap. 6.

[12] I.183: *Peter of Cornwall's Book*, 226–53, chap. 5.

[13] II.893, *Peter of Cornwall's Book*, 248, chap. 5; and II.891: *Peter of Cornwall's Book*, 248, chap. 5, (a story told by the brethren who had heard it from Hervey).

[14] I.183: *Peter of Cornwall's Book* 226, chap. 5; and II.894: *Peter of Cornwall's Book*, 252–53, chap. 5: Peter and Benedict knew each other well; for example, King John appointed both of them to visit Archbishop Stephen Langton on his behalf in 1210. See *Peter of Cornwall's Book*, 16, 20, and 219.

[15] I.205: *Peter of Cornwall's Book*, 236, chap. 5.

devil), but had died anyway a few days later without proper penance (IV.101). The other three stories were told by Premonstratensians (III.49, IX.50, XII.47).[16] Only one, however, concerns their order. A certain Premonstratensian priest told Caesarius about a pious scribe from Arnsburg[17] whose hand had been found intact twenty years after his death (XII.47).

Storytelling practices of the Canons Regular demand further research. What is clear for now is that they were avid readers of the stories of others. Below, I provide an overview of surviving manuscripts of the three major Cistercian *exempla* collections that belonged to the Canons and Canonesses Regular: Augustinian Canons, Premonstratensians, and Croisiers (Canons Regular of the Order of the Holy Cross).

Regular Canons' Manuscripts of the Dialogus miraculorum

B   Bern, Burgerbibliothek, 333, 13th century. Dist I–X. – Rommersdorf abbey (Premonstratensians)

Bo   Bonn, Universitäts- und Landesbibliothek, S 297, 15th century (1434) – Canonesses Regular of Nieuwe Nonnenklooster of Sint Dionysius ten Huse ter Lelyen (Amsterdam)

Bs1   Basel, Universitätsbibliothek, A I 34, 15th century (1446). Version B. – Canons Regular of Saint Leonhard (Basel)

Cl   Colmar, Bibliothèque municipale, 57 (24), 14th century. Dist. I–X. Version E. – Isenheim in Alsace (Canons Regular of Saint Anthony of Vienne)

Co   Cologne, Historisches Archiv, GB f° 87, 15th century (1440) – Canons Regular of the Order of the Holy Cross, Cologne

---

[16] The order of the Canons Regular founded in 1120 by Saint Norbert of Xanten.

[17] There were three Premonstratensian monasteries in Arnsberg. Caesarius gave no further detail.

Ko   Koblenz, Landeshauptarchiv, Best. 701 Nr. 152, 15th century (1470) – Canons Regular of Saint George (Niederwerth near Koblenz)

Li1   Liège, Bibliothèque du Séminaire Épiscopal, 6 N 11, 15th century (1467). Dist. VII–XII – Canons Regular of the Order of the Holy Cross, Liège

Li2   Liège, Université de Liège, Bibliothèque Générale de Philosophie et Lettres, MS. 86, 15th century. Dist. I–VI – Canons Regular of the Order of the Holy Cross, Liège

M5   Munich, Bayerische Staatsbibliothek, Clm 5106, 15th century (1463–66). Dist I–X. Version B. – Canons Regular of Bernried

M6   Munich, Bayerische Staatsbibliothek, Clm 7545, 15th century (1480). Version B. – Canons Regular of Indersdorf

M7   Munich, Bayerische Staatsbibliothek, Clm 5504, 15th century. Version B. – Canons Regular of Dießen am Ammersee

O   Osnabrück, Bischöfliches Archiv, Hs. Frenswegen 21, 15th century (1459). Dist. I–VI – Canons Regular of Sankt Marienwolde (Frenswegen). The manuscript was given to the monastery by Hinricus Brumzel, a canon of Osnabrück's cathedral.

Pl   Sankt Paul im Lavanttal, Benediktinerstift, Cod. 61/4, 14th century (1394). Version C. – Canons Regular of Neunkirchen am Brand (according to the crossed-out *ex-libris*)[18]

St   Strasbourg, Bibliothèque nationale et universitaire, 41 (Latin: 39), 15th century (1461). Dist. VII–XII – Canons Regular of Sankt Marienwolde (Frenswegen). The

---

[18] The manuscript was donated to Spital am Pyhrn in 1437 by Friedrich von Aufseß (bishop of Bamberg in 1421–1431). See Herbert Paulhart, ed., *Mittelalterliche Bibliothekskataloge Österreichs*, vol. 5, *Oberösterreich* (Aalen: Scientia Verl., 1971), 107–13; the *Dialogus* is on p. 109: *item Cesarium de miraculis.*

manuscript—the second part of the Osnabrück
MS.—was given to the monastery by Hinricus
Brumzel, a canon of Osnabrück's cathedral.

Ut1   Utrecht, Universiteitsbibliotheek, Cat. 176, 13th century. Dist VII–XII – Canons Regular of Saint Mary
and the Twelve Apostles, Utrecht

Ut2   Utrecht, Universiteitsbibliotheek, Cat. 177, last
quarter of the 14th century – Canons Regular of
Saint Mary and the Twelve Apostles, Utrecht

Ut3   Utrecht, Universiteitsbibliotheek, Cat. 179, 3rd quarter of the 15th century (or 1st quarter of the 16th century) – Canons Regular of Saint Mary and the
Twelve Apostles, Utrecht

Vo   Vorau, Augustiner-Chorherrenstift, Cod. 172 (olim
CXV), 15th century. Dist. I–X. Version E. – Canons
Regular of Vorau

W1   Vienna, Österreichische Nationalbibliothek, Cod.
Ser. n. 12796, 15th century – Canons Regular of
Rooklooster

W2   Vienna, Österreichische Nationalbibliothek, Cod.
Ser. n. 12774, 15th century (1425–1450) – Canons
Regular of Saint Mary (Bethlehem), Herent

Lost or unidentified manuscripts

Aachen, Stadtbibliothek, 49, 15th century (1468), written by a
Dietrich Kloker, probably a Canon Regular of Saint John the
Baptist in Aachen. The manuscript was lost during WW II.[19]

An unidentified manuscript from Rebdorf, Eichstätt (Canons Regular)[20]

---

[19] See Fritz Wagner, "Der Codex Nr. 49 der Stadtbibliothek Aachen," in
Studia codicologica, ed. Kurt Treu (Berlin: Akademie, 1977), 503–9.
[20] See the catalogue in Bernhard Bischoff and Paul Ruf, eds., *Mittelalterliche Bibliothekskataloge Deutschlands und der Schweiz*, vol. 3/1, *Bistum Augsburg*

Regular Canons' Manuscript of Herbert's
Liber visionum et miraculorum

Paris, Bibliothèque nationale de France, lat. 14655, first half of the 13th century – Canons Regular of Saint Victor, Paris (*ex-libris* from the 17th century)

Regular Canons' Manuscripts of the *Exordium Magnum*

Berlin, Staatsbibliothek zu Berlin, Preußischer Kulturbesitz, theol. lat. fol. 171, 15th century (1473) – Canons Regular of the Order of the Holy Cross, Emmerich

Brussels, Bibliothèque Royale de Belgique, II 2333 (3874), 15th century – Canons Regular of Rooklooster

Liège, Université de Liège, Bibliothèque Générale de Philosophie et Lettres, 200, 15th century (around 1480) – Canons Regular of the Order of the Holy Cross, Liège

Liège, Université de Liège, Bibliothèque Générale de Philosophie et Lettres, 227, 15th century – Canons Regular of the Order of the Holy Cross, Huy

Trier, Stadtbibliothek, 1212/509 4°, 15th century (1472) – Canons Regular of Eberhardsklausen (Trier)

There are significant similarities between the transmission patterns of the *Dialogus* and the *Exordium* in the milieu of the Canons Regular, such as the area of their distribution and the period of time when they were most popular. As for Herbert's *Liber*, it seems not to have received much attention from Canons Regular.

Already in the thirteenth century at least two manuscripts of the *Dialogus* were possessed by Canons Regular. A thirteenth-century manuscript of the *Dialogus* of possible Cistercian origin (MS B) once belonged to the Premonstratensian abbey of Rommersdorf, situated just twenty-eight miles from

---

(Munich: Beck, 1932), 272 and 276. The catalogue (15th / 16th century) is in alphabetical order.

Heisterbach. Heisterbach and Rommersdorf had occasional connections. In 1205, Gevard, abbot of Heisterbach, acted with Abbot Reiner of Rommersdorf as mediator in the conflict between the counts of Sayn and Count Dietrich of Landsberg.[21] Another thirteenth-century manuscript of the *Dialogus* (Ut1) belonged to the Augustinian priory of Saint Mary and the Twelve Apostles (Sint-Maria en de Twaalf Apostelen) in Utrecht, founded in 1290–1292. Heisterbach Abbey had connections to the region. In Caesarius's time, at least two Heisterbach monks came from Utrecht (see I.18; IV.15). Caesarius also mentions a certain canon from Utrecht as a source (I.38). Besides, Heisterbach Abbey had property not far away from the city, in Dordrecht and Sliedrecht.[22] The Utrecht manuscript belongs to the "*Hermannus*" manuscript family[23] and is textually very close to the manuscripts from Clairvaux. It could, therefore, have been copied from an early version of the *Dialogus* from Heisterbach. The *Dialogus* seems to have appealed to the taste of the canons from Sint-Maria en de Twaalf Apostelen. They had at least three manuscripts of the *Dialogus*, dating from the thirteenth, fourteenth, and fifteenth centuries (MSS. Ut1, Ut2, Ut3).

The real success of Cistercian *exempla* collections among the Canons Regular, however, came between the end of the fourteenth and the beginning of the fifteenth centuries. Remarkably, all the communities that copied or acquired the *Dialogus* or the *Exordium* in this period were influenced either by the *Devotio moderna*, initiated by Geert Groote (1340–1384), or by similar spiritual reform movements.[24]

---

[21] Swen H. Brunsch, *Das Zisterzienserkloster Heisterbach von seiner Gründung bis zum Anfang des 16. Jahrhunderts* (Siegberg: Franz Schmitt, 1998), 320.

[22] Brunsch, *Das Zisterzienserkloster Heisterbach*, 173–74.

[23] See above, pp. 49–51.

[24] Scholars have already pointed out the relevance of the *Dialogus* to the adepts of the *Devotio moderna*, although in a somewhat different context, namely the translation of the *Dialogus* into Middle Dutch, made in the Northern Low Countries. See Jasmin Hlatky, "On a Former Mayor of Deventer:

Having started as a semi-religious movement of lay persons (Brothers and Sisters of the Common Life), the *Devotio moderna* in a short while became essentially a movement of priests and canons, spread by the Congregation of Windesheim.[25] It offered an important alternative to the Observance within the large religious orders and, at the same time, a way to accommodate and to navigate religious aspirations of laymen and secular clergy.[26] Many communities in possession of Cistercian *exempla* collections were members of the Congregation of Windesheim. For example, in 1423 the aforementioned monastery of Sint-Maria en de Twaalf Apostelen in Utrecht joined the Chapter of Neuss, which was absorbed by the Windesheim Congregation

---

Derick van den Wiel, the *Devotio moderna* and the Middle Dutch Translation of the *Dialogus miraculorum*," in *The Art of Cistercian Persuasion in the Middle Ages and Beyond*, ed. Victoria Smirnova, Marie Anne Polo de Beaulieu, and Jacques Berlioz (Leiden: Brill, 2015), 211–26; Jasmin Hlatky, "Hoe die nouicius vraecht: Die mittelniederländische Überlieferung des *Dialogus Miraculorum* von Caesarius von Heisterbach," PhD diss., Westfälischen Wilhelms-Universität zu Münster, 2006, available at https://d-nb.info/101764327X/34. Another Middle Dutch translation of the *Dialogus* was made in the South. It is considered to have been linked to Flemish nunneries, and its relation to the *Devotio moderna* is unclear. One of the three surviving manuscripts (MS. Paris, Bibliothèque Mazarine, 781) can be traced back to a community involved in this reform movement. This manuscript, copied in 1574, belonged to the Canonesses Regular of Sint-Elisabeth op de berg Sion in Brussels. The monastery had close connections with the convents touched by the *Devotio moderna*, such as Groenendael Priory or the Rooklooster. The canonesses from Saint Elisabeth wanted to join the Chapter of Windesheim, but in 1436 Pope Eugene IV prohibited further admission of female communities.

[25] Wilhelm Kohl, "Die Windesheimer Kongregation," in *Reformbemühungen und Observanzbestrebungen im spätmittelalterlichen Ordenswesen*, ed. Kaspar Elm (Berlin: Duncker & Humblot, 1989), 83–106, esp. 96.

[26] See Bert Roest, "Die *Devotio Moderna* als Medium und Element: Abschlussbemerkungen über Arten der Annäherung an ein historisches Phänomen," in *Die Devotio Moderna: Sozialer und kultureller Transfer (1350–1580)*, ed. Iris Kwiatkowski and Jörg Engelbrecht, vol. 2, *Die räumliche und geistige Ausstrahlung der Devotio Moderna—Zur Dynamik ihres Gedankengutes* (Münster: Aschendorff, 2013), 254–62, esp. 249.

in 1430. Among the monasteries that joined the chapter of Windesheim were Frenswegen (in 1400, as the first German Augustinian monastery to do so), Rooklooster and Bethlehem in Herent (both in 1412), Niederwerth (re-founded in 1428 by the canons from the Bethlehem monastery in Zwolle, a member of the Windesheim chapter since 1391), *Eberhardsklausen* (1461), and Saint Leonhard in Basel (1464).

The Chapter of Windesheim was not the only congregation promoting the *Devotio moderna*. For example, Nieuwe Nonnenklooster of Sint Dionysius ten Huse ter Lelyen, founded in 1403 as a monastery of tertiary sisters, made the transition to the Augustine Rule in 1422 and became affiliated with the Chapter of Sion[27] (or Chapter of Holland, composed of seven male and seven female monasteries), which followed the Windesheim model but remained independent.

Other communities aligned themselves with different reform movements; the question of how much they were influenced by the Windesheim Congregation is debated. For example, by order of the bishop of Bamberg, Lamprecht von Brunn,[28] Neunkirchen am Brand joined the so-called Roudnice reform around 1390.[29] The Augustinian Canons of Roudnice (Raudniz), located north of Prague, promoted ideals similar to those of the *Devotio moderna*,[30] specifically the reform of monastic life, aiming to extirpate abuses and to recover the original observance of the Rule. The *Consuetudines* of Roudnice

---

[27] See Rudolf van Dijk, "De bestuursvorm van het Kapittel van Sion: Hollands verzet tegen het Windesheims centralisme," *Archief voor de Geschiedenis van de Katholieke Kerk in Nederland* 29 (1987): 166–91.

[28] Lamprecht von Brunn had close connections to Charles IV and his son Wenceslaus, king of Bohemia from 1363.

[29] Ignaz Zibermayr, "Zur Geschichte der Raudnitzer Reform," *Mitteilungen des Instituts für Österreichische Geschichtsforschung* 11, Ergänzungsband (1929): 323–53.

[30] See Johanna Schreiber, "*Devotio moderna* in Böhmen," *Bohemia: Jahrbuch des Collegium Carolinum* 6 (1965): 93–122; Eduard Winter, *Frühhumanismus: seine Entwicklung in Böhmen und deren europäische Bedeutung für die Kirchenreformbestrebungen im 14. Jahrhundert* (Berlin: Akademie-Verlag, 1964).

and Windesheim are very close, but the Bohemian movement is older than its counterpart in the Low Countries. There is a possibility that Geert Groote studied in Prague from 1358–1362, and some scholars even advance the hypothesis that he may have been inspired by the Bohemian example.[31] It seems, however, more prudent to consider the Roudnice reform as a parallel movement of renewed Augustinian piety.[32] The reform in Neunkirchen am Brand ended successfully in 1406. Other early followers of the Roudnice reform were the Canons of Saint Dorothea in Vienna, founded in 1414. In 1433, they helped to reform Vorau. In 1417, the Indersdorf monastery joined the movement and itself became an important center of reform in Bavaria. Bernried and Dießen am Ammersee joined the Indersdorf reform in 1433 and 1441 respectively.[33]

Another example of parallel reform efforts is the Order of Canons Regular of the Holy Cross or Crosiers (according to tradition, founded by Theodore of Celles in 1210). Many exchanges took place between Crosiers, Canons from the Congregation of Windesheim, and the Brethren of the Common Life. Thomas à Kempis mentioned that Crosiers—along with Cistercians—studied in the school of Johannes Cele in Zwolle.[34] Helmicus Amoris from Zutphen (general of Crosiers in 1415–1433) asserted that his order often accepted as members those who had started their religious life among Brothers of the

---

[31] Engelbrecht Wilken, "War Geert Grote in Prag? Zur Frage der Beziehung Grotes zum Vorhussitismus—eine Problemskizze," in *Sborník prací Filozofické fakulty brněnské univerzity. E, Řada archeologicko-klasická* 41, E37 (1992): 171–85.

[32] Winter, *Frühhumanismus.*

[33] Franz Machilek, "Die Raudnitzer Reform der Augustiner-Chorherren im 14./15. Jahrhundert: Unter besonderer Berücksichtigung des böhmisch-mährischen Stamms und des Neunkirchen-Indersdorfer Zweigs der Reformbewegung," in *Reformen vor der Reformation: Sankt Ulrich und Afra und der monastisch-urbane Umkreis im 15. Jahrhundert*, ed. Gisela Drossbach and Klaus Wolf (Berlin: De Gruyter, 2018), 33–74.

[34] Thomas à Kempis, *Chronica Montis Sanctae Agnetis*, in *Opera Omnia Thomae Hemerken a Kempis* 7, ed. Michael Joseph Pohl (Freiburg im Breisgau: Herder, 1922), 509.

Common Life.[35] Some books possessed by Crosiers also attest to the early connections between the Crosiers from Huy and Cologne, and the Brothers of the Common Life in Deventer.[36] However, many scholars see the inner reform of the Crosiers not as a result of the Windersheim's influence, but rather as a simultaneous reform effort.[37] It started in 1410 at the initiative of Johannes van Merode, procurator of the monastery in Venlo, and of his brother Arnold, a canon from Liège and a sigillifer, keeper of the seal, of John III, duke of Bavaria-Straubing, then the bishop of Liège. Under the new general, Libertus Janssen van Bommel, prior of Saint Agatha in Cuijk, the Order set a course for stricter monastic life, which included the observance of *vita communis*, personal poverty, silence, and fasting, in accordance with the first statutes of the order,[38] as well as the unification of statutes and liturgy. In 1410–1430, the monasteries of the Low Countries and Germany (Rhineland)[39] were reformed, but it took longer to reform French and English houses.

---

[35] Kaspar Elm, "Entstehung und Reform des belgisch-niederländischen Kreuzherrenordens: ein Literaturbericht," in *Mittelalterliches Ordensleben in Westfalen und am Niederrhein* (Paderborn: Bonifatius, 1989), 246.

[36] See Jean-Paul Depaire, "La bibliothèque des Croisiers de Huy, de Liège et de Namur," unpublished mémoire de licence, University of Liège, 1969–1970, 1:57, 58; Jacques Stiennon, "Introduction à l'étude des *scriptoria* des croisiers de Liège et de Huy au XVe siècle," in *Les manuscrits des Croisiers de Huy, Liège et Cuyk au XVe siècle* (Liège: Maison Desoer, 1951), 28–29.

[37] Michael Oberweis, "Die niederrheinischen Kreuzherren und ihre Beziehungen zu den 'Brüdern vom Gemeinen Leben,'" in *Die Devotio Moderna: Sozialer und kultureller Transfer*, 2:157–68, esp. 159–60. The scholarly discussion about the origins and goals of the Crosier reform is summed up by Kaspar Elm in "Entstehung und Reform des belgisch-niederländischen Kreuzherrenordens," *Zeitschrift für Kirchengeschichte* 82 (1971): 292–313.

[38] *"ad primas Constitutiones a sede Apostolica confirmatas."* See Cornelis Rudolphus Hermans, *Annales canonicorum regularium S. Augustini, Ordinis S. Crucis*, vol. 1 (1) (Bois-le-Duc, The Netherlands: Stokvis, 1858), 95.

[39] The house in Cologne was reformed in 1420 by Helmicus Amoris from Zutphen. See Robert Haaß, *Die Kreuzherren in den Rheinlanden* (Bonn: Röhrscheid, 1932), 12.

The reformed communities of Crosiers kept the *Devotio moderna* in their view. In both the Cologne and the Liège houses, the copying of the *Dialogus* was done by people with knowledge of the *Devotio moderna* writings and with the intent of sharing it with their brethren. The *Dialogus* manuscript that belonged to the Crosiers of Liège (Li1),[40] was copied in 1467 by Godefroid Withus de Kamen († 1470), the most prolific scribe of the Liège monastery, active between 1429 and 1468.[41] It was he who introduced to the reformed monastery the main works of Geert Groote and the circle of Deventer, as well as the emblematic *Imitation of Christ* by Thomas à Kempis.

The copying of the Cologne manuscript (Cologne, Historisches Archiv, GB f° 87) began in 1440. Folios 2^r–9^r were written by Conrad von Grunenberg († 1465/66). In 1418, Conrad was a scribe in Deventer. It is not certainly known for which institution he worked, but he definitely had contacts with Brothers of the Common life in Florenshaus, founded by Florens Radewijns. Conrad then moved to Cologne and joined the Crosiers there. In 1425, he became sub-prior and librarian.[42] Under Conrad, the Cologne scriptorium copied (or acquired) works of Geert Groote, Florens Radewijns, Thomas à Kempis, Geert Zerbolt van Zutphen, Johannes de Schoonhoven, and Dirc van Herxen. According to Thomas Kock, the library of the Cologne Crosiers had the most comprehensive collection of *Devotio moderna* writings.[43] There were also a number of manuscripts containing *excerpta* from the *Dialogus*—for ex-

---

[40] See Depaire, *La bibliothèque des Croisiers*, 2:254.

[41] About him see Depaire, *La bibliothèque des Croisiers*, 1:76, 96.

[42] Martina Schöler, *Ama nesciri: Spuren des Wirkens des Bibliothekars Conradus de Grunenberg († 1465/66) in der Bibliothek der Kölner Kreuzbrüder* (Cologne: Erzbischöfliche Diözesan- und Dombibliothek, 2005); see biography on pp. 36–37.

[43] Thomas Kock, "Zerbolt inkognito: auf den Spuren des Traktats 'De vestibus pretiosis,'" in *Kirchenreform von unten: Gerhard Zerbolt von Zutphen und die Brüder vom gemeinsamen Leben*, ed. Nikolaus Staubach (Frankfurt am Main: Lang, 2004), 177.

ample MS. Cologne, Historisches Archiv, GB 8° 40, made under the supervision of Conrad, which contains the *Soliloquium animae* by Thomas à Kempis, the fourth book of the *Imitatio Christi*, different texts related to the Eucharist, among them five somewhat shortened *exempla* from the *Dialogus* (IX.8, 38, 63, and 64, and X.2), and another seven *exempla*, probably from the lost part of the *Libri VIII miraculorum*.[44] In the Cologne house of Crosiers, the *Dialogus* was not only copied and read but also used to compose new collections.

Textually, the manuscripts from Cologne and Liège are very close, sharing both common variants and omissions; however, according to the probe collation, the manuscript from Liège was not copied from that of Cologne. They all belong to the branch of the textual tradition "*in civitate Lemovicensi,*"[45] and in the second part of the *Dialogus* they all call the Monk and the Novice *Cesarius* and *Apollonius*.

All manuscripts of the *Dialogus* and the *Exordium* that belonged to the reformed communities were copied after the adoption of reform, in the context of flourishing book production.[46] Thus the fifteenth-century success of the Cistercian *exempla* collections was largely due to the interest of reform-seeking Canons Regular, mostly—but not exclusively—in the framework of the *Devotio moderna*.

The propagation of the reform may or may not have concurred with the transmission of the *Dialogus* among reformed houses of the Canons Regular. For example, Rooklooster, along

---

[44] On this manuscript see Joachim Vennebusch, "Unbekannte Miracula des Caesarius von Heisterbach," *Annalen des Historischen Vereins für den Niederrhein* 184 (1981): 7–19. Other manuscripts from the Cologne monastery that contain excerpts from the *Dialogus* are Cologne, Historisches Archiv, GB f° 86; GB f° 104; GB 4° 37; GB 4° 74; GB 4° 192; GB 8° 99; GB 8° 144.

[45] See pp. 51–53 above.

[46] Book copying was considered to be an important spiritual exercise; see Thomas Kock, *Die Buchkultur der Devotio moderna: Handschriftenproduktion, Literaturversorgung und Bibliotheksaufbau im Zeitalter des Medienwechsel* (Frankfurt am Main: Lang, 2002), 18, 90; Dupaire, *La bibliothèque des Croisiers*, 1:57.

with Groenendael and Korsendonk, formed a chapter in 1402; Bethlehem in Herent and Barberendaal in Tienen joined them in 1410. Two years later this chapter was absorbed by the Windesheim Congregation. According to the probe collation, the manuscript that belonged to Bethlehem (MS. W2) may have been copied from that of Rooklooster (MS. W1).[47] By contrast, MSS. M6 from Indersdorf and Pl from Neunkirchen are not related,[48] although the reform in Indersdorf was inspired and put into action by brothers from Neunkirchen am Brand. In another example, Bernried monastery joined the Indersdorf reform, but the manuscript from Bernried (Munich, Bayerische Staatsbibliothek, Clm 5106) was copied earlier than that of Indersdorf, and from the same exemplar as the manuscript that belonged to the Cistercians from Aldersbach (Bayerische Staatsbibliothek, MS. Clm 2687). The manuscript from Indersdorf is connected to the manuscript from Aldersbach by way of MS. Munich, Bayerische Staatsbibliothek, 5504, from Dießen am Ammersee.[49]

MS. Bonn, Universitäts- und Landesbibliothek, S 297, from the Nieuwe Nonnenklooster of Sint Dionysius ten Huse ter Lelyen, stands apart, and not only because it was read in a female community. It was written in 1434, according to the colophon on fol. 98ᵛ, by a certain Johannes Eggairt filius Johannis, not certainly identified. Textually, the manuscript is very close to (but not copied from or to) MS. The Hague, Koninklijke

---

[47] The manuscript from Rooklooster is quite close to the manuscript Charleville-Mézières, Bibliothèque Municipale, 233 (dating from 1397), from the Mont-Dieu Charterhouse, itself under the influence of the *Devotio moderna*. See Véronique Beaulande-Barraud, "Foi de chartreux: la 'dévotion moderne' au Mont-Dieu," *Revue historique ardennaise* 46 (2014): 13–28.

[48] The manuscripts transmit different versions of the *Dialogus*: Version B (M6), and Version C (Pl). Textually, the manuscript from Neunkirchen is very close to the Benedictine manuscripts that originated in Melk, Kremsmünster, Tegernsee, etc.; see below.

[49] See the stemma in Karl Drescher, ed., Einleitung to *Hartliebs Übersetzung des* Dialogus Miraculorum *von Caesarius von Heisterbach* (Berlin: Weidmannsche Buchhandlung, 1929), xi.

Bibliotheek, 73 E 36, from Eiteren (a Cistercian abbey in the province of Utrecht), and MS. Soest, Wissenschaftliche Stadtsbibliothek, Cod. 13, which belonged to the Dominican Wilhelm Hanstein, and later to the Dominican house in Soest.[50] Additionally, the MS Ko from Saint George (Niederwerth near Koblenz) is extremely close to one from Himmerod (Be1), but according to the probe collation, it was not copied from it.

While copying of the *Dialogus* may not have been part of the reform-related interactions between Augustinian houses, it was nurtured in the reform climate. But why were the *Dialogus* and the *Exordium* so appealing to the Canons Regular involved in the *Devotio moderna* or similar spiritual reform movements? Or, in other words, how did the Canons Regular make their own the *exempla* that circulated among thirteenth-century Cistercians? How did these *exempla* correspond to their own agenda?

It seems logical to assume that the Canons Regular, being priests, appreciated the potential of Cistercian *exempla* as tools to disseminate a religious message. It should, however, be recalled that the question of their involvement in preaching activities is not simple. On the one hand, Bynum stresses that twelfth-century treatises on spiritual advice did not necessarily equate the apostolic life or clerical status with the right or obligation to preach.[51] On the other hand, Canons Regular were often attached to urban churches and had preaching and teaching duties. One can once again mention Jacques de Vitry as an

---

[50] These manuscripts share the following important omissions: in the first *distinctio* chapters 41, 42, and 43 are omitted, and chapter 40 ends after *"Et adiecit: Cum defunctus fuero, apparebit in me unde stupeatis, et divinae virtuti gratias merito referatis."* In *distinctio* VI, *De simplicitate*, the last chapter is missing. In *distinctio* X as many as seventeen chapters concerning the miracles of the animal world are omitted.

[51] The majority of canonical authors of the twelfth century do not define canons as preachers (see Bynum, Docere verbo et exemplo, 18–20). Canons Regular of the time also embraced the cloistered life and the idea of spiritual withdrawal (Bynum, Docere verbo et exemplo, 90–92).

example of a preaching Canon Regular. The marginal annotations in MS. Ba, from Saint Leonhard in Basel, may suggest its connection to the preaching context. For example, a marginal rubric on fol. 123ᵛ indicates "*In festo annuntiationis,*" and on fol. 131ʳ, "*In festo nativitatis Beate Virginis.*" A similar guess may be advanced for MS. Munich, Bayerische Staatsbibliothek, Clm 5106, from Bernried. Besides the *Dialogus*, it contains the *Tractatus de modo praedicandi* (with the *incipit* "*Omnis homo naturaliter scire desiderat*") and the late thirteenth-century Franciscan compilation known as the *Flores temporum*, conceptualized as a tool for preparing homilies and sermons.[52] The text of the *Dialogus* itself, however, does not contain any specific annotations (like those meant to easily find an *exemplum* suitable for the sermon being prepared) that could reinforce this hypothesis.

When *Devotio moderna* started spreading more widely, things became somewhat more complicated. Groote was himself a successful preacher (though banned from preaching in 1383 by the bishop of Utrecht); however, only a few of the first-generation devotees were known to preach in public. We should not overestimate the role played by the *Devotio moderna* in contemporary preaching.[53] The adepts of *Devotio moderna* put special emphasis not on preaching but on book copying, seen as both a spiritual exercise and a way of religious persuasion. The catchphrase "*fratres non verbo sed scripto predicantes*" ("brothers who preach not with spoken but with written words")—as Brothers of the Common Life from Saint Michael in Rostock characterized themselves—comes to mind.[54] Gabriel

---

[52] Hiram Kümper, "Flores temporum," in *Encyclopedia of the Medieval Chronicle*, ed. Graeme Dunphy and Cristian Bratu (Leiden-Boston: Brill, 2010), 1:625.

[53] Thomas Kock, "Zwischen Predigt und Meditation: Die Kollationalia des Dirc van Herxen," in *Predigt im Kontext*, ed. Volker Mertens (Berlin: De Gruyter, 2013), 399–420.

[54] The colophon in the *Sermones Discipuli de tempore* (1476) printed by the Brothers of the Common Life of Saint Michael in Rostock: "*Huius igitur zeli*

Biel, the famous theologian and preacher in Mainz, who in 1468 became provost of the Brethren of the Common Life in Butzbach, stated in his *De communi vita clericorum* that in the church of God, there are those who take care of the souls of others and those who preach with the voice, whereas his fellow adepts of the *Devotio moderna* are silent: they preach by writing and strive after the multiplication of books.[55] The copying of the *Dialogus* can easily be seen as belonging to the paradigm of written preaching. I suppose, however, that the Canons Regular used the *Dialogus* primarily for their own personal instruction. As priests living like monks and trying to achieve the ideals of the *vita canonica*, they may have been sensitive to Cistercian persuasion, centered on the monastic life that had been reformed in accordance with the true spirit of the Benedictine Rule.

In fact the *Dialogus*'s manuscripts belonging to Canons Regular contain many marginal notes highlighting passages on the *vita regularis*. Avoiding prayers, and somnolence during the night offices, seem to have been crucial problems. In the manuscript Sankt Paul im Lavanttal, Benediktinerstift, Cod., 61/4 from Neunkirchen am Brand (Pl), a *nota* on fol. 47ᵛ marks the story about a monk who, being afraid of catching cold, stayed in bed for three successive days and missed the prayers.

---

cupientes fore consortes nos fratres presbiteri et clerici viridis horti in Rostock ad sanctum Michaelem non verbo sed scripto predicantes" (cited in Georg Christian Friedrich Lisch, "Buchdruckerei der Brüder vom gemeinsamen Leben zu St. Michael in Rostock," *Jahrbücher des Vereins für Mecklenburgische Geschichte und Altertumskunde* 4 (1839): 45.

[55] "*Sunt alii in ecclesia Dei, quibus regendarum animarum cura est commissa, alii, qui linguis loquantur et verbum Dei voce predicant. Nos velut extrema vasa domus Dei velut infirma membra corporis ecclesiastici recumbimus in novissimo loco atque extremum locum eligimus et, qui voce tacemus, scripto predicamus damusque operam, ut sancti libri et sacre littere multiplicentur et veniant in usus plurimorum*" (cited, removing editorial marks, in Gerhard Faix, *Gabriel Biel und die Brüder vom Gemeinsamen Leben: Quellen und Untersuchungen zu Verfassung und Selbstverständnis des Oberdeutschen Generalkapitels* [Tübingen: Mohr Siebeck, 1999], 363).

This was, of course, the work of the devil (IV.28).[56] The readers of MS. W2, from Bethlehem, highlighted two stories on the punishment of somnolent monks. These are chapters IV.29 (in which the crucified Christ from the crucifix turned his back on a monk who used to doze between prayers) and IV.38 (in which the crucified Christ punched a monk who used to sleep in choir), at fol. 77^r and fol. 80^r respectively. In the same manuscript, a note on fol. 250^v marks the advice given by the spirit of a clairvoyant monk to a lay brother in VIII.96: "*Dic priori ut sollicitus sit circa excitandos fratres, ne dormiant dum pro defunctis cantant*" ("Tell the prior that he should be diligent to wake up brothers lest they sleep while praying for the dead"). Fol. 51^v of MS. W1, from Rooklooster, highlights a sentence from IV.38: "*Monachus accidiosus nauseam Deo prouocat et angelis sanctis*" ("A slothful monk is disgusting to God and the holy angels").

Another shared concern was monastic food. A reader of the manuscript from Neunkirchen am Brand (P1) marked on fol. 60^v the idea that adjustment to simple monastic food is God's great gift: "*Magnum Dei donum est, quando uiris delicatis, postquam conuersi fuerint ad Christum, incondita pulmentaria leguminum uertuntur in conuiuium*" ("It is a great gift of God when men accustomed to delicate food, after having converted to Christ, find unseasoned leguminous porridge as delicious as a festive meal" [IV.77]). In the manuscript from Bethlehem (W2), on fol. 96^v is highlighted the "parable" of the three grains of pepper that make simple monastic food tasty. The three grains are long vigils, manual labor, and the impossibility of getting anything else (IV.78). Then on fol. 97^v in the same manuscript, a *nota* marks the story about Christ's making the insipid monastic bread delicious by dipping it in his wounds (IV.80). On fol. 98r, another *nota* draws attention to the story of a lay brother who gnawed the wooden floor in his sleep. He thought that the wood was meat offered to him by the devil

---

[56] References, if not stated otherwise, are to Strange's edition.

(IV.83). A reader of the manuscript from Rooklooster (W1) highlights on fol. 60ᵛ the opinion of Caesarius according to which a monk sins more by avoiding legumes because of health concerns than by eating too much of them (IV.78).

Judging by the readers' notes, Canons Regular were also concerned about such issues as dangers of postponing one's confession,[57] disordered sleeping,[58] or "indiscreet fervor."[59] A reader of the manuscript from Bethlehem (W2) left several *notae* to draw attention to the following offenses against communal life: murmuring, slander, envy, negligence (fol. 303ᵛ), and another one highlighted reluctance to work (fol. 307ᵛ). According to the vision of Ysenbard, prior in Himmerod, these sins appeared as stains on the robes of glory that otherwise virtuous monks wear in the afterlife (XI.3). The same reader highlighted on fol. 76ᵛ a remedy against strained relationships within a community, suggested by Rudolf, Caesarius's teacher in the cathedral school of Cologne. Rudolf told his pupils about a religious brother who had defeated the hatred of one of his fellows by showing him the utmost affection (IV.26).

Canons Regular also highlighted Caesarius's observations related to the concept of teaching *verbo et exemplo*. A reader from Bethlehem marked on fol. 10ʳ of MS. W2 the following passage: "*Qui alium verbo uel exemplo ad bene vivendum informat, hunc profecto tanquam proprium filium Christo generat*" ("The person who teaches others, by word or deed, how to live a better life bears them for Christ as his own sons" [I.20, see 1 Cor 4:15 and Phlm 10]). A reader from Rooklooster highlighted

---

[57] MS. W2, fol. 5ʳ: an angel appeared to a prior in the form of the monk whose confession had been postponed (I.6).

[58] MS. W2, fol. 127ᵛ: a demon in the form of a nun kissed a lay brother who slept in an inappropriate way (V.33).

[59] MS. W1, fol. 196ʳ: an obstinate monk often showed an indiscreet fervor, much to the concern of his abbot. A *nota* marks the remark of the Novice: "*Ista recitari deberent monachis qui ex indiscreto feruore sibi et aliis inutiles fiunt*" (XII.29).

Caesarius's answer to the Novice's question of whether or not one may show his gift of tears to others (MS. W1, fol. 22^v): *"Si ei placet, ut alij lacrimas eius videant, quatenus per eas edificentur, ipse tamen humilitatem custodiat in corde, meretur; sin autem, demeretur"* ("If he wants others to see his tears in order to instruct them while keeping humility in his heart, it is meritorious; if not—quite the opposite" [II.21]). The same reader also pointed to the necessity of maintaining a good appearance (fol. 46^r): *"Unde studendum est omnibus, religiosis maxime et claustralibus, ut sic se in uerbis, in gestibus, in uestimentis, et in ceteris omnibus, que ad usum exteriorem pertinent, exhibeant, ne apud seculares in vicio superbie notabiles fiant"* ("All people, especially religious and monks, should behave in such a manner that their words, gestures, clothes, and other external things will not be considered proud by laymen" [IV.11]).

"Imitation of Christ" is also often noted in the *Dialogus*. Thus readers of MS. W1 from Rooklooster perceived comparisons of the monastic life to the crucifixion in chapters I.6 (fol. 3^v) and VIII.18 (fol. 131^r). Monks, explains Caesarius, conform their lives to Christ's passion by their obedience, patience, humility, and rejection of possessions and their own will.[60]

The content highlighted by the readers is of course not limited to problems of the cloistered life. A reader from Bethlehem, for example, noted on MS. W2, fol. 172^v, the receipt of the remedy against mange given to Adam from the abbey of Loccum by the Virgin Mary herself (VII.24), and, on fol. 49^r, the legend about Goth women, banished from their tribe because of their deformity, who mated with demons and had children with them. Their children, it says, were ancestors of the Huns (III.12). Nevertheless, the main focus of the readers seems to

---

[60] A lay brother from Loccum saw Christ on the cross, and near him fifteen other crucified persons—ten monks and five lay brothers—from his own abbey. When he asks who they are, Christ explains that those are the only ones from the congregation whose lives are conformed to his passion (VIII.18).

have been Caesarius's insights into the dangers and benefits[61] of the *vita communis* and spiritual practices like prayer[62] and psalmody.[63]

However revealing, the notes in the manuscripts do not speak for the entire readership. Some manuscripts, like the one from Liège, have no (or very few) notes. It would be erroneous to conclude that the parts of the *Dialogus* left without highlighting were irrelevant. For example, many stories from the *Dialogus* deal specifically with priests and the priesthood. One might even have the impression that Caesarius thought of priests (and not only of monk-priests) as one of his implicit audiences. In chapter IX.6 he expresses through the mouth of the Novice the desire to reach all priests with the message conveyed by the *exemplum* in question: "*Si sacerdotes omnes talia audirent, auditisque crederent, puto quod plus quam modo deifica sacramenta honorarent!*" ("If all priests could listen to such words and believe them, I believe that they would honor the divine sacrament better than they do these days!") The *exemplum* tells the story of a priest who wanted to use the Host as a charm and found himself unable to leave the church.

In the same *distinctio* on the Eucharist, in IX.26, Caesarius discusses the conduct of priests: a priest, he says, should be

---

[61] See the notes in MS. Pl, whose reader often reflected on the difficulties of the *vita regularis*, but also on its benefits. For example, on fol. 173[r], a *nota* marks the following passage from chapter XI.12: "*Ego vobis dico, quod beatus est monachus ille siue conuersus, qui bene uno anno, uel mense, uel quod minus est una ebdomada, in ordine conuersatus est.*"

[62] For example, a *nota* in MS. W1, on fol. 10[r] marks "*Nichil debetis dicere in oratione, sed tantum cogitare de Saluatoris natiuitate, passione et resurrectione et alijs que uobis nota sunt*" (I.35), and the rubric *nota oratio* on fol. 199[r]: "*Habebam consuetudinem ut quociens transirem coram crucifixo, hanc dicerem orationem: Domine per illam amaritudinem quam propter me sustinuisti in cruce, maxime quando anima tua egressa est de corpore tuo, miserere anime mee in egressu suo*" (XII.51).

[63] See MS. W1, fol. 71[r]: "*consulo, ut cum stamus ad psallendum, circumspecti simus et intenti, feruentes et humiles, ne meritum sancti feruoris exstinguat uicium superbe vociferationis*" (V.5).

chaste and literate.[64] An illiterate priest, however, can compensate for the lack of preaching abilities by providing a good example: "*Quod si sibi commissos illuminare non valent verbo praedicationis, ad divinum amorem illos accendere studeant exemplo bonae conversationis*" ("If they are unable to illuminate their flock with the word of preaching, they should strive to kindle them to the love of God by the example of their good life").

The *exempla* about priests and priesthood, although not specifically marked in the studied manuscripts, must have contributed to the popularity of the *Dialogus* among the Canons Regular.

Another appealing aspect of the *Dialogus* could have been the wide range of role models offered by Caesarius to his readers. The adepts of *Devotio moderna* advocated reform by seeking inspiration in exemplary figures from the past.[65] Apart from the supreme example of Jesus Christ, Thomas à Kempis listed several categories of pious people who had imitated Christ to perfection and thus could serve as model for the novices.[66] Imitation therefore emerges as one the most important strategies for carrying on the inner reform. The primary role models for these devotees were the Desert Fathers.[67] Johannes Busch in his *Chronicon Windeshemense* praised the Windesheim Canons as monks of renewed Palestinian devotion, Theban obedience, and Egyptian fervor, new disciples of Saint Antony and

---

[64] "*Gloria vitae sacerdotalis in duobus praecipue consistit, castimonia videlicet et scientia. Debet enim castus esse et litteratus.*"

[65] On this aspect see Mathilde van Dijk, "*Performing the Fathers* in the 'Devotio Moderna,'" in *Die Devotio Moderna: Sozialer und Kultureller Transfer (1350–1580)*, ed. Iris Kwiatkowski and Jörg Engelbrecht, vol. 2, *Die räumliche und geistige Ausstrahlung der Devotio Moderna – Zur Dynamik ihres Gedankengutes* (Münster: Aschendorff, 2013), 227–44.

[66] Mathilde van Dijk, " 'Persevere! . . . God Will Help You!': Thomas à Kempis's Sermons for the Novices and His Perspective on Pastoral Care," in *A Companion to Pastoral Care in the Late Middle Ages (1200–1500)*, ed. Ronald J. Stansbury (Leiden: Brill, 2010), 380.

[67] See van Dijk, "*Performing the Fathers.*"

Saint Macarius.[68] Here one can easily draw a parallel with Cistercians, who also sought to reinvent primitive monasticism by rigorously following the Rule of Saint Benedict.

It is no wonder that the *Vitae patrum* was among the all-time reading favorites in the reformed communities. In his *De sacris libris studendis*, Groote insisted on reading the *Instituta sanctorum patrum* and the *Collationes patrum*.[69] Johannes Busch gave a list of the books diligently collected by the earlier brothers from Windesheim, exemplary in their passion for sacred literature, and included among them *Collationes patrum*, *Instituta patrum*, and *Vitae patrum*.[70] Although not officially recommended as a must read, hagiographic collections containing the lives of illustrious persons from other religious orders were appreciated by the reform-seeking canons. Among the manuscripts that belonged to the Crosiers from Liège, there was, for example, the *Liber Vitasfratrum* by Jordan of Quedlinburg (MS. Liège, Université de Liège, Bibliothèque générale de Philosophie et Lettres, 191). In MS. Li1, the *Dialogus* was combined with the *Vitae fratrum ordinis praedicatorum* and the *Chronica ordinis fratrum praedicatorum*.

For a reader looking for exemplary figures, the *Dialogus* was an abundant source of inspiring characters: abbots and simple monks, novices and lay brothers. The models to be found in Cistercian *exempla* collections could have been perceived as altogether more attainable or reachable than those from the *Vitae patrum*. After all, the white monks had already proved themselves to be successful imitators of primitive monasticism. In the situation when a "literal imitation was not the point,

---

[68] *Des Augustinerpropstes Johannes Busch Chronicon Windeshemense und Liber de reformatione monasteriorum*, ed. Karl Grube (Halle: Hendel, 1886), 27.

[69] The list was included by Thomas à Kempis in his *Dialogus novitiorum* II.18: *Thomas a Kempis Opera Omnia*, ed. Michael J. Pohl (Freiburg: Herder, 1992), 7:91.

[70] See the first version of the *Chronicon Windeshemense*, partially published by Victor Becker, "Eene onbekende kronijk van het klooster te Windesheim," in *Bijdragen en Mededelingen van het Historisch Genootschap* 10 (1887): 402–5.

and could be even undesirable,"[71] Cistercian *exempla* may not only have offered models to imitate, but also have taught how to reinvent and adapt these models, in short, how to deal with both the ups and the downs of communal life.

The desired return to apostolic ideals was certainly not easy to achieve. To push forward the reform of the Order of the Holy Cross, Johannes of Merten, the successor of Libertus Janssen van Bommel, had to seek the help of Pope John XXIII. The pope gave him a special letter (from May 19, 1413) to use against resisting priors and brothers and, if necessary, to call upon the secular authorities.[72] The observance of the *vita communis* met particular resistance among the Crosiers. According to a 1418 decision of the general chapter, a brother from a community that did not respect the *vita communis* was permitted to move to another one.[73] As late as 1466, the general chapter renewed this decision, a clear sign that despite the apparent success of the inner reform at this time, some aspects remained wanting.[74] In the context of this difficult return to the ideals of observance, the *Dialogus*, with its praise of visitations and communal life, may have offered valuable encouragement for those struggling to accept the changed collective identity. For the partisans of the reform, the *Dialogus* may have served as a valuable tool for persuasion.

Caesarius, in fact, often addressed in both sharp and humorous ways the difficulties of monastic life and the consternation it could cause. One instance is the story about a knight who was terrified of lice (IV.48). When a friend encouraged him to convert to the monastic life, the knight answered that he would happily come to the Order except for the lice. His friend said to him: "*Och fortem militem! Qui in bello diaboli non timuit gladios,*

---

[71] Van Dijk, "Performing the Fathers," 229.

[72] See Robert Haaß, *Die Kreuzherren in den Rheinlanden* (Bonn: Röhrscheid, 1932), 11–12.

[73] Haaß, *Die Kreuzherren*, 13.

[74] Haaß, *Die Kreuzherren*, 14.

in militia Christi timere debet pediculos? Auferent tibi nunc pediculi regnum Dei?" ("O what a strong knight! One who did nor fear the swords in the battle of the devil should fear lice in the army of Christ? Will the lice take away from you the kingdom of heaven?"). By this witty provocation the monk succeeded in persuading his friend to join the Order.

The success of the *Dialogus* among the Canons Regular invites consideration of the rich potential of Cistercian *exempla* to support an inner religious reform. In the specific context of the desired change, conceptualized as a return to the origins, the stories from the late twelfth and the early thirteenth centuries regained their popularity and became inspiring. The *Dialogus* provided its readers with instructive and handy *sententiae* and with exemplary figures they could recognize and identify with. It could therefore serve both as a tool for propagating the reform and as a means of auto-construction of the religious self among the adherents of the renewed devotion.[75]

---

[75] See Anton G. Weiler, "La construction du soi dans les milieux de la *devotio moderna*," in *La dévotion moderne dans les pays bourguignons et rhénans des origines à la fin du XVIe siècle: rencontres de Colmar-Strasbourg (29 septembre au 2 octobre 1988)* (Neuchâtel: Centre Européen d'Études Bourguignonnes, 1989), 9–16.

10

Benedictines, Carthusians, and Mendicant Friars

Benedictines

Despite well-known frictions between Cistercians and Cluniacs, both white and black monks appreciated a good *exemplum* and exchanged stories. The Cistercian Engelhard of Langheim sent his *Libellus miraculorum* to Erbo, the abbot of the Benedictine abbey of Prüfening. A number of stories from the *Dialogus* were originally told to Caesarius by Benedictines (II.31, IX.50, X.11, X.62, XII.53). After all, their own storytelling tradition was rich enough to fill the famous *De miraculis* (1135–1156) by Peter the Venerable, abbot of Cluny. It seems, however, that the *De miraculis* did not become a hit among Cistercians: only two manuscripts among those Denise Bouthillier used for her critical edition of *De miraculis* are of Cistercian provenance.[1] Apparently the Benedictines were more welcoming towards Cistercian *exempla* collections than vice versa. But despite some early Benedictine interest in Cistercian stories, just as was true with the Canons Regular, it was not until the fifteenth century that the *Dialogus*, Herbert's *Liber*, and the *Exordium* received real attention from Benedictine readers, as

---

[1] Both date from the thirteenth century: Brussels, Bibliothèque Royale de Belgique, 7462–81 (3177), from Vaucelles; and Pelplin, Biblioteka seminarium Duchownego, 17 (27) from Pelplin. See Peter the Venerable, *De miraculis libri duo*, ed. Denise Bouthillier, CCCM 58 (Turnhout: Brepols, 1988).

is demonstrated by manuscripts of Benedictine origin or provenance:

Benedictine manuscripts of the Dialogus miraculorum

Au	Augsburg, Universitätsbibliothek, Cod. II. 1. 2°14, first half of the 15th century – Saint Mang (Füssen) – Version C
Be3	Berlin, Staatsbibliothek zu Berlin - Preußischer Kulturbesitz, MS. lat. qu. 875, 15th century (1477). Dist I–VI – Ammensleben
D	Douai, Bibliothèque municipale, 397, 15th century (1473) – Hasnon
K	Kremsmünster, Benediktinerstift, CC 54, second half of the 15th century – Kremsmünster – Version C
M2	Munich, Bayerische Staatsbibliothek, Clm 4711, 15th century – Benediktbeuern – Version C
M3	Munich, Bayerische Staatsbibliothek, Clm 18614, 15th century –Tegernsee – Dist. I–VII, Version C
M3/2	Munich, Bayerische Staatsbibliothek, Clm 18615, 15th century – Tegernsee – Dist. VIII–XII, Version C
M4	Munich, Bayerische Staatsbibliothek, Clm 3058, 15th century – Andechs – Version C
Me	Melk, Benediktinerstift, Cod. 805 (796, O 34), 15th century (1437) – Melk – Version C
Mi	Michaelbeuern, Benediktinerstift, Man. cart. 90, 15th century – Michaelbeuern – Version C (excerpts)
Tr	Trier, Stadtbibliothek, Hs. 609/2031 2°, 15th century (1462) – Sankt Marien in Trier
W4	Vienna, Österreichische Nationalbibliothek, 3785, 15th century (1453) – Mondsee
We	Weimar, Herzogin Anna Amalia Bibliothek, Q 21, 15th century. Dist. VII–XII – Ammensleben
Wü	Würzburg, Universitätsbibliothek, M. ch. f. 246, 15th century (1460–1461) – Saint Stephan (Würzburg) – Version C

Lost or unidentified manuscripts

According to the library catalogue from Saint Aegidius Abbey in Nuremberg (from the end of the fifteenth century),[2] the abbey possessed a manuscript of the *Dialogus: Dyalogus Cesarii monachi de exemplis et miraculis*. Einsiedeln Abbey (Schwyz canton, Switzerland) may also have had a copy of the *Dialogus*. On February 28, 1332, a certain Herman, the parish priest in Freienbach, mentioned the "*librum Cesarii de miraculis*" among the books that he intended to give to the abbey.[3] The inventory of Saint Emmeram Abbey in Regensburg, composed by Konrad Pleystainer (1449/1452), mentions the *Excerpta ex dyalogo Cesarii*, in the same volume with the *Tractatus magistri Hainrici de Hassia qui intitulatur cordiale quatuor novissimorum*.[4]

Benedictine Manuscripts of the Liber

Kremsmünster, Benediktinerstift, CC 253, end of the 13th century (1292) – Kremsmünster

Melk, Benediktinerstift, Cod. 320 (623, L 48), 15th century (1440?) – Melk

Vienna, Schottenstift (Benediktiner), Bibliothek, Cod. 143 (Hübl 64), 15th century – Scottish Abbey in Vienna

Vienna, Österreichische Nationalbibliothek, Cod. 3650, 15th century (1475–76) – Mondsee

Vienna, Österreichische Nationalbibliothek, Cod. 3798, 15th century (1451) – Mondsee

---

[2] Bernhard Bischoff and Paul Ruf, eds., *Mittelalterliche Bibliothekskataloge Deutschlands und der Schweiz*, vol. 3/1, *Bistum Augsburg* (Munich: Beck, 1932), 430–569.

[3] Bernhard Bischoff and Paul Lehmann, eds., *Mittelalterliche Bibliothekskataloge Deutschlands und der Schweiz*, vol. 1, *Die Bistümer Konstanz und Chur* (Munich: Beck, 1918), 28. Whether the book ended up in the abbey's library is not known.

[4] Bernhard Bischoff and Christine Elisabeth Ineichen-Eder, eds., *Mittelalterliche Bibliothekskataloge Deutschlands und der Schweiz*, vol. 4/1, *Bistümer Passau und Regensburg* (Munich: Beck, 1977), 173.

Vienna, Österreichische Nationalbibliothek, Cod. 4118, 15th
century – Mondsee

Weimar, Herzogin Anna Amalia Bibliothek, Fol max 3, 1st half of
the 15th century – Saint Peter and Paul in Erfurt

Benedictine Manuscripts of the Exordium

Berlin, Staatsbibliothek zu Berlin - Preußischer Kulturbesitz, lat.
Fol. 193, 15th century – Maria Laach (given to the abbey by
a Mathias Hey from Mayen)

Kopenhagen, Kongelige Bibliotek, Gl. Kgl. Saml. 174, 15th century
– Cismar

Trier, Seminarbibliothek, 52, 15th century (1450) – Saint Mathias
in Trier

In the light of the previous chapter's discussion, the presence of the *Dialogus* and Herbert's *Liber* in fifteenth-century
Melk invites consideration of whether interest in Cistercian
exempla collections was due to the abbey's reform activity. Melk
Abbey, founded in 1089 in Lower Austria, is known as an important center of fifteenth-century Benedictine reform. The
abbey itself was reformed in 1418[5] at the request of Albert V,
archduke of Austria. Pope Martin V appointed Nicolaus Seyringer with five other monks of Subiaco[6] to begin the reform.

---

[5] Edeltraud Klueting, *Monasteria semper reformanda: Kloster- und Ordensreformen im Mittelalter* (Münster: LIT, 2005), 27. See also Christine Glaßner, "Stift
Melk und die Melker Reform im 15. Jahrhundert," in *Die benediktinische Klosterreform im 15. Jahrhundert*, ed. Franz Xaver and Martin Thurner (Berlin:
Akademie, 2013), 75–91; Joachim Angerer, "Reform von Melk," in *Die Reformverbände und Kongregationen der Benediktiner im deutschen Sprachraum*, ed.
Ulrich Faust and Franz Quarthal (St. Ottilien: EOS, 1999), 271–313.

[6] The monastery of Subiaco underwent a series of reforms in the second
half of the fourteenth century. In 1380 the new Consuetudines Sublacenses
appeared—the basis for the Consuetudines of Melk (see Joachim Angerer,
ed., *Corpus consuetudinum monasticarum*, vol. 11/1, *Caeremoniae regularis observantiae sanctissimi patris nostri Benedicti ex ipsius regula sumptae, secundum
quod in sacris locis, scilicet specu et monasterio Sublacensi practicantur* [Siegburg:
Schmitt, 1985], esp. CLXX–CLXXX).

The pope and the duke also tasked Cistercian abbot Angelus of Rein and Carthusian prior Leonhard Paetrer of Gaming to inspect Benedictine and Augustinian monasteries. On June 30, 1418, Nicolaus Seyringer was elected the new abbot, and his five fellow monks from Subiaco joined the brethren of Melk. Then the reform began. Its goal was to establish much stricter discipline and to follow to the letter the Rule of Saint Benedict (especially provisions concerning obedience, poverty, absence of private property, uniformity of habits, observation of fasts, and enclosure).[7] Another important aspect of the Benedictine reform was the encouraging of a simplified and purified, and more internalized, daily choir service. Special emphasis was put on the psalmody: monks should sing the psalms clearly and distinctly, respecting the pauses and the rhythm of the text, without hurry. The reformers desired that the liturgy be experienced as an intense devotional practice rather than as a superfluous routine.[8]

Melk Abbey soon became the center of the reformed observance. Several monasteries followed its example, without, however, forming a congregation. Among them were the Scottish abbey at Vienna (1418), Kremsmünster (1419), Tegernsee (1426), Michaelbeuern (1434), Mondsee (1435), Benediktbeuern (1441), and Andechs (1455).[9]

---

[7] See Albert Groiss, *Spätmittelalterliche Lebensformen der Benediktiner von der Melker Observanz vor dem Hintergrund ihrer Bräuche: ein darstellender Kommentar zum Caeremoniale Mellicense des Jahres 1460* (Münster: Aschendorff, 1999), 70–80.

[8] See *Bernardi Pezii Benedictini Et Bibliothecarii Mellicensis Bibliotheca Ascetica Antiquo-Nova*, vol. 8 (Regensburg: Peetz, 1725), 548. See also Joachim Angerer, *Die liturgisch-musikalische Erneuerung der Melker Reform: Studien zur Erforschung der Musikpraxis in den Benediktinerklöstern des 15. Jahrhunderts* (Vienna: Österreichische Akademie der Wissenschaften, 1974), esp. 83–87; Petrus Becker, "Erstrebte und erreichte Ziele benediktinischer Reformen im Spätmittelalter," in *Reformbemühungen und Observanzbestrebungen im spätmittelalterlichen Ordenswesen*, ed. Kaspar Elm (Berlin: Duncker & Humblot, 1989), 28–29.

[9] Andechs Abbey was founded in 1455 with the reformed Benedictines from Tegernsee.

This being said, Melk Abbey was neither the only propagator of the reformed observance in the German-speaking area nor the first one. Kastl Abbey in Bavaria had started its reform as early as 1380. The abbey of Saint Mang in Füssen had already adopted the Consuetudines from Kastl under abbot Georg Sandauer (1397–1410). The abbey of Saint Aegidius in Nuremberg was reformed in 1418 by the monks from Reichenbach, which had itself in 1394 joined the reform started in Kastl. Another center of reform was Bursfelde abbey in Lower Saxony. Its reforming efforts resulted in the foundation of the Bursfelde Congregation in 1446. Among the members of the congregation were Cismar (1449), Saint Peter in Erfurt (1450), Sankt Marien in Trier (1455), Saint Mathias in Trier (1458), Saint Stephan in Würzburg (1459), Ammensleben (1461), and Maria Laach (1474).

Hasnon was reformed between 1466 and 1469 under the abbot Laurent d'Ivoire, who invited the monks from Florennes to put the reform in place.[10] Florennes was reformed around 1414 upon the request of the bishop of Liège, John of Bavaria, by Renier of Saint Margaret, the abbot of Saint James in Liège (1408–1436).[11] Interestingly, Florennes maintained close connections with Cistercians from Moulins and Jardinet.[12] Godefroy Godinne from Florennes, involved in the reform of Hasnon, was well acquainted with Jean Eustache († 1481), the reforming abbot of Jardinet.

To sum it up, all Benedictine abbeys in possession of Cistercian *exempla* collections were part of the Benedictine reform movement. Since many manuscripts are not dated, it is impossible to say whether they were copied or acquired before or after the official implement of the reform. The dated manu-

---

[10] Jules Dewez, *Histoire de l'abbaye de Saint-Pierre d'Hasnon* (Lille: Imprimerie de l'Orphelinat de Don Bosco, 1890), 189.

[11] Xavier Hermand, "Réformer une abbaye au XVe siècle: L'exemple de Florennes," *Revue bénédictine* 122 (2012): 342–65.

[12] Hermand, "Réformer une abbaye au XVe siècle," 361–62.

scripts, however, are all from the post-reform period, except for the copy of Herbert's *Liber* from Kremsmünster (end of the thirteenth century). The manuscript transmission itself often (though not always) concurred with the dissemination of reform. As the probe collation suggests, manuscript M4 was probably copied from those from Tegernsee. It was from Melk's exemplar, itself copied from Heiligenkreuz, that the abbey of Mondsee copied Herbert's *Liber* in 1451. The Scottish Abbey in Vienna also copied its manuscript of the *Liber* from Melk.

The *Dialogus* manuscript from Melk (Me) shows important similarities with Cistercian manuscripts from Rein and Altzella, without, however, being copied directly from them (though it is tempting to suppose that Abbot Angelus of Rein may have suggested the reading of the *Dialogus* during his visitation). Manuscript Me transmits Version C. According to the probe collation, the manuscript from Kremsmünster (K) is related to manuscript Me, probably via the manuscript from Mondsee (W4). The manuscript from Benediktbeuern (M2) is extremely close to those from Melk, Mondsee, and Kremsmünster, but was not directly copied from any of them, or they from it. The manuscripts from Tegernsee (M3 and M3/2) were copied in Benediktbeuern, as the colophon on the cover page of M3 states: *"Iste liber ist monasterij Sancti Quirini in Tegernsee et rescriptum per vnum fratrem in Benedicten Päwren loco uenerabili"* ("This book belongs to the monastery of Saint Quirin in Tegernsee and was written by a certain brother in Benediktbeuern, a venerable place"). The manuscript from Würzburg is very close to the manuscripts from Tegernsee and Benediktbeuern and could have been copied from the same exemplar as the manuscript from Benediktbeuern.

The manuscript from Saint Mang (Au), belongs to the same branch as the manuscripts from Melk, Kremsmünster, Benediktbeuern, Tegernsee, and Saint Stephan in Würzburg. This being said, the Benedictines of Saint Mang got their exemplar from the Dominicans of Nuremberg in 1463 (some fifty years after the abbey had been reformed), as the colophons on fols. 1d^v and 168^v state. Benedictines paid fifty florins for the *Dialogus* along with four volumes of the *Catholicon* by Johannes Januensis. MS. Michaelbeuern, Benediktinerstift, Man. cart. 90 (Mi), contains excerpts from *distinctiones* I, II, III, IV, and VII. This manuscript basically transmits Version C and has an addition in common with MS. Leipzig, Universitätsbibliothek, Cod. 445, from Altzella: the story *De Petro episcopo* (f. 132^r–133^r in Mi), which originated in Engelhard of Langheim's *Liber miraculorum*. The two manuscripts are definitely related. This being said, MS. Mi has the names of the Monk and the Novice (Cesarius and Apollonius), and the manuscript from Altzella does not. No intermediary manuscript has yet been identified.

The rest of the Benedictine manuscripts transmit the full version of the *Dialogus*. MS. D1 is very close to the manuscripts from Clairvaux. Of the two volumes originating from Saint Peter and Paul in Groß Ammensleben, the second (We) is close to Li1, from the Crosier monastery in Liège, whereas the first (Be3) has many individual variants; for the time being it is not possible to place it in any defined group. The Trier manuscript (Tr), copied in 1462 by Theodericus de Gorinchem, a monk of Sankt Marien, is extremely close to MS. Be1, and, as the probe collation suggests, could have been copied from it. The exact context of its copying and whether it was related to the reform, however, remain unclear.

Benedictine manuscripts of the *Dialogus* usually are either not annotated or have very few notes. The latter is the case of the manuscript from Melk. Some of its few notes are, however, very revealing. On fols. 62^v, 84^r, 127^r, and 204^r are notes made by Johannes Schlitpacher of Weilheim († 1482), one of the most prominent agents of the Melk reform.[13] Twice vicar and three

---

[13] Benedikt Konrad Vollmann, "Schlitpacher, Johannes," in *Neue Deutsche Biographie* 23 (2007): 93–94 [online version], URL: https://www.deutsche-biographie.de/pnd100966446.html#ndbcontent.

times prior of Melk, he actively participated in the reform of Saint Ulrich and Afra in Augsburg (1441/42), Ettal (1442/43), and Kleinmariazell (1446/47). Under the cardinal-legate Nicholas of Cusa, he conducted visitations of more than fifty monasteries in the church province of Salzburg. Even if Johannes's notes in MS. Me do not concern the reform agenda,[14] the very fact that he read the *Dialogus* contributes to the theory that Caesarius's work was relevant to the Benedictine reform.

The only Benedictine manuscript with a considerable number of contemporary annotations is the manuscript from Saint Quirin in Tegernsee (specifically its first part, Me3). On fol. 15ʳ, for example, the reader highlighted the importance of the monks' exemplary behavior in attracting newcomers: "*multi sine exhortacione sermonis, nullis specialibus adiudi oracionibus, per sola exempla religionis quottidie ad ordinem conuertuntur et trahuntur*" ("Every day, people are attracted into the Order not by the exhortation of sermons, not by the help of special prayers, but only by the examples of religious life" [I.20]). On fols. 124ᵛ and 125ʳ, he drew attention to both the necessity to adjust to the monastic diet and the possibility of doing so (IV.77 and IV.78).[15]

Further, the reader noted the conclusion to the story of how a Cistercian monk had been liberated from temptation by humble and profound bowing (fol. 131ʳ): "*Diabolus omnem odit humiliacionem, illam maxime, per quam homo cognoscit Deum creatorem suum et se creaturam*" ("The Devil hates all humility, and most the one in which human beings acknowledge God as their creator and themselves as creation"). There are also notes bringing attention to the salutary effects of the *Ave Maria* (fol. 64ᵛ—it chases a demon away [III.13]) and of the confession (fol. 135ʳ—it extinguishes the "*fomes peccati*" [IV.95]). In sum,

---

[14] For example, on fol. 62ᵛ, he wrote "*nomen huius prophete 3 reg 13 non exprimitur*" to comment on the following phrase: "*Homo Dei, Abdo scilicet, missus in Bethel, propter comestionem a leone occiditur*" (IV.73 in Strange's edition).

[15] See above, p. 151.

the issues that affected the reformed Benedictines seem to have been very similar to those that affected the reformed Canons Regular, especially the rigors of the ideal monastic life (such as the strict diet), the importance of combining exemplary behavior and interior devotion, the obligation both to teach others and to please God, and the indispensability of prayers. The *Dialogus* was apparently highly regarded in Saint Quirin abbey in Tegernsee.[16] The alphabetical library catalogue (1483/84) by Ambrosius Schwerzenbeck expressively presented the *Dialogus* as *egregius* and the excerpta from it as *optima*.[17] The *Dialogus's* author was honored as well. Schwerzenbeck, who added a table of contents to MS. Munich, Bayerische Staatsbibliothek, Clm 18615 (the second part of the *Dialogus*), presented Caesarius as a saint: "*Secunda pars dyalogi sancti Cesarii cysterciensis ordinis*" (fol. I^r).

The catalogue from Saint Aegidius in Nuremberg (end of the fifteenth century)[18] is not that generous with epithets. However, it mentions the *Dialogus* (call number H 42) along with the ever-popular *Vitae patrum* (call numbers H 43 and H 44). *Littera* H includes mostly sermons and devotional treatises, such as, for example, *Directorium confessorum fratris Anthonii* | *Sermo Johannis Chrisostomi de penitentia* (call number H 41).

---

[16] It is worth mentioning that Johannes Hartlieb, who translated the *Dialogus* into German, had good connections to the abbey of Tegernsee (see Reinhold Spiller, "Studien zu Ulrich Füetrer," *Zeitschrift für deutsches Altertum und deutsche Literatur* 27 [1883]: 289–93). Hartlieb's translation, however, transmits not Version C (as does the Tegernsee manuscript), but Version B. See above, Part I, p. 147, n. 49).

[17] See Günter Glauche and Hermann Knaus, eds., *Mittelalterliche Bibliothekskataloge Deutschlands und der Schweiz*, vol. 4/2, *Bistum Freising* (Munich: Beck, 1979), 776: "*Cesarii Cysterciensis* | *Dyalogus egregius inter novicium et monachum* | *cum exemplorum et miraculorum attestacione, distin-*|*ctiones quindecim* [sic]*; pars prima h 39 1o; pars 2a, h 39 2o* | *Excerpta optima ex dyalogo eius, h. 33 2o.*"

[18] Bernhard Bischoff and Paul Ruf, *Mittelalterliche Bibliothekskataloge Deutschlands und der Schweiz*, vol. 3/1, 430–569.

The catalogue from Melk (1483)[19] mentions the *Excerpta ex dyalogo Cesarii in pergamento*, under the call number E 107[20] in *Archa D*, containing hagiographic works, devotional treatises, monastic rules, different *summae*, historiography, etc., just after a certain Apiarius (E 36—*Bonum universale de apibus?*).[21] In Saint Emmeram abbey, the *Excerpta ex dyalogo Cesarii* were placed, as is explained by Konrad Pleystainer's catalogue, in the *Pulpitum vicesimum quartum*, with titles such as *Miracula beate virginis*, *Summa magistri Iohannis Beleth de divinis officiis*, *De septem sacramentis*, etc.[22]

The library of Saint Mang apparently used a very similar categorization. No surviving catalogue mentions the *Dialogus*, but some valuable information is provided by sixteenth-century call numbers. MS. Au has the call number H 17. Under the same *littera* H one finds, for example, *Vitae patrum* and *Dialogi* of Gregory the Great, *Legendae sanctorum cum exemplis*, different sermons, and glosses, and books related to (or influenced by) the *Devotio moderna*, like *Malogranatum* or *De exterioris et interioris hominis compositione* by David of Augsburg.[23] These are mostly books suitable for reading in refectory or for individual reading during Lent, or useful in preparing a sermon.

Cistercian *exempla* certainly provided the reform-aspiring Benedictines with examples of how one can follow the Rule of Benedict to the letter, as well as with engaging examples of intense inner appropriation of monastic routine, not only by reputed holy men or women, but also by ordinary members

---

[19] Theodor Gottlieb, et al., eds., *Mittelalterliche Bibliothekskataloge Österreichs*, vol. 1, *Niederoesterreich* (Aalen: Scientia, 1915), 161–261.

[20] Gottlieb, et al., *Mittelalterliche Bibliothekskataloge Österreichs*, 1:231.

[21] The Melk library also had a copy of *Alphabetum narrationum* and probably a copy of the *De oculo morali* (see Gottlieb, et al., *Mittelalterliche Bibliothekskataloge Österreichs*, 1:203 and 237).

[22] Ineichen-Eder, ed., *Mittelalterliche Bibliothekskataloge Deutschlands und der Schweiz*, 4/1:173.

[23] Christoph Roth, *Literatur und Klosterreform: die Bibliothek der Benediktiner von St. Mang zu Füssen im 15. Jahrhundert* (Tübingen: Niemeyer, 1999), 63–64, 368–69.

of the Order. Caesarius touched upon many topical issues, from the unappealing vegetarian diet to the difficulties of singing psalms clearly and in a well-coordinated manner. He approached these issues through the lenses of private devotional experiences of his fellow Cistercians, narrating them with caring, integrity, and passion. Such stories must have had a deep impact on the Benedictine monks in quest for the authenticity and renewal.

Carthusians

Among monastic communities in possession of the *Dialogus*, Carthusian monks also figure. This contemplative order was founded by Bruno of Cologne in 1084. Carthusians did not exercise the *vita communis* but lived in individual cells built around the cloister. They rarely left their cells, and their opportunities to speak with each other were even more rare. Once a week, however, Carthusian hermits were allowed to take a long walk with other members of the community and to have conversations.

The Carthusian way of life did not facilitate storytelling exchanges, whether between monks or with people outside the monastery. That fact does not mean, of course, that Carthusians had no appreciation for a good story. They were avid readers and book copyists, and among their books are some *exempla* collections. For example, the houses in Basel and Milan (Garegnano) had the *Alphabetum narrationum*,[24] the house of Bourgfontaine (in the diocese of Soissons) had an exemplar of the *Bonum universale de apibus* and a collection of the *exempla* by Jacques de Vitry,[25] and the houses in Mainz, Basel, and Wezel had Caesarius's *Libri VIII miraculorum*.[26]

---

[24] MSS. Basel, Universitätsbibliothek, B IX 7, and Milan, Biblioteca Nazionale Braidense, AD.XIV.9.

[25] See the Inventory of the Bourgfontaine Charterhouse, in Audrey Sulpice, ed., *Tombel de Chartrose* (Paris: Honoré Champion, 2014), 837–43.

[26] MSS. Oxford, Bodleian Library, Cod. Laud Misc. 540; Basel, Universitätsbibliothek, A IV 14 (donated by Antonius Rütschman, the dean at Rhe-

For the house of Bourgfontaine a certain secular clerk composed, between 1330/1334 and 1339, a collection of exemplary stories in French verse under the title *Le Tombel de Chartrose*.[27] The collection is dedicated to Eustache, prior of Bourgfontaine from 1325 to 1340, although it is not clear whether he commissioned the book.[28] The *Tombel* contains thirty-one *contes* from (or related to) the *Collationes* of John Cassian, the *Dialogi* of Gregory the Great, the *Legenda aurea* of Jacobus de Voragine, and other written sources. The majority of the Tombel's *exempla* can be found in the *Alphabetum narrationum* by Arnold of Liège, and it is certainly possible that the *Alphabetum* was the main intermediate source.

At the end of the prologue, the author invites his Carthusian friends to read the book aloud to illiterate people.[29] The idea seems strange, since Carthusians were supposed to remain in solitude and not to be involved in the pastoral care.[30] They did, however, accept guests in their monasteries, especially their donors and protectors, and in the fifteenth century this practice

---

infelden); and Xanten, Dombiliothek, s.n. (donated by Tylmann, the parish priest from Büderich). Note that in the Basel and Xanten manuscripts the *Libri VIII miraculorum* are presented as related to the *Dialogus* (Basel, fol. 131[r]: "*Istum librum composuit Cesarius Cisterciensis ut patet in prologo, et vocatur complementum Cesarii,*" and Xanten, on the flyleaf: "*Exempla Cesarij post Dyalogum suum collecta*"). The Xanten manuscript also contains the *Scala Coeli* by Johannes Gobi.

[27] See p. 170, n. 25 for the edition.

[28] At the end of the collection the author mentions that it was made under commission: "*Et pour celi qui le fist faire*" (*Tombel de Chartrose*, 647).

[29] "*j'entent a li faire prendre / par vostre main auctorité / D'estre leü et recité / A ceulx qui n'entendent la lettre*" (*Tombel de Chartrose*, 163).

[30] According to the Carthusian Customary, Carthusians preach by hands and not by mouth: "*ut quia ore non possumus, dei verbum manibus predicemus*" (Guigo I, *Consuetudines Cartusie* 28, 2–4, ed. and trans. a Carthusian [M. Laporte], SCh 313 [Paris: Cerf, 1984], 225). Although Denys the Carthusian († 1471) composed his *Sermones ad saeculares* with no express intention to deliver them personally, some monks were nevertheless opposed even to written sermons (see Denys Turner, "Why Did Denys the Carthusian Write *Sermones ad saeculares?*" in *Medieval Monastic Preaching*, ed. Carolyn Muessig [Leiden: Brill, 1998], 19–35).

became more and more common. The *Tombel* may not be the only vernacular *exempla* collection from the Carthusian milieu.

According to some scholars, the Carthusian brother Robert, who wrote the devotional treatise *Le Chastel perilleux* for his cousin, a Benedictine nun of the order of Fontevrault, may have been the same person as the compiler of the *Trésor de l'âme*, a fourteenth-century collection of 133 *exempla*.[31]

As for Cistercian *exempla* collections, Carthusians showed some interest in them, but on a lesser scale than did Canons Regular and Benedictines, as surviving manuscripts indicate:

Carthusian manuscripts of the Dialogus

Bs   Basel, Universitätsbibliothek, B VIII 18, 15th century (1404) – Saint Margarethental, Basel – Version B

ChM   Charleville-Mézieres, Bibliothèque municipale, 233, 14th century (1397). Dist I–VI. – Notre-Dame du Mont-Dieu, Raucourt, Ardennes

P   Paris, Bibliothèque nationale de France, lat. 3597, 15th century (1461). Dist I–VI. – Vauvert, Paris

U4   Utrecht, Universiteitsbibliotheek, Cat. 178, 15th century (1444) – Sint-Martens-Bos near Grammont, then Nieuwlicht or Nova Lux, Utrecht

Wr   Wrocław, Biblioteka Uniwersytecka, Akc. 1948/693 (olim Liegnitz, Petro-Paulinische Kirchenbibliothek, 30), 15th century (1457). Version C – Domus Passionis Christi, Legnica

Additionally, according to the fifteenth-century library catalog from Aggsbach (Lower Austria), the monastery had a copy of the *Dyalogus Cesarii de multis exemplis* (call number G 10[32]).

---

[31] Marie Brisson, "Frère Robert, chartreux du XIVᵉ siècle," *Romania* 87, no. 348 (1966): 543–50.

[32] Theodor Gottlieb, et al., eds., *Mittelalterliche Bibliothekskataloge Österreichs*, ed. Theodor Gottlieb, et al., vol. 1, *Niederoesterreich* (Aalen: Scientia, 1915), 594.

Carthusian Manuscripts of the Liber

Olomouc, Vědecká knihovna, M II 141, late 14th– first half of the
  15th century – Domus Vallis Iosaphat, Dolany near Olomouc
Trier, Stadtbibliothek, 1176/478 4°, 17th century – Saint Albano,
  Trier

Carthusian Manuscripts of the Exordium

Brussels, Bibliothèque Royale de Belgique, 7215–16 (3877), 15th
  century (1439) – Onze-Lieve-Vrouwe-Kapelle, Herne, Brabant
Brussels, Bibliothèque Royale de Belgique, 7237–40 (3878), 15th
  century – Sint-Sophia van Constantinopel, 's-Hertogenbosch,
  Netherlands.

Almost all the manuscripts are from the fifteenth century,
the period deeply marked by the reforming trends. Carthusians themselves did not join the monastic reform movement.
They saw themselves as simply not needing it, as is suggested
by the famous catchphrase *Cartusia numquam reformata, quia
numquam deformata* ("The Carthusian Order was never reformed, because it was never deformed").[33] As Henry of Kalkar
(† 1408) stated in his *Ortus et decursus ordinis Cartusiensis*, the
successful observance of the rule through the centuries was due
to the controlled acceptance of new members, seclusion from
the world, the distance kept between monks, and balanced
constitutiones.[34] The much-hailed stability of the Carthusian

---

[33] Jacques Dubois, "Cartusia numquam reformata," in *Dizionario degli
istituti di perfezione,* ed. Guerrino Pelliccia and Giancarlo Rocca, vol. 2 (Rome:
Edizioni Paoline, 1975), col. 803–5; Heinrich Rüthing, "Die Kartäuser und die
spätmittelalterlichen Ordensreformen," in *Reformbemühungen und Observanzbestrebungen im spätmittelalterlichen Ordenswesen,* ed. Kaspar Elm (Berlin:
Duncker & Humblot, 1989), 35–69. It should be noted, however, that Carthusians apparently did not hesitate to destroy records of transgressions; see
Jörg Sonntag, "Phantoms of Remembrance. Creative Selection in Medieval
Religious Life" (Berlin: De Gruyter, 2021), 153–69, here 163; https://doi.org
/10.1515/9783110757279-010.

[34] Rüthing, "Die Kartäuser," 37.

order did not, however, exclude either the inner change or a certain degree of involvement in the reform movements.

Praised as *regula et mensura aliarum religionum* ("rule and measure for other religious orders"),[35] Carthusians indeed exercised a great deal of influence on other reform-aspiring orders, both as role models and as active promoters, despite their secluded and contemplative way of life. Devotional writings of Groote, Florens Radewijns, and Geert Zerbolt von Zutphen are deeply rooted in the Carthusian meditative tradition.[36] On the institutional level, the Statutes of the Windesheim Chapter adopted some elements from Carthusian customs.[37] The same is true for the Bursfelde *Consuetudines*.[38] The Carthusian Leonhard Paetrer from Gaming conducted the visitation of Melk in 1418 together with the Cistercian Angelus of Rein. Among the persons involved in the reform of the Saint Aegidius in Nuremberg was the prior from the Nuremberg Charterhouse, as well as the provost from Neunchirchen am Brand.[39]

It is not possible to exclude the possibility that some Charthusian houses became acquainted with the *Dialogus* in the context of reform. The Charterhouse Mont-Dieu was under the influence of the *Devotio moderna*,[40] and manuscript ChM, which belonged to this monastery, is very close to the manu-

---

[35] Rüthing, "Die Kartäuser," 39.

[36] Otto Gründler, "*Devotio moderna atque antiqua*: The Modern Devotion and Carthusian Spirituality," in *The Spirituality of Western Christendom*, vol. 2, *The Roots of the Modern Christian Tradition*, ed. Rozanne Elder, CS 55 (Kalamazoo, MI: Cistercian Publications, 1984), 27–45. In 1374 Groote himself entered the Carthusian monastery at Monnikhuizen near Arnhem and stayed there for the next three years.

[37] Rüthing, "Die Kartäuser," 42.

[38] Edeltraud Klueting, *Monasteria semper reformanda: Kloster- und Ordensreformen im Mittelalter* (Münster: LIT, 2005), 29; Pius Engelbert, "Die Bursfelder Benediktinerkongregation und die spätmittelalterlichen Reformbewegungen," *Historisches Jahrbuch* 103 (1983): 35–55.

[39] On visitations by Carthusians, see Rüthing, "Die Kartäuser," 50–52.

[40] See Véronique Beaulande-Barraud, "Foi de chartreux: la 'dévotion moderne' au Mont-Dieu," *Revue historique ardennaise* 46 (2014):13–28.

scripts from Bethlehem (W2) and Rooklooster (W1), both members of the Chapter of Windesheim. For other manuscripts, the connections to the reform context is not established. MS. P, from the Charterhouse of Vauvert in Paris, shows some similarities with manuscript ChM but was not copied from it. Manuscript Bs was probably copied from a Cistercian exemplar. As was discussed above, this manuscript transmits Version B of the *Dialogus*, with a notable addition of the vision of Gûta from Günterstal, not attested elsewhere. The first part (Dist. I–VI) of manuscript U4, from Sint-Martens-Bos Charterhouse, is close to MS. Brussels, Bibliothèque Royale de Belgique, 551 (2120), donated in 1442 by the Franciscan Peter de Ligno to Poor Clares from Bethlehem, Ghent. Finally, manuscript Wr transmits Version C of the *Dialogus* but is not directly related to any of the studied manuscripts.

The monks from Vauvert seem to have found the *Dialogus* particularly appealing, judging by the considerable number of notes by several hands in manuscript P. One of the readers left marginal *notae* in red, mostly in *distinctio* VII, dedicated to the Virgin Mary, which is not surprising given the intensification of Marian devotional practices among the Carthusians between the fourteenth and fifteenth centuries. More Marian feasts were added to the liturgical calendar, more instances of the *Ave Maria* were prescribed for monks and nuns to recite, and so on.[41] On fol. 228v, a reader highlighted the mention of the amazing humility of Mary (VII.45, "*Mira humilitas Regine celi!*"). In this chapter, Mary in fact complied with the demand of a woman who had kidnapped the baby Jesus from a statue in order to pressure the Virgin to save her own child. The reader also drew attention to VII.50 about the Virgin Mary giving a kiss to a monk as reward for his devotion (fol. 232ᵛ) and to VII.58, where she insisted on the proper burial of a bandit who had been devoted to her, calling him her chaplain

---

[41] Yves Gourdel, "Le Culte de la très sainte Vierge dans l'ordre des Chartreux," in *Maria: Études sur la Sainte Vierge*, vol. 2, ed. Hubert du Manoir (Paris: Beauchesne, 1952), 625–78.

(fol. 236ᵛ). On fol. 214ᵛ, the reader marked the beginning of Beatrice's story in VII.34, where Caesarius briefly summarizes her devotional practices: "*Quotiens illi speciales orationes siue venias secretius offerre potuit, pro maximis deliciis reputauit*" ("Whenever she [Beatrice] offered her [the Virgin] special prayers or prostrations in secret, she thought of it as of the greatest delight"). It seems as though this reader was particularly interested in the cases of very personal interactions between Mary and her worshipers.

In other *distinctiones* this reader marked popular stories such as, for example, the one about the monk who wanted his tears to be seen by others and saw the devil instead (II.22; fol. 43ᵛ), the one about a priest who confessed his sin to a servant in a stable, with the result that a demoniac saw nothing wrong with him (III.3; fol. 55ʳ), the parable about the brothers *Date* and *Dabitur* (IV.66; fol. 112ᵛ), and harsh criticism of the modern state of the church: "*Ad hoc inquit iam devenit status ecclesie, ut non sit digna regi nisi a reprobis episcopis*" ("The state of the church is such that it deserves to be ruled only by bad bishops" [II.28; fol. 48ʳ]).

As a member of the contemplative order *par excellence*, this reader laid emphasis on the mental reading performed by Walter of Birbech (VII.38) with a marginal *nota* on fol. 224ʳ: a knight before his conversion to monastic life, Walter did not understand the reading in the refectory. So he invented his own: "*Quando manducare incipio qualiter pro me Dei filius sit ab angelo nunciatus et in vtero Virginis de Spiritu sancto conceptus mente retracto, sicque primum folium verto*" ("When I start eating, I behold in my mind how the Son of God was announced by the angel and conceived by the Holy Spirit in the Virgin's womb for me, and so I turn the first page").

On the following page (fol. 224ᵛ), another reader added a *manicula* pointing to the conclusion made by Walter: "*Talis est lectio mea cotidiana cuius finis, [finis]⁴² est prandii*" ("This is my everyday reading that ends with the meal"). Carthusian monks

---

⁴² The second *finis* is omitted in the manuscript.

seldom ate together in their refectory; they usually took their meals in the cells. Walter's technique may have been perceived as being useful, or familiar, if Carthusians from Vauvert did a similar meditation. Another reader seems to have been more interested in the stories about demons. He left the majority of his *notae* (black in a red square) in the fifth *distinctio*. This reader marked, for example, the observation that demons were more powerful around noon (V.2; fol. 132ᵛ), the story of the demon who mocked a monk who pretended to have a limp (V.6; 134ᵛ), and the explanation that demons in the form of cats, circling around chatting monks, did not dare to approach those who were serious and silent (V.6; fol. 135ᵛ). The interest of the Carthusians in the *Dialogus* was thus rather occasional. Avid readers and copyists, they could not miss such a popular, edifying book, especially given their love for monastic classics like the *Vitae Patrum* or Gregory's *Dialogi*. Despite many timely issues discussed in the stories, neither the *Dialogus* nor other Cistercian *exempla* collections became objects of intense copying inside the Carthusian order, even in the region where those collections enjoyed a considerable success among other religious communities.

Mendicant Friars

Were monastic *exempla* good for preaching? This question served as the title of the second section of the collected essays *Le Tonnerre des exemples*, which addressed monastic *exempla* collections in general and their use as sources for mendicant collections in particular.[43] As far as it concerns the *Dialogus*, the answer is definitely positive. Caesarius's stories were greatly appreciated by Dominican preachers. Arnold of Liège, the author of the famous *Alphabetum narrationum*, largely drew

---

[43] Jacques Berlioz, Pascal Collomb, and Marie Anne Polo de Beaulieu, eds., *Le Tonnerre des exemples: Exempla et médiation culturelle dans l'Occident médiéval* (Rennes: Presses Universitaires de Rennes, 2010), 103–285.

upon the *Dialogus*. It was not only his privileged source (Arnold took a total of 166 *exempla* from the *Dialogus*), but also an authoritative one. Arnold in fact always acknowledged the provenance of the *exempla* from the *Dialogus* with the reference *Refert Cesarius*. Remarkably, he did not treat the stories he borrowed from his fellow Dominicans in the same way. For example, he actively used the *Legenda Aurea* but never indicated it as his source.[44]

Johannes Gobi the Younger, another Dominican preacher and *exemplum* compiler, took many of Caesarius's *exempla* from the *Alphabetum narrationum* while apparently never having read the *Dialogus* itself.[45] He also indicated Caesarius and not Arnold as his source. Thanks to Arnold of Liège and Johannes Gobi, Caesarius's *exempla* reached a much wider audience than a monastic *exemplum* collection might have been expected to. But did Dominican friars, famous for their preaching *ad populum*, actually read the *Dialogus*? The list of surviving manuscripts of the *Dialogus* from Dominican provenance contains only four items. To my knowledge, there was no manuscript of Herbert's *Liber* or Conrad's *Exordium* in the possession of Dominican friars.

Dominican manuscripts of the Dialogus

Au   Augsburg, Universitätsbibliothek, Cod. II. 1. 2°14, first half of the 15th century. Version C – Dominicans from Nuremberg (then Benedictines of Saint Mang)

---

[44] See Elisa Brilli, "The Making of a New Auctoritas: The *Dialogus miraculorum* Read and Rewritten by the Dominican Arnold of Liège (1297–1308)," in *The Art of Cistercian Persuasion in the Middle Ages and Beyond*, ed. Victoria Smirnova, Marie Anne Polo de Beaulieu, and Jacques Berlioz (Leiden: Brill, 2015), 161–82.

[45] The library of the Saint-Maximin monastery in Provence, where Johannes lived, did not possess a copy of the *Dialogus*, although the *Alphabetum narrationum* is mentioned in the library catalog. See Marie Anne Polo de Beaulieu, "*Dialogus miraculorum*: The Initial Source of Inspiration for Johannes Gobi the Younger's *Scala coeli*?" in Smirnova, et al., *The Art of Cistercian Persuasion*, 183–210.

So   Soest, Wissenschaftliche Stadtsbibliothek, Cod.
          13, 15th century (1430–1435) – Dominican Wilhelm
          Hanstein, then the Dominican house in Soest

W3   Vienna, Österreichische Nationalbibliothek, Cod.
          14242, 15th century (1481). Version C – Dominicans
          from Brno

Wd   Vienna, Dominikanerkonvent, Cod. 196/161, 15th
          century (1450). Version C – Dominicans from Vienna

If we broaden our research and include the Franciscans, also famous preachers and compilers of *exempla* collections,[46] as well as Augustinian friars, the list does not become much longer. There are only two known surviving manuscripts of the *Dialogus* of Franciscan provenance (and none of the *Liber* or of the *Exordium*). That fact is hardly surprising, as the extant Franciscan *exempla* collections did not apparently draw upon the *Dialogus* or other Cistercian collections.

Franciscan and other Mendicant Manuscripts of the Dialogus

Ba   Bamberg, Staatsbibliothek, Msc. Patr. 59, beginning
          of the 15th century. Dist I–V. – Saint Anne monastery
          in Bamberg – Version C

Br2   Brussels, Bibliothèque Royale de Belgique, 551
          (2120), 15th century (before 1442) – donated in 1442
          by the Franciscan Peter de Ligno to the Poor Clares
          of Bethlehem, Ghent

M6   Munich, Bayerische Staatsbibliothek, Clm 8394,
          15th century – Fol. 6ʳ–11ᵛ – Augustinian friars from
          Munich

The listed manuscripts show a great deal of textual diversity. Manuscript So belongs to the same family as the manuscripts

---

[46] Jean-Claude Schmitt, "Recueils franciscains d'*exempla* et perfectionnement des techniques intellectuelles du XIIIᵉ au XVᵉ siècle," *Bibliothèque de l'École des chartes* 135 (1977): 5–22.

from Clairvaux (T1 and T2) and is textually very close to manuscripts Bo (belonging to Canonesses Regular from Amsterdam) and Ha (from the Cistercian Eiteren abbey in the province of Utrecht).

Manuscript Au transmits Version C of the *Dialogus*. The question of whether this manuscript was copied by Dominicans remains open. One piece of evidence is that it has traces of a chain. Since the Benedictines of Saint Mang did not chain their books, the chain may have been added in Nuremberg, and it is possible to assume that the manuscript was at least consulted by the Dominicans. Manuscripts Wd and W3 also transmit Version C. The two are extremely close to one another and to manuscript K from the Benedictine abbey of Kremsmünster.

The Franciscan manuscript Ba, which also transmits Version C, was apparently copied from a Cistercian exemplar, judging by its *incipit*: "*Incipit prologus in dyalogum Cesarii de miraculis in ordine nostro et extra peractis.*" According to the probe collation, it is close to the manuscripts from Rein, having the same *incipit*, and from Altzella, but it was not copied from either of them, or they from it.

As for manuscript Br2, it was first in the possession of a certain Peter de Ligno, who donated it to the Poor Clares of Bethlehem, Ghent, in 1442. As was pointed out above, this manuscript is close to manuscript U4, from Utrecht, but also to other manuscripts from the region of Brabant and Vallonia, for example, Br1 from Aulne or Na from Jardinet. Like the manuscripts from Aulne and Jardinet, this manuscript has *Cesarius* and *Apollonius* in the second part (Dist. VII–XII).

The manuscript from the house of Augustinian friars in Munich (M 6) is unique in many ways. It transmits a drastically shortened version of the *Dialogus* without the dialogical frame, significantly recalling Version E. The selection of stories, though, is different, and the prologues to each *distinctio* are retained. What is particularly striking is the fact that the compiler rewrote the Prologue to the *Dialogus* in the first-person singular, so boldly revealing Caesarius's authority, and in the third-person singular, to present his own editorial intent, as well as adding some German glosses, probably in order to be perfectly well understood by his local readers:

> *Colligite fragmenta ne pereant, id est, leset zů sammen dy drümer der speiß etc. Ego Cesarius ordinis Cisterciensis fui per abbatem meum et alios rogatus ut scriberem miracula id est die geschicht que acciderunt ut perpetuarem ea ne venirent in vergessen et putarunt quod essent dampnum irrecuperabile si talia non schriberentur vel vermerkt wurden. Ille autem qui hic nominari nult ex iam prenominato dyalogo extrahere conatus est propter se et simplices egregia dicta ex eodem libro ad edificationem simplicium non curans subtilitatem sed benignitatem quasi ille qui ex paucis libenter colligeret multa* (fol. 6ʳ).

("Gather the fragments that nothing be lost [i.e., *leset zů sammen dy drümer der speiß*, etc.]. I, Caesarius of the Cistercian Order, was asked by my abbot and many others to write down the miracles [i.e., *die geschicht*] that had happened, and to perpetuate them, so that they would not go [*in vergessen*], for it would be an irreparable loss if such stories were not written down [*vel vermerkt wurden*]. On the other hand, he who does not want to be named here tried to collect remarkable deeds from the aforementioned *Dialogus*, for himself and for the simple ones, caring not about fineness but about kindness, as one who gathers a lot from few things.")

This version transmits only the first part of the *Dialogus* (*distinctiones* I to VI). The fifth *distinctio*, *De daemonibus*, is intentionally omitted: "*Quintam distinctionem de demonibus obmisi*" (for being too sensitive for the intended audience?). It is difficult to speculate about the origin of this version, since it is so far found only in one manuscript. Judging by the presence of both the *Vita Hildegundis* and the additional story in the end of *distinctio* II (see summary in Appendix 2, pp. 279–80), it was based on Version B of the text. It is worth noting, however, that the compiler retained the chapter about the foundation of the

Cistercian Order (I.1 in Strange's edition), which may indicate a connection to the Cistercian milieu.

Earlier I insisted on the importance of the fifteenth-century reform movements for the transmission and reception of the *Dialogus* and other Cistercian *exempla* collections. The mendicant friars also strove to restore their own primitive observance, but in different ways and with different implications.

The Dominican Observant reform started with modest success. In 1399, when Raymond of Capua, the reforming general for the Roman obedience, died in Nuremberg, only a few monasteries in the province of Teutonia were reformed, among them the house in Nuremberg that had already established the regular observance in 1396. There were in fact many objections to the reform, summarized thirty years later by Johannes Nider († 1438) in his *Tractatus de reformatione status coenobitici* (1431). Many friars raised concerns that the reform would bring trouble and dissent, discourage those who wished to join the order, and cause deficiency of food and clothing in the reformed monasteries.[47] Despite such resistance, the reform continued.

The monastery in Vienna was reformed in 1434, and the monastery in Brno in 1465, by Prior Innocent from Vienna, the head of the reformed convents of the Teutonia province. The proximity of the manuscripts from Vienna, Brno, Melk, and Kremsmünster may suggest a connection to the reform context. On the other hand, the community in Soest was reformed only in 1509, previous attempts having been unsuccessful.[48] Additionally, Wilhelm Henstein is known to have been quite hostile

[47] See Eugen Hillenbrand, "Die Observantenbewegung in der deutschen Ordensprovinz der Dominikaner," in *Reformbemühungen und Observanzbestrebungen im spätmittelalterlichen Ordenswesen*, ed. Kaspar Elm (Berlin: Duncker & Humblot, 1989), 222–23.

[48] Gabriel M. Löhr, *Die Kapitel der Provinz Saxonia im Zeitalter der Kirchenspaltung: 1513–1540* (Leipzig: Harrassowitz, 1930), *25–*26.

towards the Observants,[49] so it is hardly likely that the manuscript from Soest was linked to the reform movement.

Franciscans were also endeavoring to follow a stricter observance of their Rule, especially concerning poverty, which was crucial for the identity of the order. The reforming process, however, was not without complications. In fact, the fears expressed by opponents of the Dominican observant reform came true in the Franciscan Order, as the reform brought division between the reformed Observants and the unreformed Conventuals. In 1430, John of Capistrano († 1456), one of the leading Observants, upon the order of Pope Martin V composed the so-called Martinian constitutions aiming to reunite the Conventuals and the Observants, but the majority of the Conventual houses refused to agree to them. The formal separation of the Order took place in 1517.

Franciscan Observant reform resulted from many forces acting with different emphasis. Along with the inner reform efforts, as for example that by Colette of Corbie († 1447), which were quite successful in Burgundian territory, there were also numerous interventions in the affairs of the order by the kings and nobility, who imposed reform on existing Conventual houses or sponsored new Observant foundations, especially in Germany.[50] The reform movement had different aspects: along with measures to ensure return to the Rule, some reformers promoted education to ensure better pastoral care through preaching and confession, as well as observance of devotional practices like lauda-singing or processions.[51] The focus on spirituality was also strong enough, as some scholars have

[49] Bernd Michael and Tilo Brandis, *Die mittelalterlichen Handschriften der Wissenschaftlichen Stadtbibliothek Soest* (Wiesbaden: Harrassowitz, 1990), 39.

[50] Paul L. Nyhus, "The Franciscan Observant Reform in Germany," in Elm, ed., *Reformbemühungen und Observanzbestrebungen*, 207–17.

[51] Pietro Delcorno, "*Quomodo discet sine docente?* Observant Efforts towards Education and Pastoral Care," in *A Companion to Observant Reform in the Late Middle Ages and Beyond*, ed. James Mixson and Bert Roest (Leiden and Boston: Brill, 2015), 147–84.

pointed out, to blur the distinction between the Franciscans and older monastic orders.[52]

The *Dialogus* could certainly provide enough material both for pastoral preaching and for monastic self-instruction within the Observant context. However, given the small number of manuscripts of Franciscan provenance and the differences among the houses known to have possessed the *Dialogus*, it is difficult to draw conclusions about the relations between the acquisition of the *Dialogus* and the reform activities of its Franciscan readership.

The Franciscan monastery of Saint Anna in Bamberg joined the reform initiated by the Bishop Georg von Schaumberg in 1460, that is to say, after manuscript Ba had been copied. By contrast, Colette of Corbie established the monastery of Poor Clares in Ghent in 1442 as part of her reform, aiming at restoring the observance of the original Rule of the Order. Franciscan Peter de Ligno may have made his gift of manuscript Br2 in 1442 in this context. According to the colophon on fol. 205[v] of that manuscript, Peter took the religious habit at the Poor Clares' monastery (*"dum habitum religionis assumpsit ibidem"*). Colette, in fact, desired to have four friars attached to her monasteries: the confessor of the sisters, the other priest who was his companion and confessor, and two lay brothers.[53] The same folio as that naming Peter's clothing contains some historical notes related to the history of the monastery, calling Colette *"prima reformatrix."*

If the diversity of manuscripts of Dominican and Franciscan provenance makes it difficult to characterize the reception of the *Dialogus* among the friars in unified terms, some manuscripts present themselves as interesting case studies. For example, the manuscript from Soest (So) contains not only the

---

[52] Nyhus, "The Franciscan Observant Reform," 217.

[53] Joan Mueller, "Colette of Corbie and the 'Privilege of Poverty,'" in *A Companion to Colette of Corbie*, ed. Joan Mueller and Nancy Warren (Leiden: Brill, 2016), 101–29, here 126.

Dialogus, but also Caesarius's *Libri VIII miraculorum* and the *Scala coeli* (1323–1330) by Johannes Gobi. Given the considerable length of both the *Dialogus* and the *Scala coeli*, it is surprising to see them in a single codex. It is possible that there were initially two manuscripts made by the same scribe, one with the *Dialogus* and the other with the *Scala coeli* and the *Libri VIII*,[54] which were only later bound together. At some point the codex was again split into two parts because of the damaged binding and stored as two separate manuscripts until 1955. According to the *ex libris*, this manuscript belonged to Wilhelm Hanstein, Dominican friar and professor of theology: "*Pertinet totus liber fratri Wilhelmo Hansteyn sacre pagine p[rofessori] ordinis Predicatorum domus Zozaciensis.*" Wilhelm studied in Erfurt (1444) and in Rostock (1458); he was subsequently a prior in Soest (1463–1464) and a vicar of Westphalia.[55] It is possible that Hanstein himself gave the book to the Dominican house. The manuscript has traces of a chain whose form is characteristic of the house in Soest.

The manuscript has an important number of marginal scribal annotations, such as short titles, indicating the subject of the *exemplum* in question. Most often the annotations concern vices (and sometimes virtues), especially in the fourth *distinctio*: "*de superbia*" (fol. 38[r]), "*de uana gloria*" (fol. 39[v]), "*de ira*" (fol. 41[r]), etc. In *distinctiones* XI et XII, the notes emphasize different kinds of damned sinners: "*de aduocatis*" (fol. 147[r]), "*de dolosis*" (fol. 147[r]), "*de predonibus*" (fol. 147[v]), etc. It seems that the scribe was particularly concerned with the sins of greed

---

[54] See the arguments for this hypothesis in Marie Anne Polo de Beulieu and Victoria Smirnova, "Lire et faire lire des recueils d'*exempla*: Entre persuasion cistercienne et efficace dominicaine," in *Le Texte médiéval dans le processus de communication*, ed. Ludmilla Evdokimova and Alain Marchandisse (Paris: Classiques Garnier, 2018), 133–54.

[55] About Hanstein, see Gabriel Maria Löhr, "Die Dominikaner an den ostdeutschen Universitäten," *Archivum Fratrum Praedicatorum* 22 (1952): 306; and Gabriel Maria Löhr, "Die Dominikaner an den Universitäten Erfurt und Mainz," *Archivum Fratrum Praedicatorum* 23 (1953): 251.

and usury: "*nota bene de usurariis*" (fol. 21^v), "*contra auariciam*" (fol. 49^v), "*contra auariciam religiosorum*" (fol. 50^r), "*de morte usurariorum*" (fol. 146^r), etc.

Besides vices, the scribe highlighted mentions of saints, especially in the eighth *distinctio* ("*de sancto Andrea*" and "*de sancto Iacobo*" on fol. 111^r, "*de sancto Thoma*" on fol. 111^v, etc.), their feast days ("*de festo purificacionis*" on fol. 84^r, "*de passione Domini*" on fol. 103^v), and Marian miracles ("*nomen Marie pellit timorem*" on fol. 91^v, "*nomen Marie compescit temptaciones*" on fol. 92^r, etc.). Finally, in the tenth *distinctio*, the scribe drew attention to the miraculous phenomena in the natural elements: "*de fulmine et tonitruo*" (fol. 134^v), "*de fulmine*" (fol. 134^v), "*de tonitruo*" (fol. 135^r), "*de igne*" (fol. 135^r).

The *Libri VIII* have similar marginal annotations briefly announcing the principal subject of the *exemplum* in question: "*de auaricia*" (fol. 256^v), "*de accidia*" (fol. 256^v), "*exemplum de ebrietate*" (fol. 257^r), "*de depredacione*" (fol. 263^v), "*de usura*" (fol. 263^v), "*de pena usurariorum*" (fol. 264^r). As in the *Dialogus*, the emphasis is on vices, especially on greed and usury.

It seems possible, judging by the marginal annotations, that the manuscript was used or intended to be used in the context of *cura animarum*, probably as a preaching aid. The scribe not only added the marginal notes discussed above, but also made an additional table of contents on fol. I^r. This table repeats the titles of the *distinctiones* (*de conversione*, etc.) as well as the marginal annotations. The *Dialogus* thus became handier and easier to search, as is required for a preaching tool.

Manuscript Wd, from Vienna, also has a number of remarkable particularities. It was written by a certain Fridericus de Lichtenfelβ in 1450 (according to the colophon on fol. 162^r), who has not been certainly identified. Probably he was the same Fridericus Keil de Liechtenfels attested in the University of Vienna in 1444.[56] On fol. I*^{r} there is an important note of

---

[56] Franz Gall, et al., eds., *Die Matrikel der Universität Wien* (1377–1450) (Graz-Vienna- Cologne: Böhlau, 1956), 1:240 (1444 II R 21, *Natio Renensium*).

ownership, but unfortunately only partial, because the folio is damaged: "*Ille liber dialogi miraculorum . . . Cenam fratribus ordinis pre . . . domini 1459 finitus.*" The mention of *cena* might suggest refectory reading, even though the manuscript has traces of a chain, which indicates its use as a reference work. The surviving catalogue of the community's library (1513) does not, unfortunately, give any specifics about the *Dialogus*'s eventual use there. Caesarius's collection is mentioned among the books *In pulpito F anteriori superiori* under call number F 31, along with the *Vitae patrum*, lives of saints, and historiographic works like a *Cronica Polonie* and a *Hystoria Romana*[57] Curiously, on fol. 1ʳ, the manuscript presents Caesarius as an abbot: "*Incipit prologus in dialogum miraculorum Cesarii abbatis,*" so adding authority to the work.

The manuscript also has an important number of marginal notes, mostly summarizing the content of the story in question. For instance, in *distinctio* X, *de miraculis*, one reader left the notes "*de cruce non combusta*" (fol. 136ʳ; X.32 in Strange's edition), "*de meretrice*" (fol. 136ʳ; X.34), or "*de piscatore fornicario*" (fol. 136ᵛ; X.35). Such annotations not only emphasize the stories that caught the attention of a particular reader but also compensate for the absence of the proper chapter titles. The three aforementioned chapters, for example, are presented in the manuscript as "*Exemplum de quodam ciue,*" "*Exemplum notabile,*" and "*Exemplum aliud de piscatore,*" which do not facilitate the consultation of the manuscript, already seriously encumbered by the absence of a table of contents.

In *distinctio* XI, *de morientibus*, another reader made similar, though more detailed, annotations. Sometimes they also indicate potential addressees of the *exemplum* and its effects. For example, "*Nota mirabile exemplum pro eis qui religionem post multa peccata ingrediuntur atque pro consolacionem eorum qui religiosis in fine vite aduocant*" ("Note the miraculous *exemplum*

---

[57] Theodor Gottlieb, et al., eds., *Mittelalterliche Bibliothekskataloge Österreichs*, vol. 1, *Niederoesterreich* (Aalen: Scientia, 1915), 333.

for those who enter religion after having committed many sins, and for the consolation of those who at the end of their lives advocate for monks" [fol. 146ʳ; XI.17]).

The notes by a third reader not only summarized the content of some *exempla* but also appreciated Caesarius's theological and pastoral insights, especially—but not exclusively—those related to the theme of contrition, for example: "*quid differentia inter culpam et peccatum*" (fol. 12ʳ), "*quot sunt species contricionis*" (fol. 13r), "*de utilitate contricionis*" (fol. 13ʳ), etc. Even though such annotations do not run consistently through the entire manuscript (surprisingly, there are no annotations in *distinctio IX, de corpore et sanguine Christi*), they do make it easier to consult and to draw upon. Despite all the differences between the manuscripts from Soest and from Vienna, their readers' attitudes have much in common.

Caesarius's *exempla* were undeniably "good for preaching," even if the *Dialogus* itself was probably far from an ideal preaching tool. Not only did Arnold of Liège and Johannes Gobi use Caesarius's *exempla* in their collections, but other famous Dominican compilers did as well, like John Bromyard († 1352) in his *Summa predicantium* and Johannes Herolt († 1468) in his *Promptuarium exemplorum*. However, mendicant friars had no specific interest in acquiring the *Dialogus*, probably because Arnold of Liège had already done the job of extracting the most interesting and useful stories and conveniently organizing them alphabetically, or perhaps because Caesarius's work did not particularly resonate with the life of mendicant friars and their ways of constructing identities. Despite all this, a popular book like the *Dialogus* still had a chance to catch friars' attention and to be eventually used as edifying reading or even as preaching tool.

The important number of surviving manuscripts of known origin or provenance makes it easy (and somewhat self-evident) to approach the medieval readership of the *Dialogus*

from the socio-religious perspective. My goal is not to oppose different kinds of reading, given the obvious similarities among medieval religious institutions, but to understand how the members of different religious orders assigned meaning to the *Dialogus* and made Caesarius's stories relevant for their own situation.

Even at the dawn of printing, the *Dialogus* did not lose its appeal. Readers with different backgrounds but often with similar aspirations for spiritual renewal continued to read Caesarius's stories and to make *exempla* from them by finding inspirational exemplary figures, by adhering to the communal identity forged through the narration of miraculous events, by relating to the experiences of thirteenth-century Cistercian monks and nuns, or by finding a suitable story to illustrate a doctrinal point in a sermon. The story of the *Dialogus* and its reception thus continues.

PART THREE

The Way into Modernity

11

Incunabulum Editions

The transmission and reception of medieval *exempla* collections did not end with the medieval era but continued after it—or with it, if we accept Jacques Le Goff's thesis of a Long Middle Ages that ran up to the Industrial Revolution. The reading communities that copied and transmitted the *Dialogus* continued to exist, and the demand from preachers for good, edifying stories remained strong far beyond the end of the fifteenth century.

The revolutionary arrival of print did, however, bring many profound changes in cultural production and consumption of *exempla*. The marked increase of book production, allowing significantly fewer hours of labor and allowing the circulation of (almost) identical texts and images shifted the communication paradigm. The more efficient transmission of written information gave new importance to learning by reading. Printing workshops brought new forms of intellectual and economic collaboration, as well as new ways of advertising of texts through handbills, circulars, and sales catalogues.[1] How did the changes associated with the transition to print affect the transmission and reception of *exempla* collections? Did they acquire a wider audience? Did their moral and didactic message

---

[1] Elizabeth Eisenstein, *The Printing Revolution in Early Modern Europe* (Cambridge: Cambridge University Press, 2005).

become more efficient and effective, actually influencing the increased number of people they reached?

The *Dialogus* was one of the lucky medieval *exempla* collections considered important enough to become a printed book.[2] Its *editio princeps*[3] was produced in around 1473 by Ulrich Zell († 1507),[4] a pioneer printer from Cologne. Zell studied printing at Mainz, probably with Peter Schöffer, Johannes Gutenberg's principal assistant. Zell later moved and established the first printing workshop in Cologne. His first dated work—*Liber Johannis Chrysostomi super psalmo quinquagesimo*—appeared in 1466. Before 1473, Zell published about a hundred books, eighty of them with theological content. They were mostly volumes of the so-called *theologia practica*, small treatises intended for the use of monks and members of other religious congregations, as well as of parish priests.[5] The *Dialogus* fitted perfectly into this category.

Zell's *editio princeps* of the *Dialogus* is an in-folio volume printed in Gothic characters (Type 2:115G). The text covers 310 folios with double columns of 35 lines. There is no specific printer's mark or colophon, which was typical for the early Cologne printing production (for the Cologne printers, self-

---

[2] On *incunabulum* editions of medieval *exempla* collections, see Nicolas Louis, "L'exemplum en pratiques: production, diffusion et usages des recueils d'exempla latins aux XIIIe–XVe siècles," PhD dissertation, École des Hautes Études en Sciences Sociales Facultés Universitaires Notre Dame de la Paix, 2013), 144–53. Available online: https://tel.archives-ouvertes.fr/tel-00860685/document.

[3] ISTC No. ic00030000. *Gesamtkatalog der Wiegendrucke.* n° 5880. Available online: http://www.gesamtkatalogderwiegendrucke.de/docs/GW05880.htm.

[4] Jakob Schnorrenberg, "Zell, Ulrich," in *Allgemeine Deutsche Biographie* 45 (1900): 19–21.

[5] Severin Corsten, "Die Blütezeit des Kölner Buchdrucks," *Rheinische Vierteljahrsblätter* 40 (1976): 135. Corsten underlines the fact that that it was characteristic for the second generation of Cologne printers to print books for the university, for instance Koelhoff (139).

awareness came later).[6] Zell's edition, however, has some particularities, probably introduced with the intention of personalizing it—specifically additional *explicits* in *distinctiones* III[7] and IX.[8] After the latter *explicit*, Zell left the second column and following verso blank. As of today, thirty-nine copies, full or fragmentary, are known to be in public institutions. Which manuscript did Zell use as the basis for his *editio princeps*? Since in the last six *distinctiones* of his edition the Novice is called *Apollonius* and the Monk *Cesarius*, the second part of the base manuscript belonged to the branch "*In civitate Lemovicensi*" of the "*Quidam princeps*" family.[9] Among the manuscripts from this branch are Br1 from Aulne, Na from Jardinet, Br2 from Bethlehem in Ghent, Co from the Crosiers' house in Cologne, and Li1 from the Crosiers' house in Liège. According to the probe collation, however, none of these manuscripts was the base text for Zell's edition.

The first part of the edition (*distinctiones* I–VI) belongs to another branch of the textual tradition (not "*In civitate Lemovicenci*," but "*In civitate ut opinor Wormacia*") and stands close to manuscripts Dü1 (probably from Heisterbach), Dü2 (from Altenberg), and Be1 (from Himmerod), forming the sub-branch "*Abbas sancti Trudonis.*" Once again, none of them served as basis for Zell's edition. As was discussed above, the *Dialogus* often circulated in two volumes, and in some manuscripts the first and second parts belong to different branches of the textual tradition. The hybrid character of the *editio princeps* is therefore not surprising.

---

[6] Severin Corsten, *Die Anfänge des Kölner Buchdrucks* (Cologne: Greven, 1955), 14.

[7] "*Dyalogi miraculorum Cesarii Cisterciensis monachi in valle sancti Petri. Tertia distinctio de confessione. Explicit feliciter. Deo gratias*" (unpaginated).

[8] "*Cesarii Cisterciensis monachi in valle sancti Petri, quae vulgo Heysterbachum dicimus. Nona distinctio de venerabilissimo sacramento corporis et sanguinis domini nostri Jhesu Christi. Explicit feliciter. Deo Gratias*" (unpaginated).

[9] See Part II, p. 49–52.

Where did the idea to print the *Dialogus* come from? The Crosiers from Cologne may have contributed to Zell's interest in Caesarius's work. Not only did they possess a copy of the *Dialogus* (Co), but they were probably involved in the development of printing in the city[10] and had some important *incunabula* in their library.[11] Besides, Zell donated some books to the community, as we know from the colophon of the *Sermones viae et veritatis* by Lucas Patavinus: *"Hunc librum cum pluribus aliis reperimus ex parte magistri Ulrici impressoris pie memorie, ut fideliter pro eo et suis oremus quatinus in librum uite nomen eius scribatur"* ("We received this book, along with many others, from master Ulrich, the master printer of pious memory, so we will pray faithfully for him and his relatives until his name is written in the Book of Life").[12] It is therefore possible that the initiative for printing the *Dialogus* may have been if not directly inspired, at least encouraged by the book-loving Cologne Crosiers, who appreciated Cistercian *exempla* and were interested in printed books. Unfortunately, it is unknown whether they themselves had a printed copy of the *Dialogus*.

---

[10] Corsten, *Die Anfänge des Kölner Buchdrucks*, 31. In 1462, Nicolaus de Haarlem, from the Cologne Crosier house, became prior in Hoorn. The master printer Arnold Therhoernen, who probably learned the art of printing with Zell, also came originally from Hoorn. It is not impossible that Nicolaus negotiated the opening of Therhoernen's workshop in Cologne. He also maintained a relationship with the Cologne Crosiers and may, according to Corsten, have encouraged them to explore the world of printed books. See also Hans Lülfing, "Hoernen, Arnold ter," in *Neue Deutsche Biographie* 9 (1972): 356–57; available online: https://www.deutsche-biographie.de/pnd137661495.html#ndbcontent.

[11] For example, the *Philobiblion* of Richard de Bury, first printed in Cologne in 1473 (Rudolf Juchhoff, "Aufgang und Blütezeit des Kölner Buchdrucks," in *Fünf Jahrhunderte schwarze Kunst in Köln*, ed. Adam Wienand [Cologne: Bibliophilen-Ges, 1953], 12). On the library of the Cologne Crosiers, see also Robert Haaß, *Die Kreuzherren in den Rheinlanden* (Bonn: Röhrscheid, 1932), 79; and Joseph Theele, "Einzeltypenstempel auf Kölner Einbänden," in *Gutenberg-Jahrbuch* 1 (1926), 9–13, 10.

[12] Juchhoff, "Aufgang und Blütezeit," 12.

The book of sermons given by Zell to the Crosiers was printed not by him but by another Cologne printer, Johann Koelhoff the Elder († 1493).[13] Koelhoff, who originated from Lübeck, probably studied printing in Venice with Wendelinus de Spira before moving to Cologne. Koelhoff's first published book—*Praeceptorium divinae legis* by Johannes Nider—dates from 1472. Zell and Koelhoff entertained close relationships, both professional and personal. Koelhoff even employed Zell on some occasions.

In 1481, Koelhoff printed the second edition of the *Dialogus*,[14] from the text of the first edition. It is an in-folio in Gothic characters (Type 7:95G), with the text covering 268 single-column folios of thirty-eight lines. In contrast to Zell's edition, Koelhoff's ends with a colophon: "*Impressique per me Johannem Koelhoff civem Colonie anno domini MCCCCLXXXI*" ("Printed by me, Johannes Koelhoff, citizen of Cologne, in 1481"). Currently fifty-nine copies (full or fragmentary) are known in public institutions.

The attention paid to the *Dialogus* by two competing master printers—even though on friendly terms—indicates the kind of demand for a book that justified their investment. With the arrival of the printing process, the *utilitas* of an *exempla* collection inevitably became the subject of commercial evaluation by the master printer, the new key figure in the production of books—who was responsible for obtaining money and estimating the markets.[15] Both Zell and Koelhoff had printed other *exempla* collections before the *Dialogus*. Zell, for example, had printed both Herolt's *Promptuarium exemplorum* in 1474 (reprinted in 1477 and 1478) and the *Gesta romanorum* in 1472

---

[13] Hans Lülfing, "Koelhoff, Johann d. Ä.," *Neue Deutsche Biographie* 12 (1980): 318–19. Available online: https://www.deutsche-biographie.de/gnd 102507554.html#ndbcontent.

[14] ISTC No.: ic00031000. *Gesamtkatalog der Wiegendrucke*, n° 5881. Available online: http://www.gesamtkatalogderwiegendrucke.de/docs/GW05881 .htm.

[15] Eisenstein, *The Printing Revolution*, 28.

(reprinted in 1482). Koelhoff had printed the *Bonum universale de apibus* in 1479 and the German *exemplum* collection *Der Große Seelentrost* in 1474 and 1489.

The Cologne book market seems to have been favorable to *exempla* collections. But to what extent did the move to printing affect the readership of the *Dialogus*? A small number of printed copies of the *Dialogus* belonged to the religious communities that had already contributed to the transmission of Caesarius's *exempla* collection and, unsurprisingly, especially among Cistercians. Himmerod Abbey owned Koelhoff's edition of the printed *Dialogus*,[16] bound with Johannes Zainer's edition of *De abundantia exemplorum* (*De dono timoris*) by Humbert of Romans[17] and a fifteenth-century manuscript collection of forty-eight *exempla*.[18] Two incunabula (both by Koelhoff) now in Düsseldorf University Library probably originated at Heisterbach[19] and Altenberg.[20] The library of the Vorau monastery of Canons Regular still possesses a copy of Koelhoff's edition,[21] and the incunabulum now in Liège (Zell's edition)[22] may well have originated in the Crosier house in Liège.

The majority of the *Dialogus*'s incunabula, however, come from monasteries that are not known to have possessed its manuscripts. A copy of Koelhoff's edition still belongs to the abbey of Wettingen (Salem's daughter) in Bregenz,[23] and a

[16] The incunabulum was sold in 2015. For the catalogue, see *Venator & Hanstein Bücher Graphik Autographen Auktion 136, 25. September 2015 Köln*, available online: http://venator-hanstein.de/assets/Pdfkataloge/Katalog _136.pdf.

[17] Ascribed in the edition to Albertus Magnus and published between 1478 and 20.VI.1481 in Ulm (*Gesamtkatalog der Wiegendrucke*, n° 00581. ISTC ia00217000).

[18] See the description in *Venator & Hanstein*, 286–87.

[19] Düsseldorf, Universitäts- und Landesbibliothek, an O. u. G.H.366 (Ink).

[20] Düsseldorf, Universitäts- und Landesbibliothek, Gult. G. 228 (Ink).

[21] See: https://www.gesamtkatalogderwiegendrucke.de/docs/GW05881 .htm.

[22] Liège, Bibliothèque du Séminaire Épiscopal, 6. E. 19.

[23] Bregenz, Zisterzienserabtei Wettingen-Mehrerau, Mehrerau WW 112 ca.

copy of Zell's to Bornem abbey, successor of Hemiksem (Villers' daughter).[24] Another copy of Zell's edition once belonged to the Cistercian women's monastery of Kentrop near Münster.[25] Kentrop was under the care of the abbey of Altenberg, and, taking into account Altenberg's long-lasting interest in Caesarius's *exempla*, it is safe to assume that Kentrop acquired the printed *Dialogus* at the suggestion or with the help of Altenberg. Eucharius Prey, a Cistercian monk-priest from Kaisheim (Lucelle's daughter) had a copy of Koelhoff's edition in 1544.[26] Before Prey, this book had belonged to a Brother Niedher from Neresheim (the Benedictine abbey of Saints Ulrich and Afra), who had received it from Alexius Strigel, a brother from Dillingen. In 1592 the book landed—as a gift—in the possession of a Daniel Lesher. Then it came into the possession of Leonhard Wölflin from Dillingen (attested in 1595 as a parish priest in Buchold), and then to Heinrich von Knoeringen, bishop of Augsburg. Finally, the book arrived in the library of the Jesuit University of Dillingen. Another interesting testimony to Cistercian reception of the printed *Dialogus* comes from a later period. In 1663, a certain Brother Paul from the Cistercian abbey of Zlatá Koruna (Goldenkron, the daughter of Heiligenkreuz) in southern Bohemia acquired an exemplar of Koelhoff's edition on the order of his abbot, Bernhard Pachmann (1661–1668).[27]

Besides the abbey of Neresheim mentioned above, Benedictine readership of *Dialogus*'s incunabula included monks from the abbey of Chemnitz,[28] where a copy of Koelhoff's edition

---

[24] See https://www.gesamtkatalogderwiegendrucke.de/docs/GW05880.htm.

[25] Bonn, Universitäts- und Landesbibliothek, Inc 298.

[26] Munich, Bayerische Staatsbibliothek, 2 Inc.c.a. 1041.

[27] Praha, Národní knihovna ČR, 40 F 24.

[28] Chemnitz was reformed in 1464 upon the initiative of the bishop of Meissen, Dietrich III von Schönberg. See Rittenbach Willi and Siegfried Seifert, *Geschichte der Bischöfe von Meissen 968–1581* (Leipzig: St Benno, 1965), 329.

was kept until 1543, when it was moved to the university library in Leipzig.[29] A copy of Zell's edition was owned by Saint Peter and Paul Abbey in Erfurt;[30] for information that this abbey also had a manuscript of Herbert's *Liber*, see above.

The presence of incunabulum editions of the *Dialogus* is also attested in several Crosiers monasteries. The houses of Marienfrede in Hamminkeln and Sint-Agatha in Cuijk each possessed a copy of Zell's edition,[31] and the Crosiers from Roermond had a copy of Koelkoff's edition.[32] Several congregations of Canons Regular also had incunabula of the *Dialogus*: a copy of Koelkoff's edition once belonged to the Canons Regular of All Saints' Monastery in Olomouc,[33] and a copy of Zell's edition now in the Museum Meermanno-Westreenianum (The Hague) was left to the Saint Leonard Priory of the Canons Regular near Liège by Anthonius Esterneel († 1483), a canon in Liège. Another copy of Zell's edition, now in the City Library of Trier,[34] belonged originally to the Canons Regular from Eberhardsklausen, who also had a manuscript of the *Exordium magnum*. Also now in the City Library of Trier is a copy of Koelhoff's edition[35] originally from the Premonstratensian abbey of Steinfeld, and the Premonstratensian abbey of Berne in Heeswijk still owns another copy of the same edition.[36]

Female readership of the printed *Dialogus* was small, but not negligible. Henricus Münden († 1490), the corn clerk (Kornschreiber) of Hildesheim cathedral and a canon of the secular collegiate Church of the Holy Cross, gave a copy of

[29] Leipzig, Universitätsbibliothek, C-14.

[30] Erfurt, Universitätsbibliothek, Dep. Erf. I. 4° 100.

[31] Marienfrede: Düsseldorf, Universitäts- und Landesbibliothek, Gult. G. 191 (Ink). Sint-Agatha's copy is still kept in the monastery.

[32] New Haven, Yale University Library, BEIN Zi +1048.3.

[33] Olomouc, Vědecká knihovna, II 48.309–II 48.310.

[34] Trier, Stadtbibliothek, Inc 1095 4°.

[35] Trier, Stadtbibliothek, Inc 747 4°.

[36] See https://www.gesamtkatalogderwiegendrucke.de/docs/GW05881.htm.

Koelhoff's edition to the monastery of the Sisters of the Order of Saint Mary Magdalene, also of Hildesheim.[37] From 1232, these Sisters lived according to the Augustinian rule and, with other Augustinian houses in the Northern Germany, were reformed under the assignment of the Council of Basel from January 25, 1435. In 1440, Johannes Busch, one of the leaders of the Windesheim reform, confirmed that the monastery was in good state.[38] Augustinian nuns from Marienbrink in Coesfeld, North Rhine-Westphalia, had a copy of Zell's edition of the *Dialogus*.[39] Marienbrink, founded in 1424, was initially a house of the Sisters of the Common Life, but in 1479, the community adopted the Augustinian rule. The house in Coesfeld was under the care of the house of the Brothers of the Common Life in Münster, an important book-copying center.[40] The Brothers from Münster also had a copy of Zell's edition,[41] which may suggest that the exemplar from Marienbrink was acquired under the influence of the Münster Brothers. Houses of the Brothers of the Common Life in Rostok[42] and Chełmno[43] also owned copies of Koelhoff's printed edition of the *Dialogus*.

Carthusian readership of the *Dialogus* remained small in the early period of printing. Only three incunabula survive from Carthusian monasteries—the Gaming Charterhouse near

[37] The Hague, Koninklijke Bibliotheek - Nationale Bibliotheek van Nederland, KW 171 B 2 [1].

[38] Josef Dolle, *Niedersächsisches Klosterbuch: Verzeichnis der Klöster, Stifte, Kommenden und Beginenhäuser in Niedersachsen und Bremen von den Anfängen bis 1810* (Bielefeld: Verlag für Regionalgeschichte, 2012), 2:745.

[39] Budapest, Magyar Tudományos Akadémia Könyvtár és Információs Központ, Inc. 72.

[40] Wolfgang Oeser, "Die Brüder des gemeinsamen Lebens in Münster als Bücherschreiber," *Archiv für Geschichte des Buchwesens* 5 (1964): 197–398.

[41] London, British Library MS. IB. 2988.

[42] Göttingen, Staats- und Universitätsbibliothek, 4 PATR LAT 1336/80 INC.

[43] Pelplin, Biblioteka Diecezjalna, Ink Fol. 466.

Scheibbs in the Mostviertel of Lower Austria had Koelhoff's,[44] the Charterhouse in Nuremberg also had Koelhoff's edition, left them by the will of Hermann Schedel (see below),[45] and the Charterhouse in Mainz had a copy of Zell's edition.[46] As for the mendicant friars, the only Dominican community known to have possessed a printed copy of the *Dialogus*, in this case Zell's, is the house in Dortmund.[47] By contrast, Franciscan readership grew significantly larger in the period of early printing than it had been in the manuscript period. Tertiaries from Saint Nicholas in Jüchen (Bedburdyck) owned a copy of Zell's edition,[48] and Observants from Greifswald and Bielefeld as well as Capuchins from 's-Hertogenbosch each had a copy of Koelhoff's.[49] Johannes Becker, a Franciscan friar from Rostock, bought a copy of Koelhoff's edition and presented it to his community.[50] The Observant friars from Wittenberg received their copy (also Koelhoff's edition) in 1504 as a bequest from Thammo Loesser, a canon and scholasticus in Meißen and archdeacon in Lusitz.[51] In 1535, the book was in the Bibliotheca Electoralis, founded by Frederick the Wise, elector of Saxony. A copy of Koelhoff's edition that once be-

---

[44] Wien, Österreichische Nationalbibliothek, Ink 10.G.6.

[45] Nürnberg, Historisch-Wissenschaftliche Stadtbibliothek, Theol. 427. 2.

[46] Now in the Gutenberg-Museum (Mainz).

[47] Cambridge, MA, Harvard University, Houghton Library (US), Inc 890 (15.2).

[48] Cologne, Diözesan- und Dombibliothek, Inc. d. 54. Saint Nicholas Tertiary house in Jüchen, founded in 1401, became a regular monastery in 1427 under the order of Dietrich von Moers, archbishop of Cologne. See Georg Allmang, *Geschichte des ehemaligen Regulartertiarierklosters St. Nikolaus 1400–1911* (Essen: Fredebeul & Koenen, 1911).

[49] Greifswald, Bibliothek des Geistlichen Ministeriums, 1558.1; Münster, Universitäts- und Landesbibliothek, Inc. 239; and Archivum Capuccinorum Hollandiae 's-Hertogenbosch respectively.

[50] Rostock, Universitätsbibliothek, Fg-36.

[51] Jena, Thüringer Universitäts und Landesbibliothek, 2 Op.theol. IV,41 (1).

longed to the Recollects from Nivelles[52] was also in all likelihood given to them by an individual donor.[53] A copy of Zell's edition now in the Bodmer Foundation once belonged to an unknown Franciscan community.[54]

The majority of the Franciscan houses that owned incunabula of the *Dialogus* were Observant, although there is no single pattern in their relationship to the Observant reform(s), except in the case of the houses in Greifswald, Wittenberg, and Rostock, which were reformed in 1480, 1489, and 1490 respectively by the Provincial Eberhard Hillemann († 1490), an active adept of the Martinian reform.[55] Was the reading of the *Dialogus* encouraged as part of Observant spiritual formation?[56] The Observants are in fact known for having developed substantial libraries. In comparison with non-Observant Franciscan book collections, the Observant ones tended to have more works of moral theology, as well as large numbers of sermon collections and preaching aids.[57] Fitting into both categories, the *Dialogus* may have been seen as a valuable acquisition, especially given its popularity in the German area.

The provenance of some incunabula indicates that the printed *Dialogus* was read in communities not known to have possessed its manuscripts. For example, the Carmelites from

[52] The monastery in Nivelles was initially the house of the Conventual Franciscans. In 1524, according to the wish of Margaret of Austria, it was handed over to Recollects, the reform branch of the Order.

[53] Brussels, Bibliothèque Royale de Belgique, INC B 63 (RP). The first provenance of the book is indicated as follows: "*Sum mre Guillam. Pontiam*" (not identified).

[54] Cologny (Switzerland), Fondation Bodmer, Inc. Bodmer 60.

[55] Ferdinand Doelle, *Die Martinianische Reformbewegung in der sächsischen Franziskanerprovinz (Mittel- und Nordostdeutschland) im 15. und 16. Jahrhundert* (Münster in Westf.: Aschendorff, 1921).

[56] The house in Wittenberg, however, received its copy from a donor who did not belong to the community.

[57] See the chapter "Franciscan Libraries and the Access to Books," in Bert Roest, *A History of Franciscan Education (c. 1210–1517)* (Leiden-Boston-Cologne: Brill, 2000), 212–13.

Malines, Belgium, owned a copy of Zell's edition,[58] as did the Celestines from Metz.[59] The Canons Secular as well seem to have taken some interest in the *Dialogus*. As was mentioned above, Henricus Münden, a canon of the Holy Cross Collegiate in Hildesheim, owned a printed copy of the *Dialogus*. Petrus Roden († 1483), a canon of the Magdeburg cathedral, bequeathed his exemplar of the *Dialogus* (Koelhoff's) to the cathedral school.[60] Incunabula of the *Dialogus* were also owned by the canons of the Saint-Dié Cathedral (Zell's),[61] of the Merseburg Cathedral (Zell's),[62] of the Kielce Cathedral (Koelhoff's),[63] and of the collegiate Church of Saint Leonhard in Frankfurt am Main (Koelhoff's).[64]

The age of print did not significantly change the readership of the *Dialogus*, although it seems to have become somewhat more diverse. Cistercians maintained their interest in the *Dialogus*, and some communities even procured a printed copy in addition to the manuscript already in their possession. At the same time, the number of incunabula of Franciscan provenance almost equals those from Cistercian monasteries. Another important aspect to consider is the increasing number of individuals who owned the *Dialogus*, among them renowned humanists, scholars, and book collectors.

In addition to the already-mentioned Leonhard Wölflin, Thammo Loesser, and Henricus Münden, a Heinrich Bentz

---

[58] Paris, Bibliothèque Mazarine, Inc 1232.

[59] Paris, Bibliothèque nationale de France, Rés. D 1327.

[60] Halle (Saale), Universitäts- und Landesbibliothek Sachsen-Anhalt, Ne 1193 z/1 4°. See Ilse Schunke, "Einbände des Magdeburger Domgymnasiums," *Zentralblatt für Bibliothekswesen* 78 (1964): 671–72.

[61] Saint-Dié, Bibiliothèque municipale, Inc. 114.

[62] Fritz Juntke, *Die Wiegendrucke der Domstiftsbibliotheken zu Merseburg und Naumberg* (Halle [Saale]: Niemeyer, 1940), 29.

[63] Andrzej Kwaśniewski, "Księgozbiór kapituły kieleckiej w świetle inwentarza z 1598 roku," *Archiwa, Biblioteki i Muzea Kościelne* 99 (2013): 43–92 (esp. 83).

[64] Frankfurt (Main), Universitätsbibliothek, Inc. qu. 1286.

bought a copy of Koelhoff's edition[65] in 1483 for 32 kreutzers.[66] The incunabulum from the House of the Brothers of Common Life in Chełmno was in the sixteenth century owned by a certain Mathias Kliepka. The exemplar of Zell's edition now in the Darmstadt University Library[67] initially belonged to the *doctor utriusque juris* Peter Rinck († 1501), rector of Cologne University.[68] A book collector and monastic patron, Rink wanted his books to be distributed *"zo der Eren gotz wyt ind breydt buyssen und bynnen collen"* ("to the glory of God far and wide outside and in Cologne"); as a result, some volumes came into the possession of the Franciscans from Brühl and of the Regular Canons from Gaesdonk, near Goch.[69] The *Dialogus* was apparently not among them, though, according to the provenance of the incunabulum in question.

Another copy of Zell's edition[70] belonged to a Guillaume Marcel, bursary of the College of Navarre (Paris), but the date of his ownership is unfortunately unspecified. As of 1586, a certain Johannes Wylych had the copy of Koelhoff edition now in the Düsseldorf University Library.[71] Hermann Schedel, doctor and humanist († 1485), who possessed an impressive seven hundred volumes, bequeathed his copy of Koelhoff's edition[72]

---

[65] Rottenburg, Priesterseminar, En 6.

[66] A coin and unit of currency in the southern German states.

[67] Darmstadt, Universitäts- und Landesbibliothek, Inc IV 322.

[68] Hermann Knaus, "Zum Kölner gotischen Bucheinband: Die Meister des Johann Rinck und des Peter Rinck," in *Börsenblatt für den deutschen Buchhandel* 26/23 (1970): 665–72; reprinted in Hermann Knaus, *Studien zur Handschriftenkunde: Ausgewählte Aufsätze*, ed. Gerard Achten (Munich-New York: Saur, 1992), 235–45. In 1636, the book was bequeathed by Caspar Wulfradt to the collegiate Church Saint Maria ad Gradus in Cologne.

[69] Heinz Martin Werhahn, "Die Bücher des Dr. Peter Rinck," in *Kölner Schule: Festgabe zum 60. Geburtstag von Rudolf Juchhoff*, ed. Hermann Corsten and Gerhart Lohse (Cologne: Greven, 1955), 181–88.

[70] Paris, Bibliothèque Mazarine, Inc D 166.

[71] Düsseldorf, Universitäts- und Landesbibliothek, Cult. G. 288.

[72] Nürnberg, Historisch-Wissenschaftliche Stadtbibliothek, Theol. 427. 2°. See Christine Sauer, "Handschriften und Inkunabeln aus dem Besitz Hermann und Hartmann Schedels in der Stadtbibliothek Nürnberg," in *Hartmann*

to the Charterhouse in Nuremberg, along with the "*Speculum humanae vitae, Sermones Ruperti de adventu Domini, Soliloquium Isidori, Franciscus Petrarka und anders.*"[73] Gerwin von Hameln († 1496), municipal clerk in Braunschweig, collected a remarkable private library of 336 volumes, including a copy of Zell's edition.[74] In Gerwin's library were patristic works, treatises on practical theology and spirituality (for example, the *Elucidarium* by Honorius Augustodunensis and the *Compendium theologicae veritatis* by Hugo Ripelin of Strasbourg), texts by classical and humanist writers (e.g., Seneca's *Epistulae ad Lucilium* and Petrarch's *De vita solitaria*), works on medicine and astrology, and a number of sermon collections, *artes praedicandi*, and preaching aids, like the *Repertorium morale* by Pierre Bersuire. Not a preacher himself, Gerwin von Hameln made these books available for the preachers from the Saint Andrew parish church in Braunschweig. He bequeathed his library to Saint Andrew in his will.[75]

Individual owners were sometimes members of monastic communities, such as Eucharius Prey, the owner of Kaisheim's version. Before converting to monastic life, Prey was a student in Ingolstadt (in 1513). He also possessed a copy of the *Manipulus curatorum*, published by Koelhoff.[76] It is not known whether he acquired the printed *Dialogus* before joining the Kaisheim brethren or as a member of the community. Private book ownership within the monastery was not uncommon in

---

Schedel (1440–1514), Leben und Werk: Akten, ed. Franz Fuchs (Wiesbaden: Harrassowitz, 2016), 242, Nr. 28.

[73] Bernhard Bischoff and Paul Ruf, eds., *Mittelalterliche Bibliothekskataloge Deutschlands und der Schweiz*, vol. 3/1, *Bistum Augsburg* (Munich: Bayerische Akademie der Wissenschaften, 1932), 801.

[74] Braunschweig, Stadtbibliothek, Inc 168.

[75] See Anette Haucap-Nass, *Der Braunschweiger Stadtschreiber Gerwin von Hameln und seine Bibliothek* (Wiesbaden: Harrassowitz, 1995).

[76] Pierre Aquilon, "La réception du *Manipulus curatorum* dans le monde germanique (1474–1500)," in *Le cabinet du curieux: culture, savoirs, religion de l'Antiquité à l'Ancien Régime*, ed. Witold Konstanty Pietrzak (Paris: Classiques Garnier, 2013), 205.

the late medieval-early modern period and could coexist with the traditional collective use.[77] Monks, especially university trained, often brought their books to the monastery. They could donate their books to the community, but sometimes they were also allowed to take their books with them when they left.[78] Another example of private book ownership within a monastery, though from a later time, is the incunabulum thought to be from Heisterbach, which belonged to a certain Henricus Scheffer, in all probability the lay brother Henry Scheffer († 1653), who was brother of the abbot of Heisterbach, Franz Scheffer (1628–1661).[79] Private owners of the *Dialogus* often donated or bequeathed their copies to religious establishments. Books such as the *Dialogus* were a good investment in one's salvation. During the owner's lifetime they could serve as tools of spiritual formation, and when donated or given in a will, they ensured prayers for the donor's soul. As Gerwin von Hameln stated in his copy of the *Dialogus*: "*Orate pro Gherwino de Hamelen donatore*" ("Pray for Gerwin von Hameln, the donor" [fol. 3ʳ]). Donors, however, did not necessarily take into consideration the actual needs and reading interests of the chosen monastery, often just looking for good hands in which to leave their valuable possessions.[80] Consequently, to a certain degree the donors shaped the reading of the community in question by their own literary preferences and understanding of the efficacy and suitability of the book-gifting.

---

[77] David N. Bell, "Monastic Libraries: 1400–1557," in *The Cambridge History of the Book in Britain*, vol. 3, *1400–1557*, ed. Lotte Hellinga (Cambridge: Cambridge University Press, 1999), 229–54, esp. 233–34.

[78] Christian Alschner, "Die Säkularisation der Klosterbibliotheken im albertinischen Sachsen (Mark Meißen, Leipzig und Pegau)," PhD dissertation, Karl-Marx-Universität, Leipzig 1969, 36. Available online https://slub.qucosa .de/api/qucosa%3A824/attachment/ATT-0/?L=1.

[79] See Ferdinand Schmitz, ed., *Urkundenbuch der Abtei Heisterbach* (Bonn: Hanstein, 1908), 83 (a selection from the *Memoriale defunctorum maxime religiosorum et conversorum Heisterbacensium*).

[80] Alschner, *Die Säkularisation der Klosterbibliotheken*, 70.

In the late fifteenth and sixteenth centuries, Caesarius's *exemplum* collection was read in roughly the same region where the manuscripts had circulated. But this being said, manuscripts of the *Dialogus* still competed for readers' attention. As annotations left by sixteenth-century readers suggest, the manuscript copies continued to be read. One example is MS. Tr, from the Benedictine abbey of Sankt Marien in Trier. In 1571, a brother not only made some marginal annotations but also asked future readers to pray for him: *"O frater quicunque hunc librum lecturus es ora pro me miserrimo peccatore ut Deus michi propicietur"* ("Oh brother, whoever you are, who will read this book, pray for me, a most miserable sinner, for God's mercy upon me" [fol. 164ᵛ]). His name, unfortunately, was erased from the manuscript.

Unsurprisingly, the circulation of the printed *Dialogus* was mostly limited to the area that remained Roman Catholic after the Reformation. Although the printing process facilitated the distribution of the *Dialogus* in terms of greater availability of copies, the political and religious situation of the Reformation era confined the book to Catholic regions. The *Dialogus* was not simply ignored by Protestant readers, but—as I will show further—actively rejected and severely criticized.

Before moving forward, I should mention one particular text that contributed significantly to the reception of the *Dialogus* in the sixteenth century and later. It is the *Liber de scriptoribus ecclesiasticis*, published in 1494 by the Benedictine Johannes Trithemius († 1516), abbot of Sponheim and Saint James's Abbey in Würzburg. The *Liber*, the first monumental biblio-biographical catalog, presents Caesarius among other important ecclesiastical writers, all the while praising his life and works:

> *Caesarius monachus in Heisterbach ordinis Cisterciensis, natione teutonicus Coloniensis agrippinae diocesis, vir devotus et in disciplina regulari praecipuus atque in divinis Scripturis longa exercitatione studiosus, composuit ad instructionem novitiorum quorum institutor erat, simplici et aperto sermone non nulla opus-*

*cula quorum lectio devotis et simplicioribus fratribus non est
spernenda.*

(Caesarius, a Cistercian monk in Heisterbach, of the German nation, in the diocese of Cologne, a pious man, distinguished in monastic discipline and assiduous in long-running
study of the Divine Scripture, wrote in a simple and clear
style many works, the reading of which should not be neglected by devout and more simple brothers.)[81]

Trithemius then described the *Dialogus* as an "*opus prolixus
de miraculis et visionibus diversis suo tempore factis in Germania,
quod ad imitationem papae Gregorii praenotavit*" ("a long work
on various miracles and visions that happened in Germany in
his time, which he named in imitation of the Pope Gregory"),
and, finally, gave a short list of Caesarius's other works, namely
the Sunday homilies, homilies for saints' feasts,[82] and an unidentified *Sermones ad novitios*, mentioned vaguely and without
incipit.

Did Trithemius himself have a copy of the *Dialogus*? It is
possible, given the fact that he cited the work's *incipit*: "*Colligite
fragmenta ne.*" Besides, he is known for having assembled a
very rich library during his abbacy in Sponheim. Because of
the losses that the library suffered in the later period, its exact
content is, unfortunately, unknown.[83] The 1517 inventory of
the books bequeathed by Trithemius to the Saint James monastery does not mention any work by Caesarius.[84]

---

[81] Johannes Trithemius, *Liber de scriptoribus ecclesiasticis* (Basel: Amerbach,
1494), fol. 63ᵛ.

[82] Parts two and three of Caesarius's large homiletic collection *Moralitates
evangeliorum*, published in 1615 by Johannes Andreas Coppenstein.

[83] See Michael Embach, "Johannes Trithemius OSB (1462–1516) und die
Bibliothek von Kloster Sponheim—mit einem Blick auf die Vita Juttas von
Sponheim (1092–1136)," in *Zur Erforschung mittelalterlicher Bibliotheken:
Chancen—Entwicklungen—Perspektiven*, ed. Andrea Rapp (Frankfurt am Main:
Klostermann, 2009), 101–36.

[84] Ivo Fischer, "Der Nachlaß des Abtes Johannes Trithemius von St. Jakob
in Würzburg," *Archiv des historischen Vereins von Unterfranken und Aschaffenburg*
67 (1928): 41–82.

Trithemius played an important role in the Benedictine reform of the fifteenth century, as one of the main representatives of the Bursfelde congregation (Sponheim joined it in 1470, under Trithemius's predecessor Johannes Kolenhausen), and he participated in the general chapter and effectuated numerous visitations.[85] Among many other monasteries, he inspected Saint Stephan Abbey in Würzburg, which possessed a manuscript of the *Dialogus*.

Thanks to Trithemius, Caesarius's work became an integral part of the church's literary history.[86] The *Liber de scriptoribus ecclesiasticis* tangibly shaped the reception of the *Dialogus* by highlighting Caesarius's exemplary life and the simplicity and clarity of his style, as well as by presenting the supposed audience of the *Dialogus* as pious and simple brothers. Over time these characteristics became commonplace, cited over and over again.

---

[85] See Klaus Arnold, *Johannes Trithemius (1462–1516)* (Würzburg: Schöningh in Komm, 1971), 22–35.

[86] There is no mention of Conrad of Eberbach or of Herbert of Clairvaux in the *Liber de scriptoribus ecclesiasticis*.

12

Jacob Fischer's Edition (1591) and the Controversy over Miracles

Toward the end of the sixteenth century, incunabula of the *Dialogus* became a rarity, but the demand persisted. At least, so Jacob Fischer of Harlem assures us in the Foreword *Ad catholicum virtutis studiosum lectorem*, which accompanied his 1591 edition of the *Dialogus* under the title *Illustrium miraculorum et historiarum memorabilium libri XII*.[1] Fischer was a chaplain of Saint Bavo Cathedral in Haarlem. In 1581, he fled the persecution of priests and found refuge in Himmerod. The abbot at that time, Johannes Roder of Saint Vith (1581–1596), not only offered haven to Fischer but also sponsored his studies. In 1586, Fischer became a doctor in theology.

In Himmerod, Fischer first composed the commentary to the *Catechism* of Peter Canisius in 1582 and the *Expositio canonis missae* in 1586,[2] before committing himself to the edition of the

---

[1] *Illustrium miraculorum et historiarum memorabilium lib. XII, Ante annos fere CCCC a Caesario Heisterbachensi, ordinis Cisterciensis . . . accurate conscripti . . . nunc ab innumeris mendis, quibus incuria veterum scriptorum & chalcographorum scatebant, diligenter repurgati, & recens in lucem editi* (Cologne: Mylius, 1591): *"Prodit denue, non semel quidem olim, typus euulgatus Caesarius, sed postrema, ut videtur, editio in annum a Christo servatore nostro nato 1481, incidit, cuius cum iam vix pauca, eaque non nisi in peruetustis bibliothecis reperientur exempla"* (prefaces in this work are not paginated).

[2] See Ambrosius Schneider, "Skriptorium und Bibliothek der Cistercienserabtei Himmerod im Rheinland: zur Geschichte klösterlichen

Dialogus. He did not start from scratch, though, but followed in the footsteps of Tilmann Bredenbach († 1587), canon of Saint Gereon and professor of theology in Cologne, an ardent adherent of the Council of Trent. Bredenbach apparently greatly valued the efficacy of *exempla*, as he himself composed an *exemplum* collection called *Sacrae collationes* in eight books, published in Cologne in 1584, designed to strengthen the faith of Roman Catholics in the face of Protestantism. The *Sacrae collationes* enjoyed a considerable success and were reprinted six times between 1584 and 1609. The *Dialogus* was among the many sources used by Bredenbach, as is acknowledged in the *Catalogus auctorum quibus in Collationibus sacris usi sumus* (the catalogue of the authors used in these *Collationes*).[3] Bredenbach did not limit himself to drawing upon the *Dialogus*, however, but decided to publish it whole. He was about to negotiate the publishing of his text when he died, before having finished the edition.

Textually, the 1591 edition follows the incunabulum version of the *Dialogus*. The names of the interlocutors have been unified: all twelve *distinctiones* have *Caesarius* and *Apollonius*. Besides proofreading Bredenbach's text, Fischer also made some emendations with the use of a manuscript version, although, as he himself admits, not the oldest and not the best—probably MS. Be1, from Himmerod.[4]

Fischer dedicated the edition to his benefactor, Abbot Johannes Roder. In his dedication letter, Fischer insisted on the effectiveness of the *Dialogus* in kindling devotion and encouraging Catholic faith.[5] He also emphasized that Caesarius had

---

Bibliothekswesens im Mittelalter," *Bulletin of the John Rylands Library* 35 (1952/53): 202.

[3] Tilmann Bredenbach, *Collationes sacrae* (Cologne: Cholinus, 1584), n.p.

[4] *"Caesarius ipse . . . ex quodam manu scripto codice, licet nec vetustissimo, nec correctissimo, non uno loco emendatus"* (*Ad catholicum virtutis studiosum lectorem*, unpaginated).

[5] *"magnum tamen haec eius scripta ad permouendas mentes catholicorum, eorum praesertim, qui pietatis atque uirtutis studio flagrant, momentum habent"* (*Epistola dedicatoria*, unpaginated).

greatly praised the abbey of Himmerod and the piety of its monks,[6] thereby conveying the relevance of the *Dialogus* to Himmerod's collective identity.

Fischer's target audience was, of course, much wider than one Cistercian community. In addition to the dedication letter, he included in the book the *Letter to the Catholic Reader*, which served as its preface. Once again, he underlined the potential of Caesarius's book as a tool of religious (self-)instruction. The preface then assumed an apologetic tone. Fischer admonished his readers not to pay attention to the unfair criticism of a certain follower of Huldrych Zwingli (*homo zwinglianus*), who had ridiculed the *Dialogus* for being full of fables. That was a lie, assured Fischer, so it should not perturb a Catholic reader.[7]

The aforementioned "homo zwinglianus" was Johannes Jacobus Frisius († 1611),[8] who wrote in his addition to the *Bibliotheca universalis* by Conrad Gessner, "*Caesarius monachus in Heisterbach ordinis Cisterciensis, Germanus, scripsit opus prolixum de miraculis et visionibus diversis suo tempore factis in Germania, Dialogorum de variis lib. 12. In his Dialogis omnia sunt plena fabularum, ut patet ex Meffrethi Hortulo Reginae*" ("Caesarius, a German Cistercian monk from Heisterbach, wrote a long work on various miracles and visions that happened in Germany in his time—the Dialogue on different [subjects] in twelve books. In this Dialogue everything is full of fables, as one can conclude from the *Hortulus Reginae* by Meffret").[9] This contains one

---

[6] "*Deinde ipse Caesarius, qui uestrum hoc Hemmenrodense . . . monasterium mirifice praedicat . . . uirtutes religiosorum eius prolixe persequens*" (*Epistola dedicatoria*, unpaginated).

[7] "*Nihil proinde mouebit Catholicum lectorem, illa hominis Zuingliani iniqua censura, dum scribit in his dialogis omnia fabularum plena esse*" (*Ad catholicum virtutis studiosum lectorem*, unpaginated).

[8] Arthur Richter, "Frisius, Johann Jakob," *Allgemeine Deutsche Biographie* 8 (1878): 107. Available online: https://www.deutsche-biographie.de/pnd120538504.html#adbcontent.

[9] *Bibliotheca instituta et collecta, primum a Conrado Gesnero . . . amplificata, per Iohannem Iacobum Frisium* (Zürich: Christophorus Froschouerus, 1583), 129.

particularly interesting detail: to describe the *Dialogus*, Frisius quoted Johannes Trithemius: "*opus prolixus de miraculis*," etc. Another point to highlight here is the mention of the *Hortulus Reginae*, also known as the *Sermones Meffreth*, a bestselling Roman Catholic sermon collection, written between 1443 (*Pars de sanctis*) and 1447 (*Pars hiemalis* and *Pars aestivalis*). Meffreth, a priest from Meissen, did indeed use a number of Caesarius's *exempla*.[10] While accusing Caesarius of telling fables, Frisius apparently did not read the *Dialogus* itself, but got the impression secondhand.

Attacking Catholic miracles and visions was a trend among Protestant writers and editors. From the very beginning, Luther was critical of the veneration of the saints and of their confirming miracles. In the *An den Christlichen Adel deutscher Nation von des Christlichen standes besserung* (1520) he compared the worship directed to the saints to the idolatries of Israelites following the time of the Patriarchs.[11] Denouncing the false miracles and devotions of Catholicism, in 1562 Hieronymus Rauscher († 1569) published a successful collection of Catholic miracle stories or "papist lies": "*Hundert auserwelte, grosse, vnuerschempte, feiste, wolgemeste, erstunckene, Papistische Lügen.*"[12] After the first hundred "lies" (*Centuria prima*) came the editions of four additional *Centuriae*.[13] Among these so-called lies are a number of stories from the *Dialogus*—for ex-

---

[10] For example, in the *Pars hiemalis* (Munich: Henricus, 1612), XI.59 (p. 117), II.17 (p. 204), V.39 (p. 127).

[11] *Deutsch-Deutsche Studienausgabe*, vol. 3, *Christ und Welt*, ed. Hellmut Zschoch (Leipzig: Evangelische Verlagsanstalt, 2016). For more details on Luther and miracles see Philip M. Soergel, *Miracles and the Protestant Imagination: The Evangelical Wonder Book in Reformation Germany* (Oxford: Oxford University Press, 2012), 33–66.

[12] Regensburg: Geißler, 1562.

[13] Rudolf Schenda, "Hieronymus Rauscher und die protestantisch-katholische Legendenpolemik," in *Volkserzählung und Reformation: ein Handbuch zur Tradierung und Funktion von Erzählstoffen und Erzählliteratur im Protestantismus*, ed. Wolfgang Brückner and Mathilde Hain (Berlin: Schmidt, 1974), 179–259, esp. 183–87.

ample, that a Catholic priest threw a pyx with the Host in the river in order to unmask the heretics pretending to perform miracles—with the help of the devil, of course (I.14),[14] and that the Virgin Mary restored to a priest his tongue, cut off by heretics (I.12).[15] Rauscher did not mention Caesarius, and it is unlikely that he had ever read the *Dialogus*. His probable source was the anonymous *Speculum exemplorum*, published in 1481 in Deventer.[16] The *Speculum exemplorum*, organized roughly by author, contains 103 *exempla ex Cesario* (*liber* VI). Being very popular, this collection assured—as had the *Alphabetum narrationum* earlier—a wider circulation of Caesarius's *exempla* and, not less important, the recognizability of his name.

Andreas Hondorff († 1572), a Protestant pastor from Droyssig (near Zeitz, Saxony-Anhalt) in 1568 published the *Promptuarium exemplorum*, a very successful *exemplum* collection.[17] The *Promptuarium* is organized thematically according to the Ten Commandments and was intended to serve as preaching tool.[18] The title recalls the collections by Martinus Polonus and Johannes Herolt. Hondorff knew both works well and used them as sources, mostly to deride false Catholic beliefs. In the

---

[14] Chap. IX.12 in the *Dialogus*.

[15] Chap. VII.23 in the *Dialogus*.

[16] Schenda, "Hieronymus Rauscher," 200–206. On the *Speculum exemplorum* see Reiner Alsheimer, "Speculum exemplorum," in *Enzyklopädie des Märchens: Handwörterbuch zur historischen und vergleichenden Erzählforschung*, ed. Kurt Ranke and Rolf Wilhelm Brednich, vol. 18 (Berlin: De Gruyter, 2007), col. 961–68 (esp. col. 961–65).

[17] See Heidemarie Schade, *Das Promptuarium exemplorum des Andreas Hondorff: volkskundliche Studien zum protestantischen Predigtexempel im 16. Jahrhundert* (Darmstadt: Studentenwerk Darmstadt, 1966); Philip M. Soergel, *Miracles and the Protestant Imagination*, 154–67.

[18] "*Damit ich nun in meinem Predigampt bisweilen wenn es Gottes wort erfordete und nötig were derselben Exempel wenig einführen köndte*" ("Because I wanted a handy supply of *exempla* that, while fulfilling my duties as a preacher, I might use when required by God's Word"). See *Vorrede an den Leser* (Foreword to the reader) in Andreas Hondorf, *Promptuarium Exemplorum: Historienn vnd Exempel buch: Aus Heiliger Schrifft, und vielen andern bewerten und beglaubten Geistlichen und Weltlichen Büchern und Schrifften gezogen* (Leipzig, 1568).

section dedicated to the Sixth Commandment (You shall not commit adultery), he added some *exempla* under the title *Mendacia monachorum*, where one finds the well-known story of Beatrice the Sacristan (*Dialogus* VII.34) indirectly borrowed from Herolt's *Promptuarium Discipuli de miraculis Beatae Mariae Virginis*.[19] For Hondorff, this story was one of the *"lügerliche Exempel damit die liebe Jungfraw Maria von den groben lügenhafftigen Papisten mehr geunehret denn verehrt worden"* ("deceitful *exempla* by which the papist liars do not honor the blessed Virgin, but dishonor her").[20]

Not all Catholic *exempla*, however, were despised. Some were too good—purposeful and edifying—not to be used. When Hondorff needed *exempla* about ungrateful children for his section four, dedicated to the Fourth Commandment (Honor your father and your mother), he used stories from the *Promptuarium* of Herolt.[21] The selection opens with the story about an ungrateful son's being punished by having a toad fix itself to his face (Sermon 24).[22] Herolt cited Caesarius as his source:[23] *"Unde legitur in dialogo Caesarii,"* although in the *Dialogus* (VI.22) the son was punished by a snake and not by a toad. This version of the story, in fact, originates from the *Bonum universale de apibus*, II.7.4.[24] An interesting detail: in the end, Thomas of Cantimpré reported that brother Johannes de Magno Ponte had seen the man with the toad in Paris. Herolt also mentioned the testimony of Johannes, whereas Hondorff simply said that the story had happened in Paris, then gave a reference to the *Dialogus*: *"Dieses findet man auch im Decalogo*

---

[19] Hondorff, *Promptuarium exemplorum*, fol. 272^v–73^r.

[20] Hondorff, *Promptuarium exemplorum*, fol. 274^r.

[21] Hondorff, *Promptuarium exemplorum*, fol. 158^v.

[22] Johannes Herolt (Discipulus), *Sermones Discipuli de Tempore . . . cum promptuario exemplorum* (Mainz: apud Joannem Albinum, sumptibus Bernardi Gualteri 1612), 139.

[23] He mentioned Caesarius a total of seven times; see Annemarie Brückner, "Herolt, Johannes," in *Enzyklopädie des Märchens*, vol. 6, ed. Ines Kölhler–Zülch (Berlin-Boston: de Gruyter, 1990), cols. 858–63, here col. 862.

[24] *Bonum universale de apibus* (Douai: Bellerius, 1627), 150–52.

[sic!] *Caesarii"* ("One also finds this in the Decalogue by Caesarius").[25] Finally, in another Protestant *exempla* collection, the *Epitome historiarum christlicher ausgelesener Historien* published in 1576 by Wolfgang Büttner († 1596?), Caesarius was cited as the one who affirmed that the events had happened in Paris: *"Dreizehen jahr hat er die scheußliche Kröte also getragen vnd ist wie Caesarius bezeuget dis werck zu Pariß geschehen vnd das selbst von viel Leuten aus hohem vnd niderm Stande gesehen"*[26] ("For thirteen years he had this dreadful toad on his face; as Caesarius attests, the event took place in Paris and was seen by many people from high and low society"). When necessary, Caesarius's name could still be used as an authoritative reference, with no negative connotations.

In sum, then, Protestants were well aware of the persuasive potential of exemplary narratives and did not hesitate to borrow from Catholic *exemplum* collections, even while mocking the miracle stories that promoted Catholic doctrine. In Protestant *exempla* collections of the sixteenth and seventeenth centuries, Caesarius, along with Johannes Herolt, became the most cited medieval author of *exempla*.[27]

But Catholics had to respond to Protestant attacks on the *Dialogus*. In 1562, Martin Eisengrein († 1578), professor of theology in Ingolstadt, attacked Rauscher in a public sermon,[28] faulting him for spreading lies and calumnies. Peter Canisius († 1597) also dedicated a sermon to the scandalous book.[29] According to Canisius, Rauscher probably invented the lies himself (*"fortassis et ipse finxit"*).[30]

But the true response to this campaign against Catholic *exempla* collections came with massive publishing activity.

---

[25] Hondorff, *Promptvarivm exemplorvm*, fol. 158ᵛ.

[26] *Epitome historiarum christlicher ausgelesener Historien* ([s.l.], 1576), 277.

[27] Brückner, "Herolt, Johannes," col. 836.

[28] Printed in 1563 and 1565. See Schenda, "Hieronymus Rauscher," 195.

[29] *Beati Petri Canisii . . . Epistulae et Acta*, vol. 3, *1561–1562*, ed. Otto Braunschweiger (Freiburg im Breisgau: Herder, 1901), 635–40.

[30] *Beati Petri Canisii . . . Epistulae et Acta*, 3:636.

Johannes Nas († 1590), for example, published six anti-Protestant *Centuriae*. Not only did he defy Rauscher's slander, but he also included in his *Centuriae* an important number of miraculous stories where Protestants acted dishonestly or were humiliated. For example, when the Lutherans from Augsburg failed to exorcise a demon from a girl, the exorcism was successfully performed instead by a Catholic priest named Simon Scheibenhart.[31]

The publishing enterprise of Jacob Fischer belonged to this polemical context. His ideal reader was apparently aware of and concerned about the controversy around Catholic *exempla* in general and those by Caesarius in particular. Fischer thus did his best to assure readers that the *exempla* in question were not lies, that is to say that they were perfectly consistent with Catholic doctrine. Indeed, he remarked, it is impossible to praise the writings of Caesarius without praising Catholic doctrine on the Eucharist, on the sacrifice of the Mass, on the sacraments of penance, anointing of the sick, holy orders, and baptism, on the invocation of saints, on purgatory, and on monastic and other religious congregations.[32]

As for the people who criticize the abundance of miracles and visions in the *Dialogus*, Fischer declares, they think of themselves as intelligent, but in fact they are not. If they know that such stories can be found in the writings of the most serious doctors of the church, they are shameless, because they prefer their own judgment to the sharper one of learned authorities. And if the accusers do not know that the stories are found in those writings, then they are just reckless, because they thoughtlessly judge things they do not understand. Prudent Catholic readers, therefore, should not be afraid to put faith in miracles and visions reported by Caesarius and righ-

---

[31] Johannes Nas, *Das Antipapistisch eins vnd hundert: Außerleßner, gewiser, Euangelischer Warhait: bey wölchen (als bey den früchten der Baum) die reyn lehr soll und muß erkan[n]t werden* (Ingolstadt: Weißenhorn, 1570), fol. 42ᵛ–48ʳ.

[32] "*Laudare scripta haec Caesarii non potuit, nisi simul laudaret dogmata catholica . . .*" (*Ad catholicum virtutis studiosum lectorem*, unpaginated).

teously to condemn those who reject all revelations as fiction-al.[33] Certainly not all miracles and visions are trustworthy, and Fischer's ideal reader was supposed to be able to distinguish those that were suspect from the genuine or, rather, to recognize the authority behind them. If accepted church fathers had published similar miracles, who could accuse Caesarius of telling lies?

In the times of booming bio-bibliographical catalogues, interest in Caesarius's persona was par for the course. Fischer added to his edition Caesarius's biography (*Vita Caesarii*), using Trithemius's notice and the biographical information from the *Dialogus*. Caesarius's narrative about himself not only provided enough details to compose an extended biographical notice but also promoted the *Dialogus*'s ethos of authenticity, expressed through Caesarius's posture as one who faithfully transmits information from reliable witnesses without adding anything fictional. Given all the controversy around the *Dialogus*, it is no wonder that Fischer highlighted Caesarius's happy quote—"*Testis est mihi Dominus*, etc."—by putting it on a separate page.

Elsewhere in the preface, Fischer elaborates:

> *Deumque testem invocare, nihil omnino a se confictum in hos libros relatum esse: quod ipso quoque tacente, res ipsa loquitur, dum non tantum quod gestum sit, sed etiam a quo, quo loco, quoque tempore et a quibus demum illud acceperit, tam accurate recenset, idque simpliciter absque omni verborum fuci, nullis non solum hyperbolis, sed nec amplificationibus, nuda scilicet apertaque oratione veritatis amica utens.*

> (And he invoked God as witness that not a single thing in these books had been invented by him, and while he himself is silent, the matter speaks for itself. Indeed, he indicated with great accuracy not only what had happened, but also

[33] "*Quod vero ad visiones et revelationes attinet . . . sciat Catholicus lector, ut prudentiae est non timere quibusvis revelationibus fidem adhibere*" (*Ad catholicum virtutis studiosum lectorem*, unpaginated).

by whom, where, and when, and who had told him about it. And he did it simply, without any verbal frills, not only without hyperboles, but also without amplifications, that is to say, by using bare and clear speech, which is a friend of the truth.)

Caesarius's scrupulous indication of places, names, and sources, often omitted by medieval scribes and editors, as I showed above, became a key feature of Fischer's strategy to promote the trustworthiness of the *Dialogus* and an important instrument of the construction of exemplarity. A medieval miracle story not from a universally approved source apparently needed to be historicized in order to be persuasive. A vague story about a certain priest or a certain monk could be perceived as suspiciously close to an invention.

Fischer also offered reflections on Caesarius's style. As I have demonstrated elsewhere, the language of the *Dialogus*, often considered to be simple, was in fact rather elaborate. Caesarius's Latin, while clear and correct, does have rhetorical embellishments and complex grammatical turns.[34] It was, however, not enough for sixteenth-century scholars. According to Fischer, Bredenbach corrected Caesarius's text by changing some words into some that were "more Latin."[35] Fischer nevertheless decided not to follow Brendenbach's emendations, but to give his reader "*ipsius Caesarii verba, etiam barbara et minus latina*" ("the words of Caesarius himself, even if barbaric and less Latin"). In Caesarius's defense, Fischer explains that the decline of Latin was characteristic of his times. But he also insists that Caesarius's purpose "*non fuit . . . verba sectari, sed*

---

[34] Victoria Smirnova, "Caesarius of Heisterbach Following the Rules of Rhetoric (Or Not?)," in *The Art of Cistercian Persuasion in the Middle Ages and Beyond*, ed. Victoria Smirnova, Marie Anne Polo de Beaulieu, and Jacques Berlioz (Leiden: Brill, 2015), 79–96.

[35] "*Dominus quidem Bredenbachius, modice tamen, stylum mutarat, aut verius paucula verba latiniora nonnulis locis substituerat*" (*Ad catholicum virtutis studiosum lectorem*, unpaginated).

res explicare; non linguam aut sermonem legentium perpolire, sed mores vitamque ornare et formare" ("was not to seek out words, but to explain things, not to polish the language or discourse for the readers' sake, but to adorn and inform their morals and lives"). The assumed simplicity of Caesarius's Latin created the effect of *verisimile* and—despite being a disadvantage from the standpoint of the stylistic beauty—contributed to his trustworthiness and therefore to the efficacy of *Dialogus's* didactic message.

Caesarius himself was very aware of how style reflected his authorial posture. In the prologue to the *Vita Engelberti*, one of his two hagiographic works, he stated that seeking verbal ornaments in the simple story and adorning sentences with rhetorical flowers were not suitable to his monastic profession—even if he had enough skills to do so. Judging the sweetness of oratorical jocundity less useful, he therefore decided to give an account of Engelbert's deeds and death in a simple style, using passages from Holy Scripture rather than sayings of philosophers.[36]

Reading the *Dialogus* in the seventeenth century demanded not only efforts of belief, but also of understanding. The growing time distance between the *Dialogus* and its seventeenth-century readers necessitated additional commentary. The paratext of Fischer's edition therefore includes a glossary of some medieval terms. It explains *realia* like *grangia, minuere, venia,* and *allodium,* and even some obsolete Medieval Latin words, such as *braxare.* To make his edition even more accessible to the reader, Fischer added an index of names and subjects, as well as adding marginal titles as useful instruments for organizing and rethinking the material.

---

[36] *Vita, passio et miracula s. Engelberti auctore Caesario Heisterbacensi,* ed. Alfons Hilka, *Die Wundergeschichten des Caesarius von Heisterbach,* vol. 3, *Die beiden ersten Bücher der Libri VIII miraculorum: Leben, Leiden und Wunder des heiligen Engelbert, Erzbischofs von Köln. Die Schriften über die heilige Elisabeth von Thüringen* (Bonn: Hanstein, 1937), 234.

On the whole, Fischer treated Caesarius's text with respect and did not intervene much. This attitude even earned him some criticism from Nicolaus Hees († 1702), an archivist from Himmerod, who in 1641 published the first printed history of Himmerod: *Manipulus rerum memorabilium claustri Hemmenrodensis*. In the chapter on the year of Himmerod's foundation, Hees suggests that Caesarius's dating (1134) was wrong, as according to the evidence of ancient manuscripts, the correct date was 1133. Hees wonders why this mistake was never properly addressed, let alone rectified, by Fischer, even though he had spent almost ten years in Himmerod, with access to most correct manuscripts. Fischer only corrected typographical errors, but not substance, because he was, Hees suggests, intimidated by the author's antiquity and authority.[37]

Fischer's edition enjoyed remarkable popularity and was reprinted three times. The first printing was made in Cologne in 1591 by Arnold Mylius († 1604) from Antwerp, who succeeded to the firm of Cologne printer Arnold Birckmann,[38] a publishing house with which Himmerod Abbey had connections.[39] The edition was reprinted by Birckmann in 1599, and finally, in 1605, Martinus Nutius in Antwerp made the last reprint.

Who were its readers? Luckily, some copies have owners' notes, attesting to a mostly monastic reception. A copy now in the National Library of Austria once belonged to the Augustinian canons from Saint-Nicolas-des-Prés in Tournai (Belgium); the one in the National Central Library of Rome belonged to

---

[37] Nicolaus Hees, *Manipulus rerum memorabilium claustri Hemmenrodensis, ordinis Cistertie[n]sis in archidioecesi Trevirensi* (Cologne: Henning, 1641), 5.

[38] Rudolf Schmidt, "Birckmann, Familie," in *Deutsche Buchhändler. Deutsche Buchdrucker* (Berlin: Weber, 1902), 1:63–65. The Birckmann firm had a branch printing house in Antwerp.

[39] The poet Mathias Agricius († 1613), who taught rhetoric in Himmerod, had friendly relationships with Arnold Mylius. See Leonhard Keil, "Der Dichter und Humanist Mathias Agricius von Wittlich (1545–1613). Sein Leben, sein Werdegang und seine Werke," *Trierer Zeitschrift* 2 (1927): 141–55, esp. 149.

the Feuillant monastery of Santa Pudenziana in Rome, and the one in the Cremona municipal library belonged to the Jesuit College in Cremona. One copy from the Municipal Library of Lyon had belonged to the Pauline Fathers of Bonndorf im Schwarzwald (Baden-Württemberg), and another one came to the Benedictines from Benediktbeuern, which, as we know, also owned a manuscript copy of the *Dialogus*. With Fischer's edition, the geography of Caesarius's readership became significantly wider.

In the times when Catholic articles of belief were themselves under attack from Protestants, reading medieval *exempla* collections involved an exercise of faith, an additional effort to adhere to their narrative theology. Catholic readers had not only to stick to the much-discussed dogma, but also to accept its expression through miraculous narrative. Truly to believe in the transubstantiation was hard enough, and apparently rather unorthodox stories such as the one about the priest who threw the Host in the river did not make it easier. The complex paratext created by the editor helped to win both the good will of the readers and to control their response to the book, making it an effective tool of communication and persuasion.

During the seventeenth century, the importance of Caesarius for the Cistercian Order was once more powerfully affirmed by Crisóstomo Henríquez († 1632), a Spanish Cistercian monk and ecclesiastical historian who moved to the Spanish Netherlands in 1622. Commissioned to write the history of the Cistercian Order, he visited various Belgian monasteries, including Aulne, Villers, and Dunes. The resulting *Menologium Cisterciense*—Henríquez's most influential work—was published in 1630. In it Henríquez dedicated a short notice to Caesarius, presenting him as a saintly person, even blessed with miracles:

> *In Germania beatus Caesarius prior Heisterbacensis, vir pietate et doctrina celeberrimus qui sanctorum Patrum gesta pia sollicitudine colligens, et posteritati commendans, eorum etiam vestigiis*

inhaerens, variis virtutibus et miraculis claruit, et cum magna sanctitatis opinione felicem agonem in ordine consummavit.

(In Germany the blessed Caesarius, prior of Heisterbach, a man celebrated for his piety and his learning, with pious care collected the deeds of the Holy Fathers and, bequeathing them to future generations and himself following in their steps, he shone with diverse virtues and miracles, was known for his sanctity, and passed away happily in his order.)[40]

Caesarius's writings were by then an integral part of the Roman Catholic Church's literary history in general,[41] and of Cistercian literary history in particular. Charles de Visch († 1666) in his *Bibliotheca scriptorum Sacri Ordinis Cisterciensis elogiis plurimorum maxime illustrium adornata* (1649) mentioned the recent editions of the *Dialogus* by Fischer, the edition of the *Homiliae morales* by Coppenstein (1615), and the *Vita Engelberti*, which was published twice, by Laurentius Surius in 1575 and by Aegidius Gelenius in 1633.[42] De Visch then added the locations of some other works by Caesarius or attributed to him: *Commentaria in Ecclesiasticum*,[43] reportedly in Cologne; *Chronicon episcoporum Coloniensium*[44] in Altenberg; and *Dialogus inter capitulum, monachum et novitium*[45] in the Jesuit college in

---

[40] Crisóstomo Henríquez, *Menologivm Cistertiense Notationibvs Illvstratvm* (Antwerp: Moretus, 1630), 1:324.

[41] See, for example, the corresponding entry in Antonio Possevino, *Apparatus sacer* (Venice: Soc. Veneta, 1606), 1:284–85.

[42] Gelenius owned a copy of Koelhoff's incunabulum edition. Shortly after his death, the book landed in the possession of the Jesuit college in Cologne, now Düsseldorf, Universitäts- und Landesbibliothek, H.M.V. 5 (Ink). See August Franzen, "Gelenius, Aegidius," *Neue Deutsche Biographie* 6 (1964): 173–74. Available online: https://www.deutsche-biographie.de/pnd12483 9169.html#ndbcontent.

[43] Number 36 in the *Epistola catalogica*. See Alfons Hilka, ed., *Die Wundergeschichten des Caesarius von Heisterbach*, vol. 1, *Exempla und Auszüge aus den Predigten des Caesarius von Heisterbach* (Bonn: Hanstein, 1933), 7. The work is not identified and is probably lost.

[44] Finished after the *Epistola* was completed. See Hilka, *Die Wundergeschichten des Caesarius*, 1:31.

[45] Probably the *Dialogus*.

Bruges. To give the most complete overview of Caesarius's writings, De Visch included the notice from the *Epistola catalogica* first published by Coppenstein in his *editio princeps* of Caesarius's homilies. Finally, he gave a short summary of Caesarius's life, including his reputation of sanctity.[46] Caesarius's attention to recent events was much appreciated by seventeenth-century scholars. Aubert le Mire († 1640), the author of the *Chronicon Cisterciensis ordinis* (1614), used the *Dialogus* as a source of information on the history of the Order and especially of the Abbey of Heisterbach.[47] Curiously, le Mire informed his readers that Caesarius had once been prior at Villers-en-Brabant, under Abbot Wilhelm VII, according to a manuscript chronicle from Villers.[48] This assertion resulted from the confusion with Caesarius's namesake from Villers, mentioned in the *Chronica* under the year 1197, that is to say, two years before Caesarius joined the Cistercian Order.[49] Le Mire's mistake persisted for centuries, and even won Caesarius a place in the French literary history (see below, p. 250).

Gaspar Jongelinus († 1669) refers extensively to the *Dialogus* in his *Notitia abbatiarum ordinis Cisterciensis* published in 1640,[50] as does Angel Manrique († 1649) in his *Cisterciensium seu verius*

---

[46] *Bibliotheca scriptorum Sacri Ordinis Cisterciensis elogiis plurimorum maxime illustrium adornata* (Cologne: Busaeus, 1656), 57–60.

[47] Aubert le Mire, *Chronicon Cisterciensis Ordinis, a S. Roberto abbate Molismensi primum inchoati, postea a S. Bernardo abbate Clarevallensi mirifice aucti ac propagati* (Cologne: Gualtherus, 1614), 182.

[48] "*Haec ex Chronico manuscripto Villariensi hausimus, quod ibidem exstat manuscriptum*" (Le Mire: *Chronicon Cisterciensis*, 127).

[49] Brian P. McGuire, "Friends and Tales in the Cloister: Oral sources in Caesarius of Heisterbach's *Dialogus miraculorum*," *Analecta cisterciensia* 36 (1980): 173, n. 13. See *Chronica Villariensis monasterii*, in Georg Waitz, ed., *Monumenta Germaniae Historica. Scriptores in Folio*, vol. 25, *Gesta saec. XIII* (Berlin: Weidmann, 1880), 197: "*Sub ipso [abbot Wilhelm] fuit prior nonnus Cesarius, de quo scribitur in vita domni Godefridi sacriste reconditi retro cancellum maioris altaris; de quo [Gottfried] etiam Cesarius laudabilia scribit in suo tractatu.*" See *Dialogus* I.35: *De conversione Godefridi monachi Vilariensis, et de revelationibus eius.*

[50] Gaspar Jongelinus, *Notitia abbatiarum ordinis Cisterciensis per orbem universum* (Cologne: Henningius, 1640), 2:34–37.

ecclesiasticorum annalium a condito Cistercio (1649).[51] The afore-mentioned *Manipulus rerum memorabilium claustri Hemmen-rodensis* by Nicolaus Hees was originally conceived as a contribution to Jongelinus's *Notitia abbatiarum*. Hees's work reached Jongelinus too late to be printed and was therefore published separately.[52] Some forty years after the *Manipulus*, Robert Bootz, abbot of Himmerod from 1685 to 1730, not only used the *Dialogus* a source for his major work, the *Series abbatum claustri B.M.V. de Himmenrode* (1685),[53] but also high-lighted "the renowned year" of Caesarius's conversion to the Order,[54] thus making him part of Himmerod's history.

Despite all the controversy around the *Dialogus* (or thanks to it), Caesarius's *exempla* collection enjoyed considerable vis-ibility and continued to play an important role in the construc-tion of Cistercian history and identity in times of intense development of historical studies.

In the abbey of Stams, which possessed a manuscript of the *Dialogus* (discussed above), Caesarius was held in reverence at this time. Above almost every door in the monastery were pictures of Cistercian patron saints, accompanied by Latin verses by the prior Benedict Stephani († 1672). One picture presents "*B[eatus] Caesarius prior Heisterbacensis*," with verses reading "*Gesta beatorum vigili dum digero penna / Inscius ipse alas fabrico ad astra mihi*" ("While I write down the deeds of the Blessed with my vigil pen, Myself unaware, I prepare wings that will bring me to heaven"). It seems that the "beatification"

---

[51] Angel Manrique, *Cisterciensium seu verius ecclesiasticorum annalium a condito Cistercio*, vol. 3, *Continens ab anno MCLXXIV usque ad MCCXII inclusive* (Lyon: Laurent Anisson, 1649), for example, a. 1188, chap. 7.

[52] See Ambrosius Schneider, *Die Cistercienserabtei Himmerod von der Renais-sance bis zur Auflösung, 1511–1802* (Cologne: Wienand, 1976), 108.

[53] As revealed by the title: *Series abbatum claustri B. Mariae Virginis in Him-menrode S. Ordinis Cisterciensis in Archidioecesi Trevirensi ac Memorabilium sub ipsis gestorum Ex Caesario Heisterbacensi, Annalibus Trevirensibus et Cistercien-sibus, et M.M.S.S. Himmenrodensibus eruta.*

[54] "*1199 Annus MCXCIX Conversione Cesarii Heisterbachensis viri pii, prudenti ac docti clarus notatur . . .*" (MS. Trier, Stadtbibliothek, 1720/432 4°, p. 41).

Figure 2. The Picture of Caesarius in Stams Abbey

of Caesarius, promoted by Crisóstomo Henríquez, was at least in part successful.

Besides the *Dialogus*, seventeenth-century readers were offered other Cistercian *exempla* collections. Ignatius de Ybero, Cistercian abbot of Fitero († 1612), prepared the *editio princeps* of the *Exordium magnum*, published in Fitero in 1606,[55] and incorrectly attributed it to Hélinand of Froidmont. In 1660, the Jesuit Pierre-François Chifflet († 1682) published the *Liber visionum et miraculorum* by Herbert of Clairvaux in his collection *Sancti Bernardi Clarevallensis abbatis genus illustre assertum*, along with the *De profectione Ludovici VII in Orientem* by Eudes of Deuil, the *Chronicon Clarevallense* by Alberic of Trois-Fontaines, the *Vita* of Saint Bernard by John the Hermit, and the *Vita beati Petri prioris Juliacensis*. Chifflet dedicated his edition to Pierre Henry, abbot of Clairvaux in 1654–1676, whose predecessor, Claude Largentier, had supplied the manuscripts for the edition. In the dedication letter, Chifflet informs the abbot that the published pieces not only originate from Clairvaux but also glorify it, showing that the *clear valley* indeed *miserit in coelum montes* ("raised mountains to heaven").[56] The ascetics from Clairvaux, continues Chifflet, would no doubt be kindled by these examples of the sanctity of the ancient fathers, their familiarity with God, their confidence in death, and their rewards in the afterlife. And they would thank the abbot who let those stories be brought to the light.[57] Chifflet traditionally puts his edition in the scope of communal, identity-forming reading. His short prefaces to each piece are of a historical-philological nature, focusing on what concerns their authors and the texts themselves without advertising their edifying or moral benefits. In the course of the seventeenth century, Cistercian *exempla* had become more and more objects of scholarly discourse.

---

[55] *Exordia Sacri Ordinis Cisterciensis: alterum a S. Roberto [v. Molesme], S. Alberico, & S. Stephano [Harding] primis ejusdem Ordinis fundatoribus, ante quingentos annos, alterum vero ante quadringentos ab Anonymo hactenus Monacho Clarae-Vallensi, sed revera a S. Helinando accurate conscripta* (Fitero, 1606).

[56] See Sidonius Apollinaris, "Carmen 16 Ad Faustum."

[57] *Sancti Bernardi Clarevallensis abbatis genus illustre assertum* (Dijon: Philibert Chavance, 1660), *Epistola nuncupatoria*, unpaginated.

13

Bertrand Tissier's Edition (1662)

Given the increasingly popular status of the *Dialogus*, it is
no wonder that in 1662 Bertrand Tissier († 1672), the Cistercian
prior of Bonnefontaine in the diocese of Reims, decided to
publish a new edition in the second volume of his *Bibliotheca
Patrum Cisterciensium* (also containing a new edition of the
Exordium magnum). Tissier dedicated his work to Jean Jouaud,
from 1631–1673 the abbot of Prières Abbey in the diocese of
Vannes. Jouaud was the vicar general of the Strict Observance,
and Tissier, himself a partisan of the reform,[1] clearly connected
the *Dialogus* to the context of reform by using the famous image
of teaching *verbo et exemplo*:

> *Huic enim auctori par zelus et fervor observantiae regularis fo-*
> *vendae similem te nobis exhibet. Ille siquidem, ut Novitiis, quos*
> *ad virtutem formandos susceperat, ad vitae spiritualis perfectio-*
> *nem sectandam olim stimulos adderet, ea quae in Ordine Cister-*
> *ciensi usque ad suum tempus gloriose gesta fuerant, ut idem ipse*
> *ait, enarrare, ac postmodum, universo Ordini consulens, literarum*
> *monimentis consignare curavit. Tu similiter affectus, non scripto*
> *quidem, sed exemplo (quod efficacius est) ac strictioris observantiae*
> *professione, eiusdemque instituti per multa coenobia propagatione,*

---

[1] In 1664 he managed to introduce abstinence at Bonnefontaine (with the
cooperation of the commendatory abbot Nicolas de la Lâne). See Louis J.
Lekai, *The Rise of the Cistercian Strict Observance in Seventeenth Century France*
(Washington: Catholic University of America Press, 1968), 117.

*imminutum ac tepefactum antiquum religiosae vitae fervorem
denuo accendere omni studio contendis.*

(The equal zeal and fervor for the nurturing of the regular
observance make you in our eyes similar to this author. In
former times, he—as he himself stated—narrated the glorious events that had recently happened in the Cistercian
Order to give the novices, whom he took to instruct in virtues, the stimulus to strive for the perfection of spiritual life.
Afterwards he took care to write them down for the benefit
of the entire Order. And you, driven by similar motivations,
strain with all eagerness to kindle anew the pristine fervor
of the monastic life turned feeble and lukewarm, not by
writing, but by example [which is more efficacious], by pro-
fessing the stricter observance and by propagating it among
many monasteries of the same institution.)[2]

Jouaud's reforming activities, according to Tissier, find their
reflection in Caesarius's writings and vice versa, both originating from the fervent observance of the *vita regularis*. Still,
Jouaud's lifestyle was far enough from that of the ideal abbots
portrayed in the *Dialogus*. By the time the edition appeared,
Jouaud had already lived permanently in Paris for nine years,
since 1653, having left all monastic affairs to his coadjutor and
future successor Hervé du Tertre.[3]

As was the case with Fischer, Tissier was well aware of the
backlash against the *Dialogus*. He therefore closed the edition
with the *Apologia pro Caesario*, designed to defend Caesarius
from his critics. But Tissier himself was quite critical of the
Dialogus and its narrative theology. For him, some stories were
indeed *fabulosa*, as, for example, the story of Beatrice, which
he decided not to publish at all, "*ideo . . . non potest argui*" ("so
. . . it could not be censored").[4] He similarly omitted XII.35,

---

[2] Bertrand Tissier, ed., *Bibliotheca Patrum Cisterciensium*, vol. 2 (Bonnefontaine Abbey, 1662). The dedication letter to Jean Jouaud is unpaginated.

[3] Lekai, *The Rise of the Cistercian Strict Observance*, 176.

[4] Tissier, *Bibliotheca Patrum Cisterciensium*, 2:361.

about a Benedictine nun who was a great admirer of Saint John the Evangelist and who, after her death, was helped not by him, but by Saint Benedict, the patron of the Order. By contrast, the story about an obliging demon-servant (V.36), however fabulous, could not be blamed. Only the concluding phrase—"*Dicam tibi aliud diabolicae bonitatis exemplum*" ("I will give you another example of devil's goodness")—was unacceptable. Tissier believed that Caesarius intended this phrase to be ironical ("*ironice dictum*").[5] Demons are obstinate in evil and cannot do any good to humans unless mandated to do so by God, or scheming to do harm in the future. The ending of this story had indeed already been rewritten in the *Speculum exemplorum*. In the *Dialogus*, after having been fired by his master, the demon asked to spend the money he had earned to buy a church bell: "*Peto ut ex eis nolam compares, et super tectum pauperis illius ecclesiae ac desolatae suspendas, ut per eam saltem Dominicis diebus fideles ad divinum convocentur officium*" ("I ask you to buy a bell and put in on the top of this poor and desolated church, so that this bell might convoke, at least on Sundays, the faithful to the Divine Service"). According to the *Speculum exemplorum*, the demon's intentions were indeed malicious, and his gesture led to no good: "*et hoc idcirco demon petiit, ut hi qui hactenus debitam horam officii pervenientes cum summa devotione expectabant eo quod timerent tardius ad divina mysteria concurrere, de cetero non nisi post auditum nole sonum convenirent*" ("The demon asked it so that the people who had previously awaited the time of the Divine Service with great devotion because they were afraid to be late, from then on would come only after the bell sounded").[6]

Tissier was able to exonerate some other dubious stories by finding parallels in authoritative writings. For example, he discusses at length the story about the saintly monk Wilhelm

---

[5] Tissier, *Bibliotheca Patrum Cisterciensium*, 2:360.

[6] *Speculum exemplorum* (Deventer: Richardus Pafraet, 1481), VI.57 (unpaginated).

from Heisterbach, who appeared after death to another monk and said that he was being punished (XII.37). The visionary was horrified: "*si tu es in poenis qui nunquam peccasti, quid fiet de me peccatore, meique similibus?*" ("If you who had never sinned are punished, what will happen to me, a sinner, and others like me?"). To console him, Wilhelm explained that he was suffering from not being able to see God. He did not, however, mention the fire of purgatory, which could, explains Tissier, be seen as dubious. To defend this particular story, Tissier cites testimonies from authoritative writings. For example, in the *Libri revelationum* of Saint Bridget approved by the church, one reads that the Virgin Mary told Bridget about a *presbyterus heremita* who was in purgatory but suffered no pain, only the separation from God.[7] Works of both Bede the Venerable (*Historia ecclesiastica gentis Anglorum*, lib V, cap. 12, 4–6) and Hélinand of Froidmont (*Chronicon*, lib. 45, a. 671) contain visions describing some *locus amoenus* in purgatory, and Gregory the Great speaks in his *Dialogi* about the souls of the just who were not allowed to be in the celestial mansions (IV.25). Although some sixteenth- and seventeenth-century theologians, like Francisco Suárez, had reservations about the existence of such an agreeable place in purgatory, others, like Robert Bellarmine and Gonsalvo Duranti, supported the idea. That is sufficient, concludes Tissier, to show that this particular story can be accepted as true.

In his edition, Tissier highlighted his reservations and criticism by means of his typographical choices. He printed the stories that he considered dubious (sometimes even those containing true dogmas) in a smaller font, as he stated on the title page itself. In the notes at the end of the book, he assured his readers that the fallacy of such stories would be demonstrated

---

[7] IV.127. See *Corpus Reuelacionum Sancte Birgitte* (a critical edition available online: https://riksarkivet.se/Media/pdf-filer/SanctaBirgitta_Reuelacionum_LiberQuartus.pdf).

or their probability would be measured, and if they were true or highly probable, they would be exonerated.

Both the *Apologia* and the following *Notae in Dialogum Caesarii* provide reasons that a particular *exemplum* could be considered suspect.[8] Among dubious stories one finds, for example, II.2, about a monk who left his monastery, became a robber, and committed many hideous crimes. Severely injured and about to die, he confessed his sins and, full of contrition, chose as a penitence to spend two thousand years in purgatory. He then wrote a letter to his relative the bishop, asking for prayers, and died. After two years of prayers ordered by the bishop, the dead man confirmed that he had completed his two thousand years of purgatory, and he was going to paradise. This particular story, Tissier explains in the *Notae*, is dubious because it is too vague: "*Dubia est haec narratio. Nullus enim eius author vel testis profertur, nulla persona nominatur, sed solum quidam iuvenis, quidam sacerdos, quidam episcopus, incerta dioecesis*" ("This story is dubious. There is no indication of its author or a witness, and no person is named, just a certain youth, a certain priest, a certain bishop, an unknown diocese").[9] Erudite readers of the seventeenth century not only appreciated Caesarius's attention to detail, but also seemed to disapprove of *exempla* that were too general or too vague. The efficacy of the use of indefinite pronouns to designate protagonists of an *exemplum* in order to facilitate the readers' or listeners' identification with them[10] was rejected in favor of the more reliable and solid rhetoric of historical verisimilitude.

Another problem that Tissier associated with some stories from the *Dialogus* was the possibility of inappropriate reader

---

[8] Tissier, *Bibliotheca Patrum Cisterciensium*, 2:361–64.

[9] Tissier, *Bibliotheca Patrum Cisterciensium*, 2:362.

[10] As if to tell the audience, "this certain man or certain woman may well mean you"; see for more analysis Jean-Yves Tilliette, "L'exemplum rhétorique: questions de définition," in *Les exempla médiévaux: nouvelles perspectives*, ed. Jacques Berlioz and Marie Anne Polo de Beaulieu (Paris: Champion, 1998), 43–65.

response, and especially imprudent imitation. Tissier warns against following the example set in some scandalous or extravagant stories, as for example in III.49 of the *Dialogus*, about a Benedictine abbot whose monks were quite dissolute. When he once caught them eating meat, to their surprise he joined them. Later, during chapter, the abbot confessed this sin to the prior and willingly received the punishment. The monks, afraid that the abbot would expose them, followed his example: "*Historia illa de abbate nigro carnes comedente, non est in exemplum trahenda*" ("The story about the Benedictine abbot eating meat must not be taken as a model"), wrote Tissier in the *Notae*.[11] Indiscriminately treating Caesarius's stories as *exempla* in the sense of models of conduct could be dangerous, as it could lead to the legitimization of dubious behavior, like engaging in sin in order to trigger contrition in others.

Tissier again highlights the potential danger of an exceptional story in his commentary to XI.20. This *exemplum* tells about a criminal knight who said in the last moment of his life, "*Domine miserere mei*" ("Have mercy on me, O Lord"). Shortly after his death, a demon confirmed through the mouth of a possessed man that the knight had escaped from the demons' grip by pronouncing these three words. It is nearly impossible, explains Tissier, that a sinner caught in the act of committing a crime and killed for it should repent in such a perfect manner. Such stories, unless true, should not be accepted, because they might provide the impious with justification for continuing to sin until the death, in the hope of a similar outcome.[12]

Tissier's remark puts a clear emphasis on the problematic nature of exemplarity. Many *exempla* from the *Dialogus* indeed

---

[11] Tissier, *Bibliotheca Patrum Cisterciensium*, 2:362.

[12] Tissier, *Bibliotheca Patrum Cisterciensium*, 2:364. Caesarius himself was aware of the problem of arguing in favor of a norm while displaying fascinating exceptions to the norm. In III.27 he mentioned several cases of written confessions that had been accepted as valid but were not to be taken as models: "*Simile aliquid legitur de Karolo Imperatore in Vita sancti Aegidii; sed miracula non sunt in exemplum trahenda.*"

did not fit the usual framework of imitation and reproducibility. Instead of offering a clear moral lesson or a proper model on which to construct one's religious self, they often depicted questionable acts on the margins of orthodoxy. Such high awareness of the subversive potential of medieval *exempla* was, I would argue, restricted to the reading of the *Dialogus*. In fact, in the first volume of the *Bibliotheca patrum Cisterciensium*, Tissier published the *Exordium magnum* by Conrad of Eberbach.[13] Although in the *Notae in utrumque Exordium Cisterciense* he characterizes a few stories from the *Exordium* as *"parum probabile"* ("little plausible," II.24), *"dubium"* ("dubious," III.16), *"incerta"* ("uncertain," V.7.20, 21), *"suspecta"* ("suspicious," V.12), and *"piae . . . utinam certae"* ("pious, if only they were true!" VI.5, 6), he did not use typographic means to highlight them in the text itself, nor did he feel the need to exonerate the author. Unlike Caesarius, Conrad of Eberbach was neither at the center of a controversy over miracle stories nor accused of telling ridiculous lies.

Tissier's interventions are revealing in his attempts to control readers' response to the *Dialogus*. Despite describing the *Dialogus* as a spark of fire that ignites souls for charity and improvement of religious life,[14] he maintained a critical distance from the text and in some sense encouraged his readers to do the same, while also pushing them to exercise belief in Caesarius's stories, not an easy task. The anonymous compiler of the *Collectaneum exemplorum et visionum Clarevallense*, the first known Cistercian *exempla* collection, insisted that his stories required *"fidem . . . non racionem; assensum, non argumentum; simplicem animum, non scrupulosum; deuotum, non uersutum; amicum, non insidiosum; credulum, non dubium; flexibilem, non obstinatum"* ("faith, not reason; assent, not argument, a simple

---

[13] Tissier, *Bibliotheca Patrum Cisterciensium*, 1:13–246. For his edition he used the manuscript from Foigny.

[14] Tissier, dedication letter to Jean Jouaud, *Bibliotheca Patrum Cisterciensium*, 2, unpaginated.

soul, not captious; devout, not cunning; credulous, not doubt-ful; flexible, not obstinate").[15] The ideal seventeenth-century reader—as imagined by Fischer and Tissier—had both to be always on guard not to fall for a fable and at the same time to trust in the authority of a published book.

Little-known today, Tissier's edition enjoyed a certain popu-larity, especially in France. In the volume XVIII of the *Histoire littéraire de la France*, published in 1835, it is called "the best known and the last."[16]

The reception of Early Modern printed editions of the *Dia-logus* was to a large extent shaped by other influential works. Among those, Trithemius's *Liber de scriptoribus ecclesiasticis* is the most prominent. Of great importance also were the popular—at least more popular than the *Dialogus*—sermon and *exempla* collections that used the stories from the *Dialogus* and mentioned Caesarius as the author, such as the *Sermones Meffret* and the *Speculum exemplorum*. It is through these col-lections that Protestants came to know Caesarius's stories and then to use them to expose and to mock what they called "pa-pist lies."

The Reformation, with its polemic concerning miracles and wonders, brought Caesarius into the spotlight and made him in some sense an exemplary figure. Heated debates led learned editors and publishers to question the *Dialogus*'s exemplarity. One may ask to what extent doubts about the truthfulness of Caesarius's stories were forced onto readers by Catholic edi-tors, who tried their best to defend Caesarius from the accusa-

---

[15] *Collectaneum exemplorum et visionum Clarevallense e codice Trecensi 946,* ed. Olivier Legendre, CCCM 208 (Turnhout: Brepols, 2005), 5.

[16] *Histoire littéraire de la France; ouvrage commencé par des religieux bénédictins de la Congrégation de Saint Maur, et continué par des membres de l'Institut,* ed. Pierre Daunou, Académie des inscriptions et belles-lettres, vol. 18 (Paris: Firmin Didot, 1835; repr. 1971), 198 (s.v. "Césaire d'Heisterbach").

tion of lying while also struggling with his often unorthodox narrative theology. Nevertheless, Caesarius's somewhat problematic reputation—"*Hunc scriptorem aliqui reprehendunt quasi fabulosum*" ("Some rebuke this author for being a fabulist"), as Tissier said[17]—did not prevent the *Dialogus* from becoming a sought-after source for historians. Gerardus Vossius († 1649) mentions Caesarius among historians in his *De historicis Latinis libri III* (1627).[18] And if, Vossius argues, using Caesarius's own defense strategy, something happened not exactly as it is described, it should be blamed on the informants, not on the writer. This ambiguous view of the *Dialogus* persisted in the eighteenth century.

---

[17] Tissier, *Bibliotheca Patrum Cisterciensium*, 2:359.

[18] Gerardus Vossius, *De historicis Latinis: libri III* (Lyon: Maire, 1651), 2:459 (cap. 57).

14

The *Dialogus miraculorum* and Its Modern Reception: From Derision to Fascination

The *Dialogus* was not re-edited in the eighteenth century, but Caesarius never disappeared completely from the scholarly scene. On the one hand, he was included in the catalogues or lists of ecclesiastical authors, such as the *Historia ecclesiastica veteris novique testamenti* (1734) by the French Dominican Alexander Natalis († 1724)[1] and the *Bibliotheca Scriptorum coloniensis* (1747) by the German Jesuit Hermann Joseph Hartzheim († 1767). Hartzheim not only dedicated a detailed entry to Caesarius, but also printed his *Epistola catalogica*.[2] On the other hand, Caesarius again became the object of severe criticism, as is barely surprising given the Enlightenment's condemnation of monasticism with its "ignorance" and "superstition." This time, though, it was not because the *Dialogus*'s narrative theology was considered dubious or its moral message improper. It was the author himself who was ridiculed for being naive and gullible. Caesarius became in some sense

---

[1] Alexander Natalis, *Historia ecclesiastica Veteris Novique Testamenti ab orbe condito ad annum post Christum natum millesimum sexcentesimum* (Lucca: Leonardus Venturinus, 1752), 115 ("*De scriptoribus praecipuis XIII saeculi*").

[2] Hermann Joseph Hartzheim, *Bibliotheca Coloniensis, in qua vita et libri typo vulgati et manuscripti recensentur omnium archi-dioceseos Coloniensis . . . indigenarum et incolarum scriptorum* (Cologne: Thomas Odendall, 1747), 43–45.

an exemplification of medieval superstitiousness. His famous defense line (*"Testis est mihi Dominus,"* etc.) was not working well anymore. If Alexander Natalis presented it as a proof of sincerity (*"Sinceritatem Authoris haec verba probant in Praefatione,"*)[3] many other scholars insisted that one should not simply believe everything others said.

As the French ecclesiastical historian Louis Ellies Dupin († 1719) points out rather neutrally in his *Nouvelle bibliothèque des auteurs ecclésiastiques*, it is inexcusable to trust unreliable persons too easily and to collect from their words—as Caesarius did in his work—fables and supposed histories.[4] There was also much harsher criticism. For example, Casimir Oudin († 1717), a French Premonstratensian who later in life became a Protestant, mockingly presents the *Dialogus* in his *Commentarius de scriptoribus ecclesiae antiquis* as a laughable product of the utmost naiveté: *"Hoc in opere, quam simplex fuerit Caesarius in credendo, quam facilis in fabulis scripto consignandis, nullus negabit, qui ejusmodi monachalem farraginem legerit; nullus leget qui non impense ad tantas fabulas riserit"* ("How gullible Caesarius was in believing, how easily in writing he confirmed all sorts of fables, is clear to anyone who has read the nonsensical writings of this monk. And no one will read them without laughing at such fables").[5] Oudun's derisive take on Caesarius became widely cited in later literature.

For example, in his *Bibliotheca belgica* (1739) the Belgian ecclesiastical historian Jean François Foppens († 1761) first cites Oudin—*"Hoc in opere, quam simplex fuerit Caesarius,"* etc.—then adds that because of Caesarius's gullibility, the *Dialogus* was even included in the Spanish index of prohibited books.[6] The

---

[3] Natalis, *Historia ecclesiastica*, 125.

[4] Louis Ellies Dupin, *Nouvelle bibliothèque des auteurs ecclésiastiques*, vol. 10, *Des auteurs du treizième siècle de l'Église* (Paris: Prallard, 1702), 62.

[5] Casimir Oudin, *Commentarius de scriptoribus ecclesiae antiquis* (Leipzig: Moritz Georg Weidmann, 1722), 3:80.

[6] Jean François Foppens, *Bibliotheca belgica, sive virorum in Belgio vita, scriptisque illustrium catalogus, librorumque nomenclatura* (Brussels: Foppens, 1739), 1:447.

Novus Index librorum prohibitorum et expurgatorum, published by Antonio Zapata de Mendoza in 1632, indeed mentioned Caesarius, but for an almost diametrically opposite reason. The book to be censored was not the *Dialogus,* but Conrad Gessner's *Bibliotheca universalis* with the addition by Frisius (see above, pp. 213–14). The *Index* advised deleting the passage between *"Dialogorum de variis, lib. 12"* and *"Evangeliis dominicalibus,"* that is to say, the accusation that *Dialogus* was full of fables.[7]

There were also more measured opinions, like the one of the German theologian Christian Eberhard Weismann († 1747), who after writing *"de eo varia et contraria legimus doctorum iudicia"* ("we read concerning him [Caesarius] different and controversial judgments of learned scholars"),[8] cites both favorable and negative opinions. He concludes that Caesarius still holds a place among anti-Albigensian writers in his own right.[9] And even though the French scholar Nicolas Lenglet du Fresnoy († 1755) in his *Méthode pour étudier l'histoire* (1729) agrees that the *Dialogus* was full of grotesque things that would put the monastic state to shame,[10] he still finds Tissier's edition the worst, because by censoring Caesarius's work, the editor took away the best of it.[11]

Eighteenth-century discourse about Caesarius's character had a heavy impact on the reception of the *Dialogus,* with its echoes resounding throughout the following century as writers ridiculed Caesarius as gullible and superstitious. For people interested in superstitions, however, the *Dialogus* was an

---

[7] Antonio Zapata de Mendoza, *Novus index librorum prohibitorum et expurgatorum* (Seville: Francisco de Lyra, 1632), 187.

[8] Christian Eberhard Weismann, *Introductio in memorabilia ecclesiastica Historiae sacrae novi Testamenti ad juvandam notitiam Regni Dei et Satanae* (Halle: Orphanotropheum, 1745), 1:1037.

[9] Weismann, *Introductio,* 1:1038.

[10] Nicolas Lenglet du Fresnoy, *Méthode pour étudier l'histoire* (Paris: Gandouin, 1735), 3:117.

[11] *"il en a ôté tout le sel"* (Lenglet du Fresnoy, *Méthode pour étudier l'histoire,* 3:117).

excellent source of information. For instance, the French occultist Jacques Collin de Plancy († 1881) drew from the *Dialogus* for his *Dictionnaire infernal*, a bestselling book on demonology and superstitions, first published in 1818 and reedited many times in the subsequent decades. The 1825 edition contains a short entry dedicated to Caesarius himself, presented as a monk of Cîteaux and as the author of a singular and rare book that was a curious collection of miracles in which angels, saints, and demons played the leading roles.[12] Collin de Plancy inserted in his book a number of Caesarius's *exempla*, loosely translated from the original, as for example chapter I.34 (about a necromancer who became a Cistercian after having seen the punishment of the Landgrave Ludwig in hell) in the entry on *Enfer* (Hell),[13] or chapter V.29 (about an abbot and a lay brother who passed out when they saw the devil) in the entry on Exorcism.[14]

The *Dictionnaire* aimed, as Collin de Plancy stated in the preface, to crush superstition, to fight ignorance and errors, to unveil truth, and to report lies.[15] Despite the enlightened skepticism he expressed towards beliefs and rituals, his overall attitude seemed to be that of rather ambivalent curiosity, even before his turn to Catholicism at the end of the 1830s. His embrace of the Catholic Church predictably resulted in the extensive rewriting of the *Dictionnaire*. Along with the changes introduced to the 1844 edition, there is an interesting comment concerning Caesarius. The entry on the abbot Adam, who used to see the devil,[16] opens with an explanation about times when

[12] *Dictionnaire infernal ou recherches et anecdotes sur les démons, les esprits, les fantômes, les spectres, les revenants, les loups-garoux . . .* (Paris: Librairie Universelle de P. Mongie Aîné, 1825), 2:97–98: "*Césaire ou Cesarius (Pierre)—Moine de Cîteaux, mort en 1240.*" Other entries of the *Dictionnaire* refer to Caesarius as "*d'Heisterbach*" rather than as "*de Cîteaux.*"

[13] *Dictionnaire infernal* (1825), 2:436–39.

[14] *Dictionnaire infernal* (1825), 2:485–87.

[15] *Dictionnaire infernal* (1825), 1:xxiv.

[16] The source of this story is the *Compendium de origine et gestis Francorum* by Robert Gaguin (Paris: Jean Petit, 1504), lib. VII, fol. LXIX.

people saw the devil everywhere, saying that perhaps they were not wrong. It seems, however, that those people perceived him too physically. The good and naive Caesarius of Heisterbach, Collin de Plancy continues, composed a book of prodigious stories presenting the devil as a universal machine: he showed himself relentlessly and in many tangible forms.[17] Collin de Plancy's new Catholic sensibility apparently demanded some distancing—however benevolent—from the notorious Cistercian monk whose stories were often dangerously close to the limits of orthodoxy.

At the same time, the advent of Romanticism, with its reevaluation of the Middle Ages, brought a profound paradigm shift in regard to so-called medieval superstitions, a shift that also affected the reception of the *Dialogus*, though initially not directly. In this period it was not the *Dialogus* that captured the romantic imagination, but the landscape around the abbey of Heisterbach, situated on the west side of the Siebengebirge (Seven Mountains) range.

The Siebengebirge—the highest point of the lower Rhine— served as the gateway to the "romantic Rhine" for nineteenth-century tourists. One of its hills, Drachenfels (Dragon's Rock), was especially praised for its wild beauty, which inspired Lord Byron, among others. The poem *The Castled Crag of Drachenfels* from *Childe Harold's Pilgrimage* (Canto III.lv.1) was highly influential in popularizing the Rhine scenery. In 1816, Alois Schreiber († 1841) published in the annex to his travel guide, *Handbuch für Reisende am Rhein*, some of the most popular legends of the Rhine, among them that of the Drachenfels. In ancient times, says the legend, there was a dragon's lair here. Local people used to offer human sacrifices to the dragon, usually captives. Among them once was a young Christian virgin. When the dragon approached her, she showed him a

---

[17] "*Le bon et naïf Césaire d'Heisterbach a fait un livre d'histoires prodigieuses où le diable est la machine universelle; il se montre sans cesse et sous diverses figures palpables*" (*Dictionnaire infernal* [1844], 9).

small cross, and the dragon fell dead from the rock.[18] Elsewhere in the travel guide, Schreiber curiously associated the Drachenfels with the *Nibelungenlied*, as the place where, according to local legends, Siegfried saved "a daughter of the land" from a dragon.[19] This tentative association quickly became a certainty and significantly contributed to the popularity of the region. In 1913 the "Nibelungenhalle" was opened at the Drachenfels on the occasion of Richard Wagner's centenary.

At the time that Rhine tourism was booming, the abbey of Heisterbach, suppressed in 1803, lay in ruins. Its church had been sold and torn down in 1809, and only the apse with the vestiges of the choir remained. This unfortunate destruction, however, made Heisterbach a popular place for inspiration for artists and poets, with new legends about the abbey appearing. The first edition of the *Rheinsagen aus dem Munde des Volks und deutscher Dichter* (1837) by Karl Simrock († 1876) already contains a poem about Heisterbach: *Der alte Abt* (The Old Abbot), by Christian Reinhold Köstlin († 1856). The poem (whose subject is original to Köstlin, not dating to the Middle Ages) tells of an old abbot who wanders among the graves of his brethren but cannot find his own final peace so long as the building stands.

Further editions of the *Rheinsagen* (organized geographically according to the localities of the poems) expanded the Heisterbach section. The 1841 edition for the first time adds the legend of the monk from Heisterbach with the poem *Der Mönch zu Heisterbach*, by Wolfgang Müller († 1873), from Königswinter near Heisterbach.[20] The legend is a retelling of a popular medieval *exemplum*, whose oldest known version comes from a sermon of Maurice de Sully, the bishop of Paris from 1160 to

---

[18] Alois Schreiber, *Handbuch für Reisende am Rhein: von Schafhausen bis Holland, in die schönsten anliegenden Gegenden und an die dortigen Heilquellen* (Heidelberg: Engelmann, 1816), 481–82.

[19] Schreiber, *Handbuch für Reisende am Rhein*, 84.

[20] Karl Simrock, *Rheinsagen aus dem Munde des Volks und deutscher Dichter: Für Schule, Haus und Wanderschaft* (Bonn: Weber, 1841), 154–55.

1196.[21] The story, which circulated widely in the Middle Ages, appears in many *exempla* collections, but not in Caesarius's works. It concerns a monk who once meditated on the verse *One day with the Lord is as a thousand years, and a thousand years as one day* (2 Pet 3:8). He ventured out of the abbey (in the medieval version he followed a bird), fell asleep under a tree, and woke up when the bell called for prayer. He then returned to the cloister, where he was surprised to see unfamiliar faces. The monks too were surprised to meet a stranger. Finally they remembered a story about a monk who had disappeared hundreds of years before. The monk then fully understood the truth of the Scripture, before falling dead. Müller's poem became an instant hit and secured Heisterbach's reputation as a place of legends.

But what about the *Dialogus*? Was it used as a source for the *Rheinsagen*? The answer is yes. In the first edition of the *Rheinsagen aus dem Munde des Volks und deutscher Dichter*, Simrock had already published his own poem, *Jost vom Büchl* (a name invented by Simrock),[22] inspired by chapter VIII.63 of the *Dialogus*. Caesarius had named the protagonist Karl, specifying that he was "*dives ac potens*" ("rich and powerful"). This Karl, reflecting on his heavy sins, decided to do something to counterbalance them. He therefore bought large heavy stones and offered them for the eventual renovation of the Church of the Saint Apostles in Cologne.

In the 1841 edition, Simrock added another poem of his own, *Walther von Birbach* (based on chapter VII.38 of the *Dialogus*).[23] Caesarius's chapter contains Walter's whole *Vita*, but Simrock used only the first episode, in which the knight Walter was very devoted to the Virgin Mary; once, on his way to a tournament, he entered a church to hear a Mass dedicated to her. He

---

[21] Paul Meyer, "Les manuscrits des sermons français de Maurice de Sully," *Romania* 23, no. 90 (1894): 190.

[22] Simrock, *Rheinsagen* (Bonn: Weber, 1837), 71–72 (no. 18).

[23] Simrock, *Rheinsagen* (1841), 271–73 (no. 131).

missed the tournament, but later he met many of its participants, who claimed that he had vanquished them. He understood then that the Virgin Mary had recompensed his devotion.

Finally, in 1869, Simrock not only added another poem inspired by the *Dialogus* in his *Rheinsagen*, but also, remarkably, acknowledged Caesarius as his source. The poem, entitled *Der Kirchenschlaf*, retells *Dialogus* IV.37, about a knight named Henry who spent Lent in Heisterbach. In the end, he asked the abbot to sell him a particular stone next to a particular column in the church. This stone, the knight declared, had a special power: those having trouble sleeping should lay their head on the stone, and they would immediately fall asleep. In fact the knight himself used to sleep during the prayers, confused by the devil. At the end of the poem, Simrock mentions Caesarius as a historian and as the one who wrote down this funny story: *"Der Prior war geheißen / Der Mönch Cäsarius / Den sah man sich befleißen / Als ein Historicus. / Den Wackern sollt ihr lieben: / Ihr schuldet ihm viel Dank / Er hat uns aufgeschrieben / Auch diesen guten Schwank"* ("The prior was called the monk Caesarius, known as a historian. You would like this smart guy: you owe him a lot of thanks. He wrote down this funny story for us").[24]

A poetic rewriting of the *Dialogus*'s narrative material was not limited to Germany's romantic appropriation of local history. A remarkable parallel to Simrock's adaptations appears in England, where Sabine Baring-Gould († 1924), an Anglican priest, folk-song collector, and eclectic scholar put into verse at least two *exempla* from the *Dialogus*: *The Devil's Confession* (III.26) and *The Little Scholar* (II.10, about a repentant scholar, who made a written confession and later found his sins miraculously erased). Both were published in Baring-Gould's collection of poems *The Silver Store: Collected from Mediæval Christian and Jewish Mines* (1868).[25]

---

[24] Simrock, *Rheinsagen* (Bonn: Weber, 1869), 159.

[25] Sabine Baring–Gould, *The Silver Store: Collected from Mediæval Christian and Jewish Mines* (London: Longman, Green and Co., 1868), 1–8 ("The Devil's

Simrock's poem *Der Kirchenschlaf* was dedicated to Alexander Kaufmann († 1893), the German historian and archivist, who laid the foundation for the modern *Dialogus* scholarship with his 1850 monograph, *Caesarius von Heisterbach, ein Beitrag zur Kulturgeschichte des 12. und 13. Jahrhunderts.*[26] After having presented the history of Heisterbach Abbey and Caesarius's life and works, Kaufmann reflected on the relevance of the *Dialogus*, suggesting that it represented "clearly and in a lively way" the "gloomy side" of medieval life, therefore complementing Gottfried von Strassburg's poetry, which represented its "merry and sensuous" side.[27] Remarkably, Kaufmann characterized Caesarius as a poet, underlining the picturesqueness of his writings, "so that bygone time stirs and moves in its most colorful and varied ways, mundane and wonderful, cheerful and sad, big and small, full of hope and moribund."[28] He of course highly praised Caesarius's passion for truth and attention to historical details (especially as the Rhineland was concerned), but also some stories without historical grounding, in which "the traces of vanished heathendom continue to surface."[29] In the end of his study, Kaufmann expresses the hope that Caesarius will no longer be scorned as a gullible monk (*"leichtgläubige[r] Mönch"*), but will get the attention he deserves as the author of the "oldest and the most comprehensive book of the legends of the Rhine region" (*"Verfasser des ältesten*

Confession") and 50–53 ("The Little Scholar"). Baring-Gould cited the source of the "The Devil's Confession" as Caesarius Heisterbachensis, *De Miraculis et Visionibus sui Temporis* lib, iii, c. 26, AD 1230. The title *De miraculis et visionibus sui temporis* is used in several Latin and German scholarly works translated into English in the nineteenth century, for example by Karl Rudolf Hagenbach in his 1841 *Lehrbuch der Dogmengeschichte*. Its translation by Carl W. Buch was published in 1847 as *Compendium of the History of Doctrines* (Edinburgh: T. & T. Clark, 1847), 2:103.

[26] Alexander Kaufmann, *Caesarius von Heisterbach, ein Beitrag zur Kulturgeschichte des 12. und 13. Jahrhunderts* (Cologne: Heberle, 1850).

[27] Kaufmann, *Caesarius von Heisterbach*, 37–38 (translation mine).

[28] Kaufmann, *Caesarius von Heisterbach*, 38.

[29] Kaufmann, *Caesarius von Heisterbach*, 6.

und umfangreichsten rheinischen Sagenbuchs").[30] The double vision of the *Dialogus*—as a valuable historical source and as a *Sagenbuch*—is reflected in Kaufmann's dedication of the study to historian Johann Friedrich Böhmer († 1863) and to poet Karl Simrock.

The renewed scholarly interest in Caesarius's work resulted in the first and so far the only critical edition of the *Dialogus*, published in 1851 by Joseph Strange († 1880), who specialized in genealogy and regional history. Strange's edition was primarily based on four manuscripts: Dü1, Dü2, Bo, and Co. Another two manuscripts: Ko, from the fifteenth century (1470), and the lost Aachen, Stadtbibliothek, 49, from the fifteenth century (1468), reached him too late, so he used them only in the final sheets, which were still being printed. Besides the manuscripts, Strange also used the editions by Zell, Koelhoff, and Fischer. The index to the edition (*Index in Caesarii Heisterbacensis Dialogum*) was published in 1857 in Koblenz; the second edition was printed in 1922 in Cologne.[31] Despite the limited number of manuscripts, Strange's edition provides a stable and reliable text that is still used today.

In the short preface that accompanies the edition, Strange mentions that the absence of a modern critical edition of the *Dialogus* had been deplored by many esteemed scholars, including Johann Friedrich Böhmer and Jacob Grimm.[32] Caesarius, he continues, had in fact remarkably elucidated ("*insigniter illustravit*") not only monastic life in particular, but also the private and public lives of people of the Rhine region in general. In addition, Strange points out, the *Dialogus* possesses qualities able both to win over readers' hearts in the sweetest way and to offer a rich source of information to all those interested in history. The emphasis on the ability of the

---

[30] Kaufmann, *Caesarius von Heisterbach*, 55–56.

[31] Strange's edition was reprinted, with its index, in 1966 (Ridgewood, NJ: Gregg Press).

[32] *Caesarii Heisterbacensis Dialogus miraculorum* (Cologne-Bonn-Brussels: J. M. Heberle, 1851), 1:III.

Dialogus to *"delectare"* not only shows Strange's appreciation of Caesarius's rhetoric, but also calls attention to the fact that academic reading was not entirely devoid of pleasure—as is indeed still true today.

Strange's edition cemented the importance of the *Dialogus* for cultural historians. However, nineteenth-century academic society still had some reservations, inherited from previous centuries. Editorial notes to the 1850 edition of the English translation of Mosheim's *Institutiones historiae ecclesiasticae antiquae et recentiores* (1755) casually characterize the *Dialogus* as "full of fables."[33]

French scholars were also critical. Despite an overall positive tone, the 1851 review of Strange's edition, printed in *Revue catholique*, still expressed regrets that "such a book had been published in the company of a Saint Augustine, a Saint Aloysius Gonzaga, a Saint Macarius and the models of asceticism without a word of disapproval or reservation, but with recommendations that can make justified doubt seem superfluous."[34]

Usually seen as more or less reliable in what concerns the local history of the Rhineland, the *Dialogus* still had many controversial narratives that called for reflection. The best known of these is V.21, *De haeresi Albigensium*, where Arnaud Amalric, abbot of Cîteaux and papal legate, unleashed the massacre at Béziers with the words, *"Caedite eos. Novit enim Dominus qui sunt eius,"* popularly translated in English as "Kill them all! God will know his own." The growing historical interest in the Albigensian wars and the legendary appropriation of Catharism[35] popularized the "Kill them all" phrase,

---

[33] Johann Lorenz von Mosheim, *Institutes of Ecclesiastical History: Ancient and Modern*, trans. James Murdock with additions by Henry Soames, vol. 2 (London: Brown, Green, and Longmans, 1850), 555.

[34] *Revue catholique* 8 (1850–1851): 51.

[35] See Sandrine Lavaud, "La fabrique historiographique et mythographique de la Croisade albigeoise (XIXᵉ–début XXᵉ siècle)," *Médiévales* (On-line), 74 Spring (2018). URL: http://journals.openedition.org/medievales/8325; DOI: https://doi.org/10.4000/medievales.8325.

which had made its way into many historical works, to the displeasure of some scholars. For Johann Baptist Alzog († 1878), the whole episode was nothing but a historical lie (*eine historische Lüge*), which had been told to a gullible Caesarius of Heisterbach, whose trustworthiness, he says, "people so rightfully derided."[36]

Philippe Tamizey de Larroque († 1898) is more eloquent and also more acerbic towards the *Dialogus*. He complains that Arnaud's words invaded almost every historical work,[37] as is all the more lamentable, he says, because it was taken from a book where "implausibility reaches the utmost limits of the grotesque."[38] In order to demonstrate to his readers how untrustworthy Caesarius was, Tamizey de Larroque recapitulates some stories from the *Dialogus*: X.23 (the sun is divided into three parts), I.32 (devils play with a soul as if it were a ball), II.11 (Pope Innocent demands that a woman show up before him in the same clothes she was wearing while committing a sin), etc. "All these absurdities," he concludes, "do not permit one to take this writer seriously."[39]

French historians seem to have been particularly negative about the *Dialogus*, although Caesarius was featured in the eighteenth volume of the *Histoire littéraire de la France*, published in 1835 by Pierre Daunou.[40] Caesarius became part of French literary history because of Le Mire's affirmation that he had been prior at Villers. Daunou's position on Caesarius and on the *Dialogus* is essentially neutral. He cites Oudin's acerbic criticism ("*Quam simplex fuerit Caesarius in credendo,*" etc.) but

---

[36] Johann Baptist Alzog, *Grundriss der Universal-Kirchengeschichte: zunächst für akademische Vorlesungen* (Mainz: Florian Kupferberg, 1868), 344.

[37] Philippe Tamizey de Larroque, "Un épisode de la guerre des Albigeois," *Revue des questions historiques* 1 (1866): 175.

[38] Tamizey de Larroque, "Un épisode de la guerre," 180.

[39] Tamizey de Larroque, "Un épisode de la guerre," 182.

[40] *Histoire littéraire de la France; ouvrage commencé par des religieux bénédictins de la Congrégation de Saint Maur, et continué par des membres de l'Institut*, ed. Pierre Daunou, et al., Suite du treizième siècle (Paris: Firmin Didot, 1835; repr. 1971), 18:194–201.

does not explicitly affirm it. Having described in detail the content of the *Dialogus* and its editions, Daunou then presents the *Vita Engelberti*, Caesarius's second most famous work. The life of Engelbert may have been controversial, and he had never been officially canonized, but according to Daunou, his historian (Caesarius of Heisterbach) nevertheless merits to have a place of his own in French literary history. Caesarius's contemporaries, Daunou continues, did not consider him worth much, but Trithemius spoke of him highly. Daunou's entry on Caesarius concludes with the quotation from Trithemius.[41]

From the middle of the nineteenth century onward, the *Dialogus*'s reputation as a historical source in its own right became more and more pronounced, despite echoes of the previous backlash. At the same time, the *Dialogus* was attaining a wider readership thanks to translations into German. In 1888, Alexander Kaufmann published the first part of the *Wunderbare und denkwürdige Geschichten aus den Werken des Cäsarius von Heisterbach*, with the translation of 216 *exempla*. The second part came out in 1891, with 212 *exempla*.[42] In his preface, Kaufmann observed that perception of Caesarius had finally changed to good. Just fifty or sixty years earlier, a mention of Caesarius would have caused a commiserative shrug or an invective about an author considered one of the principal exponents of medieval superstitiousness. But as cultural history and mythology were rising to the rank of science, opinions about Caesarius became more positive.[43]

Kaufmann himself, however, still found some stories from the *Dialogus* too sensitive to be published, because they were capable of offending and angering even readers not particularly prudish.[44] One example is the first episode of the *Vita domini Everhardi plebani sancti Jacobi* (IV.98), about Everhard as

[41] *Histoire littéraire de la France*, 18:201.

[42] Alexander Kaufmann, *Wunderbare und denkwürdige Geschichten aus den Werken des Caesarius von Heisterbach*, 2 vols. (Cologne: Boisserée, 1888, 1891).

[43] Kaufmann, *Wunderbare und denkwürdige Geschichten*, 1.1.

[44] Kaufmann, *Wunderbare und denkwürdige Geschichten*, 1.4.

a saintly priest who blamed young men for having carnal temptations that caused them to despair. God thus struck him with the same kind of temptation so that he could himself experience its power and be kinder to those who were struggling. When the simple monk Herman, a future abbot of Heisterbach, came to Everhard to confess his temptation and to ask for prayer, Everhard exclaimed, "I suffer from the same thing, how could I pray for you?" Herman was reassured and instructed by these words. For a nineteenth-century reader, however, the idea of a priest sharing his temptation with a penitent was disturbing. While defending and promoting the *Dialogus*, Kaufmann still censored it by omitting the story.

Kaufmann also omitted from his translation the dialogic exchanges between the Monk and the Novice and reorganized the stories geographically, as had been done in the structure of Simrock's *Rheinsagen aus dem Munde des Volks und deutscher Dichter*. These changes are consistent with Kaufmann's description of the *Dialogus* as a *Sagenbuch*. The notion of a *Sagenbuch* can in fact be seen as a key concept in understanding the reception of the *Dialogus* in nineteenth-century Germany. Franz Hirsch conclusively emphasized the association of the *Dialogus* with Rhine Romanticism when he wrote in 1883, "*Ich möchte den geistreichen Mönch von Heisterbach ohne viel Bedenken den Erfinder der Romantik des Rheins nennen*" ("Without further reservations, I would like to call the ingenious monk from Heisterbach the inventor of Rhine Romanticism").[45] Caesarius's *exempla* collection became part of the German national heritage, a mirror of the medieval German soul, a source of myths and folk tales that people might both enjoy and study as part of the culture-centered approach to the Middle Ages. Another German scholar, Mathias Bethany, wrote, "*Die Werke des Cäsarius atmen echtes deutsches Leben*" ("Caesarius's works breathe

---

[45] Franz Hirsch, *Geschichte der deutschen Literatur*, vol. 1, *Das Mittelalter* (Leipzig: Wilhelm Friedrich Hofbuchhändler, 1883), 375.

the genuine German life").[46] Despite occasional criticism, Caesarius was seen with sympathy by his compatriots.

In 1897, the *Bergischer Geschichtsverein* erected a monument in Caesarius's honor near the ruins of Heisterbach Abbey. The inscription on the stone says, "*Dem Cisterciensermönch Cäsarius von Heisterbach zur Anerkennung seiner Bedeutung für die heimische Geschichte und die Kunde des Volkslebens der Hohenstauferzeit*" ("To the Cistercian monk Caesarius of Heisterbach in appreciation of his merits for local history and studies of the life of the people in Hohenstaufen time").[47]

[46] Mathias Bethany, "Cäsarius von Heisterbach," *Monatsschrift des Bergischen Geschichtsvereins* 8 Nr 3 (1896): 173.
[47] See Fig. 1, p. xxii.

15

From the Twentieth Century to the Present Day: Academia and Popular Culture

Any overview of twentieth-century reception of the *Dialogus* must inevitably be historiographic. Medieval studies developed and diversified spectacularly in the course of the century, with the *Dialogus* studied from different critical perspectives and primarily used, to cite Karl Langosch († 1992), as an important source for the history of the Cistercian Order and its theology, but also for every aspect of contemporary life.[1] With the advent of historical anthropology in the 1970s, the *Dialogus* became sought after by scholars focusing on different aspects of medieval mentality and religious sentiment. Caesarius's work had been part of studies on medieval *exempla* since the early development of this academic area, and it continues to be explored today thanks to the recent wave of interest in monastic and especially Cistercian *exempla*.

However, despite a great deal of scholarly attention, the *Dialogus* has not been yet re-edited. Alfons Hilka († 1939) planned a critical edition of the *Dialogus* for the second volume of his three-volume monograph *Die Wundergeschichten des Caesarius von Heisterbach*. The first volume, published in 1933,

---

[1] Karl Langosch, "Caesarius von Heisterbach," in *Die deutsche Literatur des Mittelalters. Verfasserlexikon,* 2nd ed. (Berlin: de Gruyter, 1978), 1:667.

contained critically edited *exempla* and other extracts from Caesarius's sermons, while the third (1937) has the critical editions of the *Libri VIII miraculorum*, the *Vita sancti Engelberti*, and the *Vita sancte Elyzabeth Lantgravie*.[2] The second volume was never published. In 1967, Fritz Wagner († 2003) defended his Habilitation thesis *Dialogus miraculorum: Prolegomena zur Editio critica und literarhistorische Untersuchungen* at the University of Cologne, but it was never published and has unfortunately been lost.

Historiography on the *Dialogus* is not particularly large but is still impressive. The work has been summarized several times, most recently in the introduction to *The Art of Cistercian Persuasion*.[3] That historiographic overview is not repeated in this volume, notwithstanding the fact that modern research on the *Dialogus* is an inherent part of its continuous reception. Instead, what follows explores the way the *Dialogus* has influenced the modern imagination. Despite the fact that the *Dialogus*, like the majority of medieval literature, is habitually read only by scholars or students, its current reception is not limited to academia. A number of fictional works published in Germany feature Caesarius as a character, a rare achievement for a medieval author, let alone an author of a didactic collection of *exempla*.

The basis of the current pattern of reception was laid in the nineteenth century with translations into German that helped the *Dialogus* to reach readers not competent in Latin. At the beginning of the twentieth century, the *Dialogus* was fortunate

---

[2] Alfons Hilka, ed., *Die Wundergeschichten des Caesarius von Heisterbach*, vols.1, 3 (Bonn: Hanstein, 1933, 1937).

[3] For other summaries see Edmund Müller, "Caesarius von Heisterbach in der Literatur," *Unsere Liebe Frau von Himmerod* 8 (1978): 40–46; Ludger Tewes, "Der Dialogus Miraculorum des Caesarius von Heisterbach: Beobachtungen zum Gliederungs- und Werkcharakter," *Archiv für Kulturgeschichte* 79 (1997): 13–30; and the introduction to the translation by Horst Schneider and Nikolaus Nösges, *Dialogus miraculorum: Dialog über die Wunder*, Fontes Christiani (Turnhout: Brepols, 2009), 1:88–90.

enough to catch the interest of Hermann Hesse. By 1900, Hesse was already translating chapter IV.36, the famous *exemplum* about Abbot Gevard of Heisterbach, who awakened his sleepy audience by promising to tell a story about King Arthur.[4] A few years later, Hesse conceived the idea to publish selected stories from the *Dialogus* in translation. Altogether fifteen chapters from *distinctiones* I–V were published in two different articles in 1908 in the journal *März*,[5] without the framing conversations between the Monk and the Novice. Hesse perceived the dialogue as superfluous, arguing that the Monk teaches through examples and with the stories by themselves, sometimes completely forgetting to comment on them.[6] As the didactic is commonly associated with dullness, Hesse insists that the *Dialogus* is by no means a "monster of boredom" (*ein Monstrum von Langeweile*).[7] He explains that Caesarius did not ram theological definitions down the throat of his students in a dry and indigestible manner, but offered them as if in passing, in small portions.[8] While acknowledging the didactic character of the *Dialogus*, he tries to mute it and, so to speak, to de-exemplify Caesarius's stories.

In 1921, Hesse resumed his work on the *Dialogus* and published another thirteen stories from the *Dialogus* in the journal *Schwizerland*.[9] Four years later, he reprinted all his translations

---

[4] See Fritz Wagner, "Hermann Hesse and the Middle Ages," *The Modern Language Review* 77, no. 2 (April 1982): 378–86.

[5] "Cäsarius von Heisterbach," *März: Halbmonatsschrift für deutsche Kultur* 2, no. 3 (1908): 33–39; "Aus dem Dialogus miraculorum des Cäsarius von Heisterbach," *März: Halbmonatsschrift für deutsche Kultur* 2, no. 3 (1908): 131–37, 225–29, 289–91, with chapters I.3, 34; II.24, 27–29; III.49; IV.36, 37, 48, 86–88; V.17, 18.

[6] "Cäsarius von Heisterbach," 36.

[7] "Cäsarius von Heisterbach," 36.

[8] "Cäsarius von Heisterbach," 35.

[9] Hermann Hesse, "Geschichten aus dem Mittelalter: Erzählungen aus dem *Dialogus miraculorum* des Caesarius von Heisterbach, aus dem Lateinischen übersetzt von Hermann Hesse," *Schweizerland* 7 (1921): 418–29, with chapters II.22; III.25, 36; IV.60, 77; V.17, 43; VI 2.11; VII.4, 32; VIII.21, 29.

from the *Dialogus* in the anthology *Geschichten aus dem Mittelalter*, together with selected translations from the *Gesta Romanorum*.[10] In general Hesse presented both Caesarius and his works in a warm and commendatory manner. For him, the *Dialogus* was a hidden treasure of the old German literature, and Caesarius himself was a poet in his own right, unfortunately largely unknown to the general public,[11] an honest, benevolent, and good man, whose personality itself had a pedagogic effect.[12] Hesse's emphasis on Caesarius's sympathetic persona as an engaged teacher is of particular interest, because this authorial image is conveyed to the readers primarily by the dialogic frame of the *Dialogus*, which, ironically, Hesse's translations omit.

Around the same time that Hesse published his translations, another partial translation of the *Dialogus* appeared in German. The volume, translated by Ernst Müller-Holm, was published in Berlin in 1910 in the series *Verschollene Meister der Literatur* ("Forgotten Masters of Literature").[13] Somewhat condescendingly, Müller-Holm characterizes Caesarius as dependent and hidebound, but also as eager and noble spirited, through whose peculiar misapprehensions of morality he can be recognized sympathetically as a typical medieval German.[14] Apparently some stories from the *Dialogus* were still considered morally a bit scandalous, and Caesarius himself still needed an apologetic introduction to be taken seriously. As for the presentation of the *Dialogus*, Müller-Holm, like Hesse, omits the dialogue between the Monk and the Novice, because, he argues, these

---

[10] Hermann Hesse, *Geschichten aus dem Mittelalter* (Konstanz: Karl Hönn, 1925).

[11] "*ich halte ihn für einen Dichter, um den es schade ist, daß niemand ihn kennt*" ("Cäsarius von Heisterbach," 33).

[12] "Cäsarius von Heisterbach," 36.

[13] The book offers a selection of stories from each *distinctio*, 160 in all. The most often represented is *distinctio X, De miraculis*, with 23 stories, perhaps regarded as the most curious.

[14] Ernst Müller-Holm, *Caesarius von Heisterbach* (Berlin: K. Schnabel, 1910), 6.

characters are not lively, and their conversation is predominantly theoretical, so it lacks deep inner connection.[15]

In the course of the twentieth century, more German translations and re-editions appeared. The *Hundert auserlesene, wunderbare und merkwürdige Geschichten des Zisterziensers Cäsarius von Heisterbach*, by Otto Hellinghaus, published in Aachen in 1925, is largely based on Kaufmann's translation.[16] Hellinghaus points out that Kaufmann's *Wunderbare und denkwürdige Geschichten* had only a limited circulation; he addresses his own edition to a broad learned audience, including young adults of both sexes.[17] Like Kaufmann, he omits both the framing dialogue, considering it of no interest to his target readership, and some potentially objectionable stories.[18]

About fifty years later, a new partial translation by Ilse and Johannes Schneider appeared: *Die wundersamen Geschichten des Caesarius von Heisterbach*. Like other partial translations, this one also disregards the dialogic frame as being purely formal and without value of its own.[19] The majority of moral and theological explanations incorporated in the stories were omitted as well.

The later *Von Geheimnissen und Wundern des Caesarius von Heisterbach: Ein Lesebuch*, by Helmut Herles, is based on the translation by Müller-Holm. Herles's aim was finally to give

---

[15] Ernst Müller-Holm, *Caesarius von Heisterbach* (Cologne: Hegner, 1968), 8.

[16] Otto Hellinghaus, ed., *Hundert auserlesene, wunderbare und merkwürdige Geschichten des zisterziensers Cäsarius von Heisterbach* (Aachen: Deutschherren, 1925), IV.

[17] Hellinghaus, *Hundert auserlesene*, III. Interestingly, the book is organized in twelve sections according to religious subjects, somewhat resembling the composition of the *Dialogus*, e.g., *Aus dem Klosterleben; Seliges Sterben im Orden; Fromme Einfalt in der Welt*. One wonders why the selected stories still needed to be rearranged!

[18] Hellinghaus, *Hundert auserlesene*, III–IV. As for the objectionable stories, he cites Kaufmann (see above, p. 251–52).

[19] *Die wundersamen Geschichten des Caesarius von Heisterbach*, ed. and trans. Ilse and Johannes Schneider (Berlin: Union, 1972), 8.

to the readers *"ein Lesebuch, ein Volksbuch"* (a reader, a chapbook), easily available and affordable. For modern readers, Herles remarks, Caesarius's world first appears far-off, strange, and lost, and then they realize that they see themselves in it as in a mirror. It is certainly strange, he says, to read about two devils playing with a soul as with a ball, but who does not feel sometimes as though being about to become a toy for external powers?[20] The reader's response imagined by Herles is in fact very close to the construction of exemplarity. It is however questionable whether the *Dialogus* is really read in this manner today.

Finally, the first full translation together with the Latin text and a thorough scholarly introduction was published by Brepols in 2009: *Dialog über die Wunder*, by Horst Schneider and Nikolaus Nösges.[21]

The large availability of twentieth- and twenty-first-century translations has ensured the visibility of the *Dialogus* to modern and contemporary German readers. In a time of booming historical mystery and adventure novels, Caesarius and his work has caught the attention of some German writers. This being said, the modern take on Caesarius is in many ways rooted in the Rhine legends of the Romantic era. Wilifred Esch, for example, reimagined the legend of the Drachenfels in the 2002 children's book *Schandor und Cäsarius*, which features Caesarius as a good ghost who appears every full moon among the ruins of Heisterbach Abbey. He was granted this singular opportunity for life after death, the story goes, because he was

---

[20] *Von Geheimnissen und Wundern des Caesarius von Heisterbach: Ein Lesebuch*, ed. Helmut Herles, 2nd ed. (Bonn: Bouvier, 1991), 2.

[21] *Dialogus miraculorum: Dialog über die Wunder*, ed. and trans. Horst Schneider and Nikolaus Nösges, Fontes Christiani 86 (Turnhout: Brepols, 2009). A complete list of translations of the *Dialogus* appears in the bibliography to this volume, pp. 288–97. A two-volume English translation of the *Dialogus* will appear in 2023 and 2024: Ronald Pepin, trans., *Caesarius of Heisterbach: Dialogue on Miracles*, CF 89, 90 (Collegeville, MN: Cistercian Publications, forthcoming).

a brave man who helped many people.[22] He continues meeting with his friend Schandor, who, being a dragon, can live a thousand years or even more. Schandor, it turns out, was expelled by his family for being too good and inoffensive for a dragon, and his name, in fact, comes from the German *Schande*, which means *shame*. He wanted to live in a town, but after people drove him away, he hid himself in a cave in the forests of Siebengebirge, where Caesarius found him. Because Caesarius had no fear of Schandor, they became friends.

During their monthly nocturnal meetings, as Esch explains it, Caesarius and Schandor exchange stories, among them the legend of the dragon of Drachenfels, which Schandor tells. After each story, there is a brief exchange between the two characters, recalling the dialogue between the Monk and the Novice in the *Dialogus*, but the tales in the book are neither those of the *Dialogus* nor inspired by them.

Another Rhine legend appropriated by contemporary writers is that mentioned above of the monk from Heisterbach who meditated on the verse *One day with the Lord is as a thousand years, and a thousand years as one day* (2 Pet 3:8). Although the legend was not initially connected to Caesarius, it shaped his modern reception. One interesting example of the legend appears in the novel *Das Rätsel der Templer* by Martina André, published in 2007. It is about the adventures of a Templar knight named Gérard von Breydenbach, alias Gero. In 1307, just before the suppression of his order, Gero was entrusted with a mission to collect the "Haupt der Weisen" (Head of the Wise), a precious relic kept in Heisterbach. It had been brought from Jerusalem by the grand master of the order and was given into the custody of the Cistercians at Heisterbach. From this time on, the abbey always had a guardian of the relic. In 1206, the novel says, that guardian was Caesarius, the prior, known

---

[22] Wilfried Esch, *Schandor und Cäsarius: Geschichten und Abenteuer des Cäsarius von Heisterbach und des Drachen Schandor* (Bonn: Free Pen, 2002), 2.

for his interest in the phenomenon of time and for his own dark prophecies about the future.[23]

It turns out that during his initial journey, Gero was taken into the future, to 2004, where he learned that the *Haupt der Weisen* was a quantum computer that allowed the Knights Templar to travel through time, thus assuring the extraordinary success of the order. When Gero wakes up in 2004, he assumes that the clue to what had happened to him in 1307 must be in the abbey of Heisterbach. When he consults someone with an extensive knowledge in medieval history, he discovers that the abbey did indeed have the needed connection to the mystery of time-travel: the person of Caesarius himself. Caesarius is presented like this:

> Caesarius of Heisterbach was a Cistercian monk who lived in Heisterbach Abbey from 1199 to 1240. He was the prior of the abbey, and one can without a doubt characterize him as a talented writer. He also made some apocalyptic prophecies. Some people think that he predicted climate catastrophes and the third World War, and that he was a predecessor of Nostradamus. Anyway, among his writings one finds a story about a monk who fell asleep in the forest near the abbey and awoke in the same place. To his great astonishment nobody recognized him. It turns out that he had slept away not just one afternoon, but hundreds of years.[24]

This time-traveling monk, the novel assures us, really existed—it was Brother Thomas from Himmerod—and Caesarius knew him personally and turned his story into the popular legend.

Along with the attribution of the story to Caesarius of Heisterbach, the novel also affirms that Caesarius wrote prophecies. In reality, there are no prophetic texts among Caesarius's surviving works, except for an apocalyptic prophecy of a brother Simon, who announces both the advent of Antichrist and the

---

[23] Martina André, *Das Rätsel der Templer*, 4th ed (Berlin: Aufbau, 2012), 195.
[24] André, *Das Rätsel der Templer*, 446–47.

plagues awaiting the city of Cologne after it was corrupted by bad clergy (II.30). Caesarius does not identify Simon, saying, *"sed quis fuerit idem Simon, penitus ignoro"* ("I do not know who this Simon was"). Nevertheless, Caesarius seems to enjoy a solid reputation as a prophet. Several Internet sites feature him among famous prophets; the majority of these are in German, but a few are in English. One of them reads,

> Caesarius of Heisterbach was a Cistercian monk who lived in Cologne from 1180 to 1240. Caesarius foretold the rise of Napoleon and the events of the French Revolution. He also predicted the following events, still to come: "There will be no Pope, and the air will be as a pestilence, destroying men and beasts alike. Not since the creation of the world has one experienced such misfortune."[25]

Caesarius's fame as a clairvoyant results from an interesting confusion. In the nineteenth century a popular prophecy attributed to Saint Caesarius of Arles circulated, originating from the *Mirabilis liber qui prophetias reuelationesque nec non res mirandas preteritas presentes et futuras aperte demonstrat*, a collection of prophetic texts published for the first time in Paris in 1522.[26] The *Mirabilis liber* contains no mention of Saint Caesarius, but ascribes the prophecy in question to Johannes de Vatiguerro. The original version of the prophecy referred to events in France beginning in about 1354, among them civil unrest and persecution of great lords (the Jacquerie), as well as imprisonment of the king (capture by the English of the French king John II). The prophecy survives in several fifteenth-century manuscripts, in each case said to be by Johannes de Bassigniaco.

---

[25] http://www.bibliotecapleyades.net/profecias/esp_profecia01c1b.htm. See also catholicprophecy.org.

[26] *Mirabilis liber qui prophetias reuelationesq[ue] nec non res mirandas preteritas presentes et futuras aperte demonstrat* (Paris: Jean Petit, 1522), fol. I^v–lviii; see Jennifer Britnell and Derek Stubbs, "The *Mirabilis Liber*: Its Compilation and Influence," *Journal of the Warburg and Courtauld Institutes* 49 (1986): 126–49, esp. 136–37 about this prophecy.

The prophecy made quite a stir during the French Revolution, and the *Mirabilis liber* enjoyed a renewed popularity. Jacques-Barthélemy Salgues remarks in his *Des erreurs et des préjugés répandus dans les diverses classes de la société*, from 1810, that it became very much sought after and gained the status of a sacred, incomparable book, in which one finds faithful and exact history, with all the details concerning the disasters of the Revolution.[27]

Around 1790, the prophecy was finally translated into French by a certain J. A. S. Ch. under the title *Prédiction pour la fin du dix-huitième siècle, tirée du Mirabilis liber*. The preface affirms that some people attributed the prophecy in question to Saint Caesarius and others to Saint Severus.[28] The translation does incorporate some elements from the so-called Saint Severus prophecy, also drawn from the *Mirabilis liber* (*Prophetia sancti Severi Archiepiscopi*).[29]

The revolutionary authorities, trying to stop the spread of the prophecy that allegedly predicted the fall of the Directory and the revival of the monarchy, forbade the reading of the book.[30] But the *Mirabilis liber* continued to be read in secrecy, and attempts to ban it only increased the public's interest. When *Des erreurs et des préjugés* was published, the *Mirabilis liber* finally became generally available, and many curious readers, as Salgues remarks, were disappointed by its "barbaric" style and "childish" ideas, as well as by the fact that its predictions had not been realized.[31]

---

[27] Jacques-Barthélemy Salgues, *Des erreurs et des préjugés répandus dans les diverses classes de la société*, 3rd ed. (Paris: Foucault, 1823), 2:60.

[28] *Prédiction pour la fin du dix-huitieme siecle: tirée du Mirabilis liber; avec la traduction littérale à côté du texte; précédée d'une introduction qui établit la concordance des dates et des événements, avec les circonstances actuelles*, 2nd ed. (Paris: Marielle et Lebreton, 1790), 1. In Germany, the extracts from the prophecy were published in the *Tiroler Wochenblatt* 47 (1849): 192, and *Tiroler Wochenblatt* 48 (1849): 194–95.

[29] On the prophecy, see Britnell and Stubbs, "Mirabilis Liber," 134–35.

[30] Salgues, *Des erreurs et des préjugés*, 2:66.

[31] Salgues, *Des erreurs et des préjugés*, 2:67.

Doubts about the authorship of Saint Caesarius had already been expressed in 1793. In the February 15 number of *Journal historique et littéraire* an anonymous note stated that the *Liber admirablis* (*sic*) was certainly written not by Caesarius of Arles, but by Caesarius of Heisterbach. The author of the note was aware of the *Dialogus* (unsurprisingly, his opinion of it was low) and informed his readers that it had even been included in the *Spanish Index of Forbidden Books* for its excessive credulity.[32] But the confusion between Caesarius of Arles and Caesarius of Heisterbach proved persistent. The attribution of the whole *Liber mirabilis* to Caesarius of Heisterbach is found, for example, in the *Lexikon der Prophezeiungen: Analyse von 350 Vorhersagen von der Antike bis zur Gegenwart* by Karl Leopold von Lichtenfels, published in Munich as recently as in 2015, following its first edition in 2000.[33]

The "Saint Caesarius prophecy" is also ascribed to Caesarius of Heisterbach in the novel *Zeit der Dämmerung* (2009) by Wilfried Esch.[34] The story takes place around 1625, when the calamities predicted by Caesarius—destruction of churches and monasteries, pestilence, hunger, etc.—seemed to be coming true. Caesarius's prophetic gift, however, is mentioned only briefly. Instead, the novel develops a subplot around Caesarius's involvement in the events that set up the principal action in the seventeenth century.

In the novel, it is revealed that Caesarius kept a secret journal, hidden in the Saint Cassius Collegiate in Bonn. Once one of the seventeenth-century protagonists finds it, the reader of

---

[32] *Journal historique et littéraire*, February 15 (Maastricht: Cavelier, 1793): 319–21.

[33] Karl Leopold von Lichtenfels, *Lexikon der Prophezeiungen: Analyse von 350 Vorhersagen von der Antike bis zur Gegenwart* (Munich: Heyne, 2002), 93–94. To be fair, the book gives, in brackets, the name of Johann Vatiguerro: "*Diese Quelle ist höchstwarscheinlich mit der von Johann Vatiguerro (Bruder Johann vom gespaltenen Felsen, um 1340 angesetz) identisch, d. h. eine der beiden wurde zur Vorlage der anderen.*"

[34] Wilfried Esch, *Zeit der Dämmerung* (Königswinter: Lempertz, 2009), 135.

the novel discovers that since his youth Caesarius had had strange dreams, repeatedly seeing a mysterious woman putting a baby under the lime trees for somebody to find. While on pilgrimage to Rocamadour (see *Dialogus* I.17), Caesarius recognized the place from his dreams and found the baby there. He at first entrusted the foundling to the care of the nuns of Dietkirchen, Bonn, and then after the boy—named Wilfred vun de Lynde—turned seven, Caesarius brought him to Heisterbach and raised him among the novices.

As the novel continues, Caesarius, accompanied by Wilfred, took part in the Albigensian Crusade in 1209 as a chronicler and actually witnessed the siege of Béziers. In Béziers, Wilfred found a dying woman with a baby girl named Sophia, whom he himself had earlier seen in a dream. He promised the woman to bring Sophia to the Church of Saint Mary Magdalene in Rennes-le-Château. Later Caesarius and Wilfred learned that Sophia was a descendant of Jesus and Mary Magdalene, and that in fact Cathars were protectors of the holy bloodline. After this discovery, Caesarius found himself in a difficult situation, as Wilfred later explains: "Oh, my poor Master! How he must have suffered, when he had to choose between the truth and the Church!"[35]

In the event, says the novel, Caesarius did stay loyal to the Church. However, he also tried to describe the events of the Crusade as truthfully as possible, an attempt that apparently did not please Church officials. Later, the Church even purposely introduced some inaccuracies into the German translation of the *Dialogus* (invented by Esch). In the chapter concerning the circumstances of the massacre in Béziers, this "official" translation stated that the abbot "*reportedly* said 'Kill them all,'" whereas, Esch assures the reader, the word *reportedly* is absent from the original text. A more accurate translation would therefore be, "*The legate Arnauld Amalric said.*" (In reality,

---

[35] Esch, *Zeit der Dämmerung*, 539: "*Oh, mein armer Meister, wie musste er damals gelitten haben, als er zwischen Wahrheit und die Kirche wählen musste!*"

the *Dialogus* has *"fertur dixisse"*: "he reportedly said.") The novel reimagines the *Caedite eos* episode by portraying Caesarius as an eyewitness of the massacre and also as someone who was aware of its wickedness, but, being bound by duty, was unable to oppose it explicitly. Esch reinvents not only the persona of Caesarius, but also the *Dialogus* itself, which he presents as a book that contains unpleasant truths and was deliberably shaped in order to conceal them.

The *Zeit der Dämmerung* also highlights Caesarius's *Vita Engelberti*. In the novel's seventeenth-century plot, one of the characters—the Jesuit Maurus van Leuven—is asked by the prince elector and archbishop of Cologne, Ferdinand of Wittelsbach († 1650), to translate the *Vita* in order finally to canonize Engelbert. To his surprise, Maurus discovers that "Caesarius, apparently deliberately, had not mentioned any of Engelbert's good qualities."[36] The question of whether Engelbert deserved to be canonized is further discussed in the sequel *Die Hexenjäger* (2011), where one of the subplots is the investigation of Engelbert's death and his true involvement in the events surrounding the discovery of the holy bloodline. Caesarius's *Vita Engelberti* does in fact explicitly mention Engelbert's shortcomings as a bishop—that he was not a preacher, was inadequate in spiritual conversation and in biblical commentary, and in his youth was absorbed in worldly activities—but still eulogizes him as a good and righteous ruler.[37] The novel certainly exaggerates Caesarius's uncritical attitude but does not completely invent it.

Another novel that portrays Caesarius as someone involved in mysterious affairs of his times is the *Civitas A.D. 1200: Das Geheimnis der Rose* by Christoph Wolf, published in 2011. The novel tells about a precious relic (a holy nail) brought from

[36] Esch, *Zeit der Dämmerung*, 502.
[37] See my article, "No Way to Salvation for German Bishops? The Case of Saint Engelbert of Cologne," in *Saintly Bishops and Bishops' Saints*, ed. Trpimir Vedriš and John Ott (Poreč: Hagiotheca, 2012), 184–201.

Jerusalem by an enigmatic pilgrim. The pilgrim is hunted down by the evil church organization named *Die Strengen Augen Gottes* ("God's watchful eyes"), which strives to control the flow of the relics. In this novel Caesarius is a secondary character, introduced early in the novel, serving as Heisterbach's librarian. Wolf describes in detail Caesarius's love for the abbey's library—the treasury of knowledge of the history of Christianity, of the world outside Heisterbach, of the mysteries of the faith, and of ways to achieve a happy life and to understand how the world functions.[38] After being appointed as a librarian, the novel explains, Caesarius immersed himself in the work and was rarely seen outside the library. Having become pale from the lack of sunlight, the other monks nicknamed him "Ghost." He seized the opportunity his work gave him to pursue his numerous research interests, from healing arts to mysticism, from legends and myths to the verification of Christian stories, with his favorite subject Jesus' miracles. He studied pagan texts and apocrypha and was proficient not only in Latin, but also in Greek, Hebrew, Arabic, and Aramaic.[39]

At the same time, the novel explains, Caesarius was also the master of novices—one of the most famous in the Holy Roman Empire.[40] He taught the novices about the Cistercian way of life,[41] but also about calligraphy[42] and church architecture, as an admirer of the "new architectural style" (Gothic), which permitted building high, well-lit buildings with thinner columns and bigger windows.[43]

According to the plot, Caesarius receives an encoded message informing him that the Holy Nail will soon be brought to the Westerwald area, where Marienstatt, daughter house of

---

[38] Christoph Wolf, *Civitas A.D. 1200. Das Geheimnis der Rose: Ein mystischer Mittelalter-Roman* (Hamburg: Acabus, 2011), 36.

[39] Wolf, *Civitas*, 37, 40–41.

[40] Wolf, *Civitas*, 137.

[41] Wolf, *Civitas*, 38.

[42] Wolf, *Civitas*, 42.

[43] Wolf, *Civitas*, 39–40.

Heisterbach, is going to be constructed. Caesarius at once cryptically informs the founding community of this event. Once Caesarius's message has been sent, his character recedes into the background and participates in no further action, though he is mentioned several times: as an "enigmatic mystic" by his friends,[44] and as a "crank," "mad mystic," "sorcerer's apprentice," and even "sorcerer" by his foes.[45] But even some of those who blamed Caesarius for corrupting the minds of his young pupils were avid readers of the *Dialogus*.[46]

Wolf portrays Caesarius as a talented teacher, respected and loved by his students. But he also insists on Caesarius as an accomplished scholar with outstanding knowledge of ancient languages. In fact, all these novels present Caesarius as someone who was more than just a humble collector of stories told by others. Instead, he is a prophet, representative of the enigmatic Knights Templar, honest chronicler of the Albigensian Crusade, unconventional thinker, and even guardian of Christian mysteries. What is remarkable is that he is never portrayed as a storyteller. The stories from the *Dialogus* also rarely make their way into modern novels—those by Esch are an exception. Caesarius's authorial image has proved to be more appealing to modern writers of historical mystery fiction than are his stories.

From the nineteenth century onward, the *Dialogus* was hardly read within the context of religious or moral persuasion. Translations made the *Dialogus* available to the general public, especially as regarded the numerous and apparently in-demand translations into German. All of them but one, however, omitted the dialogic frame as too didactic or dull, with the result that Caesarius's own explanatory discourse was not

---

[44] Wolf, *Civitas*, 532.
[45] Wolf, *Civitas*, 148–49.
[46] Wolf, *Civitas*, 149.

available for readers unfamiliar with the Latin text. The *exempla* of the *Dialogus* eventually became isolated tales to be enjoyed as remnants of the past, offering a glimpse into the social and cultural life of the Middle Ages. The distance between the world of modern readers and that of Caesarius thus became shaped as evocative, giving the *Dialogus* an aura of a curious medieval collections of legends. At the same time, the distance itself robbed the *Dialogus* of the immediacy and relevance of its religious and moral message, and, to some extent, of its exemplarity. One could also argue, however, that scholars' continuing use of Caesarius's *exempla* to illustrate a particular aspect of the medieval worldview extends the value of the *Dialogus* as identifiable kind of *exempla* collection.

Conclusion

As the *Dialogus* emerged from Cistercian storytelling culture, it is no surprise that the white monks played a crucial role in its long-term transmission and reception, as both narrators and recipients of the stories. The *Dialogus* may not have been a must-have volume for every Cistercian monastery, but it was definitely a success. It was also an object of sometimes bold re-writings and appropriations. Remarkably, Cistercians had already started to create abridged and generalized versions of the *Dialogus* in the first half of the thirteenth century. At the same time, however, they continued to add new stories to it, as if Caesarius's own passion for storytelling encouraged his readers to write down good stories as they came to mind.

Other religious orders took an early interest in the *Dialogus*, but its real success came in the fifteenth century. In the context of the spreading movement of spiritual renewal, Caesarius's stories showed great potential for supporting efforts at reform: by depicting the Cistercian way of life as corresponding to the original monastic spirit while at the same time setting forth problems that a monk or a novice could face and overcome with the help of God and his brothers. Since the fifteenth-century reform movement did not try to create something radically new, but rather both to actualize the past in the present and to renew the present on the model of the past, Caesarius's optimistic recollections must have resonated deeply among those who aspired to broad religious change. The issues touched by Caesarius did not lose their currency with the passing of time. In later centuries religious faced issues similar to those of the fifteenth century, especially in what concerned adjustment to the strict *vita regularis* (desired by the spirit of reform). Marginal notes left by readers indicate that Caesarius's theological and pastoral reflections were highly appreciated as well. The success of the *Dialogue on Miracles* was due not only to the miracles, but also, in no small way, to the dialogue.

Unfortunately, the scope of this study has necessitated omission of many *Dialogus* manuscripts of unknown provenance, although they are no less relevant to the textual history of the *Dialogus* than those whose provenance is known, and they could also tell interesting stories. The same is true about manuscripts owned by people unaffiliated with a religious community and so mentioned here only briefly. Although such manuscripts are scarce, they indicate that the reading of the *Dialogus*, especially in fifteenth-century Germany, was not limited to religious or semi-religious communities, as is shown by the German translation made by Johannes Hartlieb, the physician in the service of Duke Albert III of Bavaria († 1460).[47]

The history of the transmission and reception of the printed *Dialogus* is no less captivating than that of its manuscripts, which reveal a great deal of continuity between them. Despite its undeniably revolutionary character, the arrival of print did

---

[47] See Elena Koroleva, "The *Dialogus miraculorum* in the Light of Its Fifteenth-century German Translation by Johannes Hartlieb," in *The Art of Cistercian Persuasion in the Middle Ages and Beyond*, ed. Victoria Smirnova, Marie Anne Polo de Beaulieu, and Jacques Berlioz (Leiden: Brill, 2015), 227–41.

not bring dramatic changes to readership of the *Dialogus*. The incunabulum editions of the *Dialogus* were unsurprisingly read mostly within religious communities in the area that remained Roman Catholic after the Reformation. This being said, at the time of emerging private libraries the printed *Dialogus* did attract the attention of private book collectors, including renowned humanists and scholars. In those cases, however, it is difficult to tell whether the work served merely as an addition to collections or was actually read by its owners.

If manuscript transmission of the *Dialogus* was marked by the scribal interactions with the text, creating several distinct versions, the crucial element of the reception of its early modern and modern editions is definitely attitudes toward Caesarius and his works. Thanks to their rich paratext, seventeenth-century editions provide a valuable glimpse into perception of the *Dialogus* by its most influential readers of that time—its editors. For both Jacob Fischer and Bertrand Tissier it was all but controversial: worthy of being printed and defended against Protestant criticism, but at the same time containing a somewhat flawed narrative theology. The faithful Catholic readership was expected both to believe Caesarius and to exercise caution while internalizing his exemplary stories.

Scholarly appreciation of the *Dialogus*, dating back to the end of the fifteenth century, then emerged in the form of bio-bibliographical notes in catalogues of ecclesiastical writers. It is therefore no wonder that an important part of scholarly discourse surrounding the *Dialogus* in fact considered Caesarius's character. Both mockery for his naive gullibility and praise for his probity and piety testify to the power of the authorial image constructed by the *Dialogus*. What is fascinating about this aspect of contemporary reception of the *Dialogus* is readers' continual confrontation with the work's ethos. Caesarius is one of the few medieval authors who acquired a reputation that durably influenced the reception of their works.

In the nineteenth century, the Romantic imagination fueled the reception of the *Dialogus* and gave it new positive overtones. Most important, the *Dialogus* was claimed as part of the German medieval heritage, not only ensuring its place in the developing field of medieval studies, but also opening the way into contemporary popular culture. While nineteenth-century poets appropriated some of Caesarius's stories, twenty-first-century novelists have not used the *Dialogus* as a source of inspiration, but instead consider Caesarius as a character within the established universe of the medieval mystery genre, along with enigmatic Knights Templar, the Grail as a link to Christ's bloodline, mysterious relics, and so on.

As opposed to many other famous medieval works, the *Dialogus* was never re-discovered in the nineteenth century, as it had never been completely forgotten. Its reputation was sometimes a matter of controversy, but it always had, and still has, the potential to capture readers' imagination. The most fascinating story that the *Dialogus* could tell is arguably that of its own journey through the ages.

Appendix I

Cited manuscripts of the *Dialogus miraculorum*, alphabetized by shelf mark. Manuscripts without *sigla* are those cited in the book above without *sigla*.

Au	Augsburg, Universitätsbibliothek, Cod. II. 1. 2°14
B	Bern, Burgerbibliothek, 333
Ba	Bamberg, Staatsbibliothek, Msc. Patr. 59
Be1	Berlin, Staatsbibliothek zu Berlin - Preußischer Kulturbesitz, Hdschr. 328
Be2	Berlin, Staatsbibliothek zu Berlin - Preußischer Kulturbesitz, MS. theol. fol. 95
Be3	Berlin, Staatsbibliothek zu Berlin - Preußischer Kulturbesitz, MS. lat. qu. 875
	Berlin, Staatsbibliothek zu Berlin - Preußischer Kulturbesitz, MS. lat. qu. 107
Bo	Bonn, Universitäts- und Landesbibliothek, S 297
Br1	Brussels, Bibliothèque Royale de Belgique, II 1067 (2121)
Br2	Brussels, Bibliothèque Royale de Belgique, 551 (2120)
Bs	Basel, Universitätsbibliothek, B VIII 18
Bs1	Basel, Universitätsbibliothek, A I 34
ChM	Charleville-Mézieres, Bibliothèque municipale, 233
Cl	Colmar, Bibliothèque municipale, 57 (24)
	Cologne, Historisches Archiv, *W 67
	Cologne, Historisches Archiv, GB 8° 194

Co	Cologne, Historisches Archiv, GB f° 87
D	Douai, Bibliothèque Municipale, MS. 397
Dü1	Düsseldorf, Universitäts- und Landesbibliothek, MS. C 26
Dü 2	Düsseldorf, Universitäts- und Landesbibliothek, MS. C27
	Eichstätt, Universitätsbibliothek, Cod. st. 450
Eb	Wiesbaden, Hauptstaatsarchiv, Abt 22, 535/6 [a]
Gd1	Gdańsk, Biblioteka Gdańska Polskiej Akademii Nauk, MS. 2155
Gd2	Gdańsk, Biblioteka Gdańska Polskiej Akademii Nauk, MS. Mar. F. 198
H	Heidelberg, Universitätsbibliothek, Cod. Sal. IX, 46
Ha	The Hague, Koninklijke Bibliotheek, 73 E 36
I	Innsbruck, Universitäts- und Landesbibliothek Tirol, Cod. 185
K	Kremsmünster, Benediktinerstift, CC 54
Ko	Koblenz, Landeshauptarchiv, Best. 701 Nr. 152
L	Leipzig, Universitätsbibliothek, Cod. 445
Li1	Liège, Bibliothèque du Séminaire Épiscopal, 6 N 11
Li2	Liège, Université de Liège, Bibliothèque Générale de Philosophie et Lettres, MS. 86
	London, British Library, Add. MS. 18346
M1	Munich, Bayerische Staatsbibliothek, Clm 2687
M2	Munich, Bayerische Staatsbibliothek, Clm 4711
M3	Munich, Bayerische Staatsbibliothek, Clm 18614
M3/2	Munich, Bayerische Staatsbibliothek, Clm 18615
M4	Munich, Bayerische Staatsbibliothek, Clm 3058
	Munich, Bayerische Staatsbibliothek, Clm 3593
M5	Munich, Bayerische Staatsbibliothek, Clm 5106
M6	Munich, Bayerische Staatsbibliothek, Clm 7545
M7	Munich, Bayerische Staatsbibliothek, Clm 5504

Me	Melk, Benediktinerstift, Cod. 805 (796, O 34)
Mi	Michaelbeuern, Benediktinerstift, Man. cart. 90
Na	Namur, Musée Provincial des Arts anciens du Namurois, Fonds de la Ville, 52
O	Osnabrück, Bischöfliches Archiv, Hs. Frenswegen 21
P	Paris, Bibliothèque nationale de France, lat. 3597 Paris, Bibliothèque Mazarine, 781
Pl	Sankt Paul im Lavanttal, Benediktinerstift, Cod. 61/4
R	Rein, Zisterzienserstift, Cod. 58
So	Soest, Wissenschaftliche Stadtbibliothek, Cod. 13
St	Strasbourg, Bibliothèque nationale et universitaire, 41 (Latin: 39)
T1	Troyes, Bibliothèque municipale, 641
T2	Troyes, Bibliothèque municipale, 592
Tr	Trier, Stadtbibliothek, Hs. 609/2031 2°
Ut1	Utrecht, Universiteitsbibliotheek, Cat. 176
Ut2	Utrecht, Universiteitsbibliotheek, Cat. 177
Ut3	Utrecht, Universiteitsbibliotheek, Cat. 179
Ut4	Utrecht, Universiteitsbibliotheek, Cat. 178
Vo	Vorau, Augustiner-Chorherrenstift, Cod. 172 (olim CXV)
W1	Vienna, Österreichische Nationalbibliothek, Cod. Ser. n. 12796
W2	Vienna, Österreichische Nationalbibliothek, Cod. Ser. n. 12774
W3	Vienna, Österreichische Nationalbibliothek, Cod. 14242
W4	Vienna, Österreichische Nationalbibliothek, Cod. 3785
Wd	Vienna, Dominikanerkonvent, Cod. 196/161
We	Weimar, Herzogin Anna Amalia Bibliothek, Q 21
Wü	Würzburg, Universitätsbibliothek, M. ch. f. 246

Z   Zwettl, Zisterzienserstift, Cod. 131
         Wrocław, Biblioteka Uniwersytecka, Akc. 1948/693

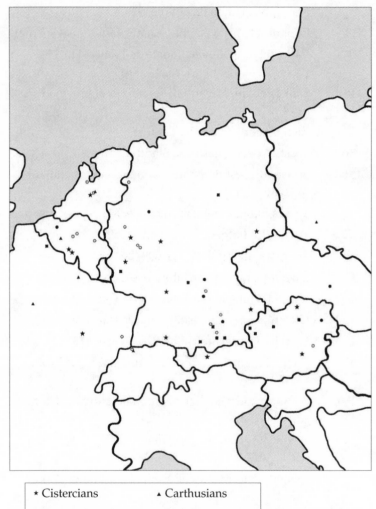

* Cistercians   ▲ Carthusians
○ Canons Regular   • Mendicant Friars
■ Benedictines
Borders are those of modern states.

Figure 3. Map of manuscripts of the *Dialogus* cited in the text

Appendix II

Summaries of nine *exempla* added to Version B of the *Dialogus*, according to MS. Heidelberg, Universitätsbibliothek, Cod. Sal. IX 46 (H).

The Abbot of Murbach (added after *distinctio* II.9)

The abbot of Murbach waged a lot of wars [*multum in gwerris desudauerit*]. Once his soldiers objected to the plundering of cemeteries, but the abbot assured them that only when they had carried out the bones of the dead would they have plundered the cemetery. When he finally fell ill and was dying, his chaplain asked him to appear after death and to reveal his destination in the afterlife. The abbot complied and informed the chaplain that he had been damned for the plundering of cemeteries.

The Repentant Usurer (added after *distinctio* II.34)

A repentant usurer, unsure how to avoid damnation, went to a bishop for advice. The bishop told him to make restitution of all that he had unjustly acquired, and to put what remained in a large chest. The usurer did as he was asked. The bishop kept the chest overnight and in the morning opened it before a crowd of people: it was full of snakes and toads. The bishop said, "This is your treasure. If you want to be purged from all your sins, throw yourself naked on these vermin." The obedient usurer jumped into the chest, and the bishop closed the lid. The next morning when the chest was opened, nothing remained but white bones shining with a splendid light.

The Demons of Cyprus (added after *distinctio* III.12)

Two kings in the region of Syria Maritima came into conflict. As a result, one forced the other to pay a tribute: ten virgins were to be sent every year to his court. After some time, the tributary rebelled and refused to pay. Ten years later, the first king attacked again and made his opponent repay the debt: one hundred virgins. On the way to the winner, the ship with the virgins landed on Cyprus, uninhabited at that time. Only demons lived there, and they corrupted the virgins. When the girls arrived at the court of the king, they all appeared very pale. A wise man figured out that they were not virgins anymore. After the girls explained what had happened to them, they were sent back to Cyprus, where they brought to the world monstrous children of both sexes. So the island became inhabited. By the will of God, the Good Thief's cross was brought there, and the demons ran away, so Cyprus turned into a Christian land with many churches.

The Brothers *Date* and *Dabitur* (added after *distinctio* IV.68)

St. Mathias's Abbey in Trier was once very hospitable, especially to Cistercians. It was rewarded with prosperity, in both temporal and spiritual things. When the new abbot ended this practice, the abbey became impoverished. No one could understand why this was happening, until a wise old monk explained that the reason was the abbey's rejection of the poor, and especially of Cistercians. It was decided then to build a house for the white monks. When St. Mathias's Abbey again became very hospitable, it was so greatly rewarded that everyone marveled. A monastery where the two brothers *Date* and *Dabitur vobis* live will never suffer want.

A Vow of Chastity (added after *distinctio* IV.103)

After having lost her parents, a rich and beautiful girl made a vow of chastity. Many men wanted to marry her, but she refused. The girl's relatives, frustrated by her adamance, robbed her of all the property. She tried to obtain help from a noble, who, captivated by her beauty, said that he was willing to give her everything in exchange for her love. The girl refused but was later compelled by her situation to accept the offer and agreed to meet the man in an orchard. She arrived first and had some time to recite the prayers in honor of the Virgin Mary, the saints, and the dead. Meanwhile, the noble appeared. God opened his eyes, and he saw the Virgin Mary with many other virgins receiving the girl's praises. Then came the saints, and then the dead. The man, terrified by the vision, asked the girl what she was doing. She explained everything, and the noble, amazed, showed her utter respect and had all her possessions returned to her.

False Coiners and the Devil (added after *distinctio* V.30)

In Weiler, in the diocese of Cologne, lived a dissolute young man named Herman who had dissipated his wealth and was desperate for money. So he left his homeland and traveled abroad, where he learned many trades, including counterfeiting. Herman returned rich and began to live in a grand style. He did not have a house, but he bought a cabin and hired an old woman to guard it. Under the cabin he dug a cave, where he installed all the equipment necessary to make false coins. Later Herman met an impoverished friend and initiated him into counterfeiting. They became partners.

One day, when they were working in the cave, the devil came to them in the form of a big black-haired man. He asked the old woman where his friends were. Not daring to betray them, she said that she had no idea. The devil replied that he would find them anyway. In the cave, he first introduced himself as the true master of counterfeiting, then killed both men. The old woman heard everything and called for people to come and see what had happened. A large crowd gathered. Both false coiners were found dead, clutching their hammers so tightly that nobody could remove the instruments.

The Vanishing Eucharist
(the first story added after *distinctio* VI)

In the times of the Emperor Otto and the Landgrave Herman [of Thuringia], there was a priest of noble birth, close to the Landgrave. He had two sons and two daughters, all married well. One year, he invited his family with their servants to celebrate Christmas and threw a big feast on Christmas Eve, which happened to be on Sunday. No one observed the Fast; everybody drank, ate, and made merry to excess. After the banquet, the priest went to bed with his mistress. The next morning, the priest was woken up by the bells ringing. He couldn't even remember which day it was until his mistress reminded him about Christmas. The priest hurried to the church. When it came to the celebration of the Eucharist, he found neither Host nor wine and had to simulate the Communion in order to avoid scandal. The same happened in another village, where he celebrated the next Mass. The priest promised the faithful to return shortly and hurried to a nearby Cistercian monastery, where he confessed all his excesses to the abbot. Upon returning to the parish, he celebrated the third Mass with a contrite heart and found three Hosts: the two that had been removed from him earlier, and the one prepared for consecration. After a few days, the priest distributed his fortune among his children, left some money to his mistress and his servants, and became a monk in the aforementioned Cistercian monastery.

The Lecherous Cleric
(the second story added after *distinctio* VI)

A lecherous cleric slept with a possessed girl. The demon, repulsed by such filth, left the girl and went to another village, where he entered the body of an old woman, all the while complaining about being forced to leave his previous receptacle. Upon hearing these lamentations, the people threatened to send for the cleric, and the demon became frantic. Indeed, when the cleric came and propositioned the old woman, the evil spirit fled shrieking.

The Knight and his Dead Master
(the third story added after *distinctio* VI)

A knight once met his dead suzerain, who asked him in the name of old friendship and mutual respect to follow him to a certain place. The knight refused to go without having consulted the abbot of Ebrach. The abbot tried to dissuade him from going and pointed out that the dead suzerain was definitely a demon. The knight, however, said that he would not act ungratefully and that he intended to go. He met with his suzerain, who assured him that nothing bad would happen to him if he would follow his directions, and warned him not to touch anything, even when asked. Then the knight was led to a place where he was received by the bishop of Würzburg, the count of Enchirsberge (Erichsberg?), and the count of Hohenlohe (Honloch). They saluted him and asked to carry a message to their friends and relatives requesting that they alleviate their pain with alms and prayers. The knight was surprised and asked what pain they were suffering, because he had noticed nothing. A count told him to approach and then lifted his garments; suddenly a huge flame burst out and badly burned the knight's face. His remorseful suzerain brought him back to Ebrach, where the knight died a few days later.

Appendix III

Other Cited Manuscripts

Auxerre, Bibliothèque municipale, 243

Auxerre, Bibliothèque municipale, 36

Auxerre, Bibliothèque municipale, 260i

Basel, Universitätsbibliothek, A IV 14

Basel, Universitätsbibliothek, AR I 2

Basel, Universitätsbibliothek, B IX 7

Basel, Universitätsbibliothek, F VI 53

Berlin, Staatsbibliothek zu Berlin - Preußischer Kulturbesitz, lat. fol. 193

Berlin, Staatsbibliothek zu Berlin - Preußischer Kulturbesitz, theol. lat. fol. 611

Berlin, Staatsbibliothek zu Berlin - Preußischer Kulturbesitz, theol. lat. fol. 171

Bern, Burgerbibliothek, 410

Brussels Bibliothèque Royale de Belgique, 7237–40 (3878)

Brussels, Bibliothèque Royale de Belgique, II 1077 (3872)

Brussels, Bibliothèque Royale de Belgique, 412–14 (3873)

Brussels, Bibliothèque Royale de Belgique, 7215–16 (3877)

Brussels, Bibliothèque Royale de Belgique, 7462–81 (3177)

Brussels, Bibliothèque Royale de Belgique, II 2333 (3874)

Cambrai, Bibliothèque municipale, 860 (764)

Cologne, Historisches Archiv, GB 8° 40

Dijon, Bibliothèque municipale, 594 (olim 349)

Dijon, Bibliothèque municipale, 610

Einsiedeln, Stiftsbibliothek, Cod. 300 (439)

Florence, Biblioteca Medicea Laurenziana, Ashburnham 1906

Graz, Universitätsbibliothek, Ms 421

Heidelberg, Universitätsbibliothek Cod. Sal. IX, 31

Heidelberg, Universitätsbibliothek, Cod. Sal. IX, 41I

Heidelberg, Universitätsbibliothek, Cod. Sal. IX, 19

Heidelberg, Universitätsbibliothek, Cod. Sal. IX, 26

Heidelberg, Universitätsbibliothek, Cod. Sal. IX, 23

Heiligenkreuz, Zisterzienserstift, Cod. 177

Heiligenkreuz, Zisterzienserstift, Cod. 323

Innsbruck, Universitäts- und Landesbibliothek Tirol, Cod. 350

Innsbruck, Universitäts- und Landesbibliothek Tirol, Cod. 25

Karlsruhe, Badische Landesbibliothek, Hs. 1016

Karlsruhe, Generallandesarchiv, 143

Königsberg, Staats- und Universitätsbibliothek, N. 1080

Kopenhagen, Kongelige Bibliotek, Gl. Kgl. Saml. 174

Kremsmünster, Benediktinerstift, CC 253

Laon, Bibliothèque municipale, 331

Leipzig, Universitätsbibliothek, Cod. 81

Leipzig, Universitätsbibliothek, Cod. 841

Leipzig, Universitätsbibliothek, Cod. 842

Leipzig, Universitätsbibliothek, Cod. 1332

Liège, Université de Liège, Bibliothèque Générale de Philosophie et Lettres, 200 C (281)

Liège, Université de Liège, Bibliothèque Générale de Philosophie et Lettres, 227 C (282)

Liège, Université de Liège, Bibliothèque Générale de Philosophie et Lettres, 191

Lille, Bibliothèque municipale, 446

Lille, Bibliothèque municipale, 447

London, British Library, Add. MS. 15723

London, British Library, Add. MS. 21616

London, Lambeth Palace Library, 51

Marienstatt, Klosterbibliothek, K. f. 3

Melk, Benediktinerstift, Cod. 320 (623, L 48)

Milan, Biblioteca Nazionale Braidense, AD.XIV.9

Munich, Bayerische Staatsbibliothek, Clm 13097

Munich, Bayerische Staatsbibliothek, Clm 2607

Munich, Bayerische Staatsbibliothek, Clm 28165

Munich, Bayerische Staatsbibliothek, Clm 3593

Munich, Bayerische Staatsbibliothek, Clm 6914

Munich, Bayerische Staatsbibliothek, Clm 7992

Olomouc, Vědecká knihovna, M II 141

Oxford, Bodleian Library, Cod. Laud Misc. 238

Oxford, Bodleian Library, Cod. Laud Misc. 540

Paris, Bibliothèque de l'Arsenal, 1156 (25 H. L.)

Paris, Bibliothèque nationale de France, lat. 3175

Paris, Bibliothèque nationale de France, lat. 13475

Paris, Bibliothèque nationale de France, lat. 14655

Paris, Bibliothèque nationale de France, lat. 15912

Paris, Bibliothèque nationale de France, lat. 16515

Paris, Bibliothèque nationale de France, nouv. acq. lat., 364

Paris, Bibliothèque nationale de France, nouv. acq. lat., 2044

Pelplin, Biblioteka seminarium Duchownego, 17 (27)

Poznań, Miejska Biblioteka, 173

Rein, Zisterzienserstift, Cod. 69

Soest, Wissenschaftliche Stadtbibliothek, Cod. 31/32

Stams, Zisterzienserkloster, Archiv, Cod. 6 (Cod. 67)

Stams, Zisterzienserkloster, Cod. 28

Trier, Seminarbibliothek, 52

Trier, Stadtbibliothek, Hs. 1176/478 4°

Trier, Stadtbibliothek, Hs. 1212/509 4°

Trier, Stadtbibliothek, Hs. 1720/432 4°

Troyes, Bibliothèque municipale, 521

Troyes, Bibliothèque municipale, 2299

Vienna, Österreichische Nationalbibliothek, Cod. 3650

Vienna, Österreichische Nationalbibliothek, Cod. 3798

Vienna, Österreichische Nationalbibliothek, Cod. 4118

Vienna, Schottenstift (Benediktiner), Bibliothek, Cod. 143 (Hübl 64)

Weimar, Herzogin Anna Amalia Bibliothek, Fol max 3

Wiesbaden, Hessische Landesbibliothek, Hs. 381

Wilhering, Zisterzienserkloster, Cod. IX 96

Xanten, Dombibliothek, s.n.

Zeitz, Stiftsbibliothek, 37 (olim Cod. XIII)

Zwettl, Zisterzienserstift, Cod. 13

Bibliography

Primary Sources

André, Martina. *Das Rätsel der Templer.* 4th ed. Berlin: Aufbau, 2012.

Barbeau, André, trans. *Césaire de Heisterbach: Le Dialogue des miracles.* Vol. 1, *De la conversion.* Voix monastiques, 6. Oka, Québec: Notre-Dame-du-Lac, 1992.

Barillari, Sonia Maura, trans. *Cesario di Heisterbach: Sui demòni.* Alessandria: Edizioni dell'Orso, 1999.

Becker, Victor, ed. "Eene onbekende kronijk van het klooster te Windesheim." In *Bijdragen en Mededelingen van het Historisch Genootschap* 10 (1887): 376–445.

Beda Venerabilis. *Histoire ecclésiastique du peuple anglais: Historia ecclesiastica gentis Anglorum.* Edited by Michael Lapidge. Introduction and notes by André Crépin. Translated by Pierre Monat. 3 vols. SCh 489, 490, 491. Paris: Cerf, 2005.

Birgitta Suecica. *Corpus Reuelacionum Sancte Birgitte.* https://riksarkivet.se/crb.

Bredenbach, Tilmann. *Collationum sacrarum libri VIII.* Cologne: Cholinus, 1584.

"Bulletin bibliographique III. Caesarii Heisterbacensis *Dialogus miraculorum.*" *Revue catholique* 8 (1850–1851): 48–51.

Busch, Johannes. *Des Augustinerpropstes Johannes Busch Chronicon Windeshemense und Liber de reformatione monasteriorum.* Edited by Karl Grube. Halle: Hendel, 1886.

Büttner, Wolfgang. *Epitome historiarum christlicher ausgelesener Historien und Geschichten.* [S.l.], 1576.

Caesarius Heisterbacensis. *Caesarii Heisterbacensis Monachi ordinis Cisterciensis Dialogus Miraculorum.* Edited by Josephus Strange. 2 vols. Cologne-Bonn-Brussels: J. M. Heberle, 1851.

Caesarius Heisterbacensis. *Caesarius of Heisterbach: Dialogue on Miracles.* Translated by Ronald Pepin. 2 vols. CF 89, 90. Collegeville, MN: Cistercian Publications, forthcoming.

Caesarius Heisterbacensis. *Dialogus miraculorum: Dialog über die Wunder.* 4 vols. Fontes Christiani 86. Edited and translated by Horst Schneider and Nikolaus Nösges. Turnhout: Brepols, 2009.

Caesarius Heisterbacensis. *Epistola catalogica.* In *Die Wundergeschichten des Caesarius von Heisterbach.* Vol. 1, *Exempla und Auszüge aus den Predigten des Caesarius von Heisterbach.* Edited by Alfons Hilka. Publikationen der Gesellschaft für Rheinische Geschichtskunde, 43.1. Bonn: Hanstein, 1933.

Caesarius Heisterbacensis. *Fasciculus moralitatis venerabilis fr. Caesarii, Heisterbacencis monachi S. Ordinis Cistertiensium . . . Nunc primum ex pervetusto M. S. Cod. ad typos elaborata: additis ad marginem lemmatis & citationibus adnotatis. Quibuscunque concionationibus: Religiosis vero imprimis utiles in spiritualibus exhortationibus instituendis.* Edited by Joannes A. Coppenstein. Cologne: P. Henningius, 1615.

Caesarius Heisterbacensis. *Libri VIII miraculorum.* In *Die Wundergeschichten des Caesarius von Heisterbach.* Vol. 3, edited by Alfons Hilka. Publikationen der Gesellschaft für Rheinische Geschichtskunde, 43, 3. Bonn: Hanstein, 1937.

Caesarius Heisterbacensis. *Vita, passio et miracula beati Engelberti Coloniensis archiepiscopi.* In *Die Wundergeschichten des Caesarius von Heisterbach,* vol. 3, edited by Alfons Hilka. Publikationen der Gesellschaft für Rheinische Geschichtskunde, 43. Bonn: Hanstein, 1937.

Canisius, Petrus. *Beati Petri Canisii . . . Epistulae et Acta.* Vol. 3, *1561–1562.* Edited by Otto Braunschweiger. Freiburg im Breisgau: Herder, 1901.

Canivez, Joseph-Marie, ed. *Statuta Capitulorum Generalium Ordinis Cisterciensis ab Anno 1116 ad Annum 1786.* 8 vols. Louvain: Revue d'Histoire Ecclésiastique, 1933–1941.

Chifflet, Pierre-François, ed. *Sancti Bernardi Clarevallensis abbatis genus illustre assertum. Accedunt Odonis de Diogilo, Johannis Eremitae, Herberti Turrium Sardiniae archiepiscopi aliorumque aliquot scriptorum opuscula, duodecimi post Christum saeculi historiam spectantia.* Dijon: Philibert Chavance, 1660.

Chronica Villariensis monasterii. Edited by Georg Waitz. Monumenta Germaniae Historica: Scriptores in Folio. Vol. 25, Gesta saec. XIII. Berlin: Weidmann, 1880.

Collectaneum exemplorum et visionum Clarevallense e codice Trecensi 946. Edited by Olivier Legendre. CCCM 208. Turnhout: Brepols, 2005.

Collectio exemplorum Cisterciensis in codice Parisiensi 15912 asseruata. Edited by Jacques Berlioz and Marie Anne Polo de Beaulieu. CCCM 243. Turnhout: Brepols, 2012.

Collin de Plancy, Jacques. *Dictionnaire infernal ou recherches et anecdotes sur les Démons, les Esprits, les Fantômes, les Spectres, les Revenants, les Loups-garoux . . . en un mot, sur tout ce qui tient aux Apparitions, à la Magie, au Commerce de l'Enfer, aux Divinations, aux Sciences secrètes, aux Superstitions, aux Choses mystérieuses et surnaturelles etc., etc., etc.* Paris: Librairie Universelle de P. Mongie Aîné, 1818–1825; Paris: P. Mellier, 1844.

Conradus Eberbacensis. *Exordium magnum Cisterciense, sive Narratio de initio Cisterciensis Ordinis*. Edited by Bruno Griesser. CCCM 138. Turnhout: Brepols, 1997.

Conradus Eberbacensis. *The Great Beginning of Cîteaux: A Narrative of the Beginning of the Cistercian Order*. Translated by Benedicta Ward and Paul Savage. Edited by E. Rozanne Elder. CF 72. Kalamazoo, MI: Cistercian Publications, 2012.

Corpus consuetudinum monasticarum. Vol. 11/1. Caeremoniae regularis observantiae sanctissimi patris nostri Benedicti ex ipsius regula sumptae, secundum quod in sacris locis, scilicet specu et monasterio Sublacensi practicantur. Edited by Joachim Angerer. Siegburg: Schmitt, 1985.

De Sainte-Marthe, Denis. *Gallia Christiana in provincias ecclesiasticas distributa*. Vol. 4. Paris: Coignard, 1728.

De Visch, Charles. "Auctarium D. Caroli de Visch ad Bibliothecam Scriptorum S. ordinis Cisterciensis." Edited by Joseph-Marie Canivez. *Cistercienser-Chronik* 38 (1926); 39 (1927).

De Visch, Charles. *Bibliotheca scriptorum Sacri Ordinis Cisterciensis elogiis plurimorum maxime illustrium adornata*. Cologne: Busaeus, 1656.

Drescher, Karl, ed. *Hartliebs Übersetzung des* Dialogus Miraculorum *von Caesarius von Heisterbach. Aus der einzigen Londoner Handschrift.* Deutsche Texte des Mittelalters 33. Berlin: Weidmannsche Buchhandlung, 1929.

Dupin, Louis Ellies. *Nouvelle bibliothèque des auteurs ecclésiastiques contenant l'histoire de leur vie, le catalogue, la critique, et la chronologie de leurs ouvrages; le sommaire de ce qu'ils contiennent: un jugement sur leur style, et sur leur doctrine; et le denombrement des differentes editions de leurs oeuvres.* Vol. 10, *Des auteurs du treizième siècle de l'Église.* Paris: Prallard, 1702.

Esch, Wilfried. *Schandor und Cäsarius: Geschichten und Abenteuer des Cäsarius von Heisterbach und des Drachen Schandor.* Bonn: Free Pen, 2002.

Esch, Wilfried. *Zeit der Dämmerung.* Königswinter: Lempertz, 2009.

Foppens, Jean François. *Bibliotheca belgica, sive virorum in Belgio vita, scriptisque illustrium catalogus, librorumque nomenclatura.* 2 vols. Brussels: Foppens, 1739.

Gaguin, Robert. *Compendium de origine et gestis Francorum.* Paris: Jean Petit, 1504.

Gerardus de Fracheto. *Vitae fratrum ordinis praedicatorum necnon cronica ordinis ab anno MCCIII usque ad MCCLIV.* Louvain: Charpentier & Schoonjans, 1896.

Gessner, Conrad, Johann Jacob Fries, Josias Simmler, Christoph Froschauer, and Robert Lumsden. *Bibliotheca instituta et collecta, primum a Conrado Gesnero: deinde in epitomen redacta, & nouorum librorum accessione locupletata, tertio recognita, & in duplum post priores editiones aucta, per Iosiam Simlerum: iam vero postremo aliquot mille, cum priorum tum nouorum authorum opusculis, ex instructissima Viennensi Austriae imperatoria bibliotheca amplificata, per Iohannem Iacobum Frisium.* Zurich: Christophorus Froschouerus, 1583.

Gesta Sanctorum Villariensium. Edited by Georg Waitz. In Monumenta Germaniae Historica: Scriptores in Folio. Vol. 25, Gesta saec. XIII. Hannover, Germany: Hahnsche Buchhandlung, 1880.

Gregorius Magnus. *Dialogi. Dialogues.* Edited by Adalbert de Vogüé. 3 vols. SCh 251, 260, and 265. Paris: Editiones du Cerf, 1978–1980.

Gregorius Magnus. *Moralia in Iob*. Edited by Marcus Adriaen. CCCM 143. Turnhout: Brepols, 1979.

Guigues Ier le Chartreux. *Coutumes de Chartreuse*. Edited and translated by a Carthusian [M. Laporte]. SCh 313. Paris: Cerf, 1984.

Hartzheim, Hermann Joseph. *Bibliotheca Coloniensis, in qua vita et libri typo vulgati et manuscripti recensentur omnium archi-dioceseos Coloniensis; Ducatuum Westphaliae, Angariae, Moersae, Cliviae, Juliaci, Montium, Comitatûs Arensbergae, Marchiae; Vestae Recklinghusanae, Territoriorum Ravensteinii, Ravensbergae, Essendiae, Werdenae, Civitatum, Coloniae, Aquarum-Grani, Tremoniae indigenarum et incolarum scriptorum*. Cologne: Thomas Odendall, 1747.

Hees, Nicolaus. *Manipulus rerum memorabilium claustri Hemmenrodensis, ordinis Cistertie[n]sis in archidioecesi Trevirensi librum unum complexus*. Cologne: Henning, 1641.

Helinandus Frigidi Montis. *Chronicon*. PL 212. Paris: Migne, 1863.

Hellinghaus, Otto, ed. *Hundert auserlesene, wunderbare und merkwürdige Geschichten des Zisterziensers Cäsarius von Heisterbach*. Aachen: Deutschherren, 1925.

Henríquez, Crisóstomo. *Menologivm Cistertiense Notationibvs Illvstratvm. Accedunt seorsim Regula, Constitutiones, et Priuilegia eiusdem Ordinis; ac Congregationum Monasticarum et Militarium quae Cistertiense Institutum obseruant*. Antwerp: Moretus, 1630.

Herbertus Claraevallensis. *Herbert von Clairvaux und sein Liber miraculorum: die Kurzversion eines anonymen bayerischen Redaktors*. Edited by Gabriela Kompatscher-Gufler. Bern: Lang, 2005.

Herbertus Claraevallensis. *Liber visionum et miraculorum Clarevallensium*. Edited by Giancarlo Zichi, Graziano Fois, and Stefano Mula. CCCM 277. Turnout: Brepols, 2017.

Herles, Helmut, ed. *Von Geheimnissen und Wundern des Caesarius von Heisterbach. Ein Lesebuch*. 2nd ed. Bonn: Bouvier, 1991.

Hermans, Cornelis Rudolphus. *Annales canonicorum regularium S. Augustini, Ordinis S. Crucis*. Vol. 1 (1). Bois-le-Duc: Stokvis, 1858.

Hervieux, Léopold, ed. *Les fabulistes latins depuis le siècle d'Auguste jusqu'à la fin du moyen âge*. Vol. 3, *Avianus et ses anciens imitateurs*. Paris: Firmin-Didot, 1894.

Hervieux, Léopold, ed. *Les fabulistes latins depuis le siècle d'Auguste jusqu'à la fin du moyen âge.* Vol. 4, *Eudes de Chériton et ses dérivés.* Paris: Firmin-Didot, 1896.

Hesse, Hermann. "Aus dem Dialogus miraculorum des Cäsarius von Heisterbach." *März: Halbmonatsschrift für deutsche Kultur* 2, 3 (1908).

Hesse, Hermann. *Geschichten aus dem Mittelalter.* Konstanz: Karl Hönn, 1925.

Hesse, Hermann. "Geschichten aus dem Mittelalter: Erzählungen aus dem Dialogus miraculorum des Caesarius von Heisterbach, aus dem Lateinischen übersetzt von Hermann Hesse." *Schweizerland* 7 (1921): 418–29.

Hirsch, Franz. *Geschichte der deutschen Litteratur von ihren Anfängen bis auf die neueste Zeit.* Vol. 1, *Das Mittelalter.* Leipzig: Friedrich, 1883.

Histoire littéraire de la France; ouvrage commencé par des religieux bénédictins de la Congrégation de Saint Maur, et continué par des membres de l'Institut. Vol. 18, *Suite du treizième siècle jusqu'à l'an 1255.* Edited by Pierre Daunou and L'Académie des inscriptions et belles-lettres. Paris: Firmin Didot, 1835.

Historia miraculorum in itinere Germanico patratorum (Vitae liber sextus). In Monumenta Germaniae Historica, Scriptores In folio. Vol. 26, Ex rerum Francogallicarum scriptoribus, edited by Georg Waitz. Hannover: Hahn, 1882.

Hondorf, Andreas. *Promptuarium Exemplorum. Historien vnd Exempel buch: Aus Heiliger Schrifft, und vielen andern bewerten und beglaubten Geistlichen und Weltlichen Büchern und Schrifften gezogen.* Leipzig, 1568.

Hopf, Karl, ed. "Sieben Wundergeschichten aus dem XIII. Jahrhundert." *Germania: Vierteljahrsschrift für deutsche Altertumskunde* 16 = *Neue Reihe, Jg.* 4 (1871): 308–16.

Humbertus de Romanis. *De dono timoris.* Edited by Christine Boyer. CCCM 218. Turnhout: Brepols, 2008.

Idungus Emmeramensis. "Dialogus duorum monachorum." In *Le moine Idung et ses deux ouvrages "Argumentum super quatuor questionibus" et "Dialogus duorum monachorum,"* edited by Robert B. C. Huygens. Studi medievali 11. Spoleto: Centro italiano di studi sull'alto medioevo, 1972.

Johannes de Cirey. *Articuli Parisienses seu instrumentum reformationis Ordinis cisterciensis.* In *Nomasticon Cisterciense seu antiquiores Ordinis Cisterciensis constitutiones.* Paris: Alliot, 1664. 678–86.

Johannes de Ellenbogen. *De vita venerabilium monachorum monasterii sui liber, Ex MS. Cod. Academicae Bibliothecae Basileensis.* Edited by Bernhard Pez. Bibliotheca Ascetica Antiquo-Nova, vol. 8. Regensburg: Peetz, 1725, repr. 1967.

Johannes Herolt (Discipulus). *Sermones Discipuli de Tempore . . . cum promptuario exemplorum.* Cologne, 1504.

Jongelinus, Gaspar. *Notitia Abbatiarum Ordinis Cisterciensis Per Orbem Universum Libros X Complexa: In qua singulorum Monasteriorum origines, incrementa Regum Principum procerum Benefactorum, aliorumque Illustrium virorum diplomata, donationes, Insignia Gentilitia Epitaphia, et id genus alia notatu digna cum ex ipsis locorum Archivis, tum ex Variis scriptoribus selecta recensentur.* 10 vols. Cologne: Henningius, 1640.

Journal historique et littéraire. 15 February. Maastricht: Cavelier, 1793.

Kaufmann, Alexander, ed. and trans. *Wunderbare und denkwürdige Geschichten aus den Werken des Caesarius von Heisterbach.* 2 vols. Cologne: Boisserée, 1888, 1891.

Lenglet du Fresnoy, Nicolas. *Méthode pour étudier l'histoire.* Vol. 3. Paris: Gandouin, 1735.

Liber lacteus: eine unbeachtete Mirakel- und Exempelsammlung aus dem Zisterzienserkloster Stams (Innsbruck, ULB, Cod. 494). Codicologia 1. Edited by Daniela E. Mairhofer. Badenweiler: Bachmann, 2009.

Luther, Martin. *An den Christlichen Adel deutscher Nation von des Christlichen standes besserung.* In Martin Luther, *Deutsch-Deutsche Studienausgabe.* Vol. 3, *Christ und Welt,* edited by Hellmut Zschoch. Leipzig: Evangelische Verlagsanstalt, 2016.

Manrique, Angel. *Cistercienses seu verius ecclesiasticae annales a condito Cistercio.* 4 vols. Lyon: Boissat & Lavrent, 1642.

McGuire, Brian Patrick, trans. and ed. *Triviallitteratur og samfund i latinsk middelalder: Caesarius af Heisterbach og hans Dialogus miraculorum.* Copenhagen: Center for Europaeiske middelalderstudier, 1982.

Meister, Aloys, ed. *Die fragmente der Libri VIII miraculorum des Caesarius von Heisterbach.* Rome: Herder, 1901.

Mirabilis liber qui prophetias Reuelationesq[ue] nec non res mirandas preteritas presentes et futuras aperte demonstrat. Paris: Jean Petit, 1522.

Miraeus, Aubertus. *Chronicon Cisterciensis Ordinis, a S. Roberto abbate Molismensi primum inchoati, postea a S. Bernardo abbate Clarevallensi mirifice aucti ac propagati.* Cologne: Gualtherus, 1614.

Mone, Franz Joseph, ed. *Quellensammlung der badischen Landesgeschichte.* Vol. 3. Karlsruhe: G. Macklot, 1863.

Müller-Holm, Ernst, ed. and trans. *Caesarius von Heisterbach.* Berlin: K. Schnabel, 1910.

Müller-Holm, Ernst, ed. and trans. *Caesarius von Heisterbach.* Cologne: Hegner, 1968.

Nas, Johannes. *Das Antipapistisch eins vnd hundert: Außerleßner, gewiser, Euangelischer Warhait: bey wölchen (als bey den früchten der Baum) die reyn lehr soll und muß erkan[n]t werden.* Ingolstadt: Weißenhorn, 1570.

Natalis, Alexander. *Historia ecclesiastica Veteris Novique Testamenti ab orbe condito ad annum post Christum natum millesimum sexcentesimum.* Lucca: Leonardus Venturinus, 1752.

Nechutová, Jana, trans. *Vyprávění o zázracích: středověký život v zrcadle exempel.* Prague: Vyšehrad, 2009.

Oudin, Casimir. *Commentarivs de scriptoribvs ecclesiae antiqvis: illorvmque scriptis tam impressis qvam manvscriptis adhvc extantibvs in celebrioribvs Evropae bibliothecis a Bellarmino, Posserino, Philippo Labeo . . . at aliis omissis, ad annum MCCCCLX vel ad artem typographicam inventam . . . ; cvm mvltis dissertationibvs, in qvibvs insigniorvm ecclesiae avtorvm opvscvla . . . examinantvr, tribvs volvminibvs cvm indicibvs necessariis.* 3 vols. Leipzig: Moritz Georg Weidmann, 1722.

Pepin, Ronald, trans. *Caesarius of Heisterbach: Dialogue on Miracles.* Intro. Hugh Feiss. 2 vols. CF 89, 90. Collegeville, MN: Cistercian Publications, forthcoming 2023, 2024.

Petrus Pictaviensis. *Sententiarum libri quinque.* PL 211. Paris: Migne, 1855.

Petrus Venerabilis. *De miraculis libri duo.* Edited by Denise Bouthillier. CCCM 58. Turnhout: Brepols, 1988.

Possevino, Antonio. *Apparatus sacer: ad scriptores veteris & novi testamenti, eorum interpretes, Synodos, & Patres latinos, ac Graecos, Horum versiones, Theologos scholasticos, quique contra häreticos egerunt, Chronographos, & Historiographos Ecclesiasticos.* Venice: Soc. Veneta, 1606.

Prédiction pour la fin du dix-huitieme siecle: tirée du Mirabilis liber; avec la traduction littérale à côté du texte; précédée d'une introduction qui établit la concordance des dates et des événements, avec les circonstances actuelles. 2nd ed. Paris: Marielle et Lebreton, 1790.

Prieto Hernández, Zacarías. *Cesáreo de Heisterbach, Diálogo de milagros.* 2 vols. Zamora: Ediciones Monte Casino, 1998.

Russelius, Henricus. *Chronicon Cruciferorum sive Synopsis memorabilium sacri et canonici ordinis sanctae cruxis.* Cologne: Kraft, 1635. Repr. Diest: Lichtland, 1964.

Salgues, Jacques-Barthélemy. *Des erreurs et des préjugés répandus dans les diverses classes de la société.* Vol. 2. 3rd ed. Paris: Foucault, 1823.

Schmitz, Ferdinand, ed. *Urkundenbuch der Abtei Heisterbach. Urkundenbücher der geistlichen Stiftungen des Niederrheins 2.* Bonn: Hanstein, 1908.

Schneider, Ilse, and Johannes Schneider, trans. and ed. *Die wundersamen Geschichten des Caesarius von Heisterbach.* Berlin: Union, 1972.

Schreiber, Alois. *Handbuch für Reisende am Rhein: von Schafhausen bis Holland, in die schönsten anliegenden Gegenden und an die dortigen Heilquellen.* Heidelberg: Engelmann, 1816.

Simrock, Karl. *Rheinsagen aus dem Munde des Volks und deutscher Dichter: Für Schule, Haus und Wanderschaft.* Bonn: Weber, 1837–1869.

Speculum exemplorum. Deventer: Richardus Pafraet, 1481.

Tabula exemplorum de habundancia adaptacionum ad omnem materiam in sermonibus secundum ordinem alphabeti ordinata: La Tabula exemplorum secundum ordinem alphabeti. Recueil d'exempla compilé en France à la fin du XIIIᵉ siècle. Thesaurus exemplorum 3. Edited by Jean-Th. Welter. Paris-Toulouse: Occitania, 1926.

Thomas à Kempis. *Chronica Montis Sanctae Agnetis.* In *Opera Omnia Thomae Hemerken a Kempis.* Vol. 7. Edited by Michael Joseph Pohl. Freiburg im Breisgau: Herder, 1922.

Thomas Cantimpratensis. *Bonum universale de apibus*. Douai: B. Belleri, 1627.

Tissier, Bertrand, ed. *Bibliotheca Patrum Cisterciensium*. 2 vols. Bonne-fontaine Abbey, 1662.

Tombel de Chartrose. Edited by Audrey Sulpice. Paris: Honoré Champion, 2014.

Trithemius, Johannes. *Liber de scriptoribus ecclesiasticis*. Basel: Amerbach, 1494.

Van Moolenbroeck, Jaap, trans. and ed. *Mirakels historisch: De exempels van Caesarius van Heisterbach over Nederland en Nederlanders*. Hilversum: Verloren, 1999.

Vincentius Bellovacensis. *Speculum Quadruplex sive Speculum Maius*. Vol. 2, *Speculum doctrinale*. Douai: Bibliotheca Mundi, 1624; repr. Graz: Akademische Druck- u. Verlagsanstalt, 1964.

Visio Edmundi monachi de Eynsham: interdisziplinäre Studien zur mittelalterlichen Visionsliteratur. Edited by Thomas Ehlen, Johannes Mangei, and Elisabeth Stein. Tübingen: Narr, 1998.

Von Essen Scott, Henry, and C. C. Swinton Bland, trans. *Caesarius of Heisterbach: The Dialogue on Miracles*. 2 vols. London: G. Routledge & Sons, 1929.

Vossius, Gerardus. *De Historicis Latinis: libri III*. Lyon: Maire, 1651.

Waddell, Chrysogonus, ed. *Cistercian Lay Brothers: Twelfth-century Usages with Related Texts*. Cîteaux: Commentarii cistercienses, Studia et Documenta 10. Brecht: Citeaux, 2000.

Weismann, Christian Eberhard. *Christiani Eberh. Weismanni Theologi Tvbingensis Introdvctio In Memorabilia Ecclesiastica Historiae Sacrae Novi Testamenti: Ad Ivvandam Notitiam Regni Dei Et Satanae Cordisqve Hvmani Salvtarem*. Halle: Orphanotropheum, 1745.

Wessel Gansfort, M. *Wesseli Gansfortii Groningensis, rarae & reconditae doctrin[a]e viri, Qui olim Lvx Mvndi vulgo dictus fuit, Opera Quae inveniri potuerunt omnia: partim ex antiquis editionibus, partim ex manuscriptis eruta*. Edited by Petrus Pappus à Tratzberg. Groningen: Iohannes Sassius, 1614.

Wolf, Christoph. *Civitas A.D. 1200: Das Geheimnis der Rose: Ein mystischer Mittelalter-Roman*. Hamburg: Acabus, 2011.

Ybero, Ignatius, ed. *Exordia Sacri Ordinis Cisterciensis: alterum a S. Roberto [v. Molesme], S. Alberico, & S. Stephano [Harding] primis ejusdem Ordinis fundatoribus, ante quingentos annos, alterum vero ante quadringentos ab Anonymo hactenus Monacho Clarae-Vallensi, sed revera a S. Helinando accurate conscripta.* Fitero, 1606.

Zapata de Mendoza, Antonio. *Novus index librorum prohibitorum et expurgatorum.* Seville: Francisco de Lyra, 1632.

Secondary Sources

Akkerman, Fokke, Gerda C. Huisman, and Arie Johan Vanderjagt, eds. *Wessel Gansfort (1419–1489) and Northern Humanism.* Brill's Studies in Intellectual History 40. Leiden: Brill, 1993.

Allen, Percy Stafford. *The Age of Erasmus: Lectures Delivered in the Universities of Oxford and London.* Oxford: Clarendon, 1914.

Allmang, Georg. *Geschichte des ehemaligen Regulartertiarierklosters St. Nikolaus 1400–1911.* Essen: Fredebeul & Koenen, 1911.

Alschner, Christian. "Die Säkularisation der Klosterbibliotheken im albertinischen Sachsen (Mark Meißen, Leipzig und Pegau)." PhD dissertation. Karl-Marx-Universität Leipzig, 1969.

Alsheimer, Reiner. "Speculum exemplorum." In *Enzyklopädie des Märchens: Handwörterbuch zur historischen und vergleichenden Erzählforschung,* edited by Kurt Ranke and Rolf Wilhelm Brednich. Berlin: De Gruyter, 2007. 18:961–68.

Alzog, Johann Baptist. *Grundriss der Universal-Kirchengeschichte: zunächst für akademische Vorlesungen.* Mainz: Florian Kupferberg, 1868.

Angerer, Joachim. *Die liturgisch-musikalische Erneuerung der Melker Reform: Studien zur Erforschung der Musikpraxis in den Benediktinerklöstern des 15. Jahrhunderts.* Vienna: Österreichische Akademie der Wissenschaften, 1974.

Angerer, Joachim. "Reform von Melk." In *Die Reformverbände und Kongregationen der Benediktiner im deutschen Sprachraum.* Edited by Ulrich Faust and Franz Quarthal. Germania Benedictina 1. St. Ottilien: EOS, 1999. 271–313.

Aquilon, Pierre. "La réception du *Manipulus curatorum* dans le monde germanique (1474–1500)." In *Le cabinet du curieux: culture, savoirs, religion de l'Antiquité à l'Ancien Régime*, edited by Witold Konstanty Pietrzak. Paris: Classiques Garnier, 2013. 197–217.

Arnold, Klaus. *Johannes Trithemius (1462–1516)*. Quellen u. Forschungen zur Geschichte d. Bistums u. Hochstifts Würzburg 23. Würzburg: Schöningh in Komm, 1971.

Baring-Gould, Sabine. *The Silver Store: Collected from Mediæval Christian and Jewish Mines*. London: Longman, Green and Co., 1868.

Becker, Peter Jörg. *Die theologischen lateinischen Handschriften in Folio der Staatsbibliothek Preußischer Kulturbesitz, Berlin (Ms. theol. lat. Fol. 598–737)*. Berlin: Staatsbibliothek, Handschriftenabteilung, 1985.

Becker, Petrus. "Erstrebte und erreichte Ziele benediktinischer Reformen im Spätmittelalter." In *Reformbemühungen und Observanzbestrebungen im spätmittelalterlichen Ordenswesen*, edited by Kaspar Elm. Berliner historische Studien 14. Ordensstudien 6. Berlin: Duncker & Humblot, 1989. 24–34.

Bell, David. N. "The Library of Cîteaux in the Fifteenth Century: *Primus inter pares* or *Unus inter multos?*" *Cîteaux: Commentarii Cistercienses* 50 (1999): 103–33.

Bell, David N. "Monastic Libraries: 1400–1557." In *The Cambridge History of the Book in Britain*. Vol. 3, *1400–1557*, edited by Lotte Hellinga and J. B. Trapp. Cambridge: Cambridge University Press, 1999. 229–54.

Bériou, Nicole. *L'Avènement des maîtres de la Parole: La prédication à Paris au XIIIᵉ siècle*. 2 vols. Collection des études augustiniennes 31. Paris: Institut d'Études Augustiniennes, 1998.

Bériou, Nicole, and Isabelle Le Masne de Chermont, eds. *Les sermons et la visite pastorale de Federico Visconti archevêque de Pise, 1253–1277*. Sources et documents d'histoire du moyen âge 3. Rome: École française de Rome, 2001.

Berlioz, Jacques. "Césaire de Heisterbach." In *Dictionnaire encyclopédique du Moyen Âge*. Vol. 1, *A–K*, edited by André Vauchez and Catherine Vincent. Paris: Éditions du Cerf, 1997.

Berlioz, Jacques. "Le récit efficace: l'*exemplum* au service de la prédication (XIIIᵉ–XVᵉ siècles)." *Mélanges de l'École française de Rome, Moyen Âge-Temps modernes* 92 (1980/1): 113–44.

Berlioz, Jacques, and Marie Anne Polo de Beaulieu. "The Preacher Facing a Reluctant Audience According to the Testimony of Exempla." *Medieval Sermon Studies* 57, no. 1 (2013): 16–28.

Berlioz, Jacques, Pascal Collomb, and Marie Anne Polo de Beaulieu, eds. *Le Tonnerre des exemples: Exempla et médiation culturelle dans l'Occident médiéval*. Rennes: Presses Universitaires de Rennes, 2010.

Bethany, Mathias. "Cäsarius von Heisterbach." *Monatsschrift des Bergischen Geschichtsvereins* 8, no. 3 (1896): 165–78.

Bird, Jessalynn. "The Religious's Role in a Post-Fourth-Lateran World: Jacques de Vitry's *Sermones ad status* and *Historia occidentalis*." In *Medieval Monastic Preaching*, edited by Carolyn Muessig. Brill's Studies in Intellectual History 90. Leiden, Boston, and Cologne: Brill, 1998. 209–29.

Bischoff, Bernhard, and Paul Lehmann, eds. *Mittelalterliche Bibliothekskataloge Deutschlands und der Schweiz*. Vol. 1, *Die Bistümer Konstanz und Chur*. Munich: Beck, 1918 (repr. 1969).

Bischoff, Bernhard, and Paul Ruf, eds. *Mittelalterliche Bibliothekskataloge Deutschlands und der Schweiz*. Vol. 3/1, *Bistum Augsburg*. Munich: Beck, 1932 (repr. 1970).

Bischoff, Bernhard, and Christine Elisabeth Ineichen-Eder, eds. *Mittelalterliche Bibliothekskataloge Deutschlands und der Schweiz*. Vol. 4/1, *Bistümer Passau und Regensburg*. Munich: Beck, 1977.

Bondéelle-Souchier, Anne. *Bibliothèques cisterciennes dans la France médiévale. Répertoire des abbayes d'hommes*. Paris: CNRS, 1991.

Bondéelle-Souchier, Anne. "Trésor des moines: Les Chartreux, les Cisterciens et leurs livres." In *Histoire des bibliothèques françaises*. Vol. 1, *Les bibliothèques médiévales du VIᵉ siècle à 1530*, edited by Claude Jolly and André Vernet. Paris: Promodis, 1989. 64–81.

Bougard, François, and Pierre Petitmengin. *La bibliothèque de l'abbaye cistercienne de Vauluisant: histoire et inventaires*. Documents, études et répertoires 83. Paris: CNRS, 2012.

Bremond, Claude, Jacques Le Goff, and Jean-Claude Schmitt. *L'Exemplum*. Typologie des sources du Moyen Âge Occidental 40. Turnhout: Brepols, 1982; re-edited Turnhout: Brepols, 1996.

Brilli, Elisa. "The Making of a New Auctoritas: The *Dialogus miraculorum* Read and Rewritten by the Dominican Arnold of Liège (1297–1308)." In *The Art of Cistercian Persuasion in the Middle*

Ages and Beyond: Caesarius of Heisterbach's "Dialogue on Miracles" and *Its Reception,* edited by Victoria Smirnova, Marie Anne Polo de Beaulieu, and Jacques Berlioz. Studies in Medieval and Reformation Traditions 196. Leiden and Boston: Brill, 2015. 161–82.

Brisson, Marie. "Frère Robert, chartreux du XIVᵉ siècle." *Romania* 87, no. 348 (1966): 543–50.

Britnell, Jennifer, and Derek Stubbs. "The *Mirabilis Liber*: Its Compilation and Influence." *Journal of the Warburg and Courtauld Institutes* 49 (1986): 126–49.

Brückner, Annemarie. "Herolt, Johannes." In *Enzyklopädie des Märchens,* edited by Ines Kölhler-Zülch. Berlin-Boston: de Gruyter, 1990. 6:858–63.

Brunsch, Swen H. *Das Zisterzienserkloster Heisterbach von seiner Gründung bis zum Anfang des 16. Jahrhunderts.* Bonner historische Forschungen 58. Siegberg: Franz Schmitt, 1998.

Bynum, Caroline Walker. Docere Verbo et Exemplo: *An Aspect of Twelfth-Century Spirituality.* Harvard Theological Studies 31. Missoula: Scholar Press, 1979.

Châtillon, Jean. *Le mouvement canonial au Moyen Âge: Réforme de l'Église, Spiritualité et Culture,* edited by Patrice Sicard. Bibliotheca Victorina 3. Paris and Turnhout: Brepols, 1992.

Cordez, Philippe. "Le lieu du texte. Les livres enchaînés au Moyen Âge." *Revue Mabillon* t. 78, n. sér., t. 17 (2006): 75–103.

Corsten, Severin. *Die Anfänge des Kölner Buchdrucks.* Arbeiten aus dem Bibliothekar-Lehrinstitut des Landes Nordrhein-Westfalen 8. Cologne: Greven, 1955.

Corsten, Severin. "Die Blütezeit des Kölner Buchdrucks." *Rheinische Vierteljahrsblätter* 40 (1976): 130–49.

De Certeau, Michel. "Reading as Poaching." In *The Practice of Everyday Life,* translated by Steven Rendall. Berkeley: University of California Press, 1984. 165–76.

Dehouve, Danièle. "Caesarius of Heisterbach in the New Spain (1570–1770)." In *The Art of Cistercian Persuasion in the Middle Ages and Beyond: Caesarius of Heisterbach's "Dialogue on miracles" and Its Reception,* edited by Victoria Smirnova, Marie Anne Polo de Beaulieu, and Jacques Berlioz. Studies in Medieval and Reformation Traditions 196. Leiden and Boston: Brill, 2015. 242–68.

Dehouve, Danièle. *L'évangélisation des Aztèques ou le pécheur universel.* Paris: Maisonneuve & Larose, 2004.

Delcorno, Pietro. "'Quomodo discet sine docente?' Observant Efforts towards Education and Pastoral Care." In *A Companion to Observant Reform in the Late Middle Ages and Beyond,* edited by James Mixson and Bert Roest. Brill's Companions to the Christian Tradition 59. Leiden and Boston: Brill, 2015. 147–84.

Depaire, Jean-Paul. "La bibliothèque des Croisiers de Huy, de Liège et de Namur." Licence dissertation. University of Liège, 1969–1970.

Dewez, Jules. *Histoire de l'abbaye de Saint-Pierre d'Hasnon.* Lille: Imprimerie de l'Orphelinat de Don Bosco, 1890.

Doelle, Ferdinand. *Die Martinianische Reformbewegung in der sächsischen Franziskanerprovinz (Mittel- und Nordostdeutschland) im 15. und 16. Jahrhundert.* Franziskanische Studien 7. Münster in Westf.: Aschendorff, 1921.

Dolle, Josef. *Niedersächsisches Klosterbuch: Verzeichnis der Klöster, Stifte, Kommenden und Beginenhäuser in Niedersachsen und Bremen von den Anfängen bis 1810.* Vol. 2, *Gartow bis Mariental.* Veröffentlichungen des Instituts für Historische Landesforschung der Universität Göttingen. Bielefeld: Verlag für Regionalgeschichte, 2012.

Dörrer, Anton. "Mittelalterliche Bücherlisten aus Tirol." *Zentralblatt für Bibliothekswesen* 51 (1934): 245–63.

Dörrer, Anton. "Weitere mittelalterliche Bücherlisten aus Tirol." *Zentralblatt für Bibliothekswesen* 56 (1939): 329–34.

Dubois, Jacques. "Cartusia numquam reformata." In *Dizionario degli istituti di perfezione.* Vol. 2, *Cambiagio – Conventualesimo,* edited by Guerrino Pelliccia and Giancarlo Rocca. Rome: Edizioni Paoline, 1975.

Duprat, Anne. "Pestes et incendies: l'exemplarité du récit de témoin aux XVIe–XVIIe siècles." In *Construire l'exemplarité: Pratiques littéraires et discours historiens (XVIe –XVIIIe siècles),* edited by Laurence Giavarini. Dijon: Éditions universitaires de Dijon, 2008. 63–83.

Easting, Robert, and Richard Sharpe, eds. *Peter of Cornwall's Book of Revelations.* Toronto: Pontifical Institute of Mediaeval Studies; Oxford: Bodleian Library, 2013.

Eisenstein, Elizabeth. *The Printing Revolution in Early Modern Europe.* 2nd ed. Cambridge: Cambridge University Press, 2005.

Elm, Kaspar. "Entstehung und Reform des belgisch-niederländischen Kreuzherrordens: ein Literaturbericht." In Kaspar Elm, *Mittelalterliches Ordensleben in Westfalen und am Niederrhein.* Paderborn: Bonifatius, 1989. 236–55.

Embach, Michael. "Johannes Trithemius OSB (1462–1516) und die Bibliothek von Kloster Sponheim—mit einem Blick auf die Vita Juttas von Sponheim (1092–1136)." In *Zur Erforschung mittelalterlicher Bibliotheken: Chancen - Entwicklungen – Perspektiven,* edited by Andrea Rapp and Michael Embach. Zeitschrift für Bibliothekswesen und Bibliographie 97. Frankfurt am Main: Klostermann, 2009. 101–36.

Engelbert, Pius. "Die Bursfelder Benediktinerkongregation und die spätmittelalterlichen Reformbewegungen." *Historisches Jahrbuch* 103 (1983): 35–55.

Fabre, Pierre-Antoine. "Readings/Lessons of the Exemplum." In *The Art of Cistercian Persuasion in the Middle Ages and Beyond: Caesarius of Heisterbach's "Dialogue on miracles" and its Reception,* edited by Victoria Smirnova, Marie Anne Polo de Beaulieu, and Jacques Berlioz. Studies in Medieval and Reformation Traditions 196. Leiden and Boston: Brill, 2015. 280–81.

Faix, Gerhard. *Gabriel Biel und die Brüder vom Gemeinsamen Leben. Quellen und Untersuchungen zu Verfassung und Selbstverständnis des Oberdeutschen Generalkapitels.* Tübingen: Mohr Siebeck, 1999.

Fischer, Ivo. "Der Nachlaß des Abtes Johannes Trithemius von St. Jakob in Würzburg." *Archiv des historischen Vereins von Unterfranken und Aschaffenburg* 67 (1928): 41–82.

Fleischer, Andrea. *Zisterzienserabt und Skriptorium: Salem unter Eberhard I. von Rohrdorf (1191–1240).* Wiesbaden: Reichert, 2004.

Formigoni, Edoardo. "Jacques de Vitry et le prieuré d'Oignies." In *Autour de Hugo d'Oignies,* edited by Robert Didier and Jacques Toussaint. Namur: Société archéologique de Namur, 2003. 37–45.

France, James. *Separate but Equal: Cistercian Lay Brothers, 1120–1350.* CS 246. Collegeville, MN: Cistercian Publications, 2012.

Franz, Adolph. *Drei deutsche Minoritenprediger aus dem 13. und 14. Jahrhundert*. Freiburg im Breisgau: Herder, 1907.

Franzen, August. "Gelenius, Aegidius." *Neue Deutsche Biographie* 6 (1964): 173–74.

Frioli, Donatella. *Lo scriptorium e la biblioteca del monastero cisterciense di Aldersbach*. Testi, studi, strumenti 3. Spoleto: Centro Italiano di Studi sull'Alto Medioevo, 1990.

Füser, Thomas. "Vom *exemplum* Christi über das *exemplum sanctorum* zum 'Jedermannsbeispiel': Überlegungen zur Normativität exemplarischer Verhaltensmuster im institutionellen Gefüge der Bettelorden des 13. Jahrhunderts." In *Die Bettelorden im Aufbau: Beiträge zur Institutionalisierungsprozessen im mittelalterlichen Religiosentum*, edited by Gert Melville and Jörg Oberste. Vita regularis 11. Münster: LIT, 1999. 27–106.

Gall, Franz, Hermine Paulhart, Willi Szaivert, Marta Szaivert, Kurt Mühlberger, and Ulrike Denk, eds. *Die Matrikel der Universität Wien*. Vol. 1, *(1377–1450)*. Publikationen des Instituts für Österreichische Geschichtsforschung. Graz, Vienna, Cologne: Böhlau, 1956.

Gastaldelli, Ferruccio. "A Critical Note on the Edition of the *Exordium Magnum Cisterciense*." CSQ 39, no. 3 (2004): 311–20.

Gecser, Ottó. "Lives of Saint Elizabeth: Their Rewritings and Diffusion in the Thirteenth Century." *Analecta Bollandiana* 127 (2009): 49–107.

Genest, Jean-François. "La bibliothèque de Clairvaux de Saint Bernard à l'humanisme." In *Histoire de Clairvaux, Actes du colloque de Bar-sur-Aube/Clairvaux, 22 et 23 juin 1990*, edited by the Association Renaissance de l'abbaye de Clairvaux. Bar-sur-Aube: Némont, 1992. 113–34.

Gesamtkatalog der Wiegendrucke. https://www.gesamtkatalogderwiegendrucke.de/.

Glaßner, Christine. "Stift Melk und die Melker Reform im 15. Jahrhundert." In *Die benediktinische Klosterreform im 15. Jahrhundert*, edited by Franz Xaver and Martin Thurner. Veröffentlichungen des Grabmann-Institutes zur Erforschung der mittelalterlichen Theologie und Philosophie 56. Berlin: Akademie, 2013. 75–91.

Glauche, Günter, and Hermann Knaus, eds. *Mittelalterliche Bibliotheks-kataloge Deutschlands und der Schweiz*. Vol. 4/2, *Bistum Freising*. Munich: Beck, 1979.

Gourdel, Yves. "Le Culte de la très sainte Vierge dans l'ordre des Chartreux." In *Maria: Études sur la Sainte Vierge*, edited by Hubert du Manoir. 2 vols. Paris: Beauchesne, 1952. 2:625–78.

Grélois, Aléxis. "Clairvaux et le monachisme féminin, des origines au milieu du XVᵉ siècle." In *Le temps long de Clairvaux: Nouvelles recherches, nouvelles perspectives (XIIᵉ–XXIᵉ siècle)*, edited by Aléxis Grélois and Arnaud Baudin. Paris: Somogy, 2016. 155–82.

Griesser, Bruno. "Agatha von Himmelspforten, eine unbekannte Cistercienserin des 13. Jahrhunderts." *Cistercienser-Chronik* 59 (1952): 100–12.

Griesser, Bruno. "Ein Himmeroder Liber miraculorum und seine Beziehungen zu Caesarius von Heisterbach." *Archiv für mittelrheinische Kirchengeschichte: nebst Berichten zur kirchlichen Denkmalpflege* 4 (1952): 257–74.

Griesser, Bruno. "Engelhard von Langheim und Abt Erbo von Prüfening." *Cisterzienser-Chronik* 71 (1964): 22–37.

Griesser, Bruno. "Engelhard von Langheim und sein Exempelbuch für die Nonnen von Wechterswinkel." *Cistercienser-Chronik* 70 (1963): 55–73.

Groiss, Albert. *Spätmittelalterliche Lebensformen der Benediktiner von der Melker Observanz vor dem Hintergrund ihrer Bräuche: ein darstellender Kommentar zum Caeremoniale Mellicense des Jahres 1460*. Münster: Aschendorff, 1999.

Gründler, Otto. "*Devotio moderna atque antiqua*: The Modern Devotion and Carthusian Spirituality." In *The Roots of the Modern Christian Tradition*, edited by E. Rozanne Elder. *The Spirituality of Western Christendom*, Vol. 2. CS 55. Kalamazoo, MI: Cistercian Publications, 1984. 27–45.

Guillaume, Caroline. "Édition d'un recueil d'*exempla* du XIVᵉ siècle, le *Speculum exemplare* ou *Liber ad status*." PhD dissertation, École des chartes, 1991.

Haaß, Robert. *Die Kreuzherren in den Rheinlanden*. Rheinisches Archiv 23. Bonn: Röhrscheid, 1932.

Haucap-Nass, Anette. *Der Braunschweiger Stadtschreiber Gerwin von Hameln und seine Bibliothek*. Wiesbaden: Harrassowitz, 1995.

Herbert, John Alexander. *Catalogue of Romances in the Department of Manuscripts in the British Museum*. Vol. 3. London: Trustees of the British Museum, 1910.

Hermand, Xavier. "*Scriptoria* et bibliothèques dans les monastères cisterciens réformés des Pays-Bas méridionaux au XVe siècle." In *Les Cisterciens et la transmission des textes (XIIe–XVIIIe siècles): Bibliothèque d'histoire culturelle du Moyen Âge 18*, edited by Thomas Falmagne, Dominique Stutzmann, Pierre Gandil, and Anne-Marie Turcan-Verkerk. Turnhout: Brepols, 2018. 79–126.

Hillenbrand, Eugen. "Die Observantenbewegung in der deutschen Ordensprovinz der Dominikaner." In *Reformbemühungen und Observanzbestrebungen im spätmittelalterlichen Ordenswesen*, edited by Kaspar Elm. Berliner historische Studien 14. Ordensstudien 6. Berlin: Duncker & Humblot, 1989. 219–71.

Hlatky, Jasmin. "Hoe die nouicius vraecht: Die mittelniederländische Überlieferung des *Dialogus miraculorum* von Caesarius von Heisterbach." PhD dissertation, Westfälischen Wilhelms-Universität zu Münster, 2006.

Hlatky, Jasmin. "On a Former Mayor of Deventer: Derick van den Wiel, the *Devotio moderna* and the Middle Dutch Translation of the *Dialogus miraculorum*." In *The Art of Cistercian Persuasion in the Middle Ages and Beyond: Caesarius of Heisterbach's "Dialogue on Miracles" and Its Reception*, edited by Victoria Smirnova, Marie Anne Polo de Beaulieu, and Jacques Berlioz. Studies in Medieval and Reformation Traditions 196. Leiden and Boston: Brill, 2015. 211–26.

Huston, Nancy. *L'espèce fabulatrice: Un endroit où aller*. Arles: Actes Sud, 2008.

Jamroziak, Emilia. "Cistercian Abbots in Late Medieval Central Europe: Between the Cloister and the World." In *The Prelate in England and Europe 1300–1560*, edited by Martin Heale. Woodbridge: Boydell and Brewer, 2014. 240–57.

Jamroziak, Emilia. *The Cistercian Order in Medieval Europe: 1090–1500*. The Medieval World. London: Routledge, 2015.

Jourdan, Julie. "Les *exempla* en image: Du *Jeu des échecs moralisés* au *Ci nous dit*." In *Quand l'image relit le texte: Regards croisés sur les manuscrits médiévaux*, edited by Sandrine Hériché-Pradeau and Maud Pérez-Simon. Paris: Presses Sorbonne Nouvelle, 2013. 233–46.

Juchhoff, Rudolf. "Aufgang und Blütezeit des Kölner Buchdrucks." In *Fünf Jahrhunderte schwarze Kunst in Köln*, edited by Adam Wienand. Cologne: Bibliophilen-Ges, 1953. 9–26.

Juntke, Fritz. *Die Wiegendrucke der Domstiftsbibliotheken zu Merseburg und Naumberg*. Die Stiftsbibliotheken zu Merseburg, Naumburg und Zeitz 1. Halle (Saale): Niemeyer, 1940.

Karpp, Gerhard. "Bibliothek und Skriptorium der Zisterzienserabtei Altzelle." In *Altzelle: Zisterzienserabtei in Mitteldeutschland und Hauskloster der Wettiner*, edited by Martina Schattkowsky and André Thieme. Schriften zur sächsischen Landesgeschichte 3. Leipzig: Leipziger Univ.-Verl., 2002. 193–233.

Kaufmann, Alexander. *Caesarius von Heisterbach, ein Beitrag zur Kulturgeschichte des 12. und 13. Jahrhunderts*. Cologne: Heberle, 1850.

Keil, Leonhard. "Der Dichter und Humanist Mathias Agricius von Wittlich (1545–1613): Sein Leben, sein Werdegang und seine Werke." *Trierer Zeitschrift* 2 (1927): 141–55.

Kelly, Stephen, and John J. Thompson. "Imagined Histories of the Book: Current Paradigms and Future Directions." In *Imagining the Book*, edited by Stephen Kelly and John J. Thompson. Medieval Texts and Cultures of Northern Europe 7. Turnhout: Brepols, 2005. 1–14.

Kesters, Hubert. "Jan van Xanten, Kruistochtprediker en Abt van Sint-Truiden." *Ons Geestelijk Erf* 28 (1954): 5–26.

Kienzle, Beverly M. "Hélinand de Froidmont et la prédication cistercienne dans le Midi (1145–1229)." In *La prédication en pays d'Oc (XIIe–début XVe siècle). Cahiers de Fanjeaux* 32 (1997): 37–67.

Kinder, Terryl N. "Where Was Pontigny's Library?" *Cîteaux: Commentarii Cistercienses* 53 (2002): 269–303.

King, Archdale Arthur. *Cîteaux and Her Elder Daughters*. London: Burns & Oates, 1954.

Klueting, Edeltraud. *Monasteria semper reformanda: Kloster- und Ordensreformen im Mittelalter.* Historia profana et ecclesiastica 12. Münster: LIT, 2005.

Knapp, Fritz Peter. "Ein vergessener Tiroler Autor des Spätmittelalters: Rudolf von Stams († 1294), Sprache und Dichtung." In *Sprache und Dichtung in Vorderösterreich. Elsass - Schweiz - Schwaben - Vorarlberg - Tirol. Ein Symposion für Achim Masser zum 65. Geburtstag am 12. Mai 1998,* edited by Guntram A. Plangg and Eugen Thurnher. Innsbruck: Wagner, 2000. 99–110.

Knaus, Hermann. "Zum Kölner gotischen Bucheinband: Die Meister des Johann Rinck und des Peter Rinck." *Börsenblatt für den deutschen Buchhandel* 26/23 (1970): 665–72.

Knippig, Richard. *Die Regesten der Erzbischöfe von Köln im Mittelalter.* Vol. 3/1, *1205–1261.* Bonn: Hanstein, 1909.

Kock, Thomas. *Die Buchkultur der Devotio moderna: Handschriftenproduktion, Literaturversorgung und Bibliotheksaufbau im Zeitalter des Medienwechsel.* Tradition - Reform - Innovation 2. Frankfurt am Main: Lang, 2002.

Kock, Thomas. "Zerbolt inkognito: auf den Spuren des Traktats 'De vestibus pretiosis.'" In *Kirchenreform von unten: Gerhard Zerbolt von Zutphen und die Brüder vom gemeinsamen Leben,* edited by Nikolaus Staubach. Tradition - Reform - Innovation 6. Frankfurt am Main: Lang, 2004. 165–235.

Kock, Thomas. "Zwischen Predigt und Meditation: Die Kollationalia des Dirc van Herxen." In *Predigt im Kontext,* edited by Volker Mertens, Hans-Jochen Schiewer, Regina Dorothea Schiewer, and Wolfram Schneider-Lastin. Berlin: De Gruyter, 2013. 399–420.

Kohl, Wilhelm. "Die Windesheimer Kongregation." In *Reformbemühungen und Observanzbestrebungen im spätmittelalterlichen Ordenswesen,* edited by Kaspar Elm. Berliner historische Studien 14. Ordensstudien 6. Berlin: Duncker & Humblot, 1989. 83–106.

Köpf, Ulrich. "Zisterziensische Spiritualität in Tirol: Die Anfänge von Stift Stams." In *Von der Via Claudia Augusta zum Oberen Weg. Leben an Etsch und Inn; Westtirol und angrenzende Räume von der Vorzeit bis heute,* edited by Reiner Loose. Innsbruck: Wagner, 2006. 177–91.

Koroleva, Elena. "The *Dialogus miraculorum* in the Light of Its Fifteenth-Century German Translation by Johannes Hartlieb." In *The Art of Cistercian Persuasion in the Middle Ages and Beyond: Caesarius of Heisterbach's "Dialogue on miracles" and Its Reception*, edited by Victoria Smirnova, Marie Anne Polo de Beaulieu, and Jacques Berlioz. Studies in Medieval and Reformation Traditions 196. Leiden and Boston: Brill, 2015. 227–41.

Kümper, Hiram. "Flores temporum." In *Encyclopedia of the Medieval Chronicle*, edited by Graeme Dunphy and Cristian Bratu. Leiden and Boston: Brill, 2010.

Kürten, Peter. *Das Stift St. Kunibert in Köln vom Jahre 1453 bis zur Auflösung*. Cologne: Janus, 1990.

Kwaśniewski, Andrzej. "Księgozbiór kapituły kieleckiej w świetle inwentarza z 1598 roku." *Archiwa, Biblioteki i Muzea Kościelne* 99 (2013): 43–92.

Lackner, Bede K. "Early Cîteaux and the Care of Souls." In *Noble Piety and Reformed Monasticism: Studies in Medieval Cistercian History 7*, edited by E. Rozanne Elder. CS 65. Kalamazoo, MI: Cistercian Publications, 1981. 52–67.

Langlois, Charles-Victor. "Simon de Vauvert." In *Histoire littéraire de la France*. Vol. 37, *Suite du quatorzième siècle*. Paris: Imprimerie nationale, 1938. 507–8.

Langosch, Karl. "Caesarius von Heisterbach." In *Die deutsche Literatur des Mittelalters: Verfasserlexikon*. Vol. I, *Aalen – Futerer*, edited by Karl Langosch, Kurt Ruh, and Gundolf Keil. 2nd ed. Berlin: De Gruyter, 1978. 1151–68.

Lau, Friedrich. "Das Kölner Patriziat bis zum Jahre 1325, II." *Mitteilungen aus dem Stadtarchiv von Köln* 10/26 (1895): 358–81.

Lavaud, Sandrine. "La fabrique historiographique et mythographique de la Croisade albigeoise (XIXe–début XXe siècle)." *Médiévales* [on-line], 74 Spring (2018). URL: http://journals.openedition.org/medievales/8325; DOI: https://doi.org/10.4000/medievales.8325.

Le Goff, Jacques. *Faut-il vraiment découper l'histoire en tranches?* La Librairie du XXIe siècle. Paris: Le Seuil, 2014.

Lehmann, Paul, Bernhard Bischoff, Paul Ruf, Christine Elisabeth Ineichen-Eder, Günter Glauche, and Sigrid Krämer, eds.

Mittelalterliche Bibliothekskataloge Deutschlands und der Schweiz. 5 vols. Munich: Beck, 1918–1990.

Lekai, Louis J. *The Cistercians: Ideals and Reality.* Kent, OH: Kent State University Press, 1977.

Lekai, Louis J. *The Rise of the Cistercian Strict Observance in Seventeenth Century France.* Washington, DC: Catholic University of America Press, 1968.

Liebers, Andrea. "Rigor ordinis—Gratia amoris. I." *Cîteaux: Commentarii cistercienses* 43 (1992): 162–220.

Liebers, Andrea. "Rigor ordinis—Gratia amoris. II." *Cîteaux: Commentarii cistercienses* 44 (1993): 36–151.

Lisch, Georg Christian Friedrich. "Buchdruckerei der Brüder vom gemeinsamen Leben zu St. Michael in Rostock." *Jahrbücher des Vereins für Mecklenburgische Geschichte und Altertumskunde* 4 (1839): 1–62.

Löhr, Gabriel Maria. "Die Dominikaner an den ostdeutschen Universitäten Wittenberg, Frankfurt-Oder, Rostock und Greifswald." *Archivum Fratrum Praedicatorum* 22 (1952): 294–316.

Löhr, Gabriel Maria. "Die Dominikaner an den Universitäten Erfurt und Mainz." *Archivum Fratrum Praedicatorum* 23 (1953): 236–74.

Löhr, Gabriel Maria. *Die Kapitel der Provinz Saxonia im Zeitalter der Kirchenspaltung: 1513–1540.* Quellen und Forschungen zur Geschichte des Dominikanerordens in Deutschland 26. Leipzig: Harrassowitz, 1930.

Loserth, Johann. *Geistlichen Schriften Peters von Zittau.* Vienna: Gerold in Komm, 1881.

Louis, Nicolas. "*Exemplum ad usum et abusum*: définition d'usages d'un récit qui n'en a que la forme." In *Le récit exemplaire (1200–1800): Actes du XXIIIᵉ colloque international de la Société d'Analyse de la Topique Romanesque, Belley 17–20 septembre 2009*, edited by Madeleine Jeay and Véronique Duché. Paris: Classiques Garnier, 2011. 17–36.

Louis, Nicolas. "L'exemplum en pratiques: production, diffusion et usages des recueils d'exempla latins aux XIIIᵉ–XVᵉ siècles." PhD dissertation. École des Hautes Études en Sciences Sociales (EHESS); Facultés Universitaires Notre Dame de la Paix, 2013.

Lülfing, Hans. "Hoernen, Arnold ter." *Neue Deutsche Biographie* 9 (1972): 356–57.

Lülfing, Hans. "Koelhoff, Johann d. Ä." *Neue Deutsche Biographie* 12 (1980): 318–19.

Mann, Jill, and Maura Nolan, eds. *The Text in the Community: Essays on Medieval Works, Manuscripts, Authors, and Readers.* Notre Dame, IN: University of Notre Dame Press, 2006.

Mazurek, Agata, and Irmgard Siebert. *Die mittelalterlichen Handschriften der Signaturengruppe C in der Universitäts- und Landesbibliothek Düsseldorf.* Wiesbaden: Harrassowitz, 2012.

McGuire, Brian Patrick. "The Cistercians and the Rise of the Exemplum in Early Thirteenth Century France: A Reevaluation of Paris BN MS. Lat. 15912." *Classica et Mediaevalia* 34 (1983): 211–67.

McGuire, Brian Patrick. "The Cistercians and the Transformation of Monastic Friendships." *Analecta Cisterciensia* 37 (1981): 1–69.

McGuire, Brian Patrick. "Cistercian Storytelling—A Living Tradition: Surprises in the World of Research." CSQ 39 (2004): 281–309.

McGuire, Brian Patrick. "Friends and Tales in the Cloister: Oral Sources in Caesarius of Heisterbach's *Dialogus miraculorum.*" *Analecta cisterciensia* 36 (1980): 167–247.

McGuire, Brian Patrick. "Les mentalités des Cisterciens dans les recueils d'exempla du XIIᵉ siècle: une nouvelle lecture du *Liber visionum et miraculorum* de Clairvaux." In *Les exempla médiévaux: nouvelles perspectives,* edited by Jacques Berlioz and Marie Anne Polo de Beaulieu. Paris: H. Champion, 1998. 107–45.

McGuire, Brian Patrick. "A Lost Clairvaux Exemplum Collection Found: The *Liber visionum et miraculorum* Compiled under Prior John of Clairvaux (1117–1179)." *Analecta Cisterciensia* 39 (1983): 26–62.

McGuire, Brian Patrick. "Taking Responsibility: Medieval Cistercian Abbots and Monks as Their Brother's Keepers." *Cîteaux: Commentarii cistercienses* 39 (1988): 249–69.

McGuire, Brian Patrick. "Written Sources and Cistercian Inspiration in Caesarius of Heisterbach." *Analecta Cisterciensia* 35 (1979): 227–82.

Meyer, Paul. "Les manuscrits des sermons français de Maurice de Sully." *Romania* 23, no. 90 (1894): 177–91.

Michael, Bernd, and Tilo Brandis. *Die mittelalterlichen Handschriften der Wissenschaftlichen Stadtbibliothek Soest: mit einem kurzen Verzeichnis der mittelalterlichen Handschriften-Fragmente von Tilo Brandis.* Wiesbaden: Harrassowitz, 1990.

Michels, Friedrich. *Geschichte und Beschreibung der ehemaligen Abtei Camp bei Rheinberg: nebst Notizen aus einer alten geschriebenen Urkunde, welche die Abtei und Umgegend betreffen.* Crefeld: Funcke, 1832.

Militzer, Klaus. *Kölner Geistliche im Mittelalter.* Vol. 1, *Männer.* Mitteilungen aus dem Stadtarchiv von Köln 91. Cologne: Historisches Archiv, 2003.

Milz, Joseph. *Studien zur mittelalterlichen Wirtschafts- und Verfassungsgeschichte der Abtei Deutz.* Cologne: Wamper, 1970.

Mittelalterliche Bibliothekskataloge Österreichs. 5 vols. Edited by Theodor Gottlieb, Paul Uiblein, Arthur Goldmann, Gerlinde Möser-Mersky, and Herbert Paulhart. Aalen: Scientia Verlag, 1915–71.

Molinier, Auguste, Henri Omont, Étienne-Symphorien Bougenot, and Philippe Guignard, eds. *Catalogue général des manuscrits des bibliothèques publiques de France: Departements.* Vol. 5, *Dijon.* Paris: Plon, 1885.

Mosler, Hans. *Altenberg.* Neustadt an der Aisch: Schmidt, 1959.

Mueller, Joan. "Colette of Corbie and the 'Privilege of Poverty.'" In *A Companion to Colette of Corbie,* edited by Joan Mueller and Nancy Warren. Brill's Companions to the Christian Tradition 66. Leiden: Brill, 2016. 101–29.

Mula, Stefano. "*Exempla* and Historiography. Alberic of Trois-Fontaines' Reading of Caesarius's *Dialogus miraculorum.*" In *The Art of Cistercian Persuasion in the Middle Ages and Beyond: Caesarius of Heisterbach's "Dialogue on Miracles" and Its Reception,* edited by Victoria Smirnova, Marie Anne Polo de Beaulieu, and Jacques Berlioz. Studies in Medieval and Reformation Traditions 196. Leiden and Boston: Brill, 2015. 143–59.

Mula, Stefano. "Gossuinus e il *Chronicon Clarevallense.*" *Herbertus* 2 (2000): 91–94.

Mula, Stefano. "Herbert de Torrès et l'autoreprésentation de l'ordre cistercien dans les recueils d'exempla." In *Le Tonnerre des exemples: Exempla et médiation culturelle dans l'Occident médiéval*, edited by Jacques Berlioz, Pascal Collomb, and Marie Anne Polo de Beaulieu. Rennes: Presses Universitaires de Rennes, 2010. 187–200.

Mula, Stefano. "I frammenti del *Liber Miraculorum* di Gossuinus. Edizione dal MS. Firenze, Laurenziana, Ashburnham 1906." *Herbertus* 3 (2002): 7–16.

Mula, Stefano. "Le Chronicon Clarevallense, la littérature exemplaire et l'ancienne bibliothèque de Clairvaux au XIIIᵉ siècle." In *Les Cisterciens et la transmission des textes (XIIᵉ–XVIIIᵉ siècles)*, edited by Thomas Falmagne, Dominique Stutzmann, Pierre Gandil, and Anne-Marie Turcan-Verkerk. Bibliothèque d'histoire culturelle du Moyen Âge 18. Turnhout: Brepols, 2018. 37–51.

Mula, Stefano. "Les *exempla* cisterciens du Moyen Âge, entre philologie et histoire." in *L'Œuvre littéraire du Moyen Âge aux yeux de l'historien et du philologue*, edited by Ludmilla Evdokimova and Victoria Smirnova. Paris: Classiques Garnier, 2014. 377–92.

Müller, Edmund. "Caesarius von Heisterbach in der Literatur." *Unsere Liebe Frau von Himmerod* 8 (1978): 40–46.

Neininger, Falko. "Caesarius von Heisterbach in Walberberg." In *Arbor amoena comis: 25 Jahre Mittellateinisches Seminar in Bonn, 1965–1990*, edited by Ewald Könsgen. Stuttgart: Franz Steiner, 1990.

Newman, Martha G. *Cistercian Stories for Nuns and Monks: The Sacramental Imagination of Engelhard of Langheim*. Philadelpha: The University of Pennsylvania Press, 2020.

Newman, Martha G. "Real Men and Imaginary Women: Engelhard of Langheim Considers a Woman in Disguise," *Speculum* 78, no. 4 (2003): 1184–1213.

Nyhus, Paul L. "The Franciscan Observant Reform in Germany." In *Reformbemühungen und Observanzbestrebungen im spätmittelalterlichen Ordenswesen*, edited by Kaspar Elm. Berliner historische Studien 14. Ordensstudien 6. Berlin: Duncker & Humblot, 1989. 207–17.

Oberweis, Michael. "Die niederrheinischen Kreuzherren und ihre Beziehungen zu den 'Brüdern vom Gemeinen Leben.'" In *Die*

Devotio Moderna. Sozialer und kultureller Transfer [1350–1580]. Vol. 2, *Die räumliche und geistige Ausstrahlung der Devotio Moderna*, edited by Iris Kwiatkowski and Jörg Engelbrecht. Münster: Aschendorff, 2013. 157–68.

O'Dwyer, Barry. "The Problem of Education in the Cistercian Order." *Journal of Religious History* 3 (1965): 238–45.

Oeser, Wolfgang. "Die Brüder des gemeinsamen Lebens in Münster als Bücherschreiber." *Archiv für Geschichte des Buchwesens* 5 (1964): 197–398.

Oppel, Hans D. "Die exemplarischen Mirakel des Engelhard von Langheim: Unterschungen und kommentierte Textausgausgabe (Teildruck)." PhD dissertation. Würzburg University, 1978.

Oppel, Hans D. "Eine kleine Sammlung cisterciensischer Mirakel aus dem 13. Jahrhundert." *Würzburger Diözesangeschichtsblätter* 34 (1972): 5–28.

Palmer, Nigel. *Zisterzienser und ihre Bücher: die mittelalterliche Bibliotheksgeschichte von Kloster Eberbach im Rheingau*. Regensburg: Schnell & Steiner, 1998.

Peyrafort-Huin, Monique. *La bibliothèque médiévale de l'abbaye de Pontigny (XIIᵉ–XIXᵉ siècles): histoire, inventaires anciens, manuscrits*. Documents, études et répertoires 60. Paris: CNRS, 2001.

Polo de Beaulieu, Marie Anne. "*Dialogus miraculorum*: The Initial Source of Inspiration for Johannes Gobi the Younger's *Scala coeli?*" In *The Art of Cistercian Persuasion in the Middle Ages and Beyond: Caesarius of Heisterbach's "Dialogue on Miracles" and Its Reception*, edited by Victoria Smirnova, Marie Anne Polo de Beaulieu, and Jacques Berlioz. Studies in Medieval and Reformation Traditions 196. Leiden and Boston: Brill, 2015. 183–210.

Polo de Beaulieu, Marie Anne. "L'exemplarité cistercienne." In *Les Cisterciens et la transmission des textes (XIIᵉ–XVIIIᵉ siècles)*, edited by Thomas Falmagne, Dominique Stutzmann, Pierre Gandil, and Anne-Marie Turcan-Verkerk. Bibliothèque d'histoire culturelle du Moyen Âge 18. Turnhout: Brepols, 2018. 239–84.

Polo de Beaulieu, Marie Anne. "L'image du clergé séculier dans les recueils d'exempla (XIIIᵉ–XVᵉ siècles)." In *Le clerc séculier au Moyen Age, actes du XXIIᵉ congrès de la Société des Historiens Médiévistes de l'Enseignement Supérieur Public, Amiens, juin 1991*, edited by Pierre Bonnassie. Publications de la Sorbonne 27. Paris: Publications de la Sorbonne, 1993. 61–80.

Polo de Beaulieu, Marie Anne. "Recueils d'exempla enluminés: textes et images pour une rhétorique de la persuasion." In *La légitimité implicite: Le pouvoir symbolique en Occident (1300–1640)*, edited by Jean-Philippe Genet. 2 vols. Paris and Rome: Éditions de la Sorbonne, École française de Rome, 2015. 1:423–56.

Polo de Beaulieu, Marie Anne. "Traces d'oralité dans les recueils d'exempla cisterciens." In *Understanding Monastic Practices of Oral Communication (Western Europe, tenth–thirteenth centuries)*, edited by Steven Vanderputten. Utrecht Studies in Medieval Literacy 21. Turnhout: Brepols, 2011. 139–57.

Polo de Beaulieu, Marie Anne, and Victoria Smirnova. "Lire et faire lire des recueils d'exempla. Entre persuasion cistercienne et efficace dominicaine." In *Le Texte médiéval dans le processus de communication*, edited by Ludmilla Evdokimova and Alain Marchandisse. Paris: Classiques Garnier, 2018. 133–54.

Polo de Beaulieu, Marie Anne, and Victoria Smirnova. "Visual Preaching in Russia (17th–19th Century)." In *Preaching and New Worlds: Sermons as Mirrors of Realms Near and Far*, edited by Timothy J. Johnson, Katherine Wrisley Shelby, and John D. Young. Routledge Studies in Medieval Religion and Culture 13. London: Routledge, 2018. 201–26.

Poncelet, Albert. "Miraculorum B.V. Mariae, quae saec. VI–XV latine conscripta sunt Index." *Analecta Bollandiana* 21 (1902): 241–360.

Reichl, Karl. "Plotting the Map of Medieval Oral Literature." In *Medieval Oral Literature*, edited by Karl Reichl. De Gruyter Lexikon Series. Berlin and Boston: De Gruyter, 2011. 3–68.

Reimann, Norbert. "Dortmund-Dominikaner." In *Westfälisches Klosterbuch: Lexikon der vor 1815 errichteten Stifte und Klöster von ihrer Gründung bis zur Aufhebung*. Vol. 1, *Ahlen – Mülheim*, edited by Karl Hengst. Münster: Aschendorff, 1992. 261–68.

Richter, Arthur. "Frisius, Johann Jakob." *Allgemeine Deutsche Biographie* 8 (1878): 107.

Roest, Bert. "Die Devotio Moderna als Medium und Element. Abschlussbemerkungen über Arten der Annäherung an ein historisches Phänomen." In *Die Devotio Moderna. Sozialer und kultureller Transfer [1350–1580].* Vol. 2, *Die räumliche und geistige Ausstrahlung der Devotio Moderna,* edited by Iris Kwiatkowski and Jörg Engelbrecht. Münster: Aschendorff, 2013. 254–62.

Roest, Bert. *A History of Franciscan Education (c. 1210–1517).* Education and Society in the Middle Ages and Renaissance 11. Leiden, Boston, and Cologne: Brill, 2000.

Roth, Christoph. *Literatur und Klosterreform: Die Bibliothek der Benediktiner von St. Mang zu Füssen im 15. Jahrhundert.* Tübingen: Niemeyer, 1999.

Rouse, Richard H., and Mary A. Rouse. *Preachers, Florilegia and Sermons: Studies on the* Manipulus florum *of Thomas of Ireland.* Studies and Texts 47. Toronto: Pontifical Institute of Mediaeval Studies, 1979.

Runde, Ingo. *Xanten im frühen und hohen Mittelalter. Sagentradition - Stiftsgeschichte – Stadtwerdung.* Cologne-Weimar-Vienna: Böhlau, 2003.

Rüthing, Heinrich. "Die Kartäuser und die spätmittelalterlichen Ordensreformen." In *Reformbemühungen und Observanzbestrebungen im spätmittelalterlichen Ordenswesen,* edited by Kaspar Elm. Berliner historische Studien 14. Ordensstudien 6. Berlin: Duncker & Humblot, 1989. 35–69.

Sauer, Christine. "Handschriften und Inkunabeln aus dem Besitz Hermann und Hartmann Schedels in der Stadtbibliothek Nürnberg." In *Hartmann Schedel (1440–1514), Leben und Werk: Akten des gemeinsam mit dem Germanischen Nationalmuseum Nürnberg, dem Verein für Geschichte der Stadt Nürnberg und dem Stadtarchiv Nürnberg am 28./29. Oktober 2014 veranstalteten Symposions im Germanischen Nationalmuseum Nürnberg,* edited by Franz Fuchs. Pirckheimer-Jahrbuch für Renaissance- und Humanismusforschung 30. Wiesbaden: Harrassowitz, 2016. 203–56.

Schade, Heidemarie. *Das Promptuarium exemplorum des Andreas Hondorff: volkskundliche Studien zum protestantischen Predigtexempel im 16. Jahrhunder.* Darmstadt: Studentenwerk Darmstadt, 1966.

Schenda, Rudolf. "Hieronymus Rauscher und die protestantisch-katholische Legendenpolemik." In *Volkserzählung und Reformation: ein Handbuch zur Tradierung und Funktion von Erzählstoffen und Erzählliteratur im Protestantismus,* edited by Wolfgang Brückner and Mathilde Hain. Berlin: Schmidt, 1974. 179–259.

Schmidt, Ludwig. "Beiträge zur Geschichte der wissenschaftlichen Studien in sächsischen Klöstern: Altzelle." *Neues Archiv für sächsische Geschichte und Altertumskunde* 18, Heft 3/4 (1897): 201–72.

Schmidt, Paul Gerhard. "Luzifer in Kaisheim. Die Sakramentsvision des Zisterziensers Rudolf (ca. 1207) und Abt Eberhard von Salem." In *Litterae Medii Aevi: Festschrift für Johanne Autenrieth zum 65. Geburtstag*, edited by Michael Borgolte and Herrad Spilling. Sigmaringen: Thorbecke, 1988. 191–201.

Schmitt, Jean-Claude. "Recueils franciscains d'exempla et perfectionnement des techniques intellectuelles du XIIIᵉ au XVᵉ siècle." *Bibliothèque de l'École des chartes* 135 (1977): 5–22.

Schneider, Ambrosius. *Die Cistercienserabtei Himmerod von der Renaissance bis zur Auflösung, 1511–1802*. Cologne: Wienand, 1976.

Schneider, Ambrosius. "Skriptorium und Bibliothek der Abtei Himmerod." Rev. Fritz Wagner. *Libri Pretiosi: Mitteilungen der Bibliophilen Gesellschaft Trier* 6 (2003): 4–12.

Schneider, Ambrosius. "Skriptorium und Bibliothek der Cistercienserabtei Himmerod im Rheinland: zur Geschichte klösterlichen Bibliothekswesens im Mittelalter." *Bulletin of the John Rylands Library* 35 (1952/53): 155–205.

Schnorrenberg, Jakob. "Zell, Ulrich." *Allgemeine Deutsche Biographie* 45 (1900): 19–21.

Schöler, Martina. Ama nesciri: *Spuren des Wirkens des Bibliothekars Conradus de Grunenberg († 1465/66) in der Bibliothek der Kölner Kreuzbrüder*. Cologne: Erzbischöfliche Diözesan- und Dombibliothek, 2005.

Schreiber, Johanna. "Devotio moderna in Böhmen." *Bohemia: Jahrbuch des Collegium Carolinum* 6 (1965): 93–122.

Schunke, Ilse. "Einbände des Magdeburger Domgymnasiums." *Zentralblatt für Bibliothekswesen* 78 (1964): 656–78.

Schürer, Markus. *Das Exemplum oder die erzählte Institution: Studien zum Beispielgebrauch bei den Dominikanern und Franziskanern des 13. Jahrhunderts*. Vita regularis 12. Münster: LIT, 2005.

Schwarzer, Joseph. "Vitae und Miracula aus Kloster Ebrach." *Neues Archiv der Gesellschaft für ältere deutsche Geschichtskunde zur*

Beförderung einer Gesamtausgabe der Quellenschriften deutscher Geschichten des Mittelalters 6/3 (1881): 513–30.

Sepp, Sieglinde. "Neuzeitliche Quellen zur Stamser Bibliotheksgeschichte." *Innsbrucker historische Studien* 6 (1983): 81–127.

Siwek, Alberich. *Die Zisterzienserabtei Salem: der Orden, das Kloster, seine Äbte*. Salem: Erzb. Münsterpfarramt, 1984.

Smirnova, Victoria. "Caesarius of Heisterbach Following the Rules of Rhetoric (Or Not?)." In *The Art of Cistercian Persuasion in the Middle Ages and Beyond: Caesarius of Heisterbach's "Dialogue on Miracles" and Its Reception*, edited by Victoria Smirnova, Marie Anne Polo de Beaulieu, and Jacques Berlioz. Studies in Medieval and Reformation Traditions 196. Leiden and Boston: Brill, 2015. 79–96.

Smirnova, Victoria. "De l'histoire à la rhétorique: Les recueils d'exempla cisterciens du Moyen Âge tardif." In *L'Œuvre littéraire du Moyen Âge aux yeux de l'historien et du philologue*, edited by Ludmilla Evdokimova and Victoria Smirnova. Paris: Classiques Garnier, 2014. 393–408.

Smirnova, Victoria. "L'exemplum médiéval dans une perspective codicologique (XIIIᵉ–XVᵉ siècle)." *Revue Mabillon* 85 (2013): 27–59.

Smirnova, Victoria. "Narrative Theology in Caesarius of Heisterbach's *Dialogus miraculorum*." In *The Art of Cistercian Persuasion in the Middle Ages and Beyond: Caesarius of Heisterbach's "Dialogue on Miracles" and Its Reception*, edited by Victoria Smirnova, Marie Anne Polo de Beaulieu, and Jacques Berlioz. Studies in Medieval and Reformation Traditions 196. Leiden and Boston: Brill, 2015. 121–42.

Smirnova, Victoria. "No Way to Salvation for German Bishops? The Case of Saint Engelbert of Cologne." In *Saintly Bishops and Bishops' Saints*, edited by Trpimir Vedriš and John S. Ott. Bibliotheca Hagiotheca 2. Poreč: Hagiotheca, 2012. 184–201.

Smirnova, Victoria. "Raconter des histoires dans une communauté soumise au silence: les Cisterciens et leurs exempla (XIIᵉ–XIIIᵉ s.)." *L'Atelier du CRH*, forthcoming.

Smirnova, Victoria, ed. *Fasciculum moralitatis: Omelie morales de Infantia Saluatoris*. Prague Medieval Studies Series. Prague: Karolinum Press, forthcoming.

Smirnova, Victoria, Marie Anne Polo de Beaulieu, and Jacques Berlioz, eds. *The Art of Cistercian Persuasion in the Middle Ages and Beyond: Caesarius of Heisterbach's "Dialogue on Miracles" and Its Reception.* Studies in Medieval and Reformation Traditions 196. Leiden and Boston: Brill, 2015.

Soergel, Philip M. *Miracles and the Protestant Imagination: The Evangelical Wonder Book in Reformation Germany.* Oxford Studies in Historical Theology. Oxford: Oxford University Press, 2012.

Spears, Russell. "Group Identities: The Social Identity Perspective." In *Handbook of Identity Theory and Research.* Vol. 1, *Structures and Processes,* edited by Seth J. Schwartz, Koen Luyckx, and Vivian L. Vignoles. New York, Dordrecht, Heidelberg, et al: Springer, 2011. 201–24.

Spiller, Reinhold. "Studien zu Ulrich Füetrer." *Zeitschrift für deutsches Altertum und deutsche Literatur* 27 (1883): 262–94.

Stiennon, Jacques. "Introduction à l'étude des scriptoria des croisiers de Liège et de Huy au XVᵉ siècle." In *Les manuscrits des Croisiers de Huy, Liège et Cuyk au XVᵉ siècle. Catalogue; exposition 24. févr. – 15 mars 1951.* Liège: Maison Desoer, 1951.

Tamizey de Larroque, Philippe. "Un épisode de la guerre des albigeois." *Revue des questions historiques* 1 (1866): 168–91.

Tewes, Ludger. "Der *Dialogus miraculorum* des Caesarius von Heisterbach: Beobachtungen zum Gliederungs- und Werkcharakter." *Archiv für Kulturgeschichte* 79 (1997): 13–30.

Theele, Joseph. "Einzeltypenstempel auf Kölner Einbänden." *Gutenberg-Jahrbuch* 1 (1926): 9–13.

Tilliette, Jean-Yves. "L'*exemplum* rhétorique: questions de définition." In *Les exempla médiévaux: nouvelles perspectives,* edited by Jacques Berlioz and Anne Polo de Beaulieu. Nouvelle bibliothèque du Moyen Âge 47. Paris: H. Champion, 1998. 43–65.

Tubach, Frederic C. *Index exemplorum: A Handbook of Medieval Religious Tales.* Folklore Fellows Communications 204. Helsinki: Suomalainen Tiedeakatemia, 1969.

Turner, Denys. "Why Did Denys the Carthusian Write *Sermones ad saeculares?*" In *Medieval Monastic Preaching,* edited by Carolyn Muessig. Brill's Studies in Intellectual History 90. Leiden: Brill, 1998. 19–35.

Van Dijk, Mathilde. "Performing the Fathers in the 'Devotio Moderna.'" In *Die Devotio Moderna: Sozialer und kultureller Transfer [1350–1580]*. Vol. 2, *Die räumliche und geistige Ausstrahlung der Devotio Moderna*, edited by Iris Kwiatkowski and Jörg Engelbrecht. Münster: Aschendorff, 2013. 227–44.

Van Dijk, Mathilde. "'Persevere!. . . God Will Help You!' Thomas à Kempis's Sermons for the Novices and His Perspective on Pastoral Care." In *A Companion to Pastoral Care in the Late Middle Ages (1200–1500)*, edited by Ronald J. Stansbury. Brill's Companions to the Christian Tradition 22. Leiden and Boston: Brill, 2010. 363–87.

Van Dijk, Rudolf. "De bestuursvorm van het Kapittel van Sion: Hollands verzet tegen het Windesheims centralisme." *Archief voor de Geschiedenis van de Katholieke Kerk in Nederland* 29 (1987): 166–91.

Van Moolenbroek, Jaap. "Wessel Gansfort as a Teacher at the Cistercian Abbey of Aduard: The Dismissal of Caesarius of Heisterbach's *Dialogus miraculorum*." In *Education and Learning in the Netherlands, 1400–1600*, edited by Koen Goudriaan, Jaap van Moolenbroek, and Ad Tervoort. Brill's Studies in Intellectual History 123. Leiden and Boston: Brill, 2003. 113–32.

Venator & Hanstein Bücher Graphik Autographen Auktion 136, 25. September 2015 Köln. http://venator-hanstein.de/assets/Pdfkataloge/Katalog_136.pdf.

Vennebusch, Joachim. "Unbekannte Miracula des Caesarius von Heisterbach." *Annalen des Historischen Vereins für den Niederrhein* 184 (1981): 7–19.

Vernet, André. "Un abbé de Clairvaux bibliophile: Pierre de Virey (1471–96)." *Scriptorium* 6, no. 1 (1952): 76–88.

Vernet, André, and Jean-François Genest, eds. *La Bibliothèque de l'abbaye de Clairvaux du XIIᵉ au XVIIIᵉ siècle*. Vol. 1, *Catalogues et répertoires*. Paris: CNRS, 1979.

Verzeichnisse altdeutscher Handschriften in der Deutschen Demokratischen Republik. Vol. 2, *Verzeichnis der altdeutschen und ausgewählter neuerer deutscher Handschriften in der Universitätsbibliothek Jena*, edited by Franzjoseph Pensel. Deutsche Texte des Mittelalters 70, 2. Berlin: Akademie-Verlag, 1986.

Vollmann, Benedikt Konrad. "Schlitpacher, Johannes." In *Neue Deutsche Biographie* 23 (2007): 93–94.

Von Meiller, Andreas, ed. *Regesta archiepiscoporum Salisburgensium: inde ab anno MCVI usque ad annum MCCXLVI: Conrad I., Eberhard I., Conrad II., Adalbert, Conrad III. und Eberhard II.* Vienna: Gerold, 1866.

Von Mosheim, Johann Lorenz. *Institutes of Ecclesiastical History: Ancient and Modern.* Vol. 2, *Medieval Period.* Translated by James Murdock, with additions by Henry Soames. 2nd ed. London: Brown, Green, and Longmans, 1850.

Wagner, Fritz. "Caesarius von Heisterbach." In *Lexikon des Mittelalters.* Vol. 2, *Bettlerwesen bis Codex von Valencia,* edited by Robert-Henri Bautier and Robert Auty. Munich and Zurich: Artemis & Winkler, 1983. Cols. 1363–66.

Wagner, Fritz. "Der Codex Nr. 49 der Stadtbibliothek Aachen." In *Studia codicologica,* edited by Kurt Treu. Texte und Untersuchungen zur Geschichte der altchristlichen Literatur 124. Berlin: Akademie, 1977. 503–9.

Wagner, Fritz. "Hermann Hesse and the Middle Ages." *Modern Language Review* 77, no. 2 (April 1982): 378–86.

Wagner, Fritz. "Studien zu Caesarius von Heisterbach." *Analecta cisterciensia* 29 (1973): 79–95.

Wathlé, Antoine, and Claude Muller. *Notre-Dame de Neubourg: Histoire d'une abbaye cistercienne de Basse-Alsace.* Dauendorf: Chez l'auteur, 2016.

Werhahn, Heinz Martin. "Die Bücher des Dr. Peter Rinck." In *Kölner Schule. Festgabe zum 60. Geburtstag von Rudolf Juchhoff. Gewidmet von den im Bibliothekar-Lehrinstitut in Köln ausgebildeten wissenschaftlichen Bibliothekare d. Jahrgänge 1951–1954,* edited by Hermann Corsten and Gerhart Lohse. Arbeiten aus dem Bibliothekar-Lehrinstitut des Landes Nordrhein-Westfalen 7. Cologne: Greven, 1955. 181–88.

Weiler, Anton G, "La Construction du soi dans les milieux de la *devotio moderna.*" In *La dévotion moderne dans les pays bourguignons et rhénans des origines à la fin du XVIe siècle: recontres de Colmar-Strasbourg (29 septembre au 2 octobre 1988),* edited by Jean-Marie Cauchies. Publication du Centre Européen d'Études Bourguignonnes, no 29. Neuchâtel: Centre Européen d'Etudes Bourguignonnes, 1989. 9–16.

Welter, Jean-Thiébaut. *L'exemplum dans la littérature religieuse et didactique du Moyen Âge.* Bibliothèque d'histoire ecclésiastique de la France. Paris-Toulouse: Occitania, 1927.

Werner, Wilfried. *Die mittelalterlichen nichtliturgischen Handschriften des Zisterzienserklosters Salem. Kataloge der Universitätsbibliothek Heidelberg 5.* Wiesbaden: Reichert, 2000.

Wilken, Engelbrecht. "War Geert Grote in Prag? Zur Frage der Beziehung Grotes zum Vorhussitismus—eine Problemskizze." *Sborník prací Filozofické fakulty brněnské univerzity. E, Řada archeologicko-klasická* 41, E37 (1992): 171–85.

Winter, Eduard. *Frühhumanismus: seine Entwicklung in Böhmen und deren europäische Bedeutung für die Kirchenreformbestrebungen im 14. Jahrhundert.* Beiträge zur Geschichte des religiösen und wissenschaftlichen Denkens 3. Berlin: Akademie-Verlag, 1964.

Worstbrock, Franz Josef. "Boto von Prüfening." In *Die deutsche Literatur des Mittelalters: Verfasserlexikon.* Vol. I, *Aalen – Futerer,* edited by Karl Langosch, Kurt Ruh, and Gundolf Keil. 2nd ed. Berlin: De Gruyter, 1978. Cols. 971–76.

Yassif, Eli. "Oral Traditions in a Literate Society: The Hebrew Literature of the Middle Ages." In *Medieval Oral Literature,* edited by Karl Reichl. De Gruyter Lexikon Series. Berlin and Boston: De Gruyter, 2011. 499–519.

Załuska, Yolanta. *Manuscrits enluminés de Dijon. Corpus des manuscrits enluminés des collections publiques des départements.* Paris: CNRS, 1991.

Zerner, Monique. "L'abbé Gui des Vaux-de-Cernay, prédicateur de croisade." In *Les Cisterciens en Languedoc. Cahiers de Fanjeaux* 21 (1986): 183–204.

Zibermayr, Ignaz. "Zur Geschichte der Raudnitzer Reform." *Mitteilungen des Instituts für Österreichische Geschichtsforschung* 11, Ergänzungsband (1929): 323–53.

Ziegler, Charlotte, and Joachim Rössl. *Zisterzienserstift Zwettl: Katalog der Handschriften des Mittelalters.* Vol. 2, *Codex 101–200.* Vienna-Munich: Schroll, 1985.

General Index

Citations are to numbers of pages and notes. Medieval names, from before roughly 1500, are alphabetized by first name; names from around or after 1500 are alphabetized by family name.

325